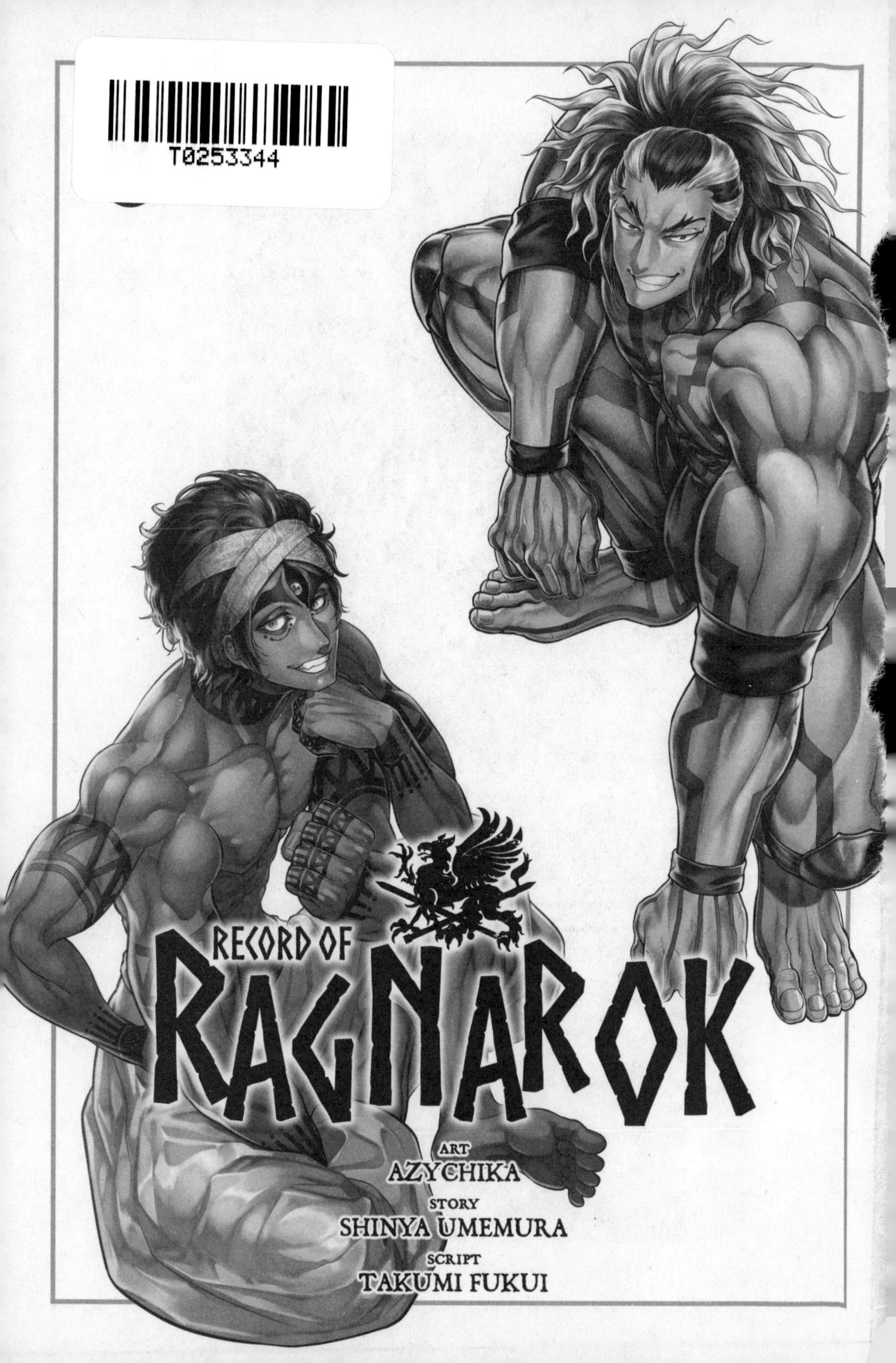
RECORD OF
RAGNAROK
ART
AZYCHIKA
STORY
SHINYA UMEMURA
SCRIPT
TAKUMI FUKUI

8

RECORD OF RAGNAROK

THE...

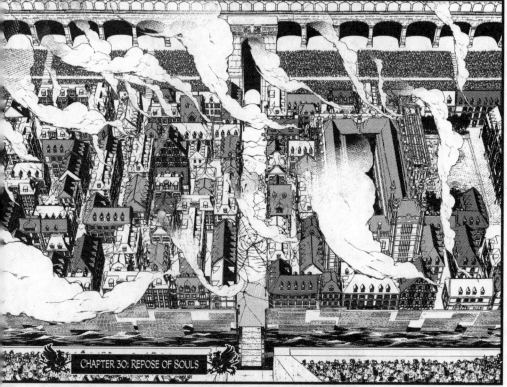

CHAPTER 30: REPOSE OF SOULS

...OF ROUND FOUR OF...

...WINNER...

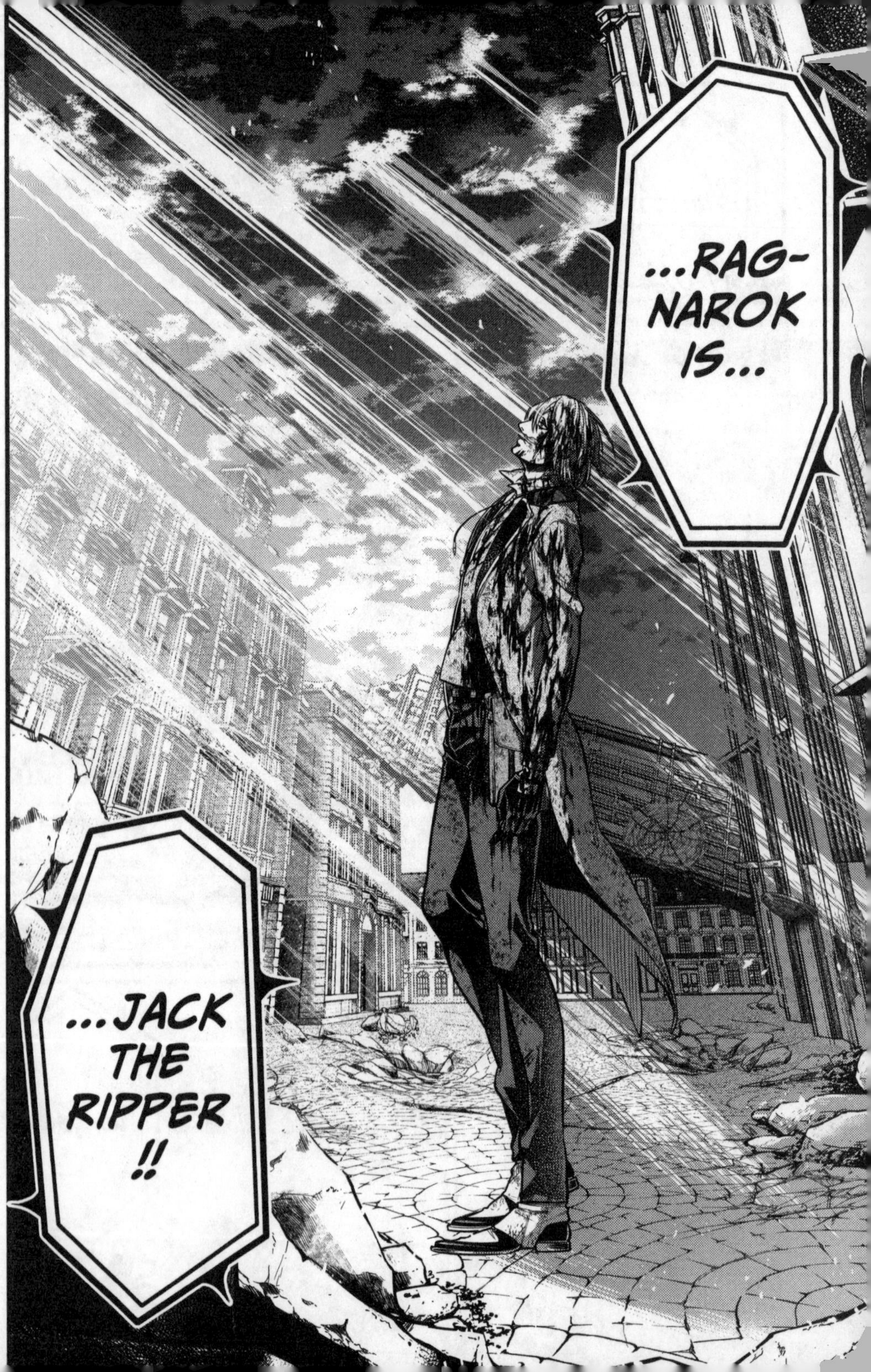
...RAG-NAROK IS...
...JACK THE RIPPER !!

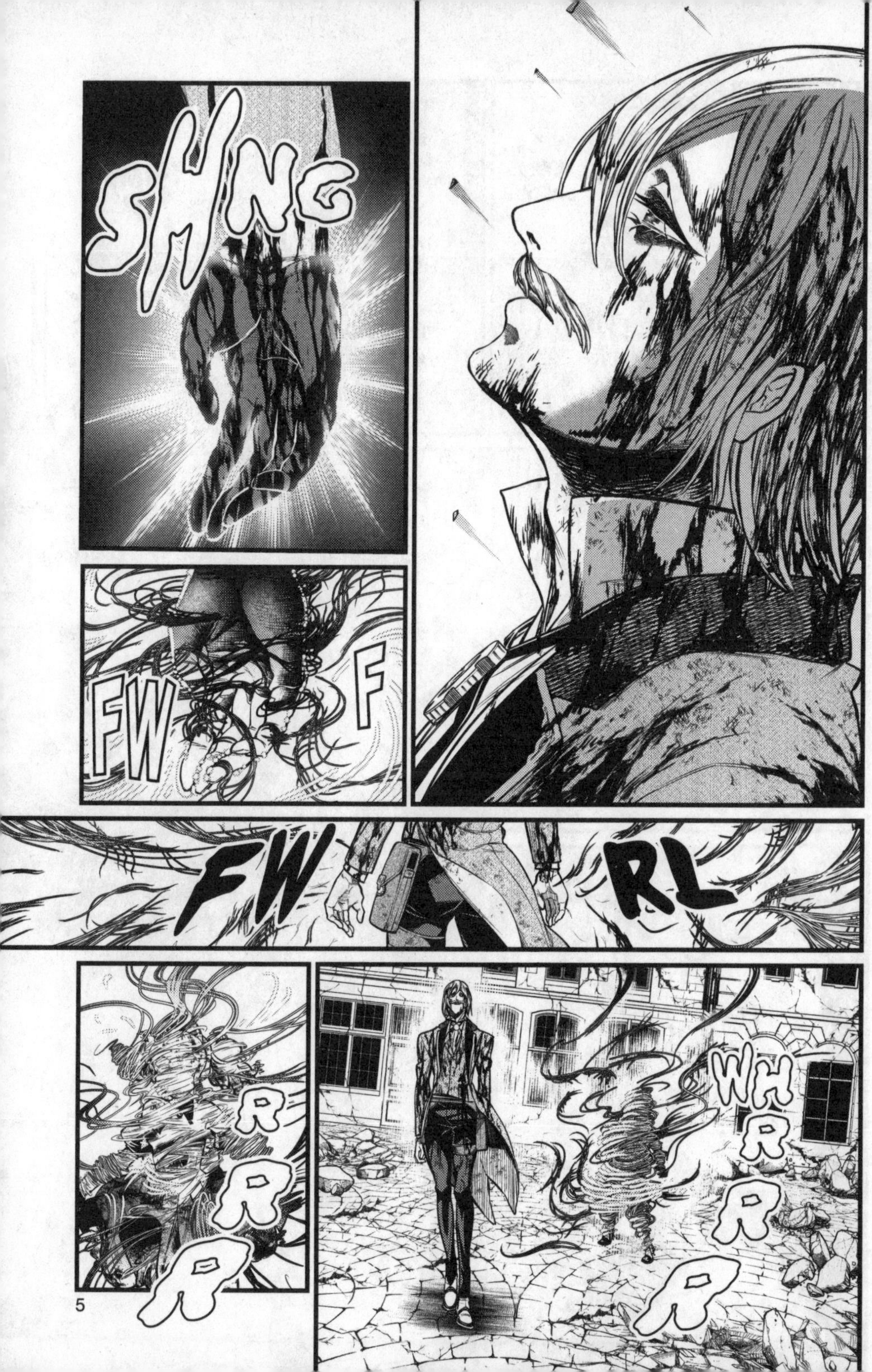
SHNG
FW F
FW RL
WH R R R
R R R

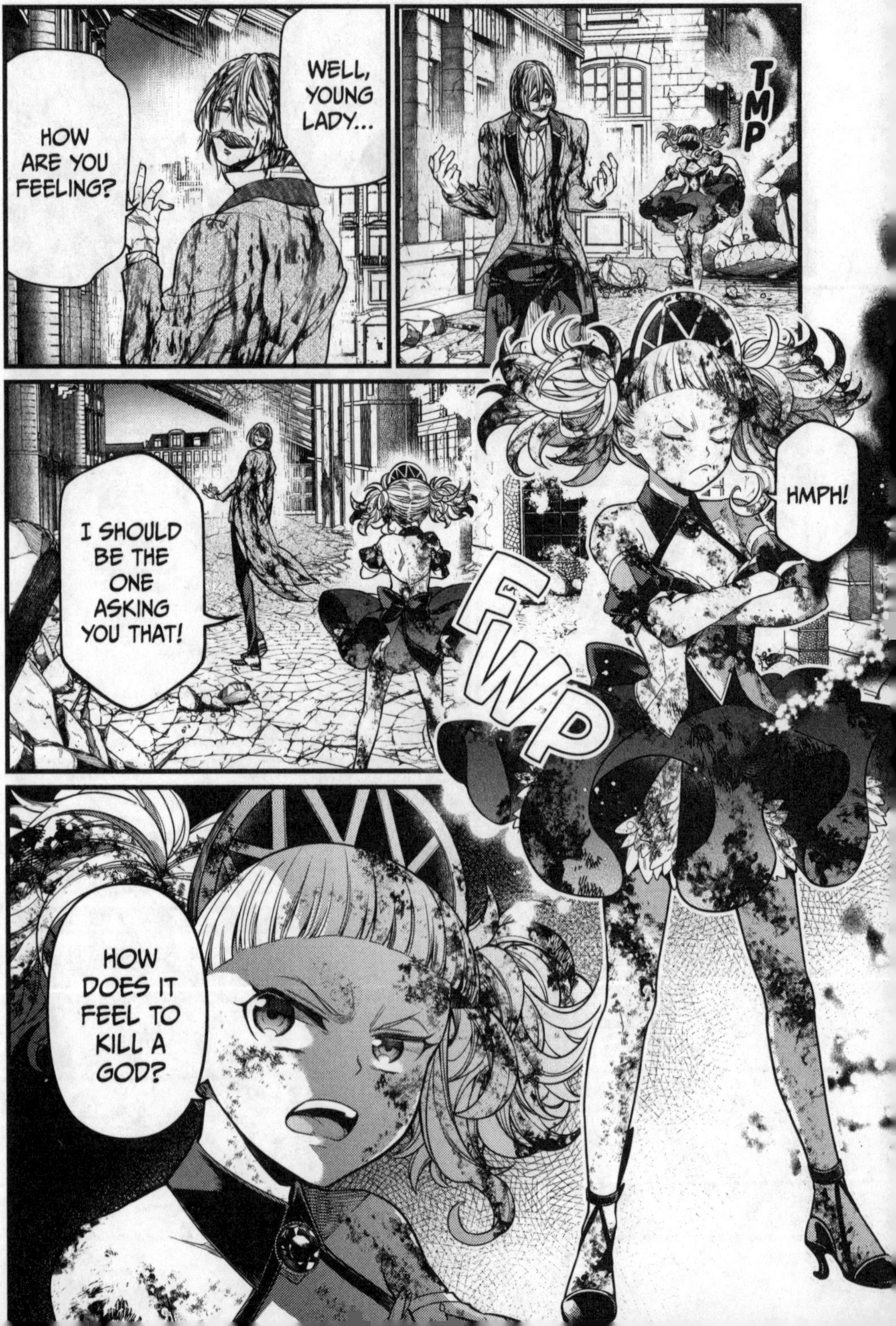
TMP
WELL, YOUNG LADY...
HOW ARE YOU FEELING?
HMPH!
FWP
I SHOULD BE THE ONE ASKING YOU THAT!
HOW DOES IT FEEL TO KILL A GOD?

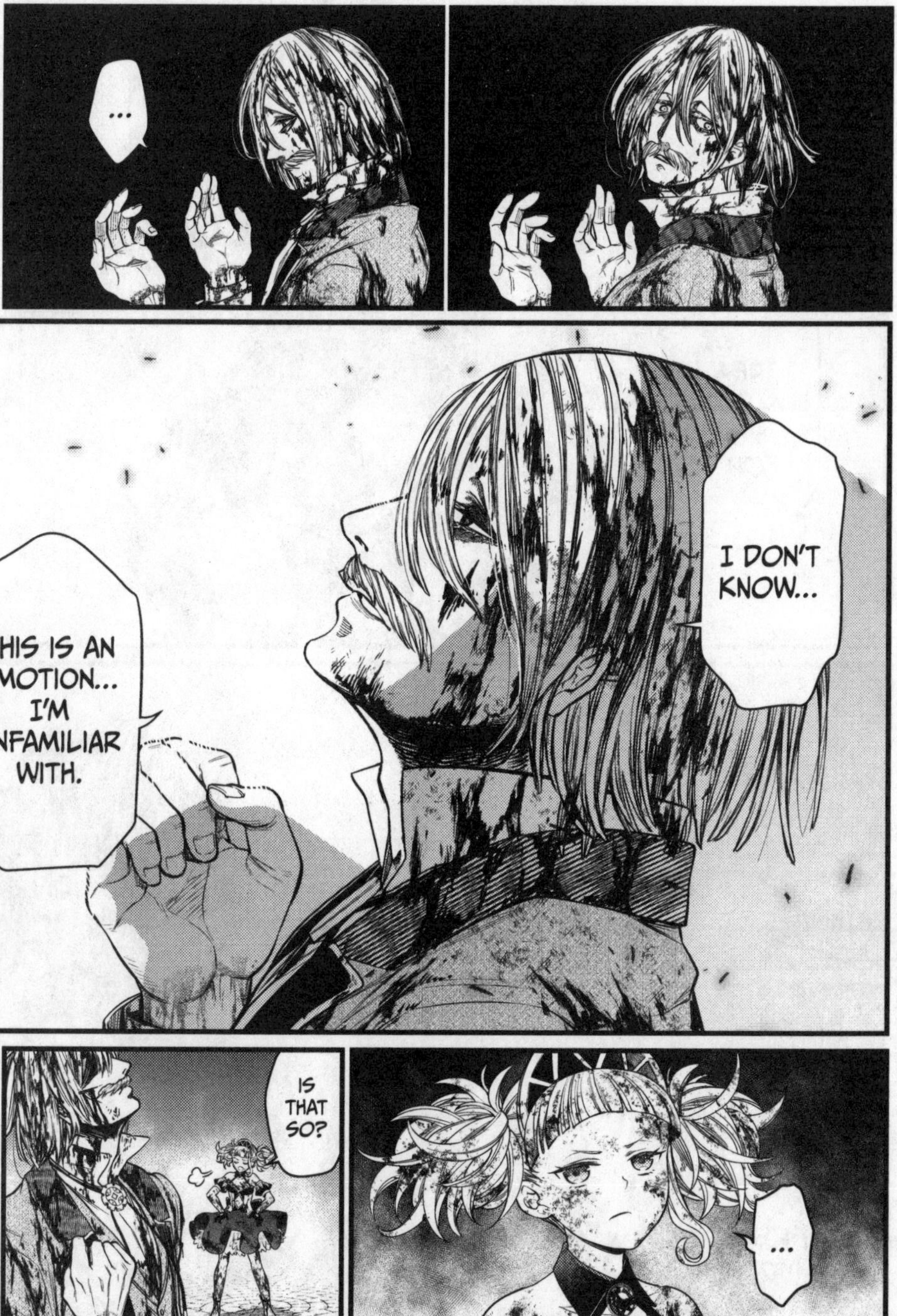
...
I DON'T KNOW...
THIS IS AN EMOTION... I'M UNFAMILIAR WITH.
...
IS THAT SO?

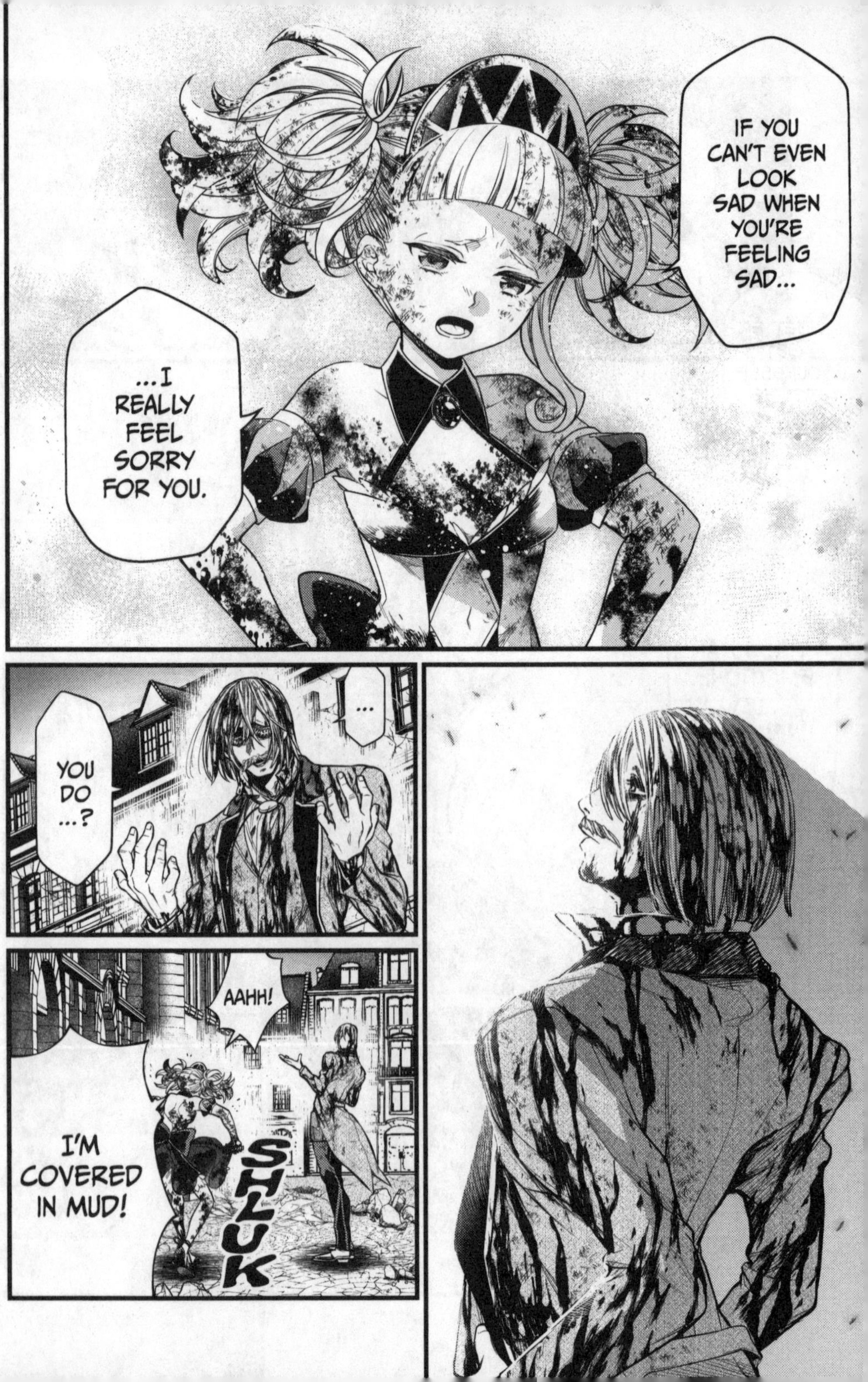
IF YOU CAN'T EVEN LOOK SAD WHEN YOU'RE FEELING SAD...
...I REALLY FEEL SORRY FOR YOU.
...
YOU DO ...?
AAHH!
I'M COVERED IN MUD!
SHLUK

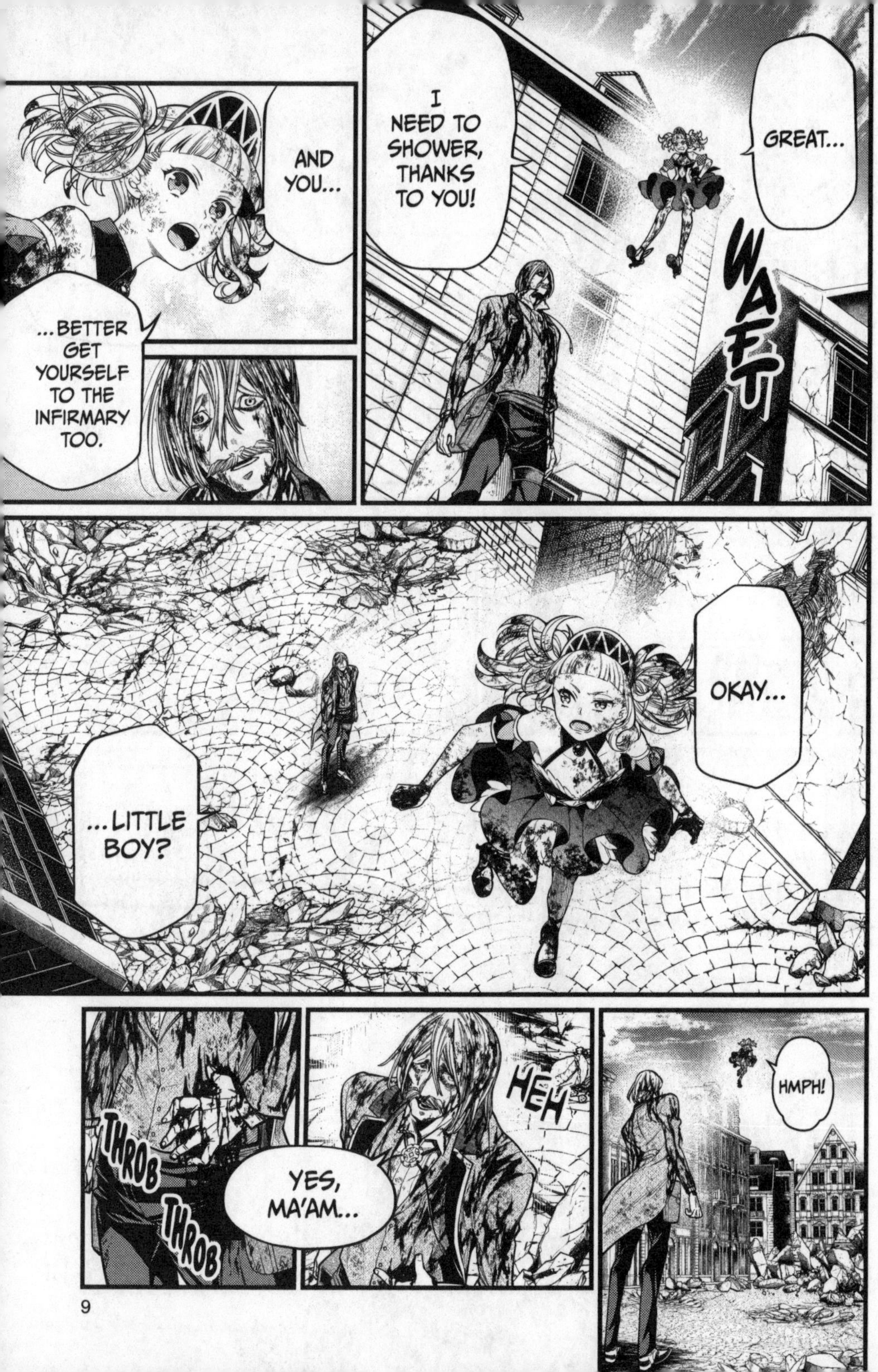
GREAT...
WAFU
I NEED TO SHOWER, THANKS TO YOU!
AND YOU...
...BETTER GET YOURSELF TO THE INFIRMARY TOO.
OKAY...
...LITTLE BOY?
HMPH!
HEH
YES, MA'AM...
THROB
THROB

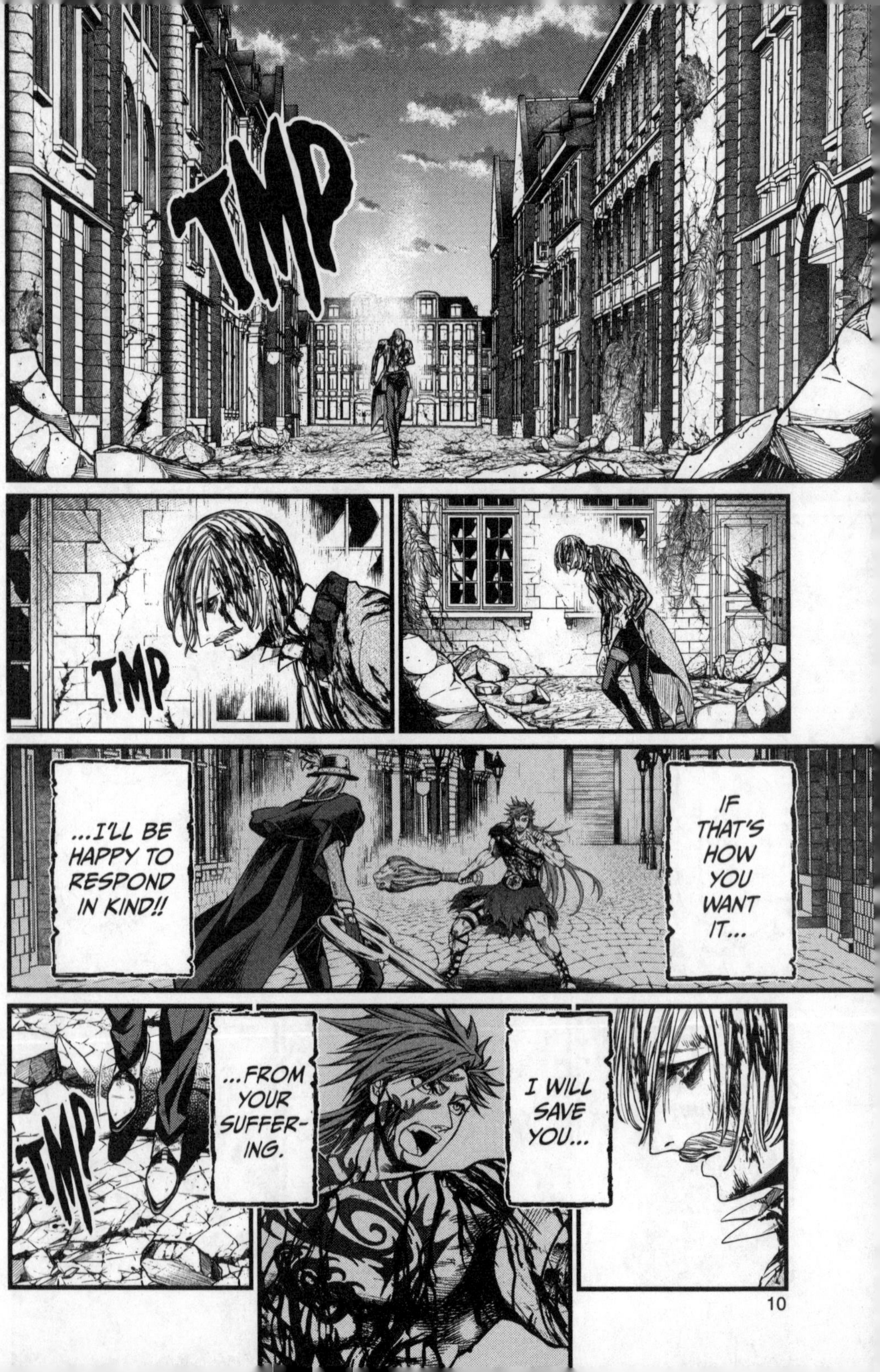
TMP
TMP
IF THAT'S HOW YOU WANT IT...
...I'LL BE HAPPY TO RESPOND IN KIND!!
I WILL SAVE YOU...
...FROM YOUR SUFFER-ING.
TMP

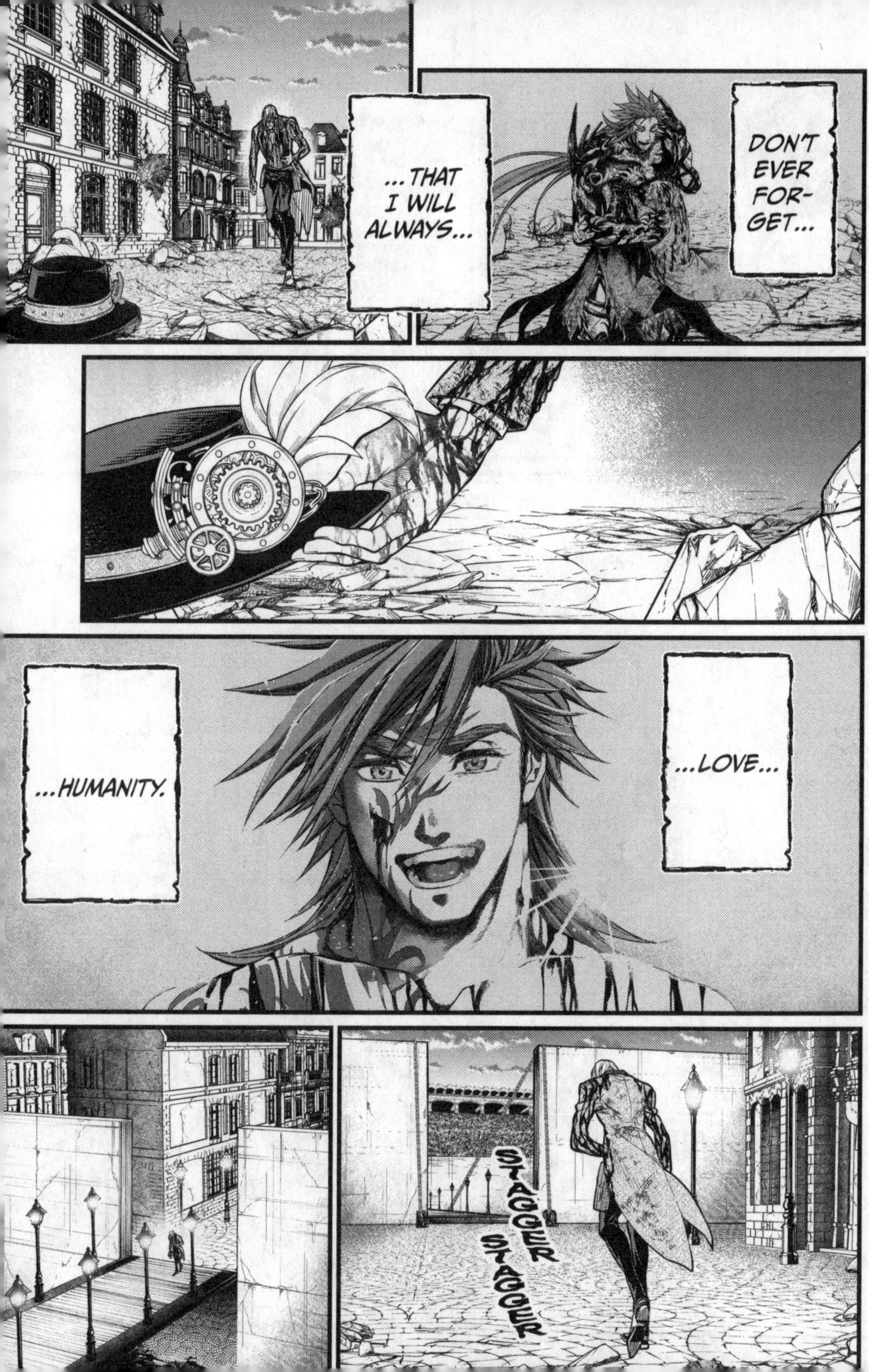
DON'T EVER FOR-GET...
...THAT I WILL ALWAYS...
...LOVE...
...HUMANITY.
STAGGER
STAGGER

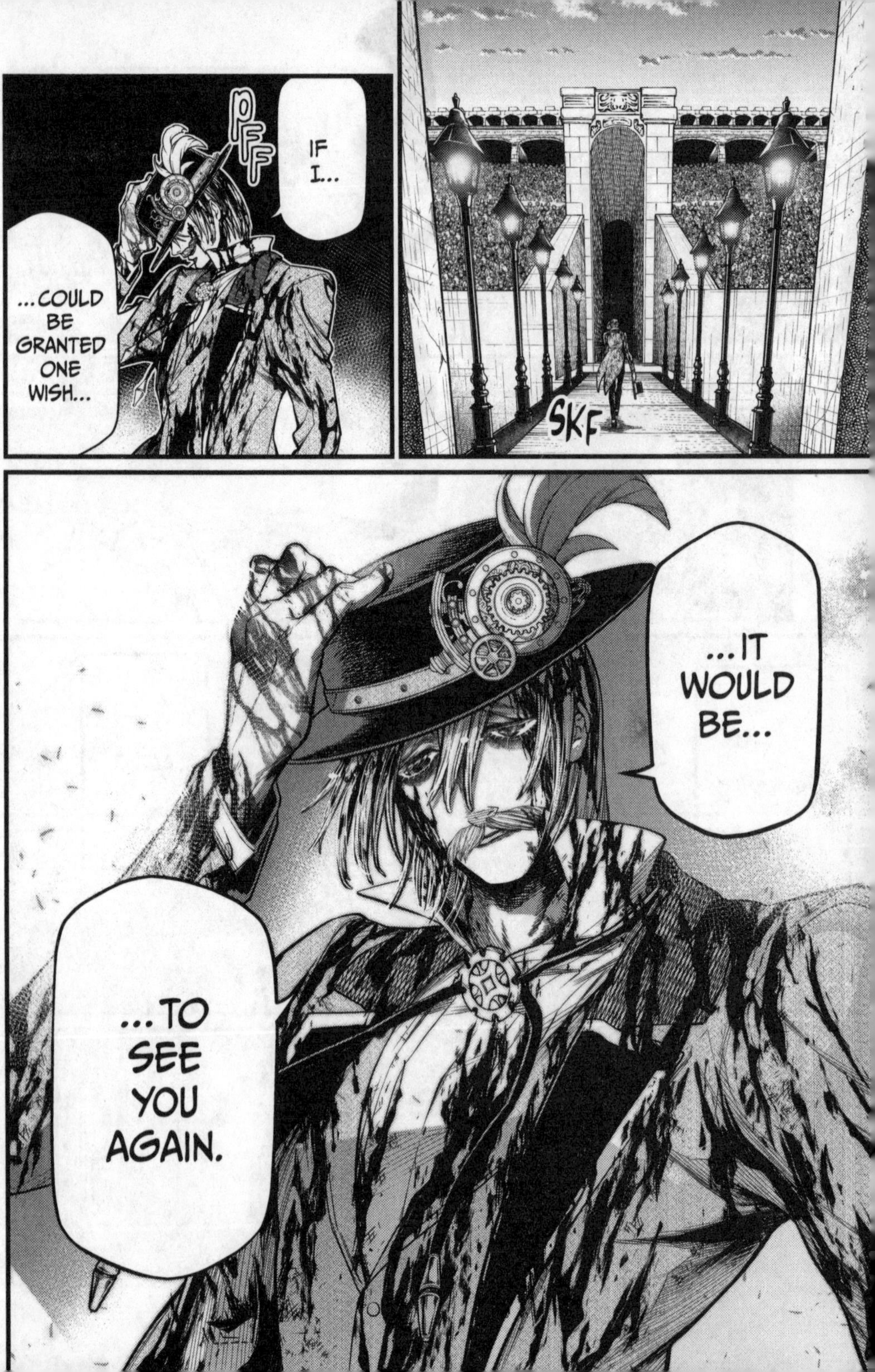
SKF
PFF
IF I...
...COULD BE GRANTED ONE WISH...
...IT WOULD BE...
...TO SEE YOU AGAIN.

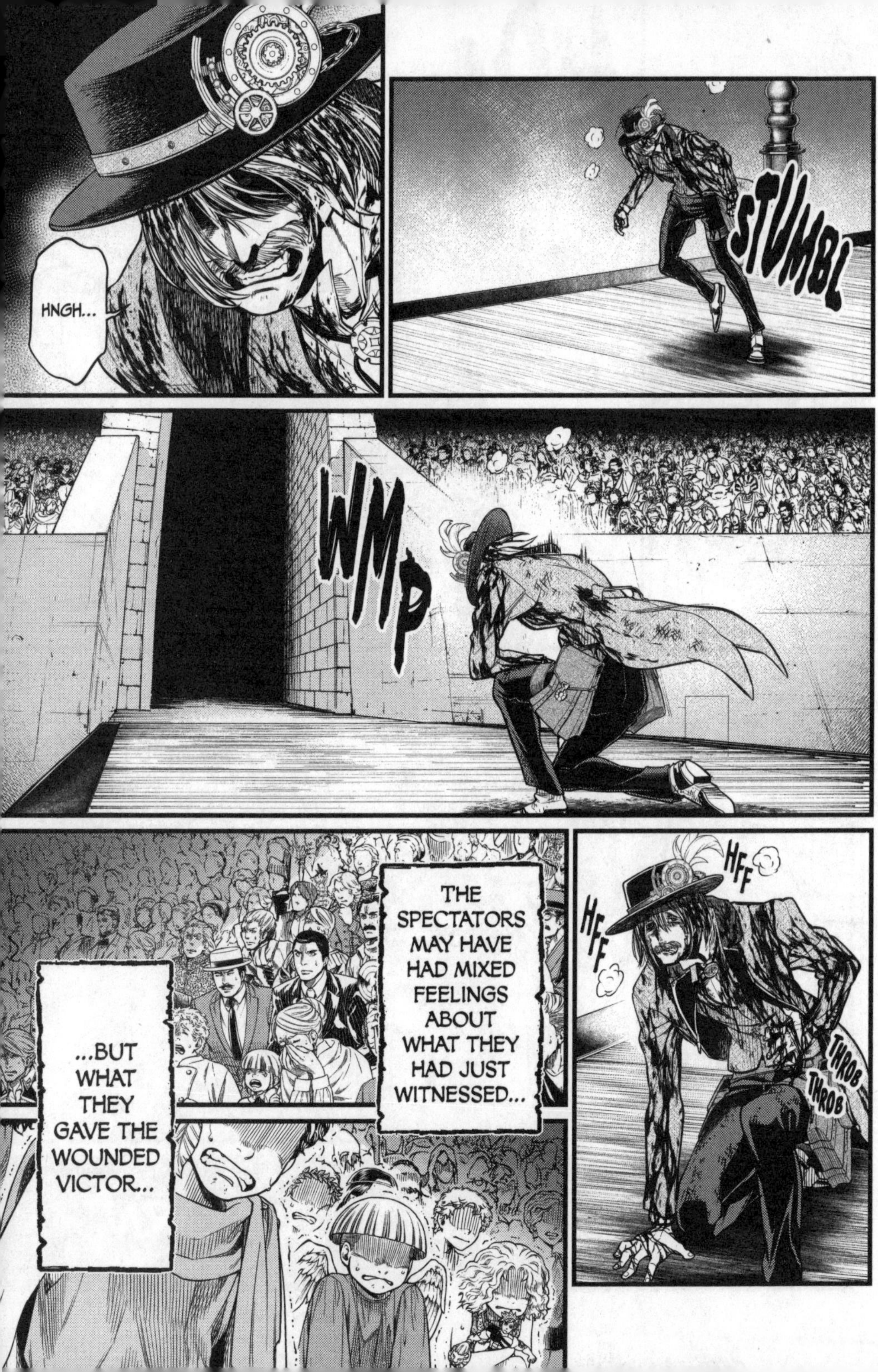
STUMBL
HNGH...
WMP
HFF
HFF
THROB THROB
THE SPECTATORS MAY HAVE HAD MIXED FEELINGS ABOUT WHAT THEY HAD JUST WITNESSED...
...BUT WHAT THEY GAVE THE WOUNDED VICTOR...

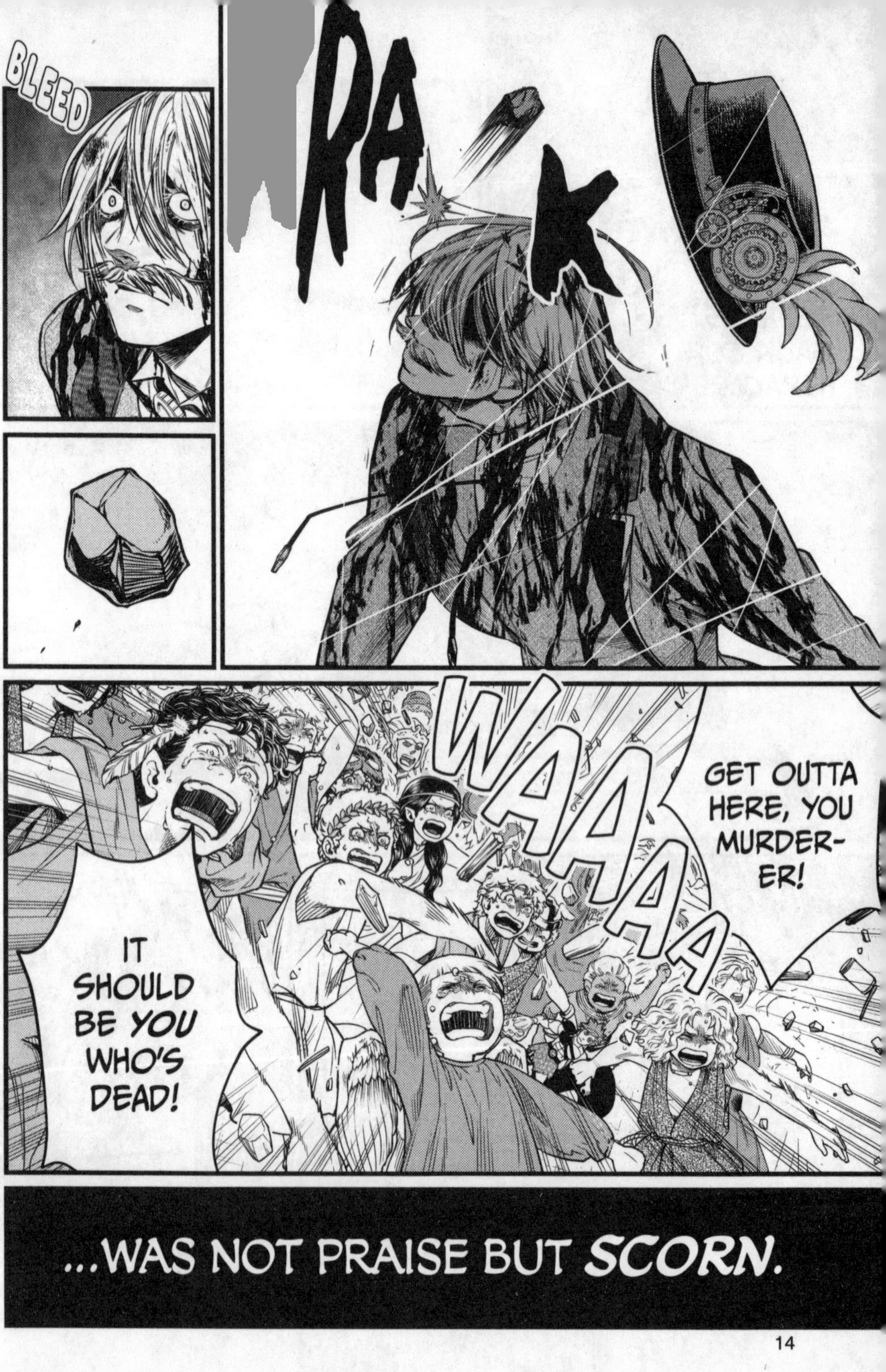
RA
K
BLEED
WAAAAA
GET OUTTA HERE, YOU MURDERER!
IT SHOULD BE YOU WHO'S DEAD!
...WAS NOT PRAISE BUT SCORN.

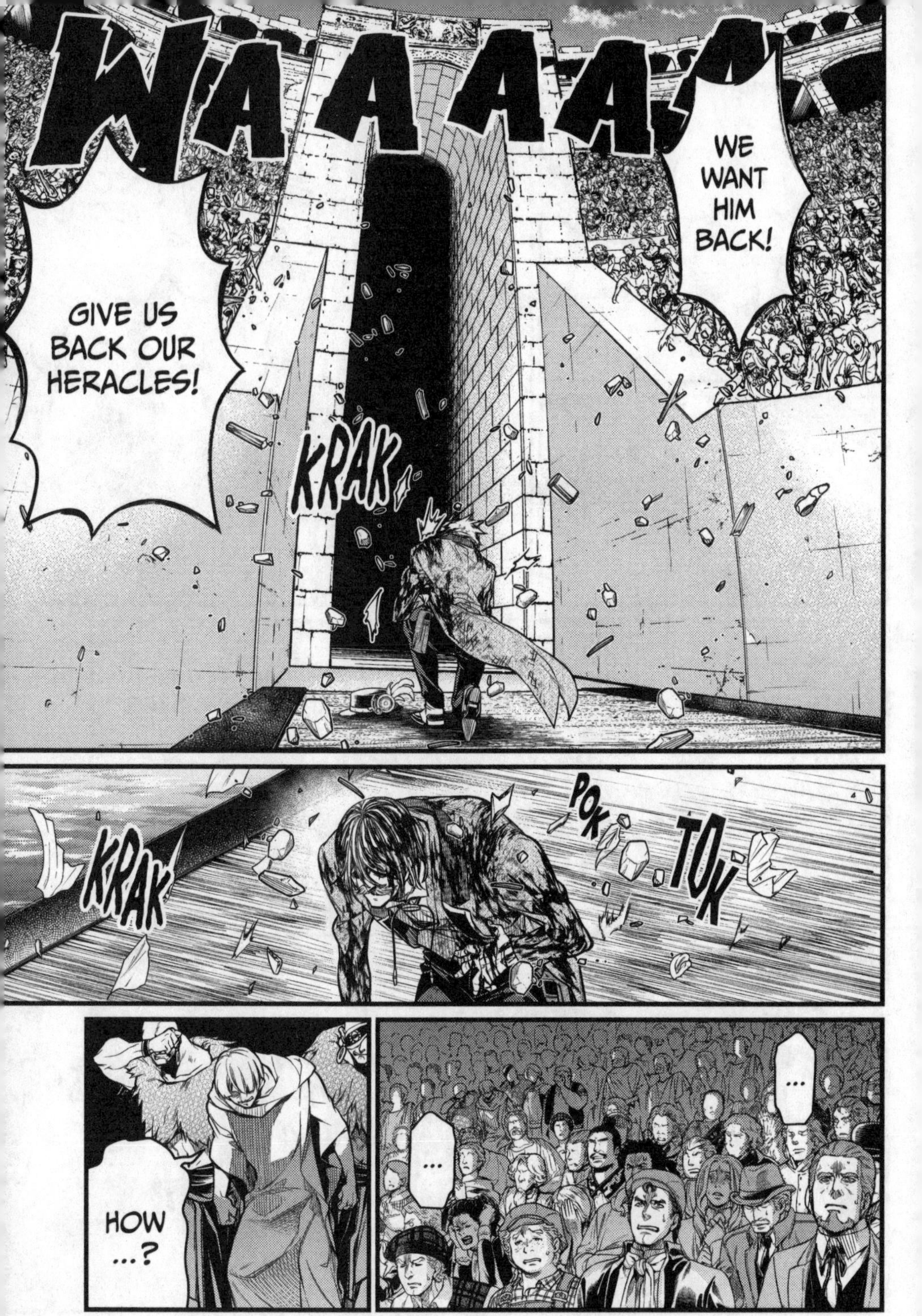

WAAAAA
WE WANT HIM BACK!
GIVE US BACK OUR HERACLES!
KRAK
POK
TOK
KRAK
...
...
HOW ...?

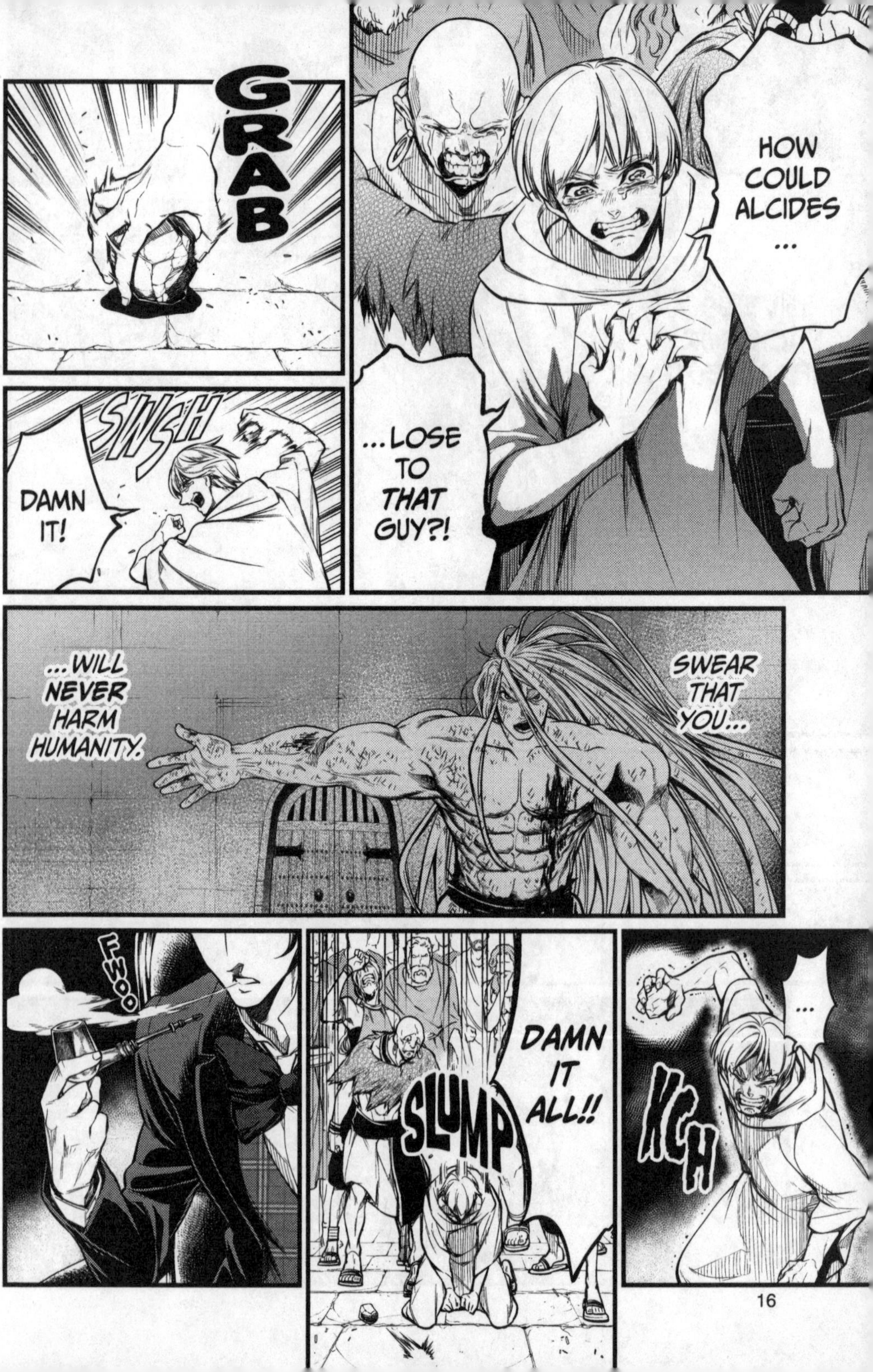
HOW COULD ALCIDES ...
...LOSE TO THAT GUY?!
GRAB
SWSH
DAMN IT!
SWEAR THAT YOU...
...WILL NEVER HARM HUMANITY.
...
KCH
DAMN IT ALL!!
SLUMP
FWOO

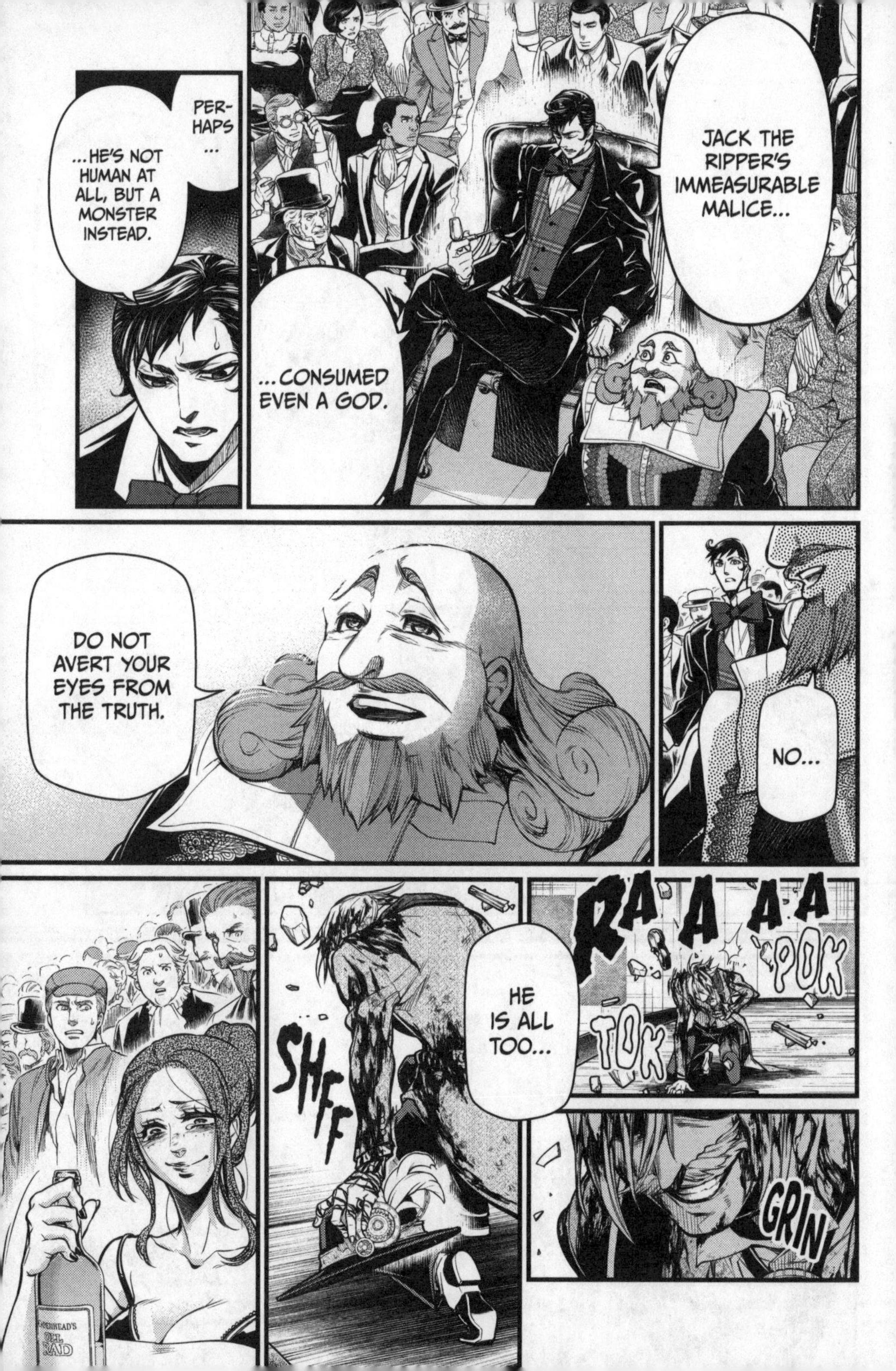
JACK THE RIPPER'S IMMEASURABLE MALICE...
...CONSUMED EVEN A GOD.
PERHAPS...
...HE'S NOT HUMAN AT ALL, BUT A MONSTER INSTEAD.
NO...
DO NOT AVERT YOUR EYES FROM THE TRUTH.
RA A A A
POK
TOK
GRIN
HE IS ALL TOO...
SHFF

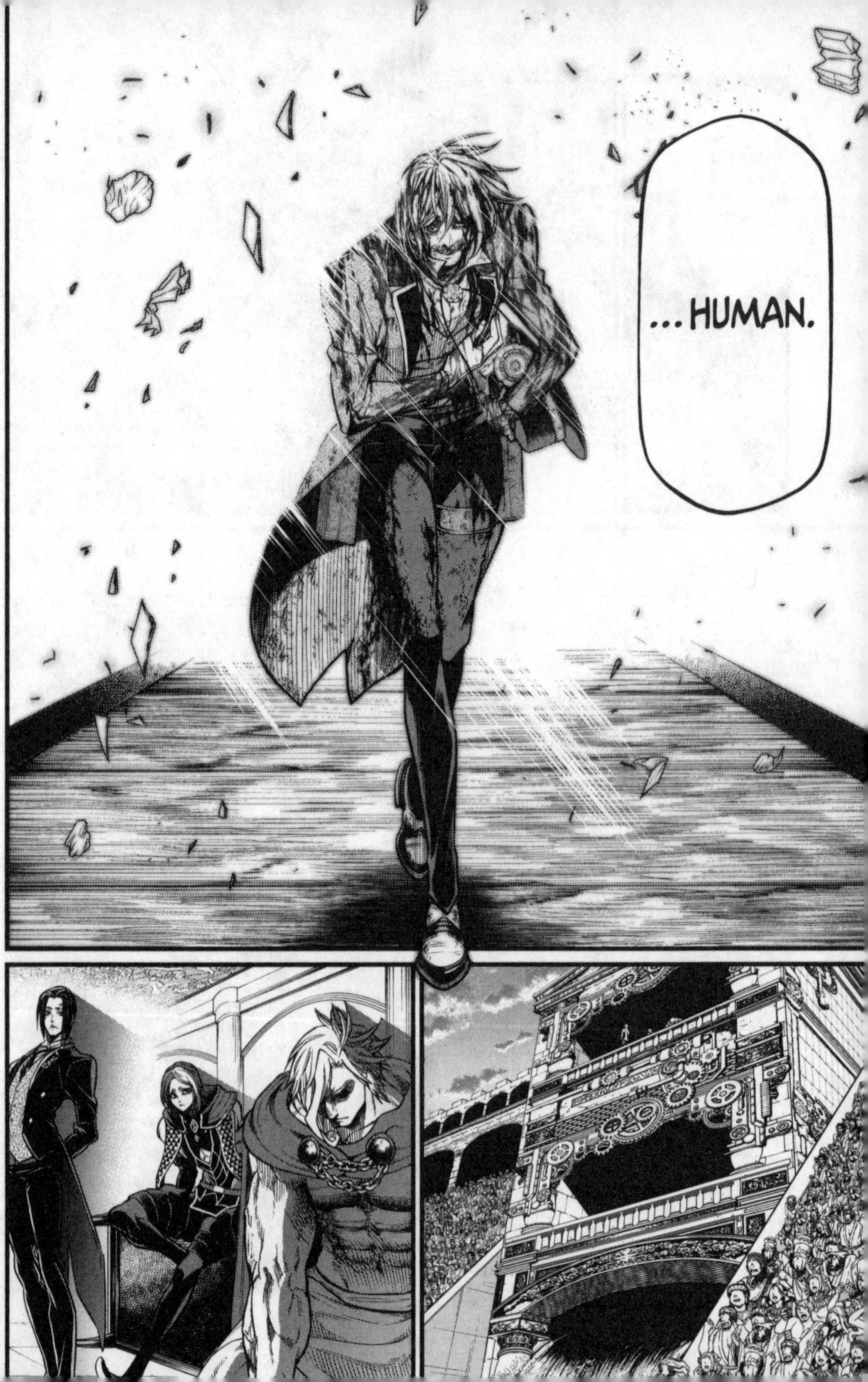
...HUMAN.

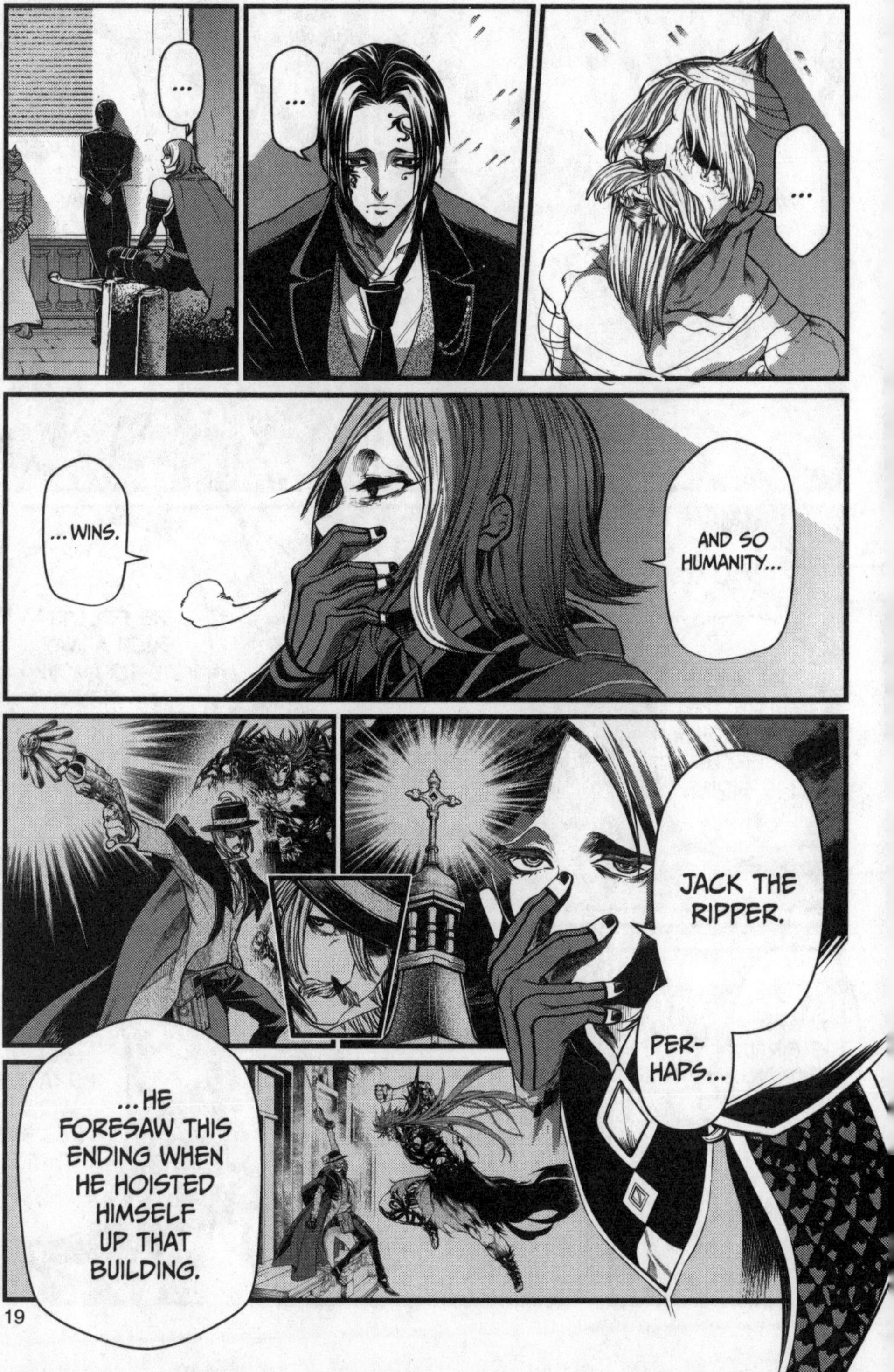
...
...
...
AND SO HUMANITY...
...WINS.
JACK THE RIPPER.
PER-HAPS...
...HE FORESAW THIS ENDING WHEN HE HOISTED HIMSELF UP THAT BUILDING.

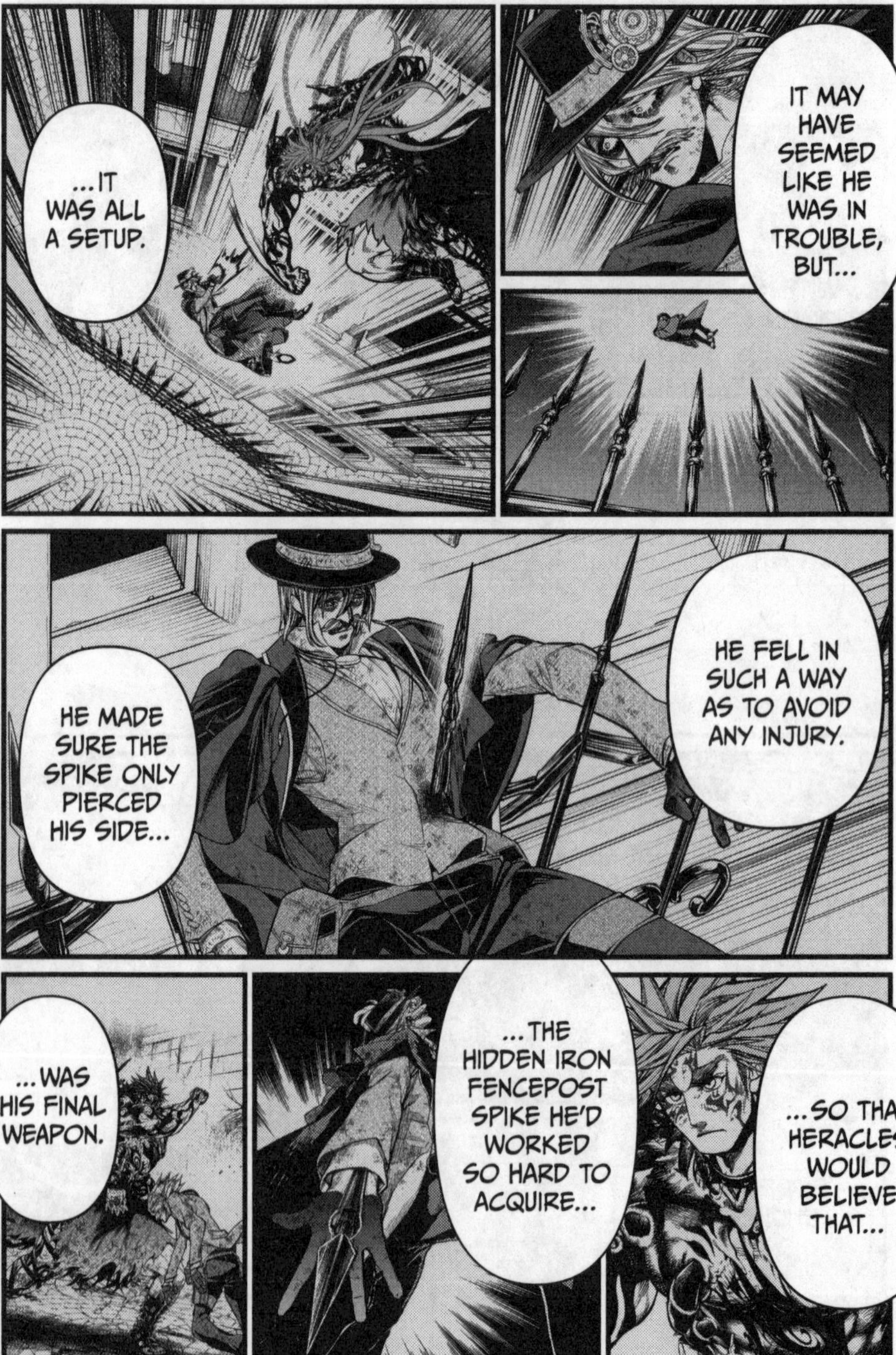
IT MAY HAVE SEEMED LIKE HE WAS IN TROUBLE, BUT...
...IT WAS ALL A SETUP.
HE FELL IN SUCH A WAY AS TO AVOID ANY INJURY.
HE MADE SURE THE SPIKE ONLY PIERCED HIS SIDE...
...SO THAT HERACLES WOULD BELIEVE THAT...
...THE HIDDEN IRON FENCEPOST SPIKE HE'D WORKED SO HARD TO ACQUIRE...
...WAS HIS FINAL WEAPON.

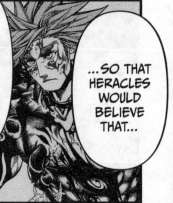

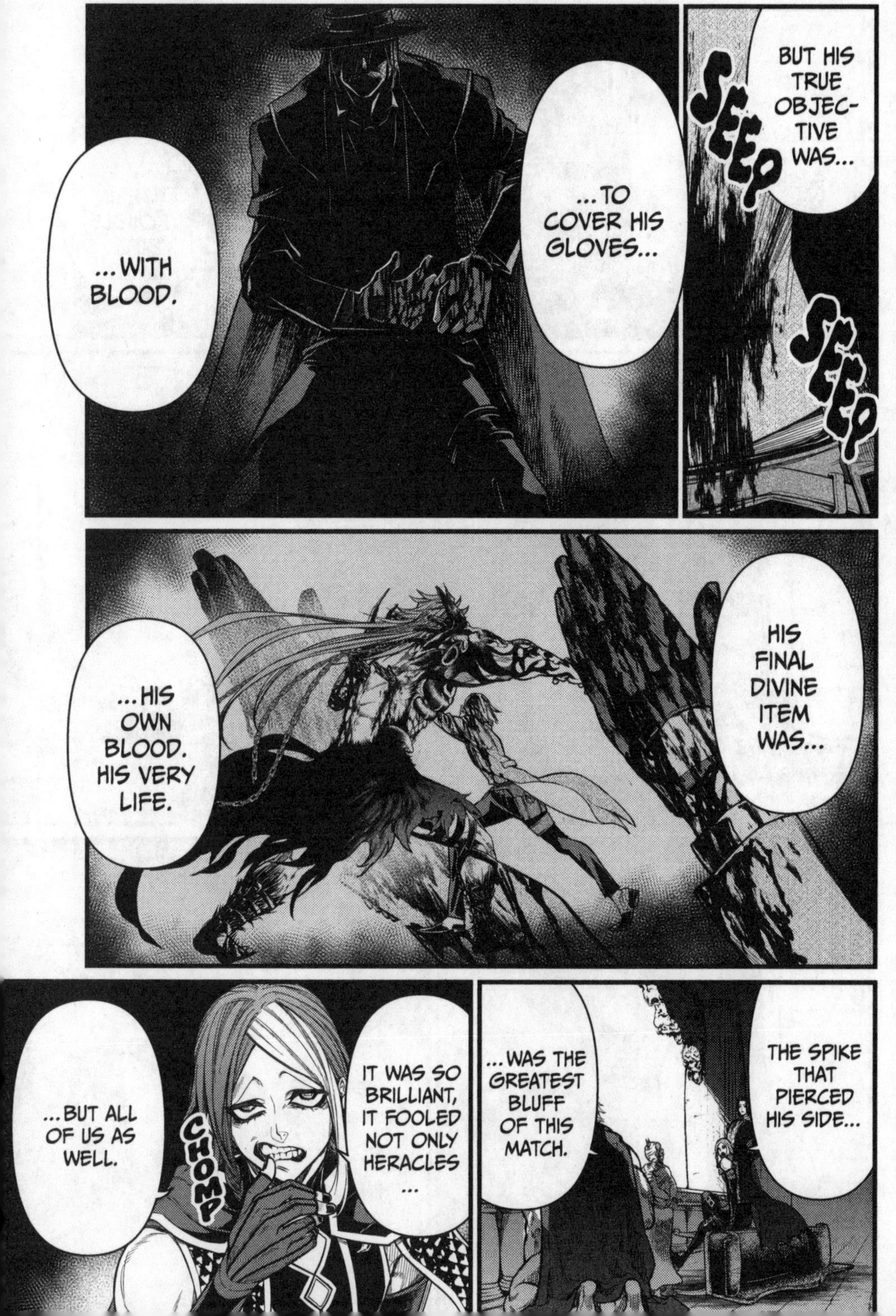
SEEP
BUT HIS TRUE OBJECTIVE WAS...
SEEP SEEP
...TO COVER HIS GLOVES...
...WITH BLOOD.
HIS FINAL DIVINE ITEM WAS...
...HIS OWN BLOOD. HIS VERY LIFE.
THE SPIKE THAT PIERCED HIS SIDE...
...WAS THE GREATEST BLUFF OF THIS MATCH.
IT WAS SO BRILLIANT, IT FOOLED NOT ONLY HERACLES ...
CHOMP
...BUT ALL OF US AS WELL.

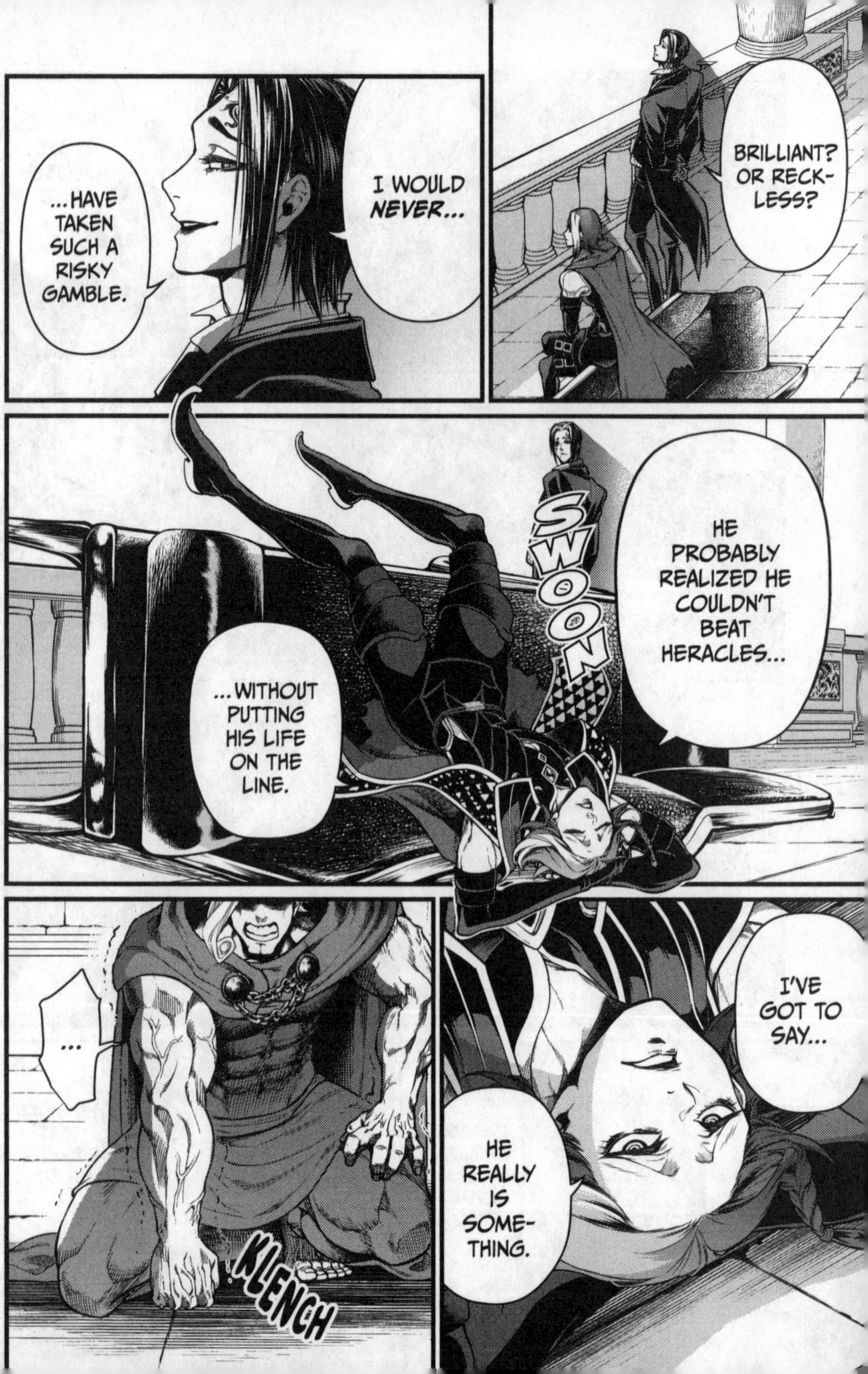
BRILLIANT? OR RECKLESS?
I WOULD *NEVER*...
...HAVE TAKEN SUCH A RISKY GAMBLE.
HE PROBABLY REALIZED HE COULDN'T BEAT HERACLES...
SWOON
...WITHOUT PUTTING HIS LIFE ON THE LINE.
I'VE GOT TO SAY...
HE REALLY IS SOMETHING.
...
KLENCH

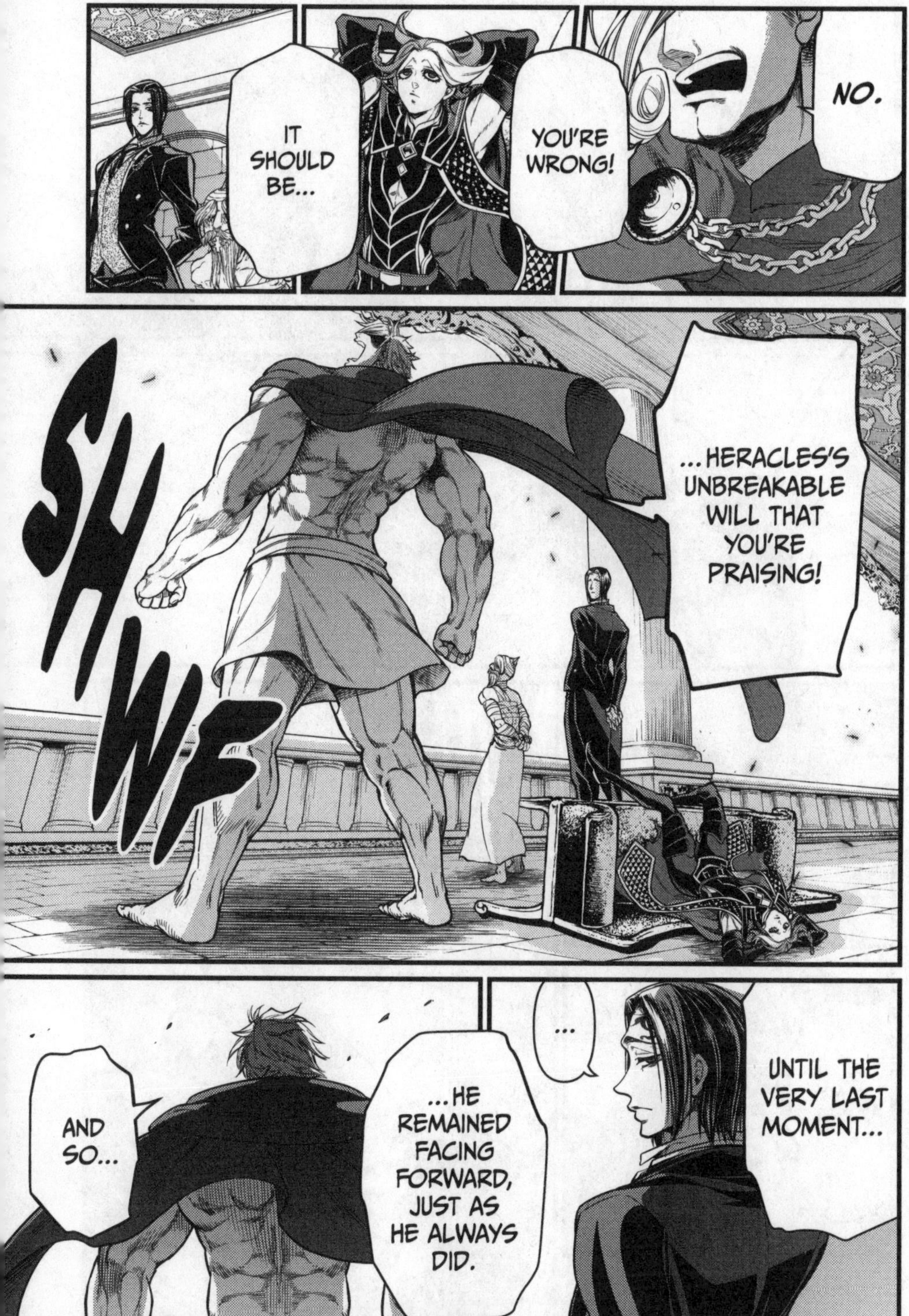
NO.
YOU'RE WRONG!
IT SHOULD BE...
...HERACLES'S UNBREAKABLE WILL THAT YOU'RE PRAISING!
SHWF
...
UNTIL THE VERY LAST MOMENT...
...HE REMAINED FACING FORWARD, JUST AS HE ALWAYS DID.
AND SO...

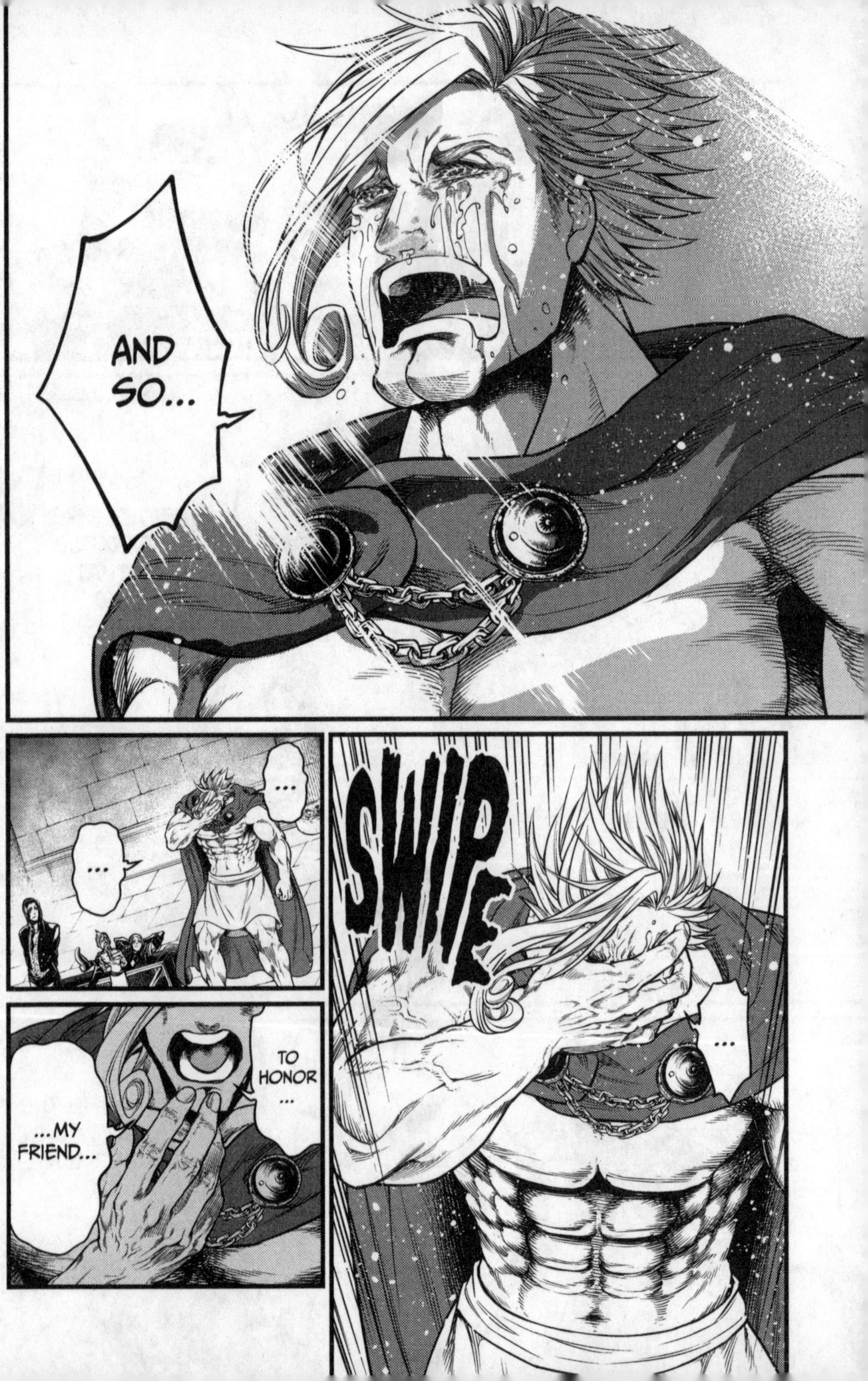
AND SO...
SWIP
...
...
...
TO HONOR ...
...MY FRIEND...

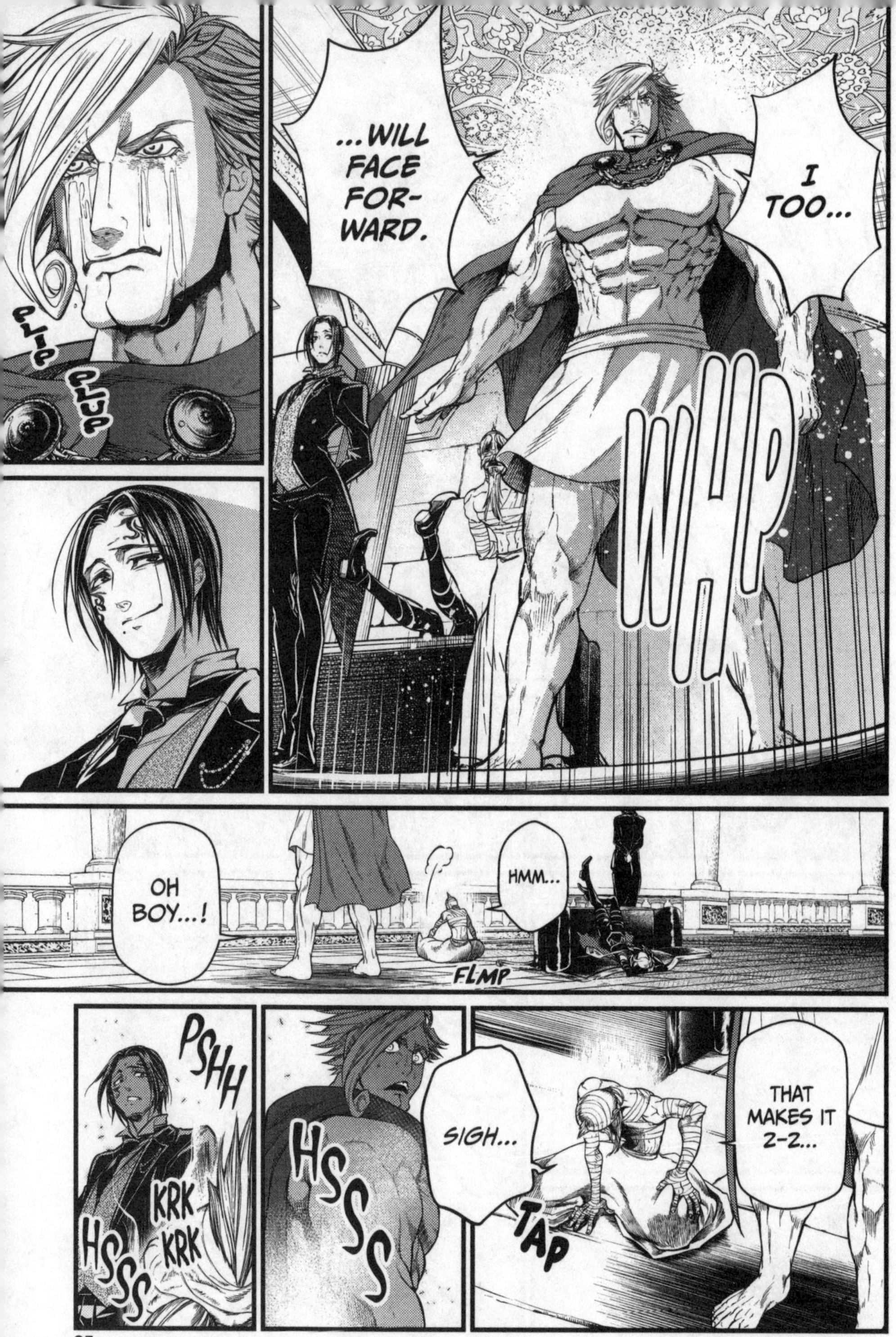
I TOO...
...WILL FACE FOR-WARD.
WHP
PLIP
PLUP
HMM...
FLMP
OH BOY...!
THAT MAKES IT 2-2...
SIGH...
TAP
HSSS
PSHH
KRK KRK
HSSS

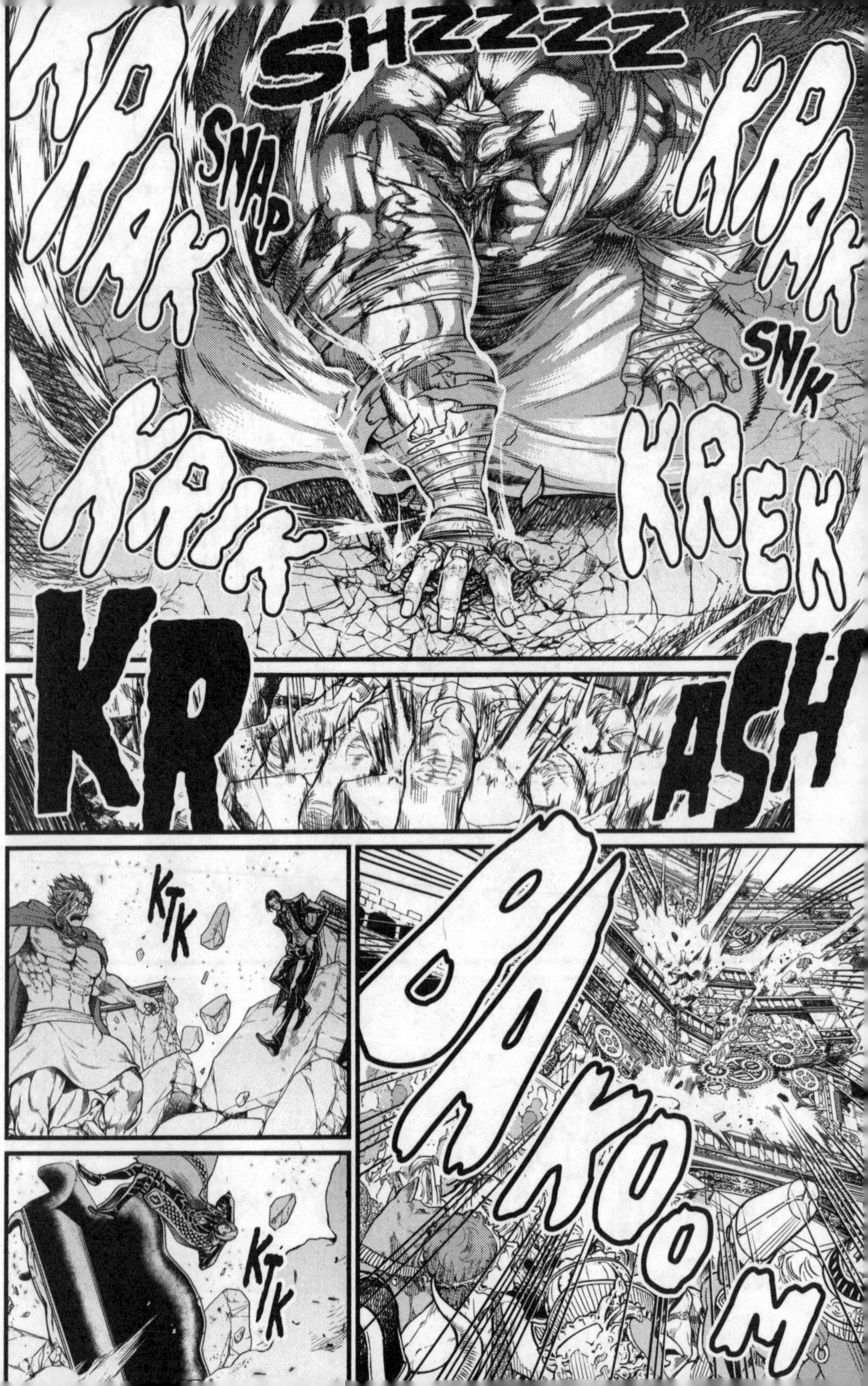
SHZZZZZ
SNIK
KREK
SNAP
KRASH
KTIK
KTIK

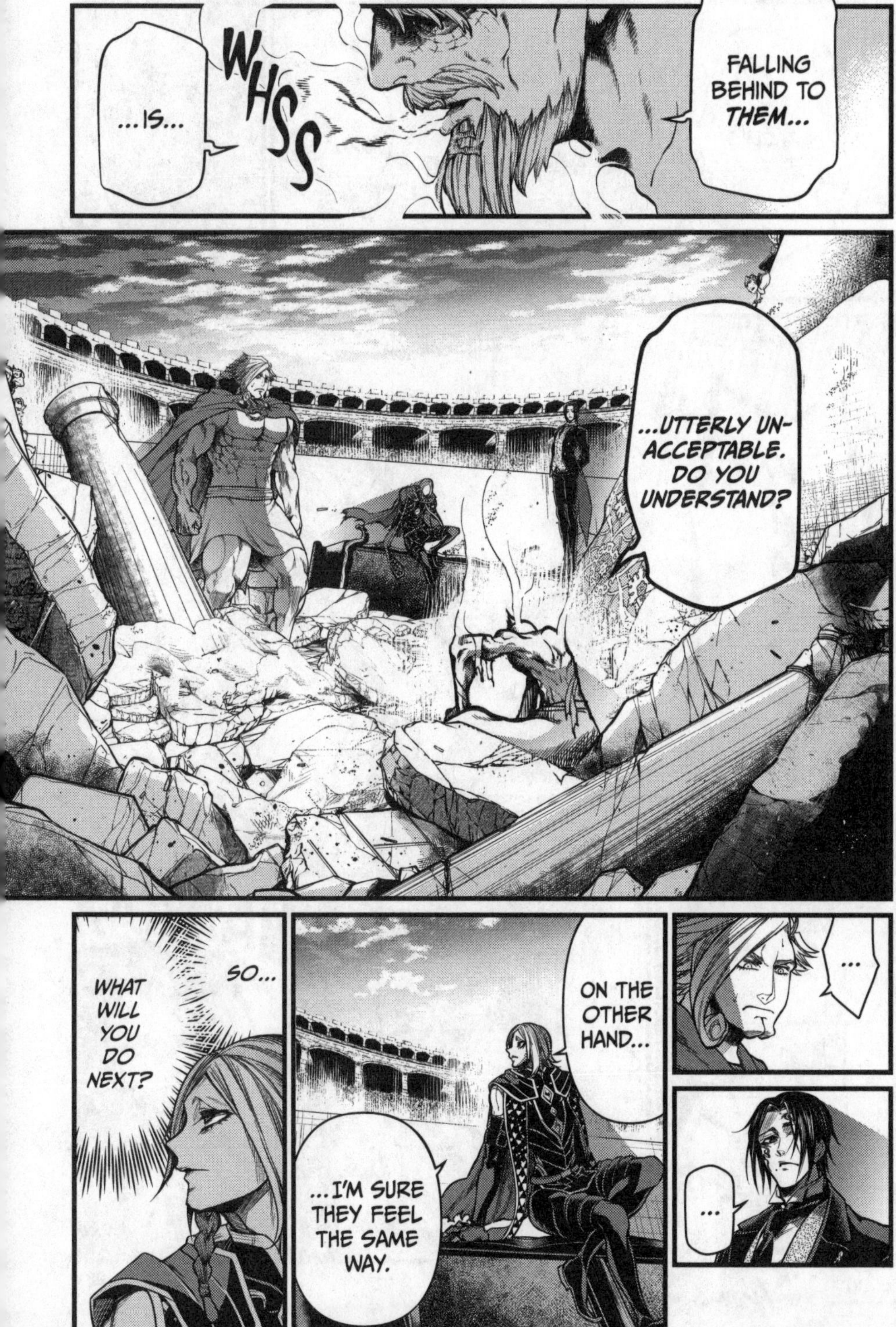
FALLING BEHIND TO THEM...
WHSS
...IS...
...UTTERLY UN-ACCEPTABLE. DO YOU UNDERSTAND?
...
...
ON THE OTHER HAND...
...I'M SURE THEY FEEL THE SAME WAY.
SO...
WHAT WILL YOU DO NEXT?

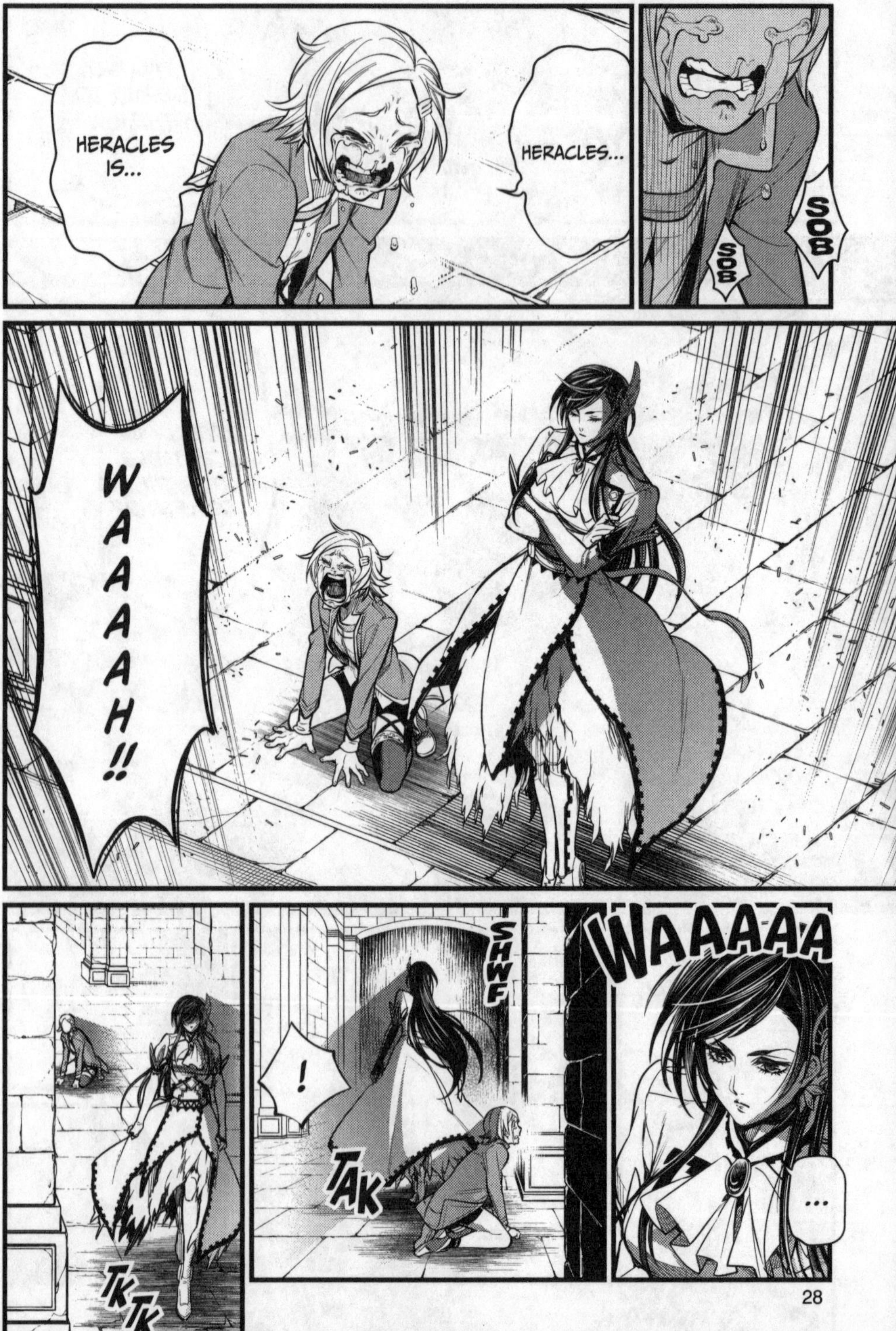
SOB
SOB
HERACLES...
HERACLES IS...
WAAAAAH!!
WAAAAA
...
SHWF
!
TAK
TKTK

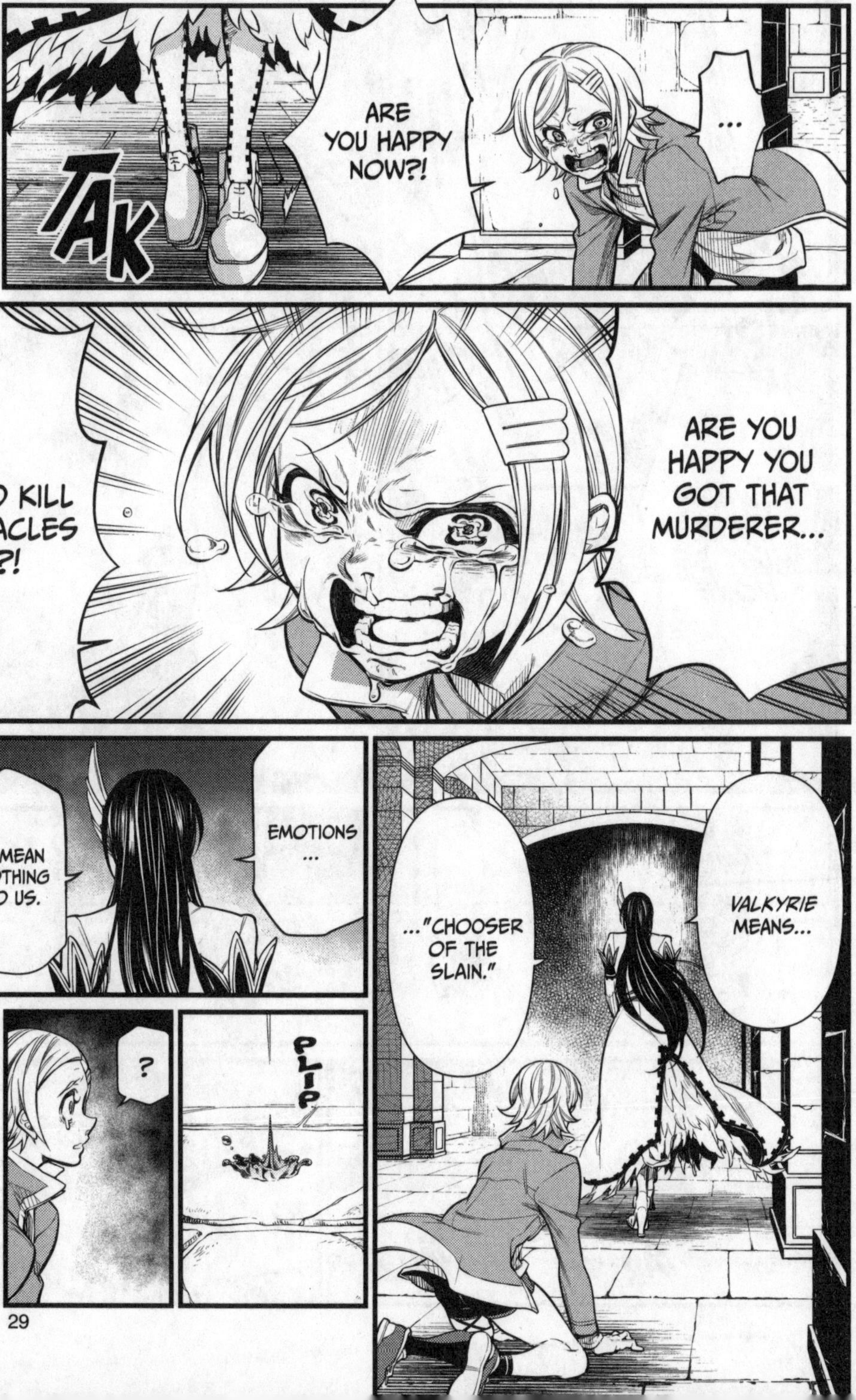
...
ARE YOU HAPPY NOW?!
TAK
ARE YOU HAPPY YOU GOT THAT MURDERER...
...TO KILL HERACLES ?!
VALKYRIE MEANS...
..."CHOOSER OF THE SLAIN."
EMOTIONS ...
...MEAN NOTHING TO US.
PLIP
?

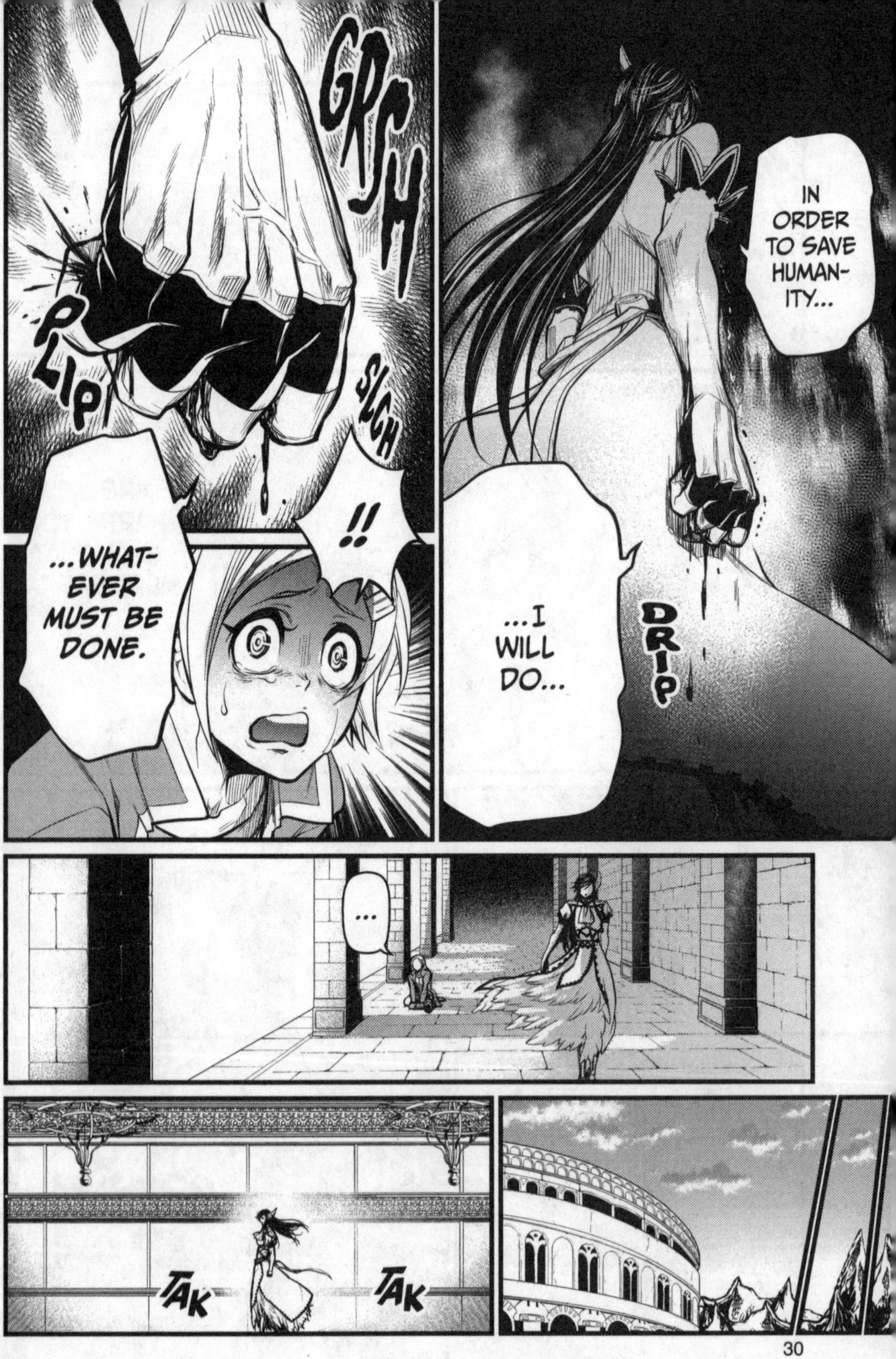
IN ORDER TO SAVE HUMAN-ITY...
...I WILL DO...
DRIP
GRPH
PLIP
SLCH
!!
...WHAT-EVER MUST BE DONE.
...
TAK
TAK

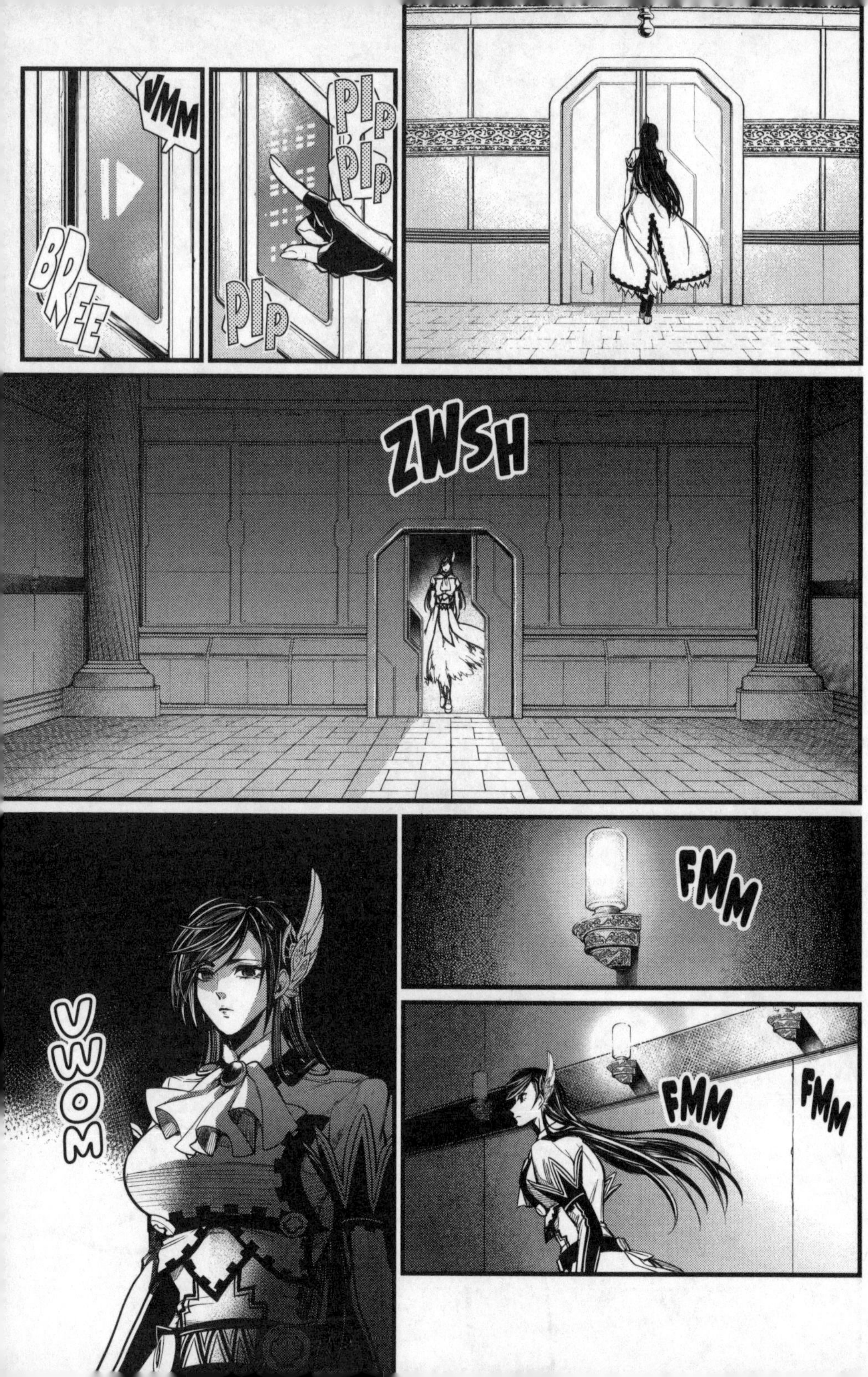
PIP PIP PIP
PIP
VMM
BREE
ZWSH
FMM
FMM
FMM
VWOM

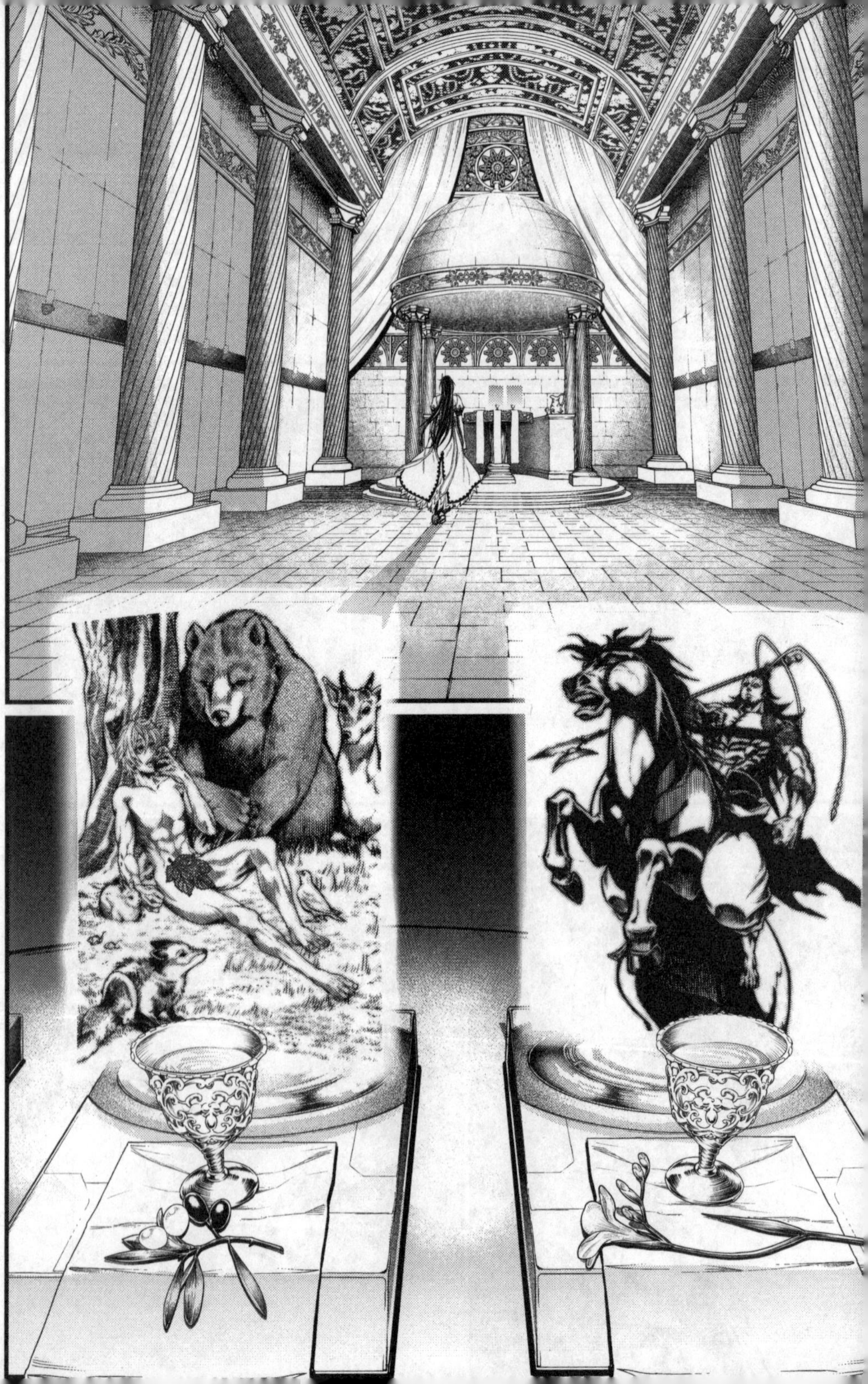

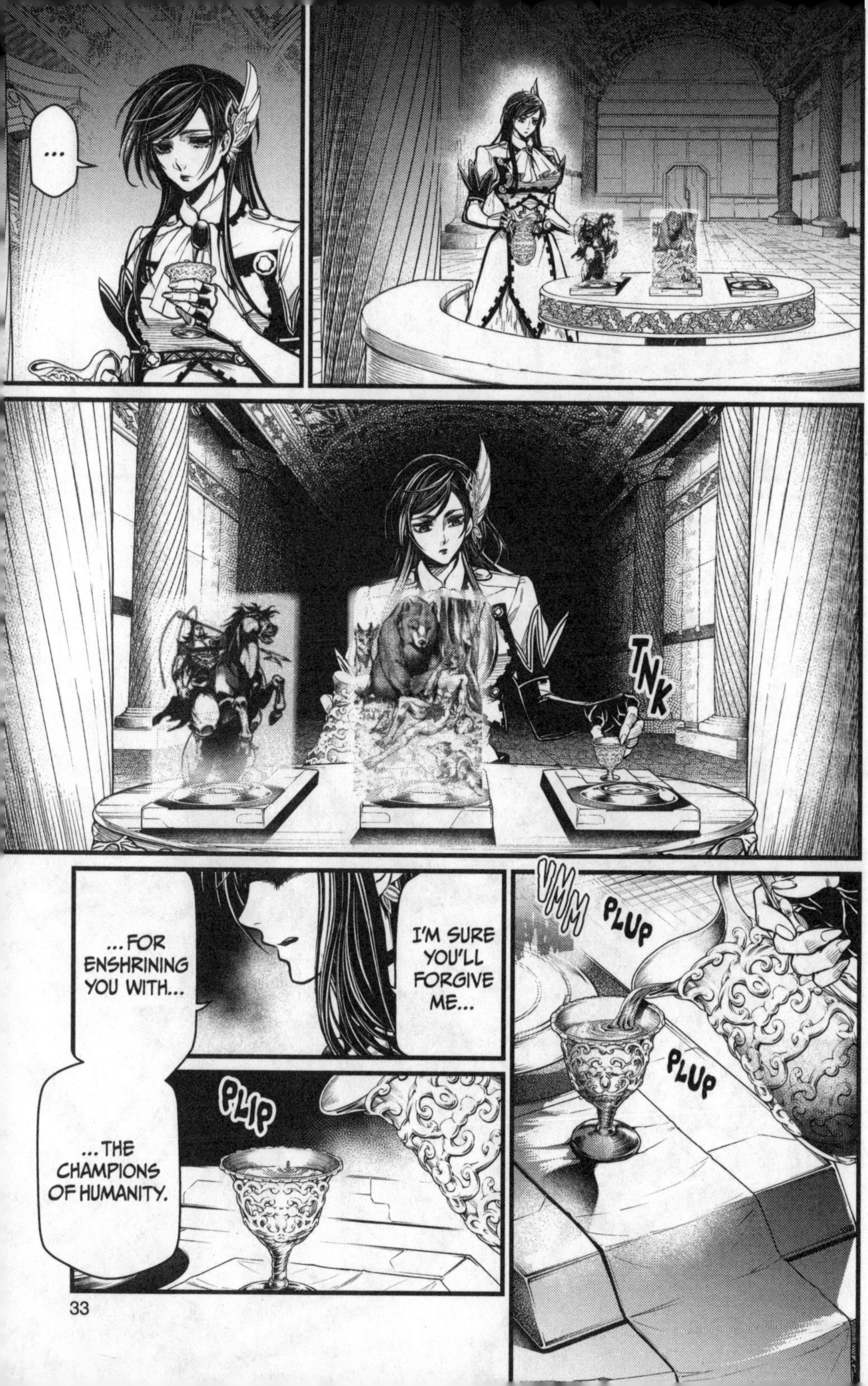
...
TNK
VMM
PLUP
PLUP
I'M SURE YOU'LL FORGIVE ME...
...FOR ENSHRINING YOU WITH...
PLIP
...THE CHAMPIONS OF HUMANITY.

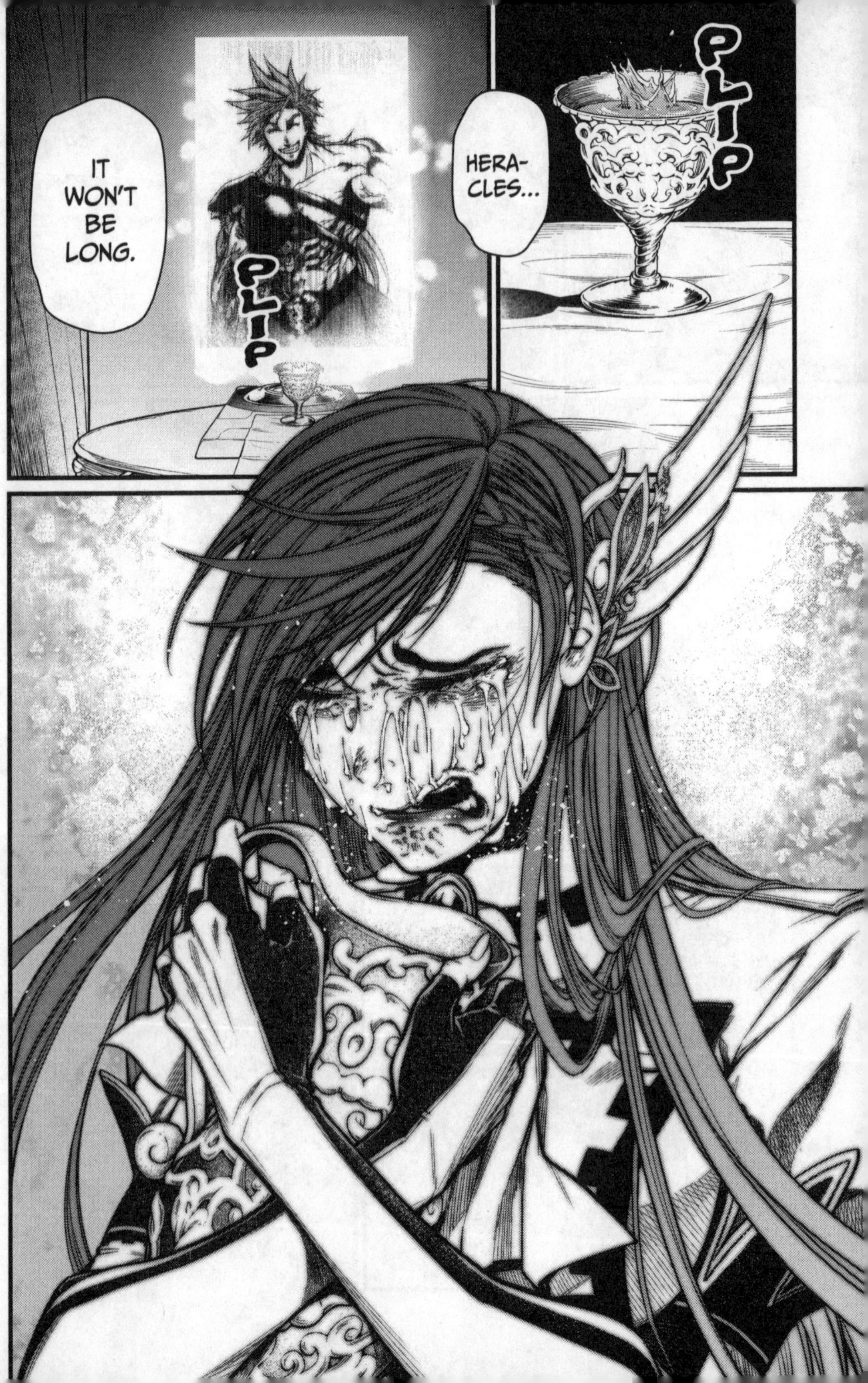
PLIP PLIP
HERA-
CLES...
IT
WON'T
BE
LONG.
PLIP

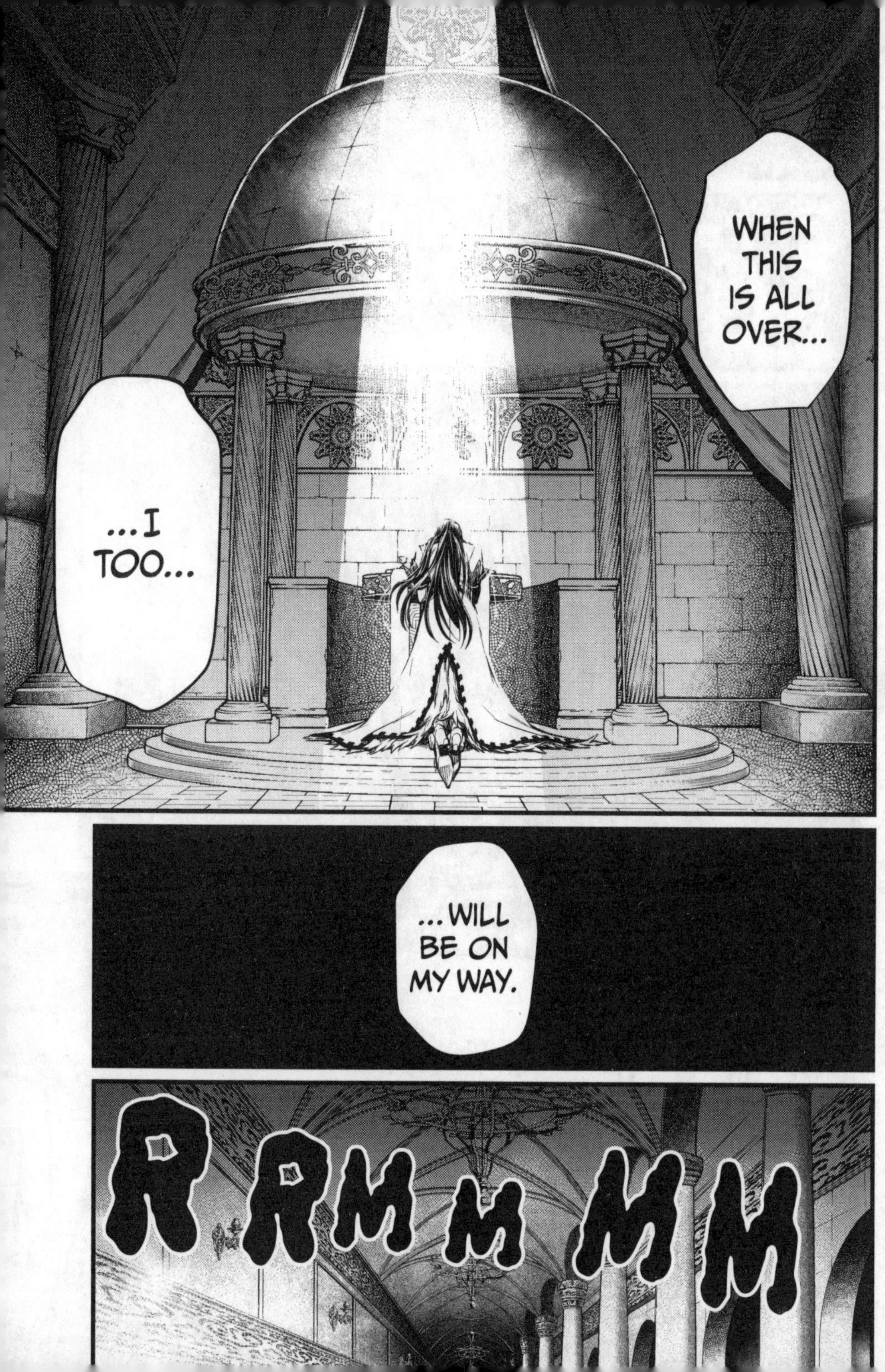
WHEN THIS IS ALL OVER...
...I TOO...
...WILL BE ON MY WAY.
RRMMMM

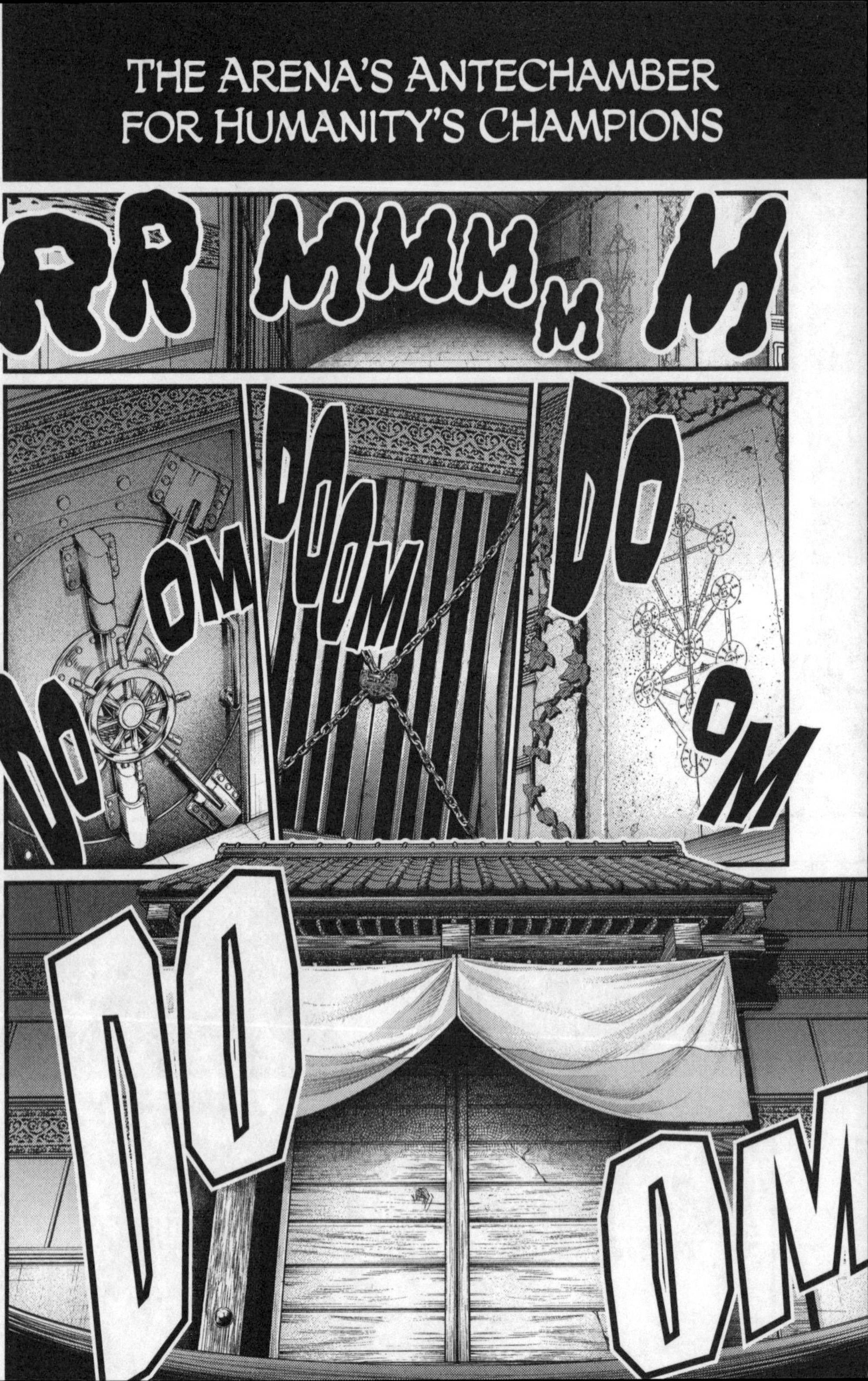
THE ARENA'S ANTECHAMBER FOR HUMANITY'S CHAMPIONS
RRMMMMM
DOOOM
DOOOM
DOOOM
DOOM

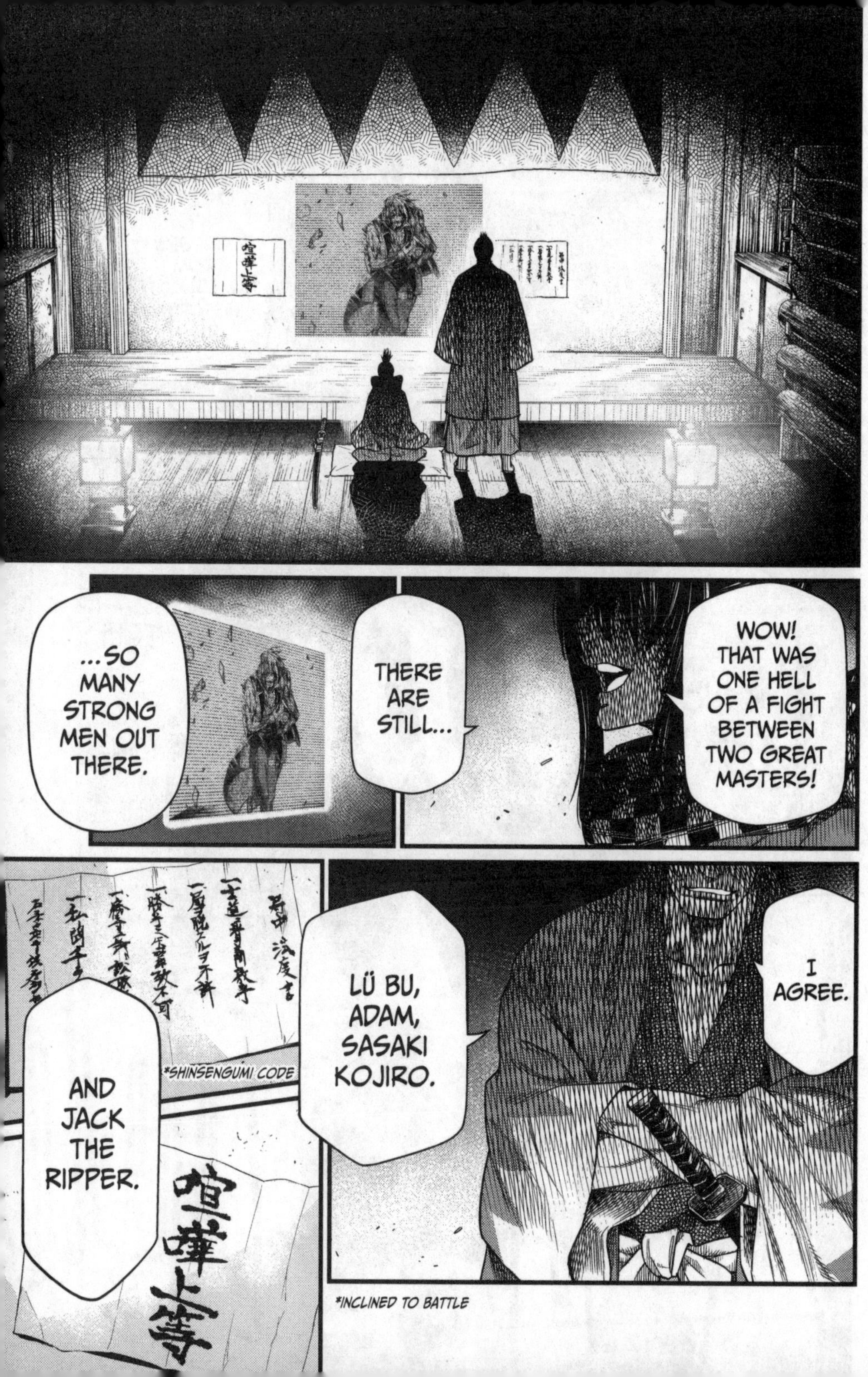
WOW! THAT WAS ONE HELL OF A FIGHT BETWEEN TWO GREAT MASTERS!
THERE ARE STILL...
...SO MANY STRONG MEN OUT THERE.
I AGREE.
LÜ BU, ADAM, SASAKI KOJIRO.
*SHINSENGUMI CODE
AND JACK THE RIPPER.
喧嘩上等
*INCLINED TO BATTLE

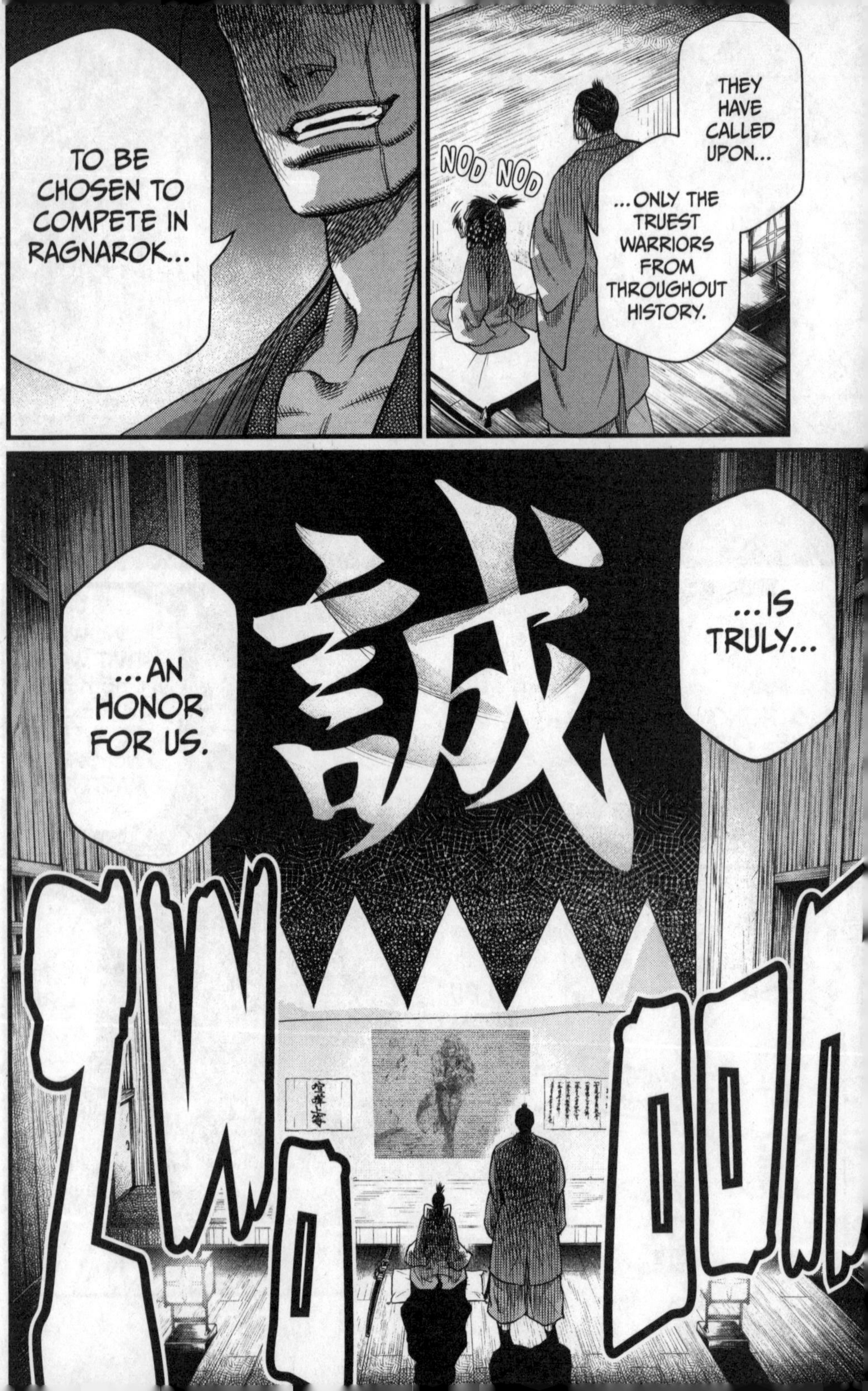
THEY HAVE CALLED UPON...
NOD NOD
...ONLY THE TRUEST WARRIORS FROM THROUGHOUT HISTORY.
TO BE CHOSEN TO COMPETE IN RAGNAROK...
...IS TRULY...
誠
...AN HONOR FOR US.

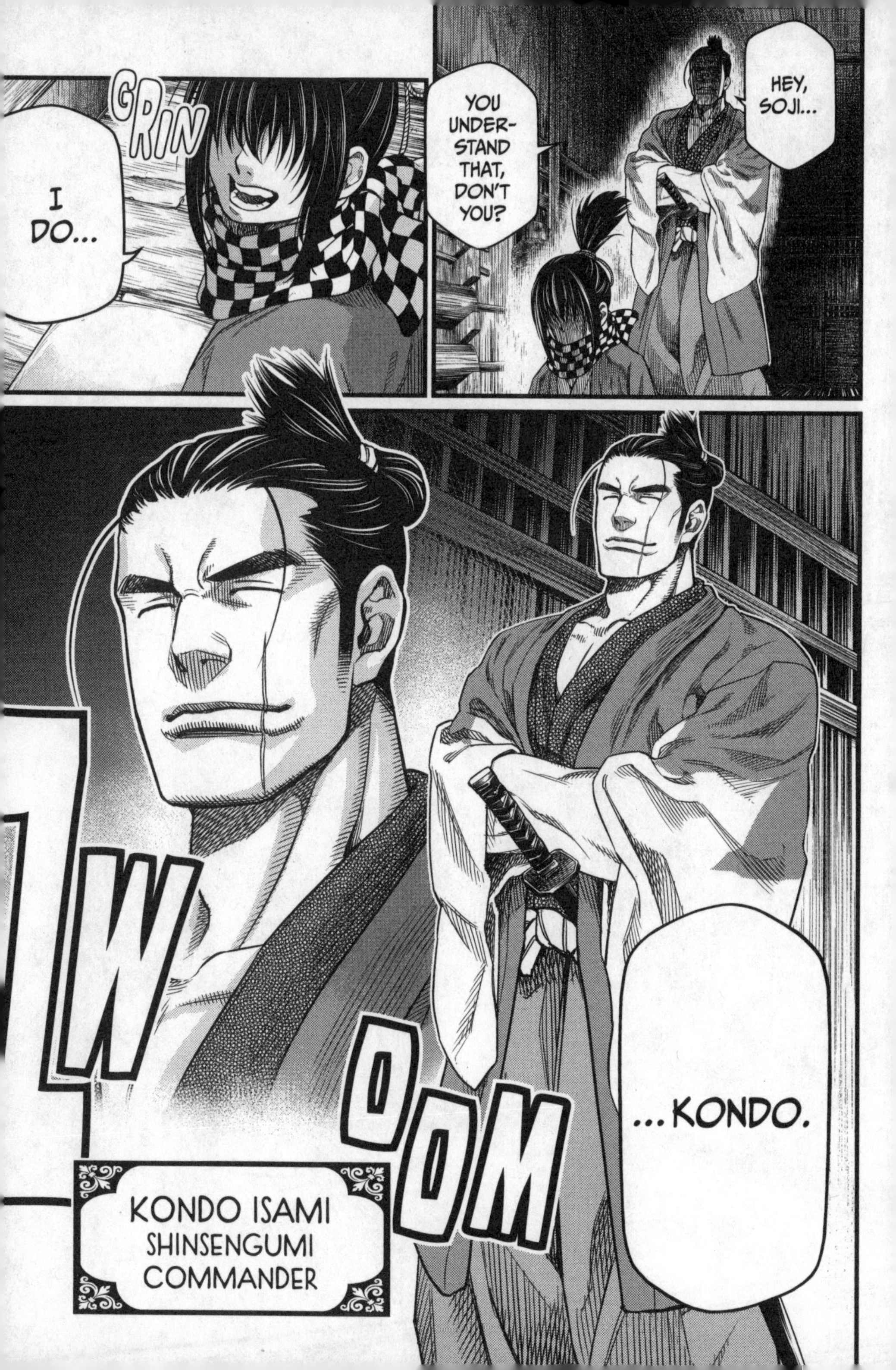
HEY, SOJI...
YOU UNDERSTAND THAT, DON'T YOU?
GRIN
I DO...
...KONDO.
WOOM
KONDO ISAMI
SHINSENGUMI COMMANDER

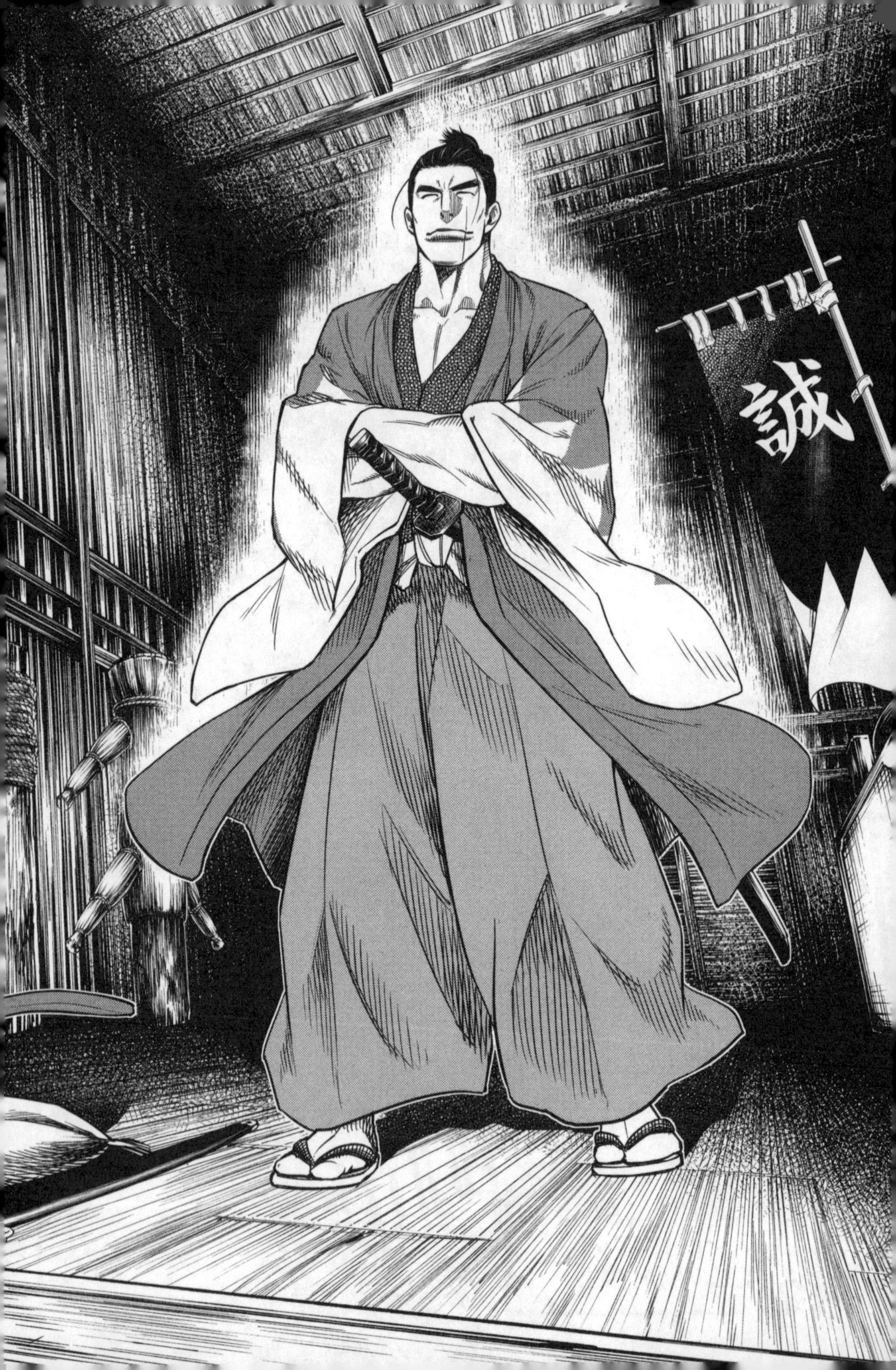
誠

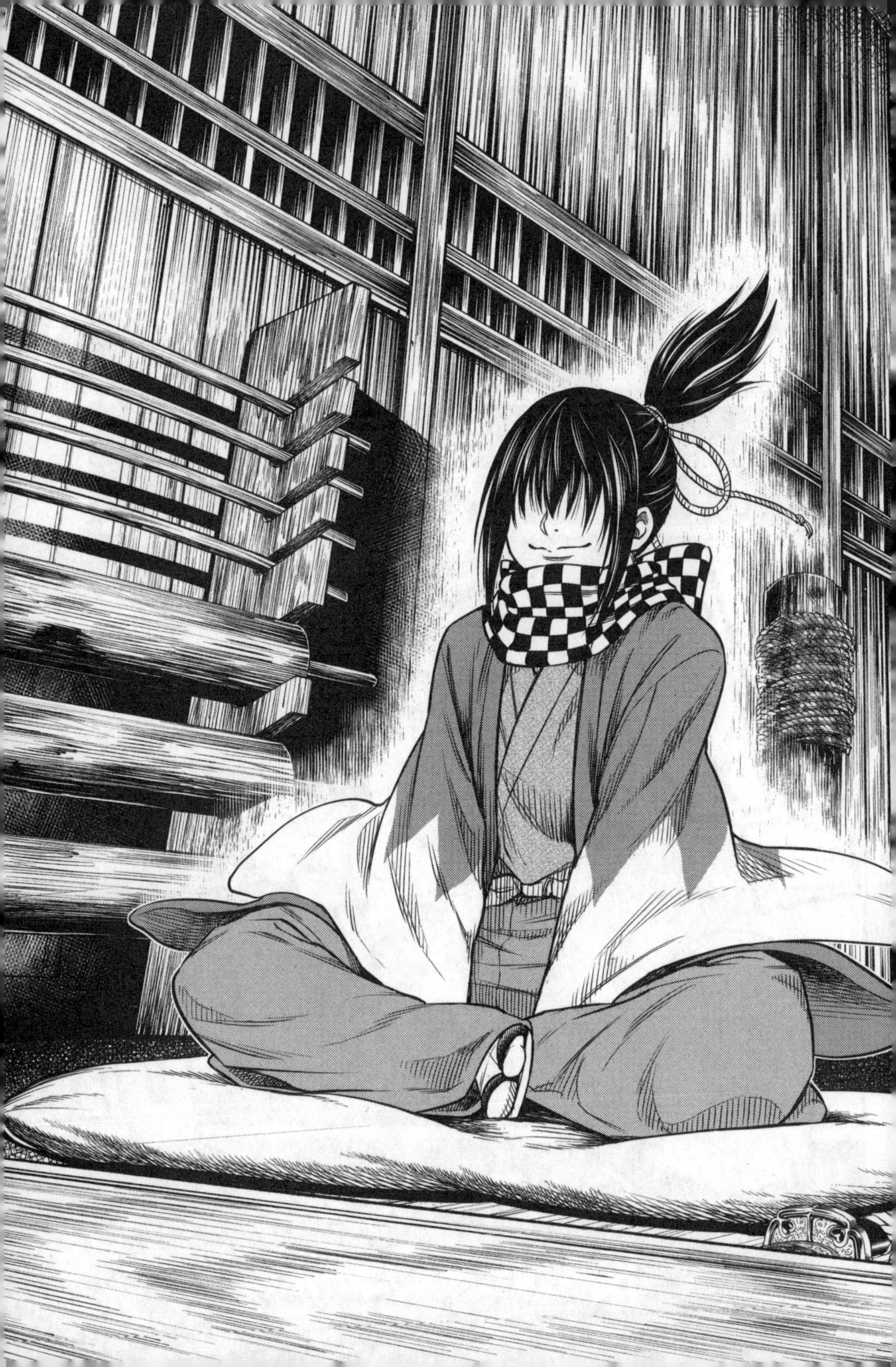

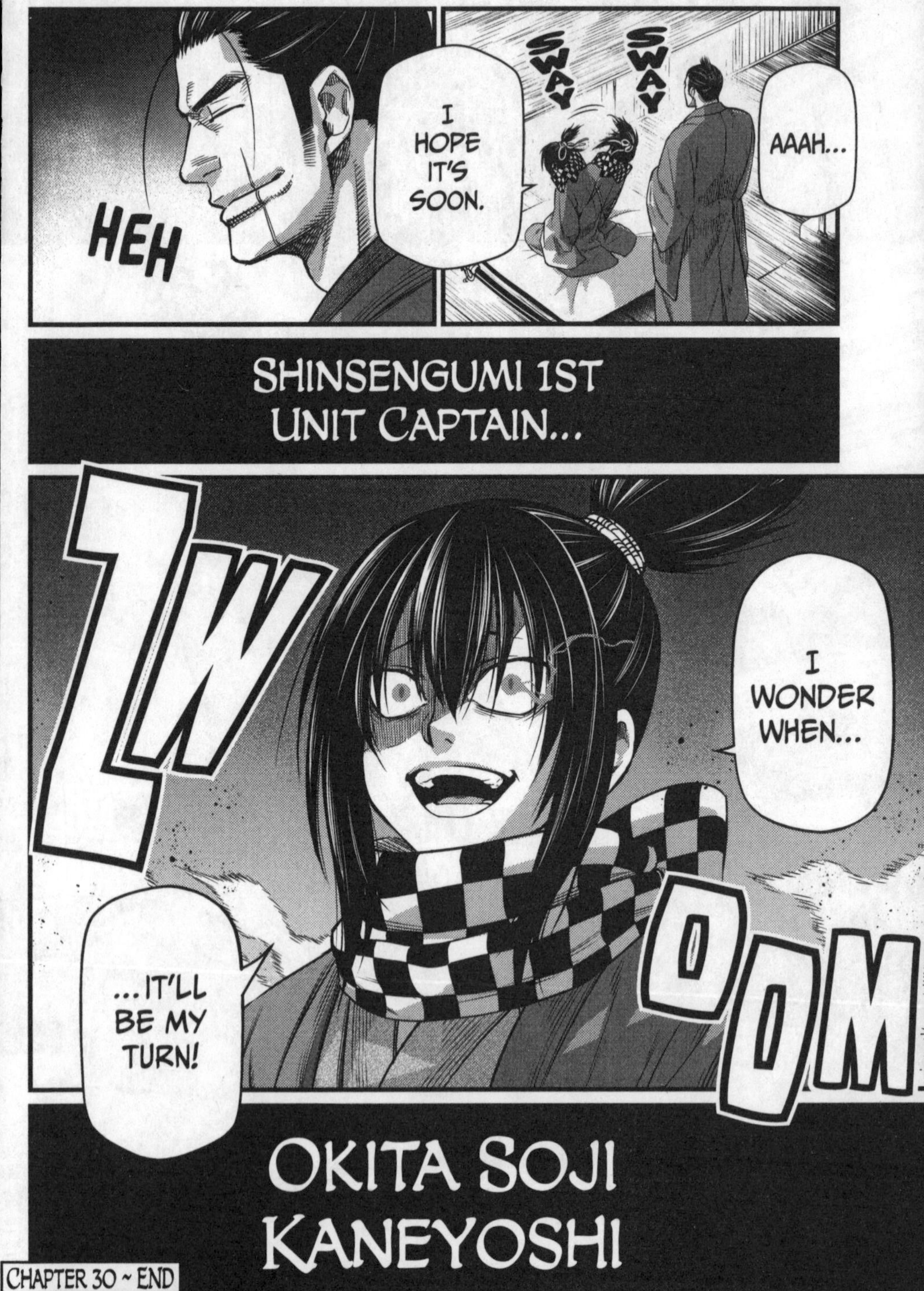
AAAH...
SWAY
SWAY
I HOPE IT'S SOON.
HEH
SHINSENGUMI 1ST UNIT CAPTAIN...
I WONDER WHEN...
ZW
OOM
...IT'LL BE MY TURN!
OKITA SOJI KANEYOSHI
CHAPTER 30 ~ END

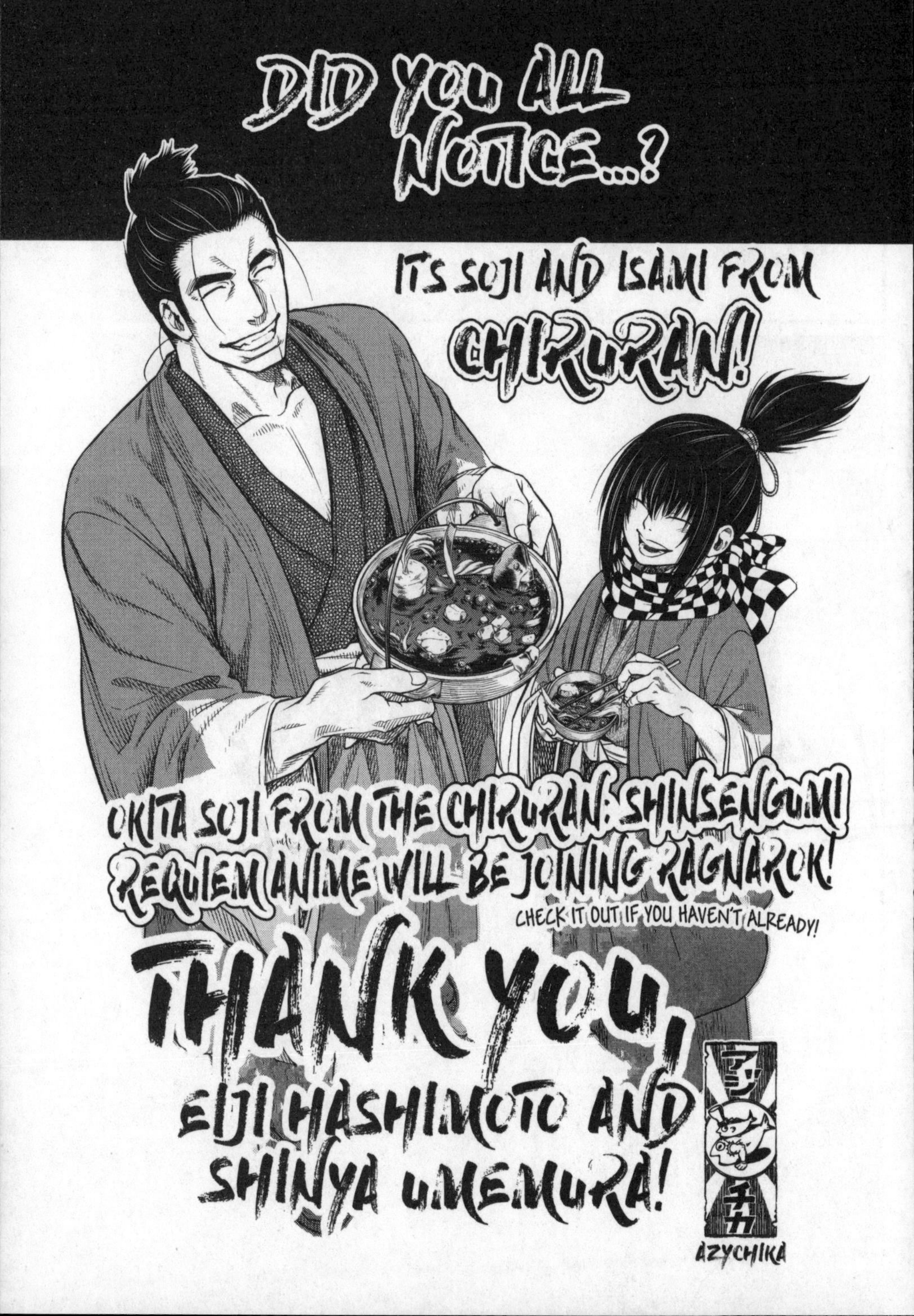
DID YOU ALL NOTICE...?
IT'S SOJI AND ISAMI FROM
CHIRURAN!
OKITA SOJI FROM THE CHIRURAN: SHINSENGUMI REQUIEM ANIME WILL BE JOINING RAGNAROK!
CHECK IT OUT IF YOU HAVEN'T ALREADY!
THANK YOU,
EIJI HASHIMOTO AND SHINYA UMEMURA!
AZYCHIKA

RECORD OF RAGNAROK

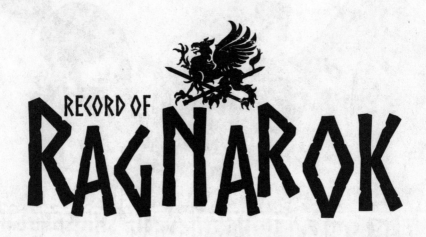

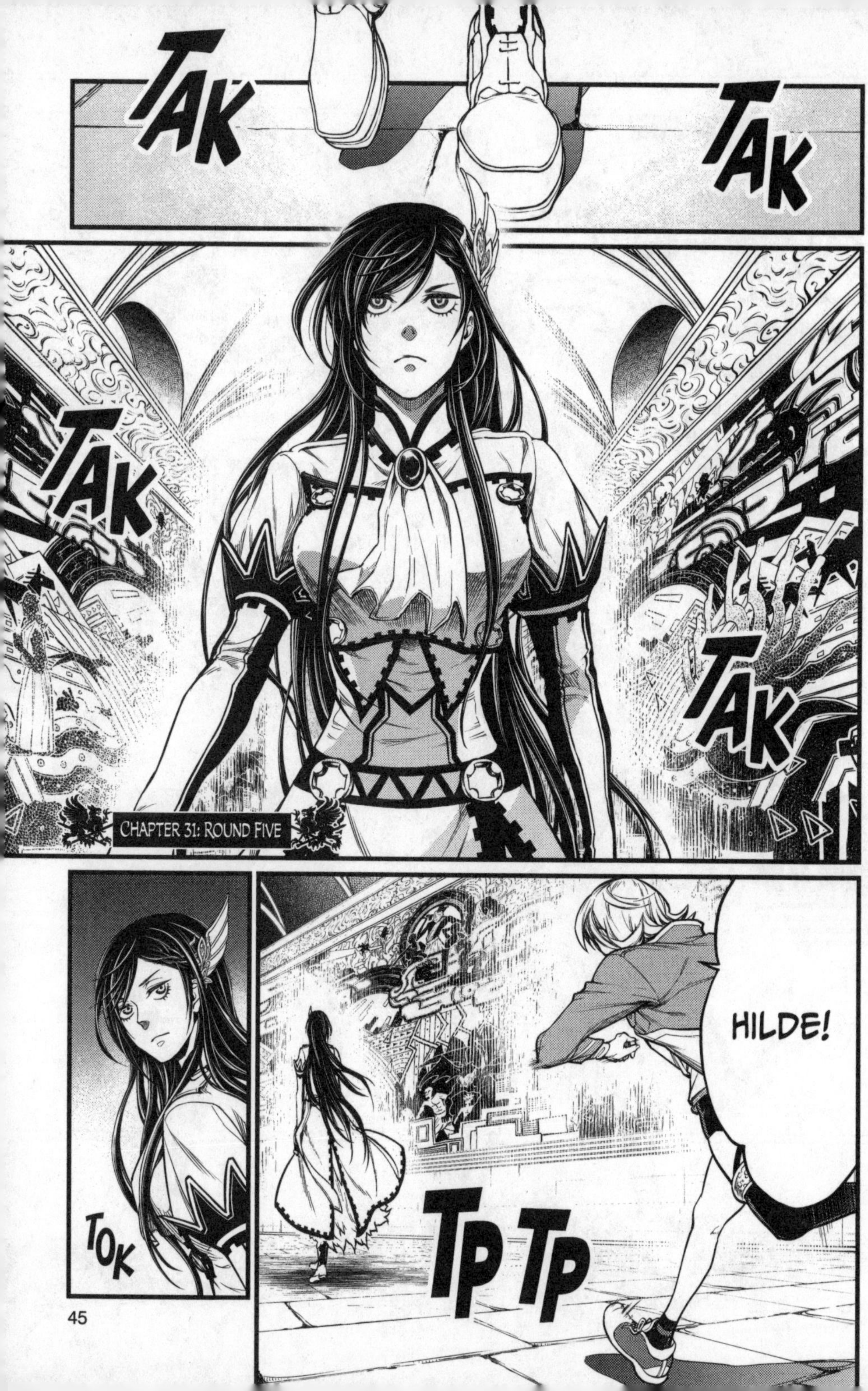
TAK
TAK
TAK
TAK
CHAPTER 31: ROUND FIVE
HILDE!
TP TP
TOK

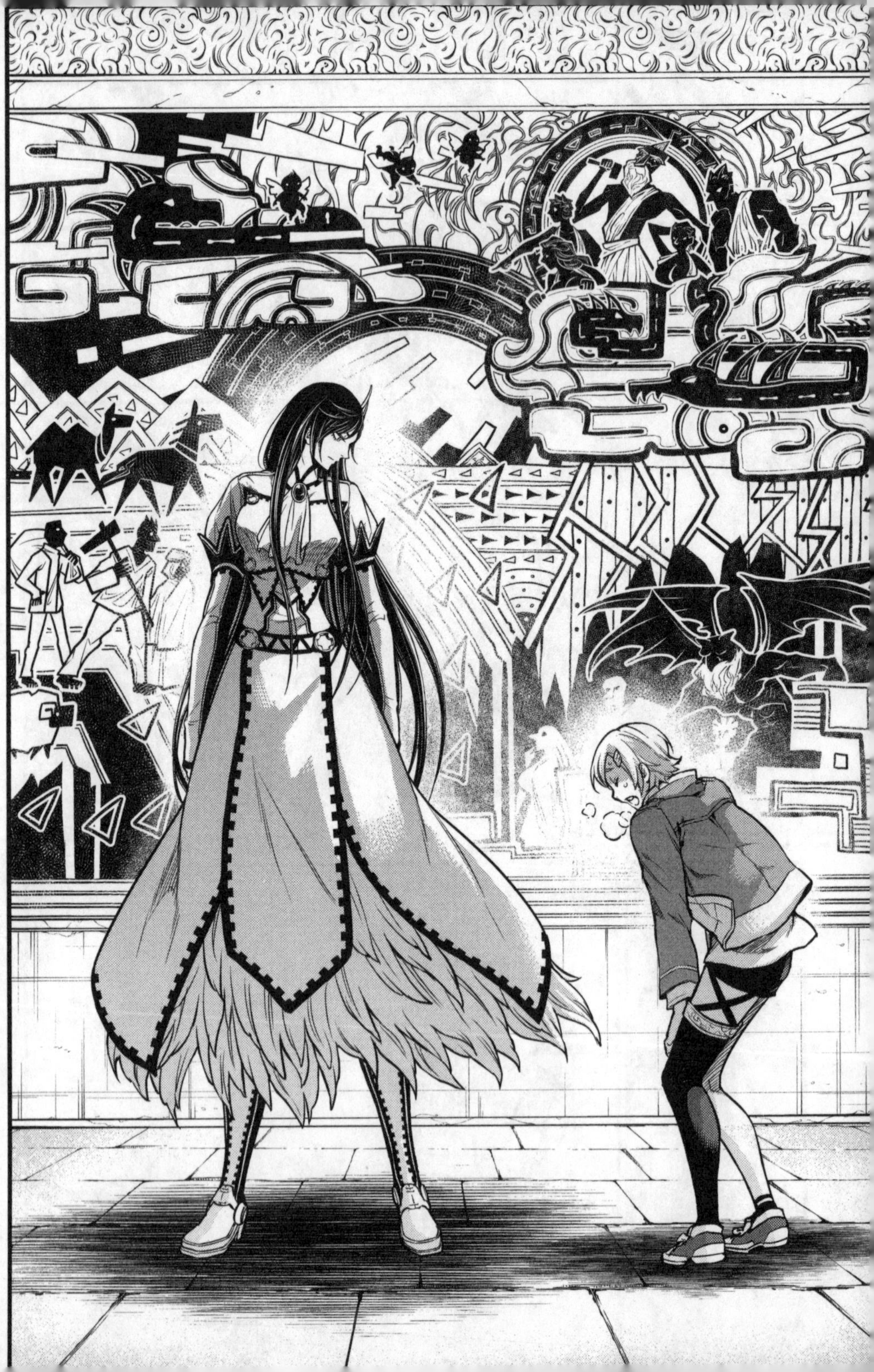

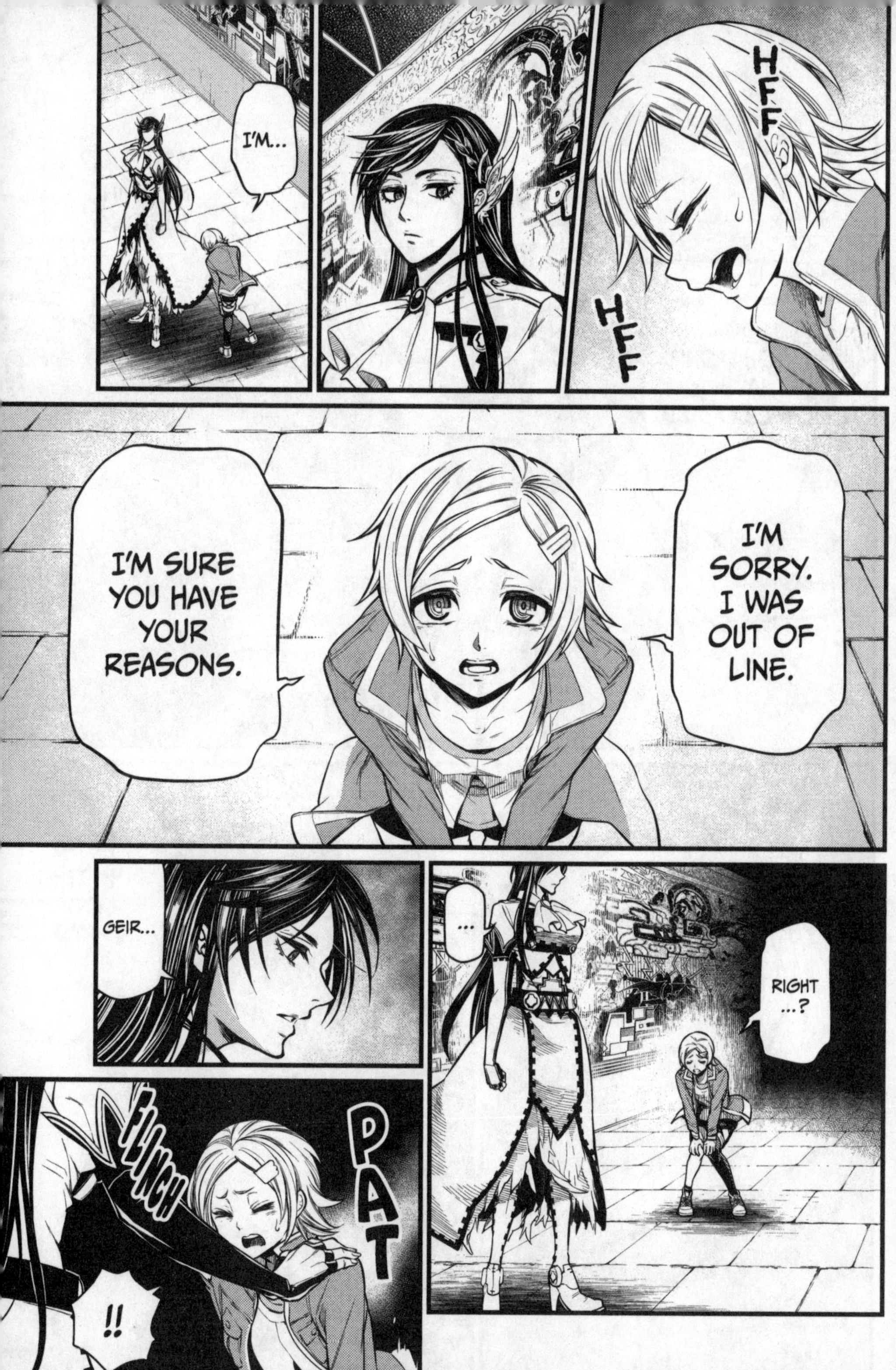
HFF
HFF
I'M...
I'M SORRY. I WAS OUT OF LINE.
I'M SURE YOU HAVE YOUR REASONS.
...
RIGHT ...?
GEIR...
PAT
FLINCH
!!

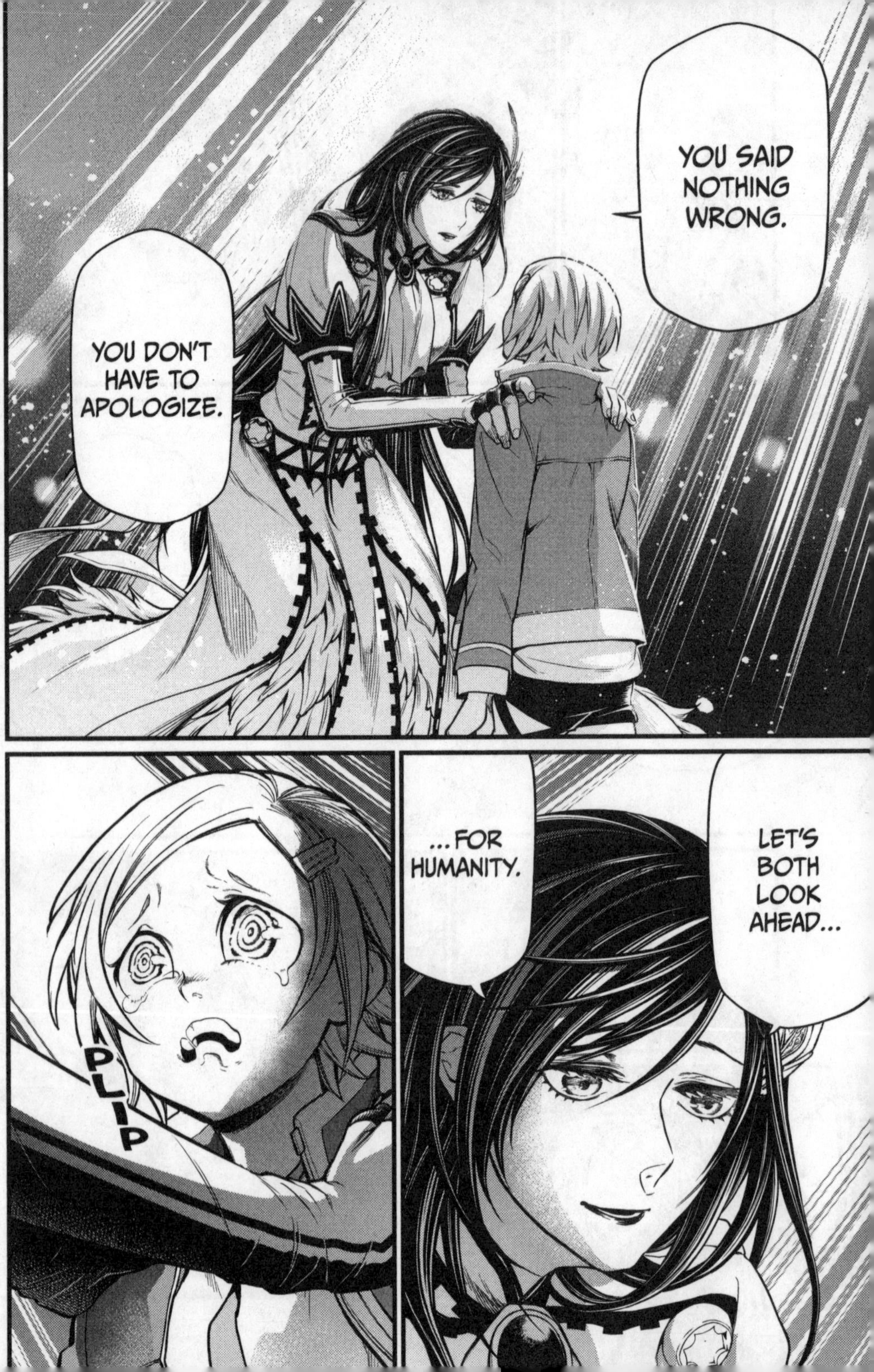
YOU SAID NOTHING WRONG.
YOU DON'T HAVE TO APOLOGIZE.
LET'S BOTH LOOK AHEAD...
...FOR HUMANITY.
PLIP

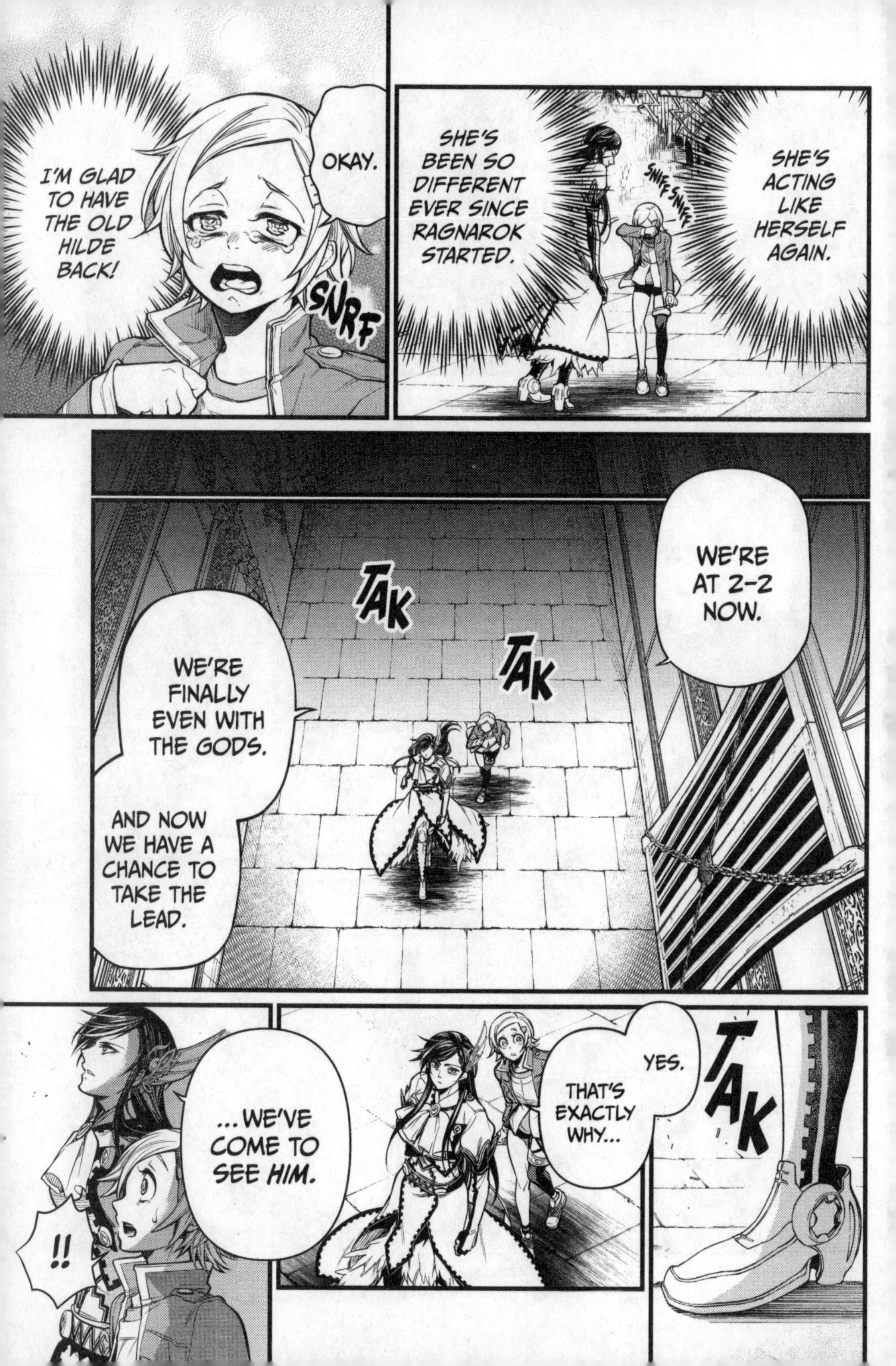
SHE'S ACTING LIKE HERSELF AGAIN.
SNIFF SNIFF
SHE'S BEEN SO DIFFERENT EVER SINCE RAGNAROK STARTED.
OKAY.
I'M GLAD TO HAVE THE OLD HILDE BACK!
SNRF
WE'RE AT 2-2 NOW.
TAK
TAK
WE'RE FINALLY EVEN WITH THE GODS.
AND NOW WE HAVE A CHANCE TO TAKE THE LEAD.
TAK
YES.
THAT'S EXACTLY WHY...
...WE'VE COME TO SEE *HIM*.
!!

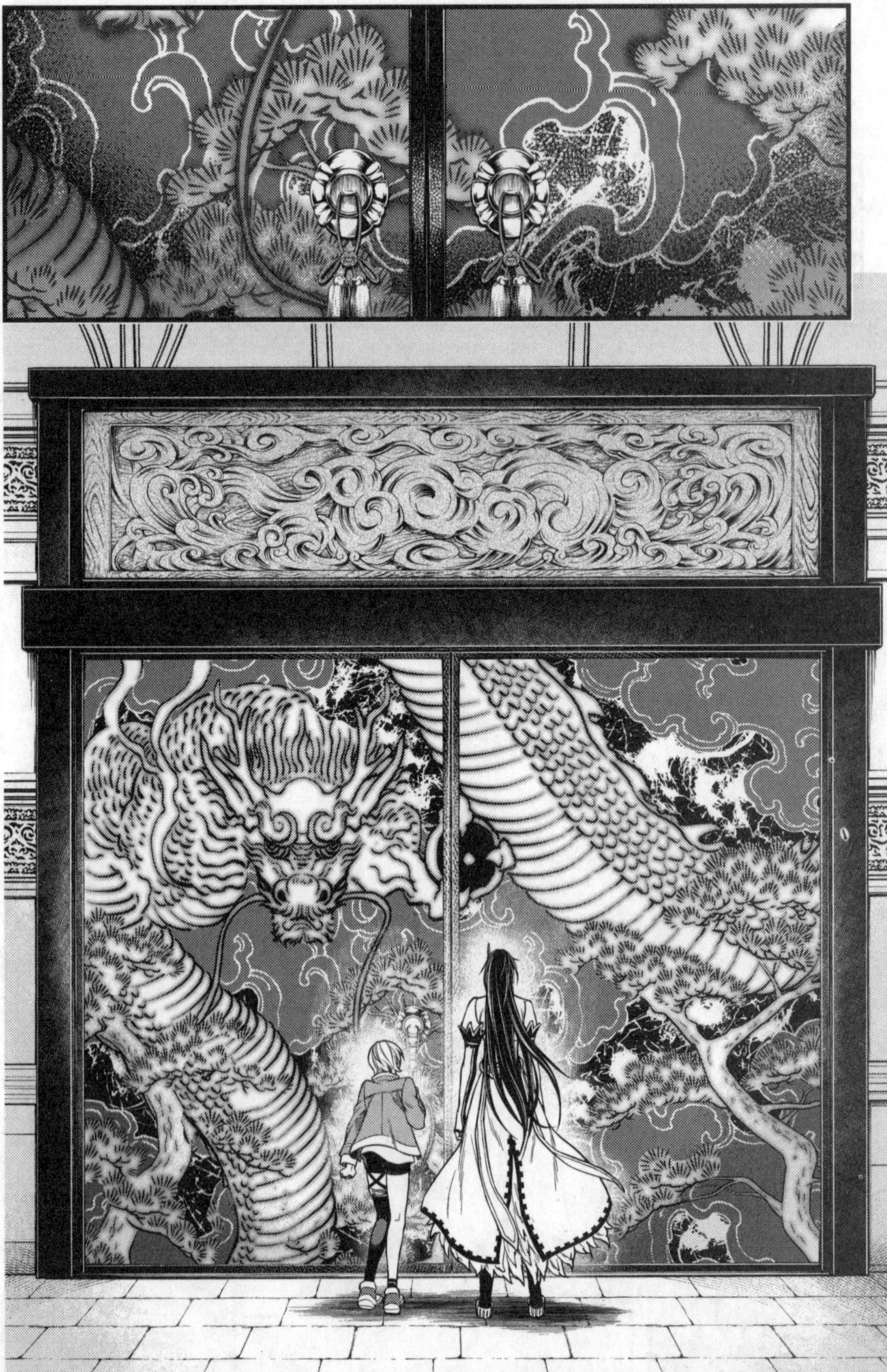

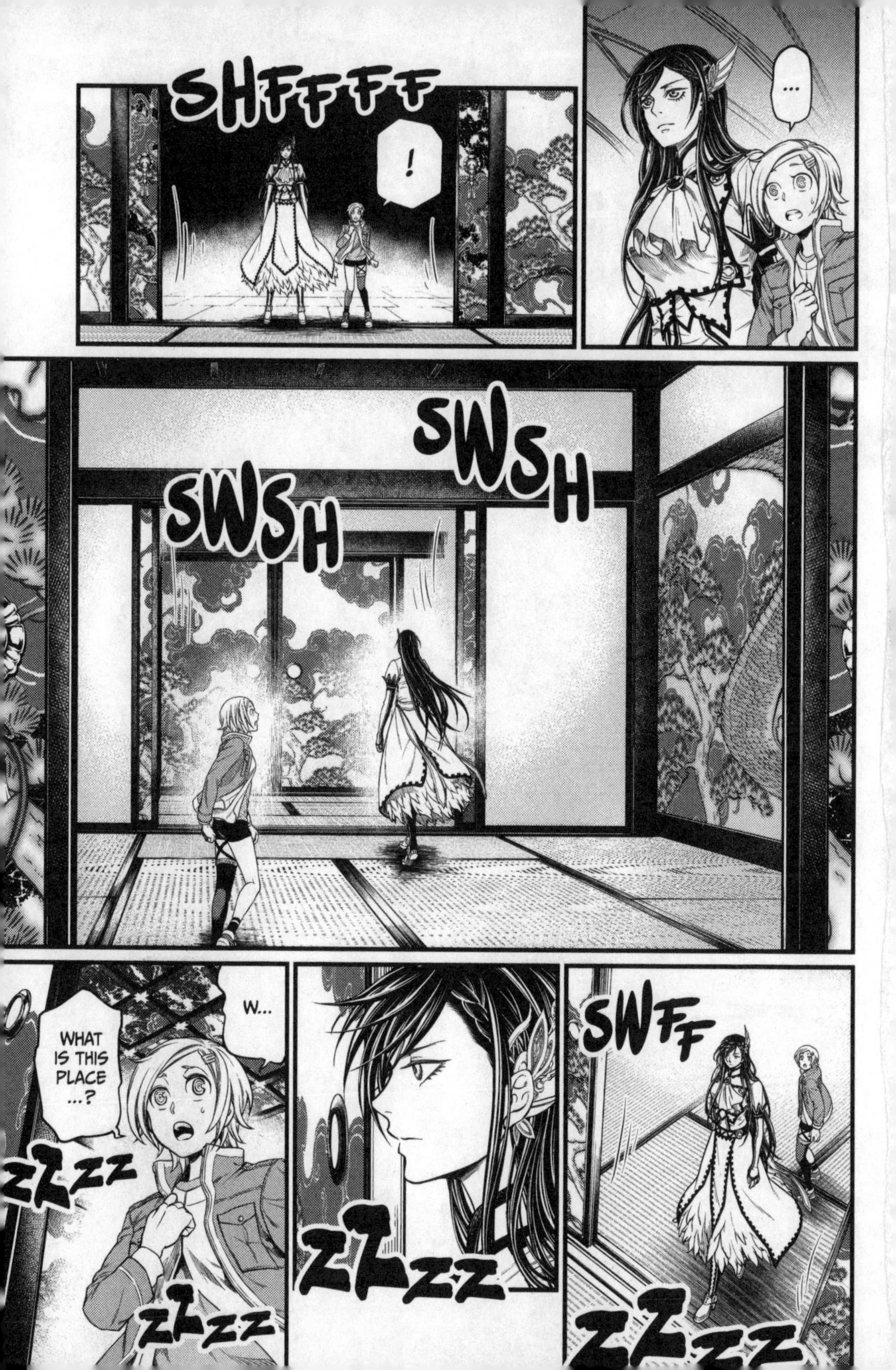
...
SHFFFFF
!
SWSH
SWSH
SWFF
ZZZZ
ZZZZ
W...
WHAT IS THIS PLACE ...?
ZZZZ
ZZZZ

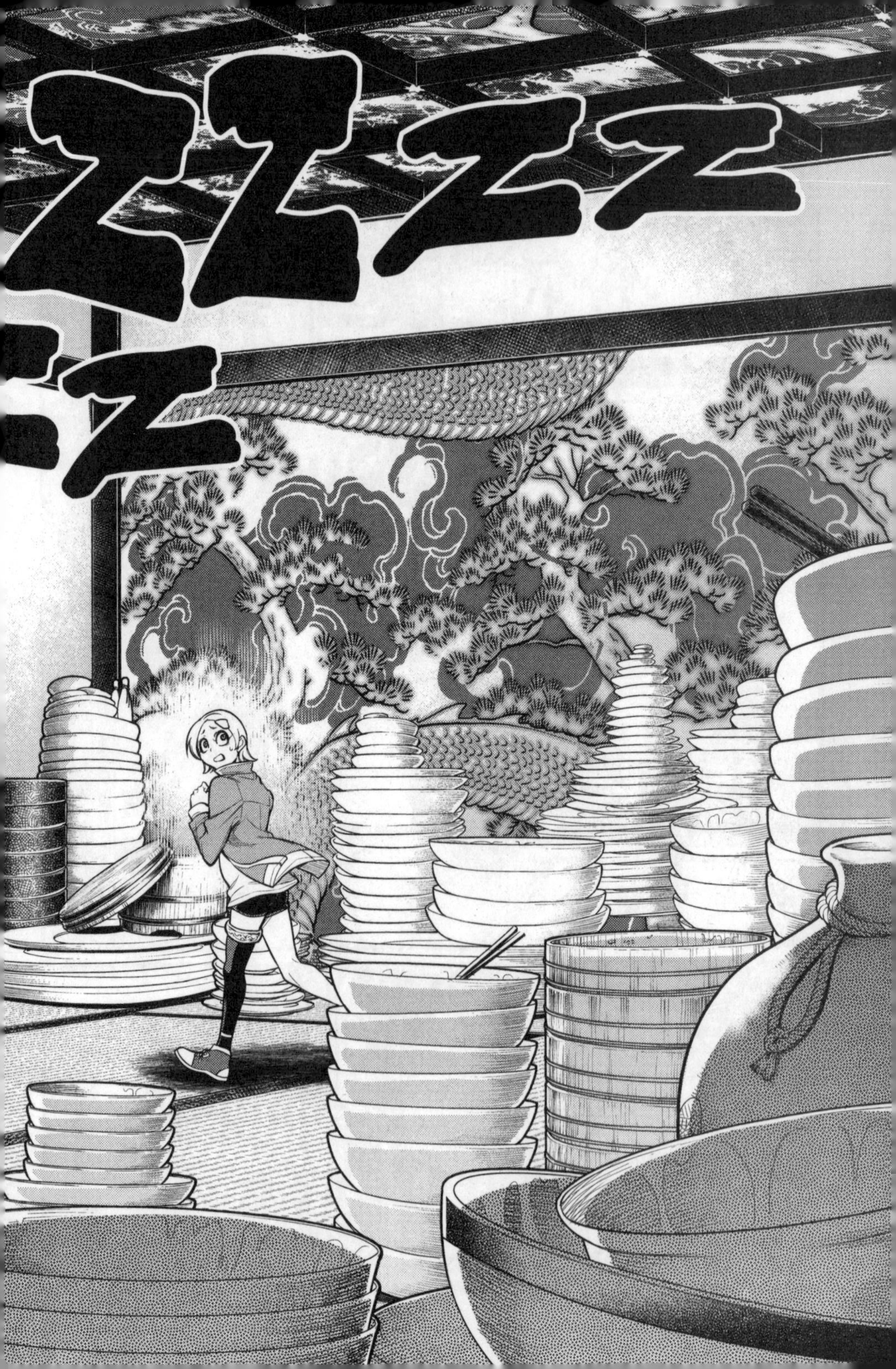
ZZZZ
Z

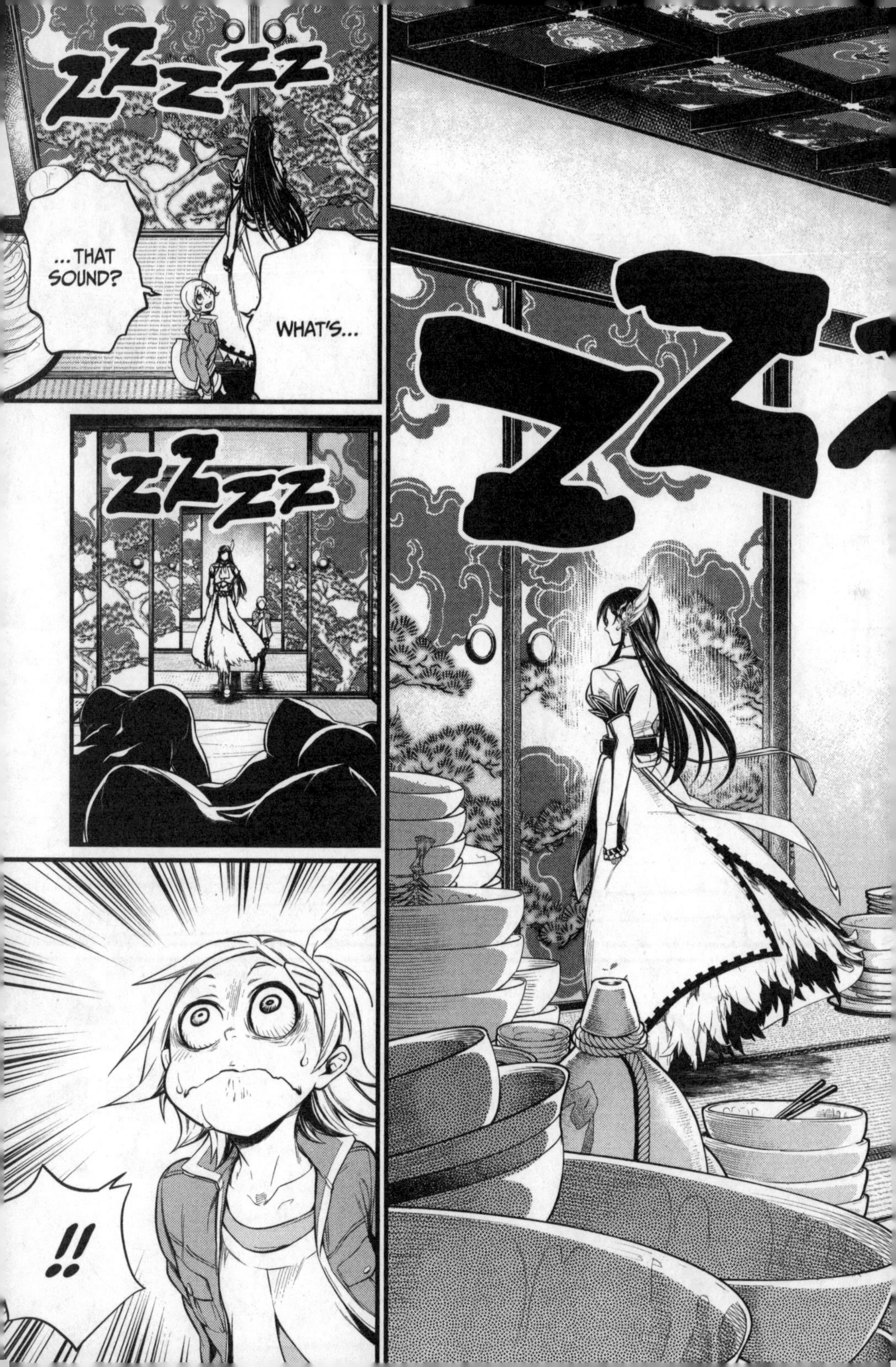
ZZ
ZZZZZZ
WHAT'S...
...THAT SOUND?
ZZZZZ
!!

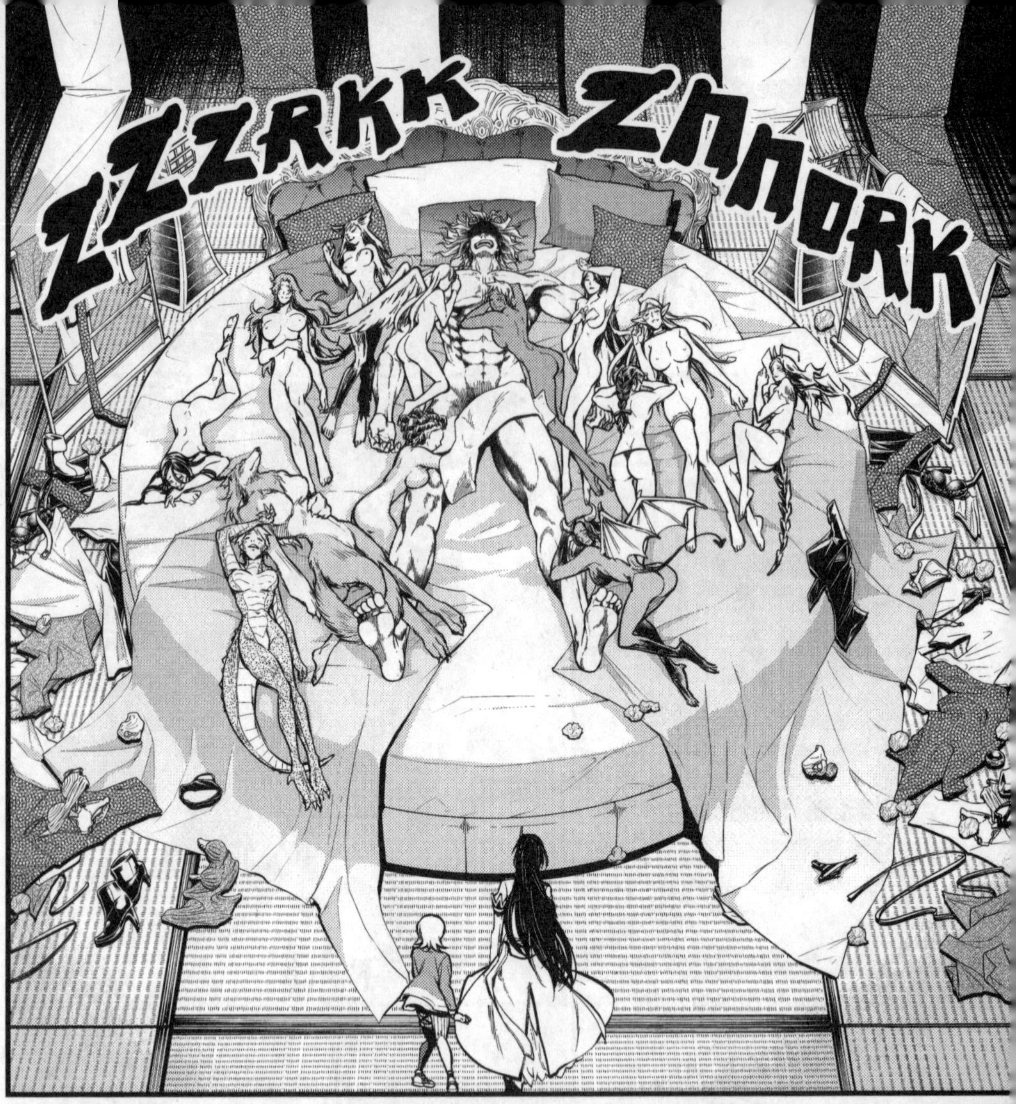
ZNNORK
ZZZRKK

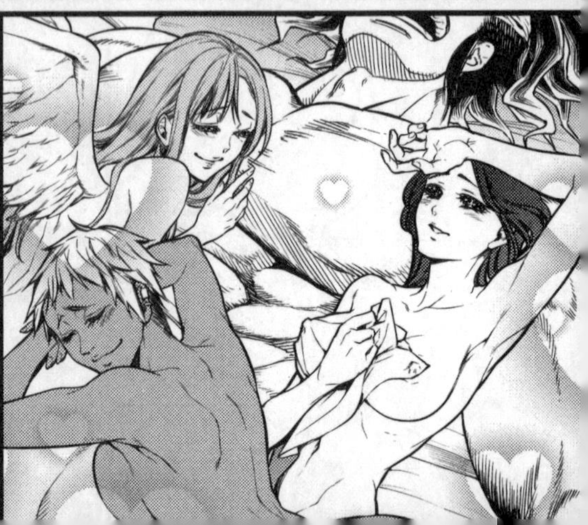

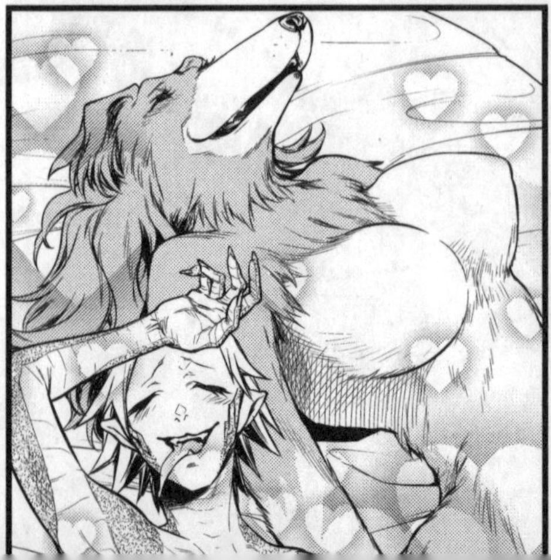

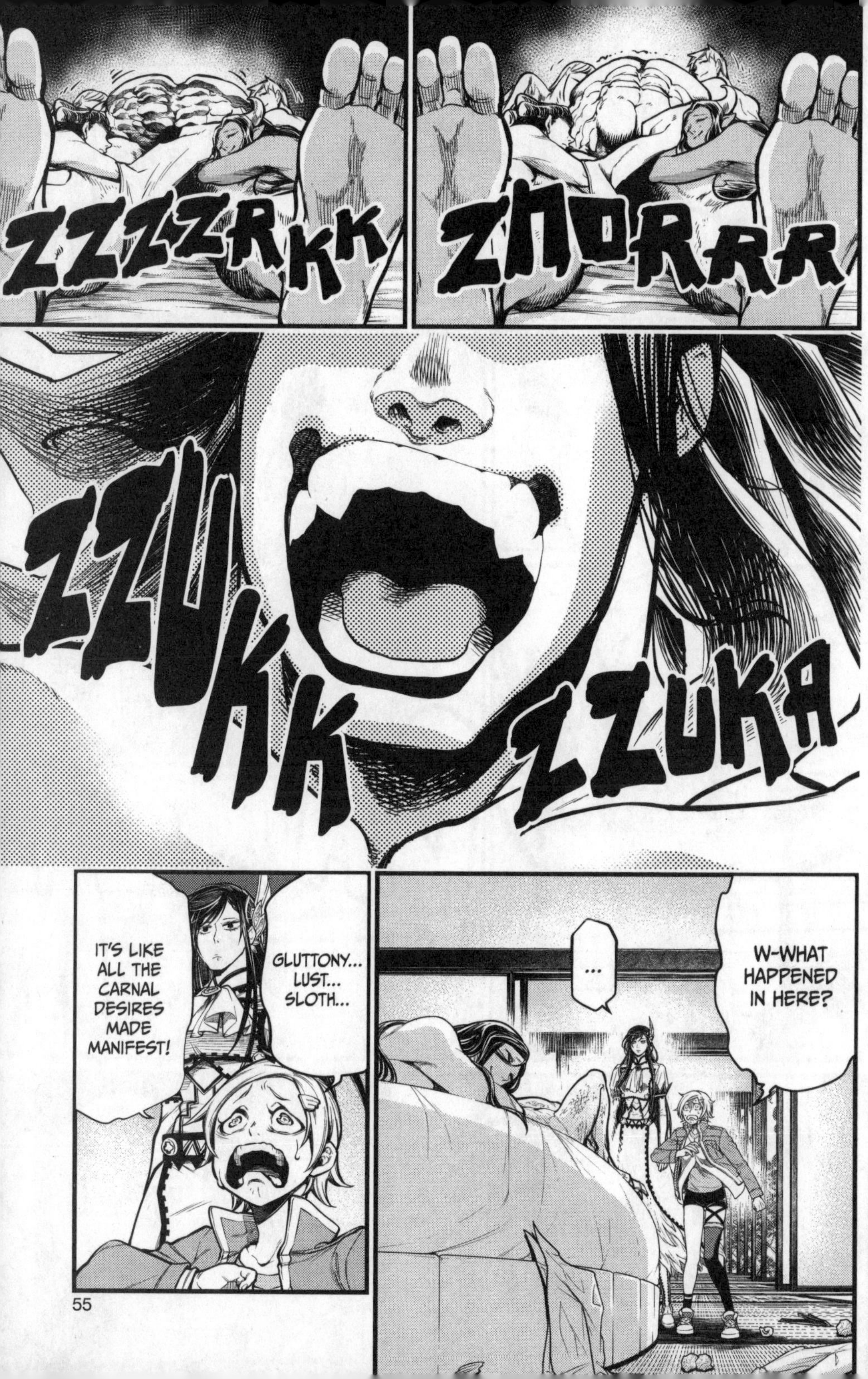
ZNORRR
ZZZZRKK
ZZUKK
ZZUKA
W-WHAT HAPPENED IN HERE?
...
GLUTTONY... LUST... SLOTH...
IT'S LIKE ALL THE CARNAL DESIRES MADE MANIFEST!

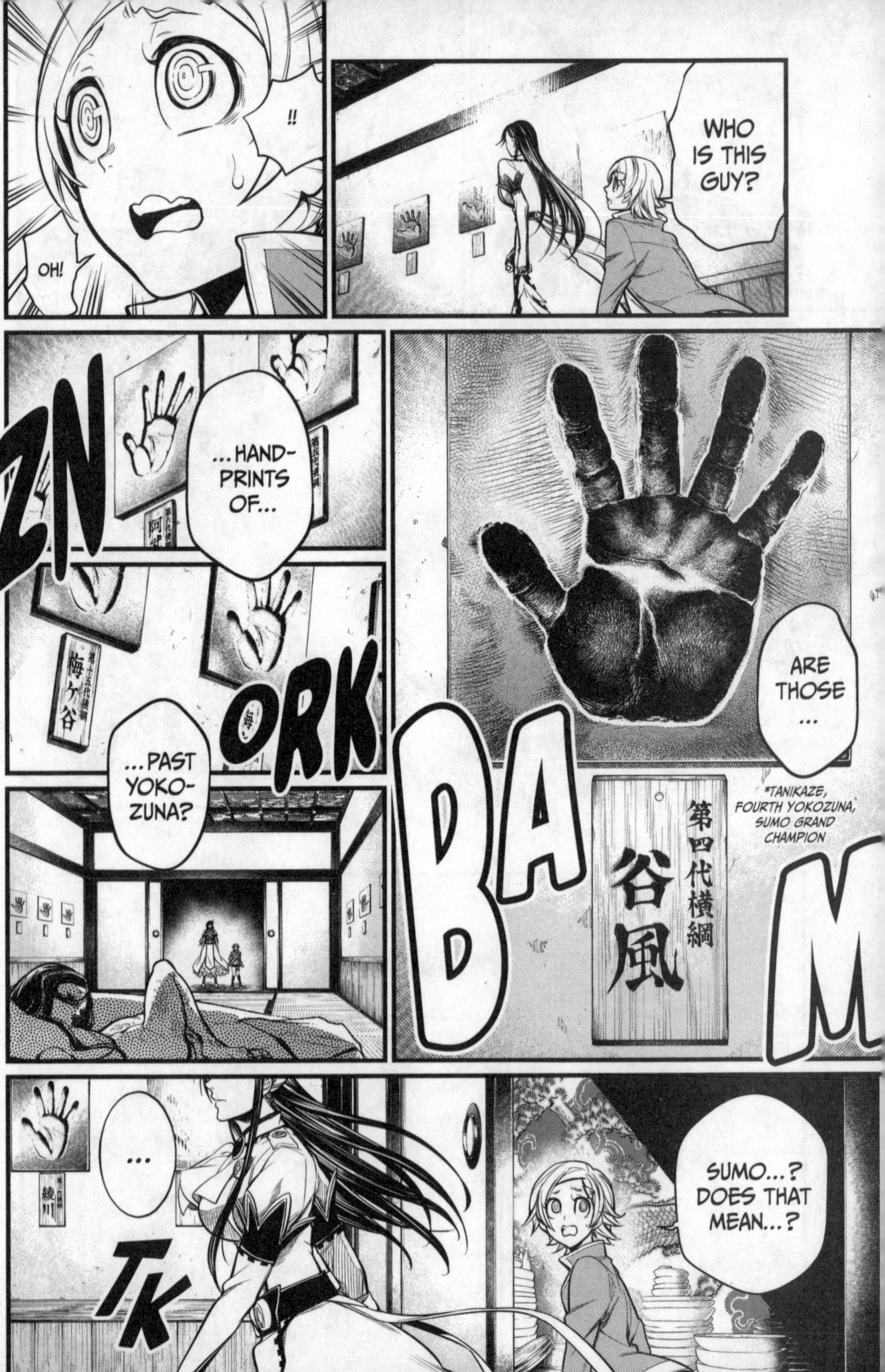
WHO IS THIS GUY?
!!
OH!
ARE THOSE ...
BAM
第四代横綱
谷風
*TANIKAZE, FOURTH YOKOZUNA, SUMO GRAND CHAMPION
...HAND-PRINTS OF...
ZN
ORK
...PAST YOKO-ZUNA?
SUMO...? DOES THAT MEAN...?
...
TK

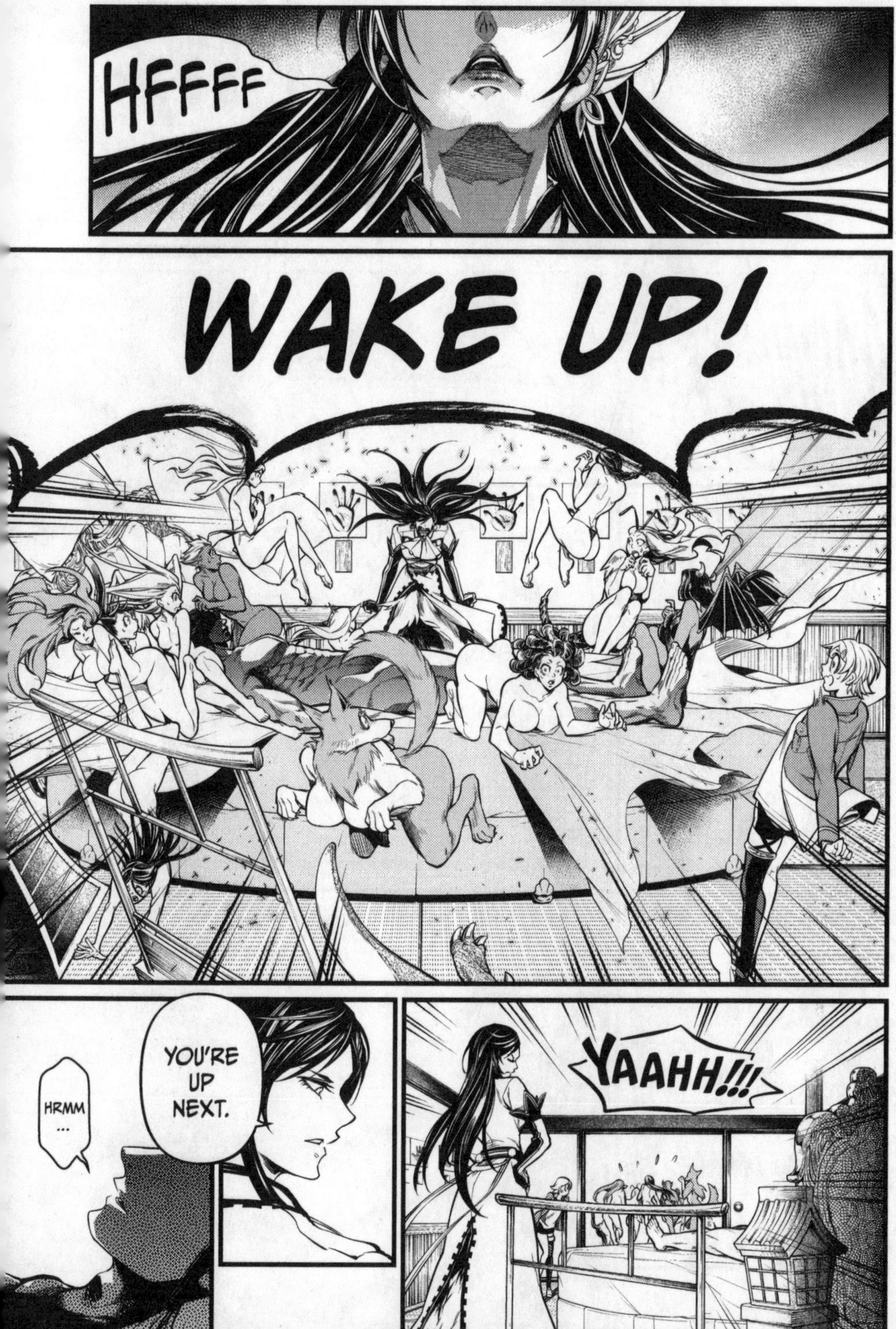
HFFFF
WAKE UP!
YAAHH!!!
YOU'RE UP NEXT.
HRMM ...

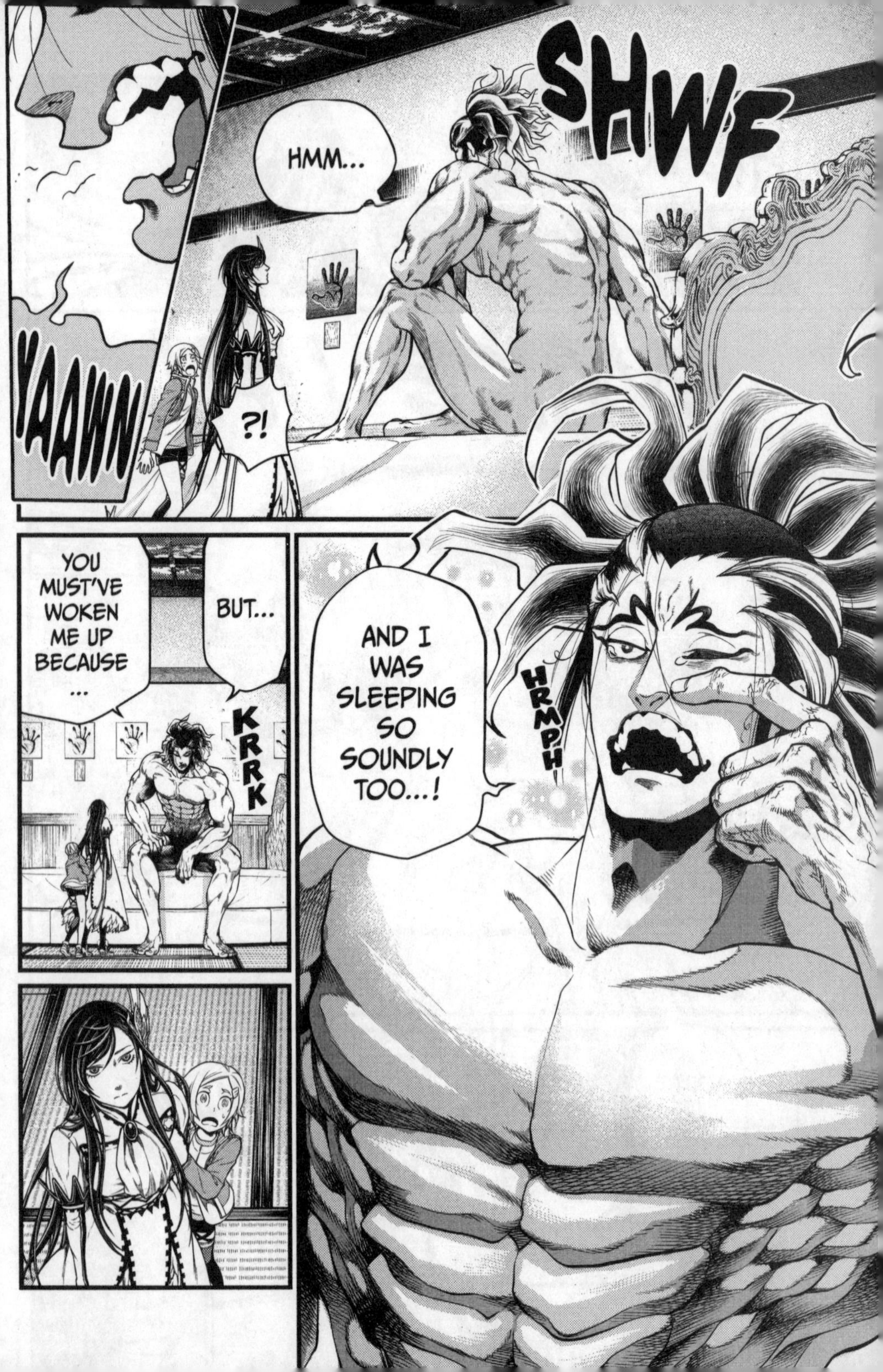
SHWF
HMM...
?!
YAAWN
HRMPH
AND I WAS SLEEPING SO SOUNDLY TOO...!
BUT...
YOU MUST'VE WOKEN ME UP BECAUSE ...
KRRK

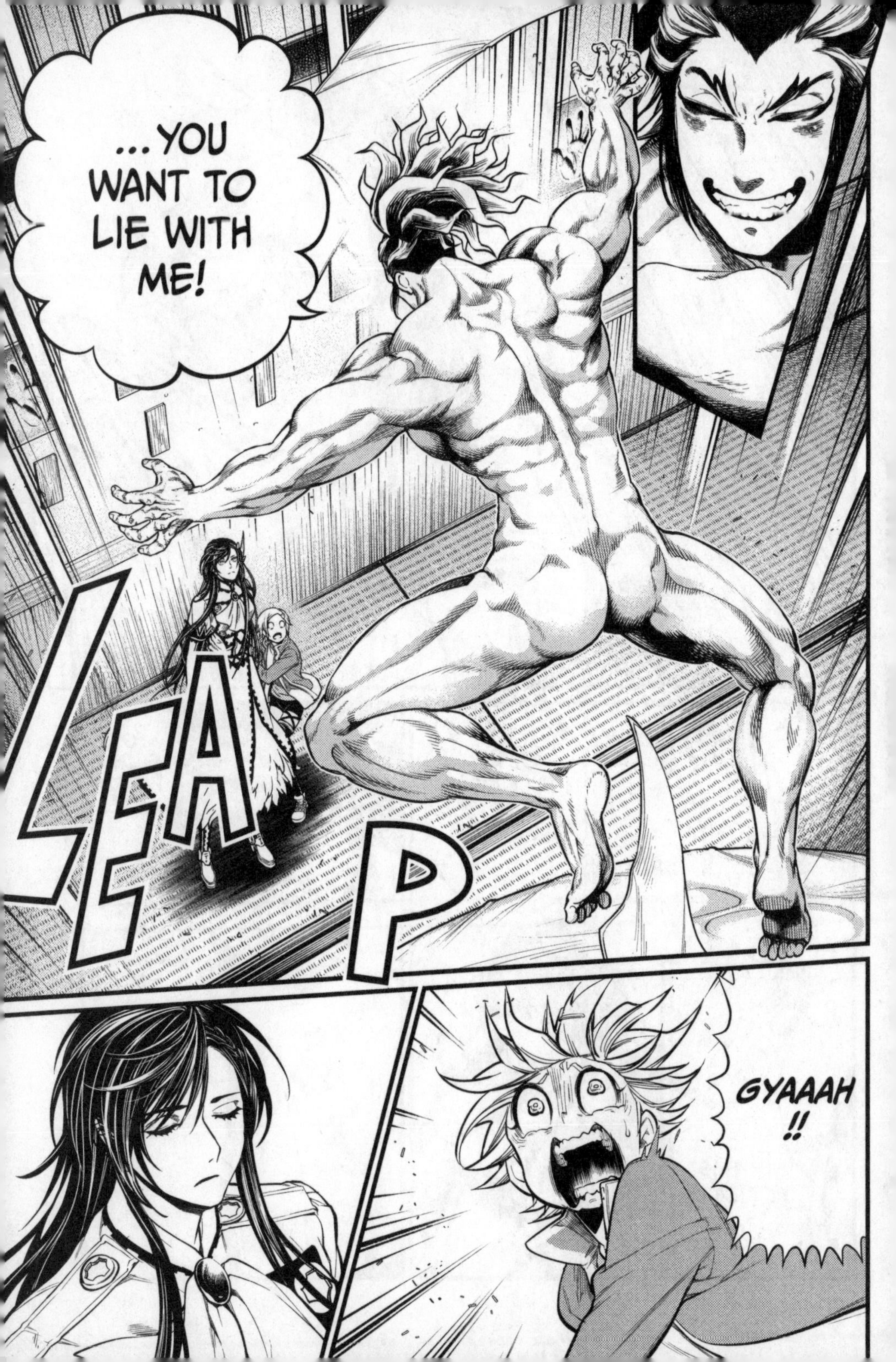
...YOU WANT TO LIE WITH ME!
LEAP
GYAAAH !!

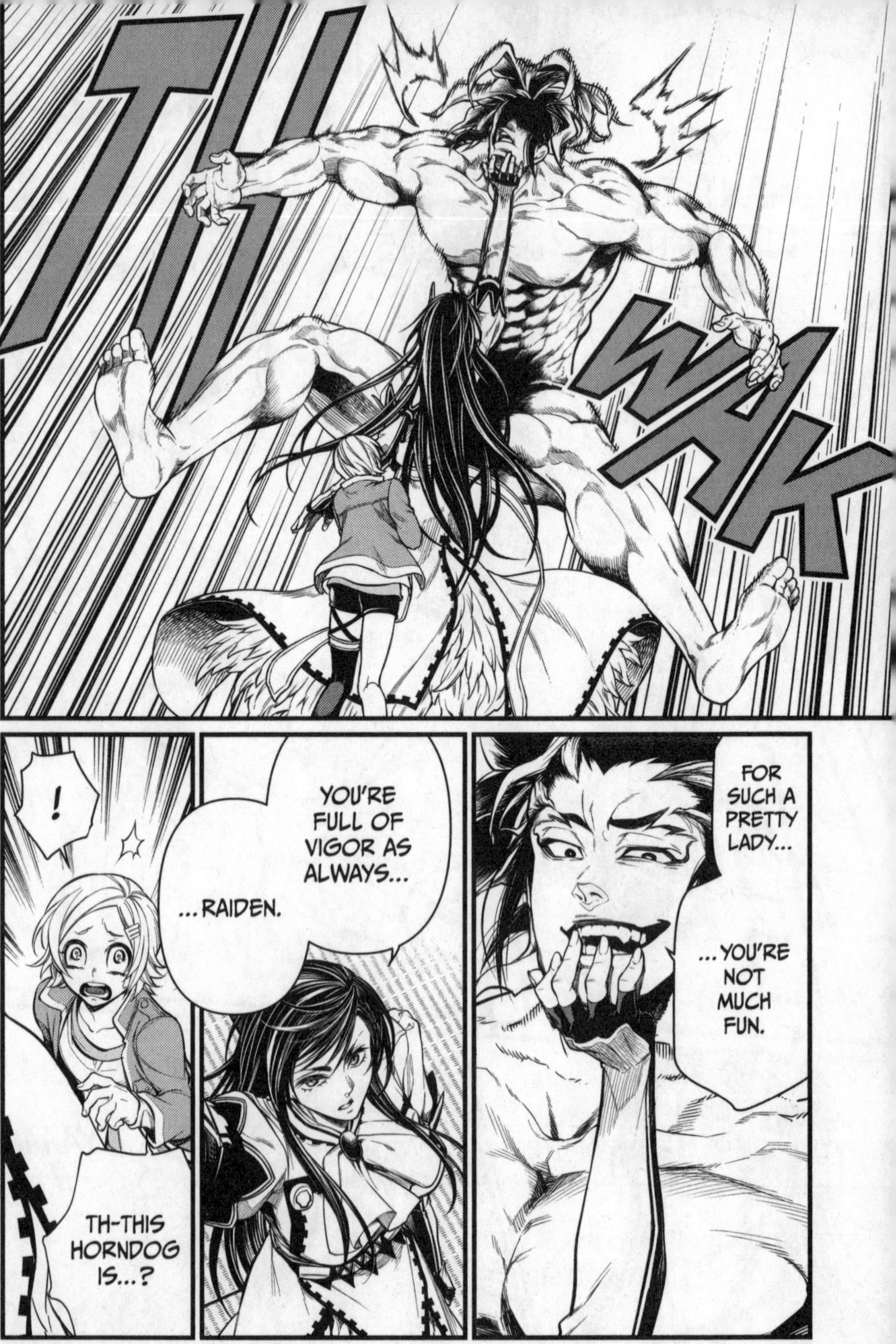
THWAK
FOR SUCH A PRETTY LADY...
...YOU'RE NOT MUCH FUN.
YOU'RE FULL OF VIGOR AS ALWAYS...
...RAIDEN.
!
TH-THIS HORNDOG IS...?

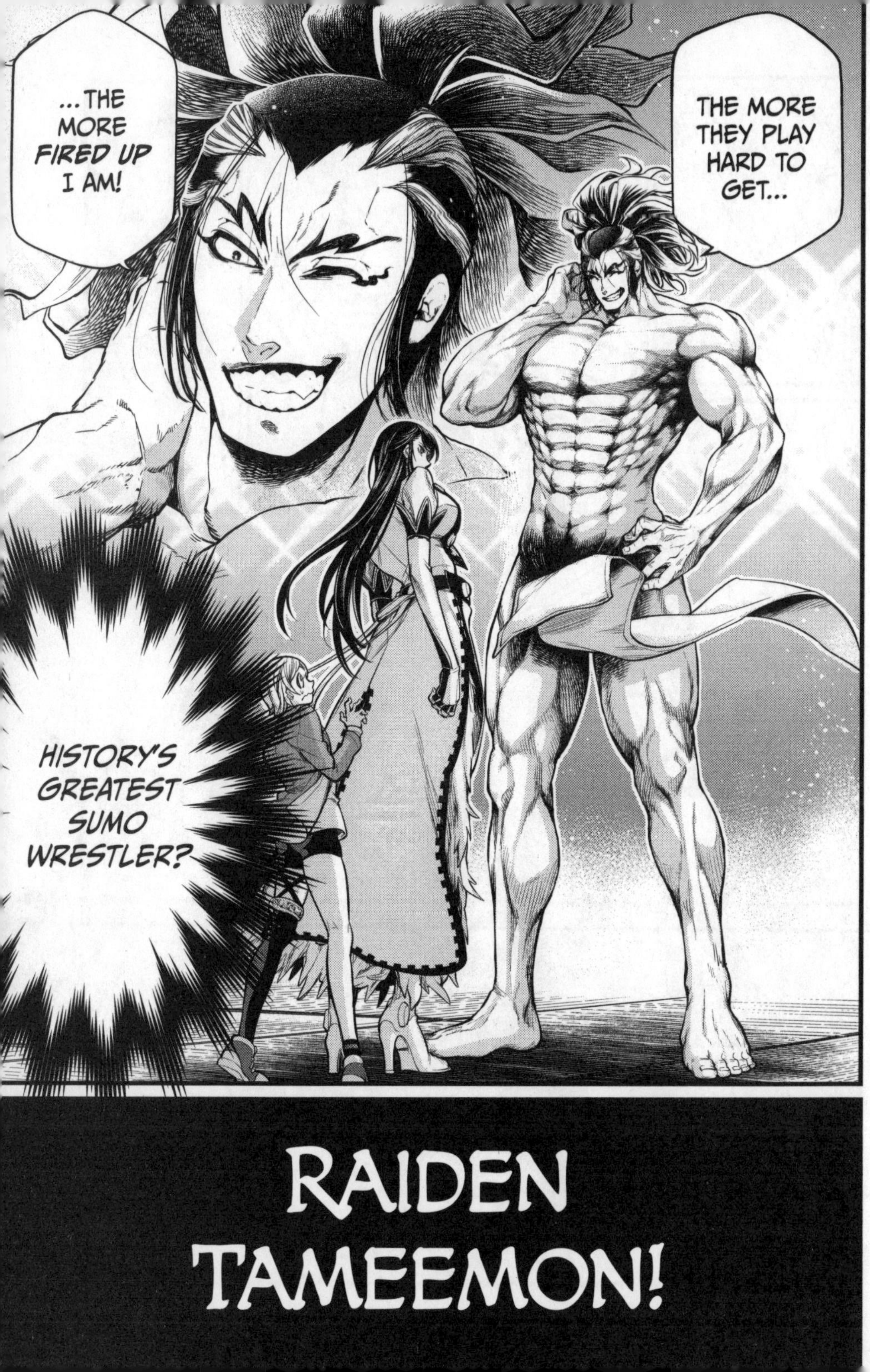
THE MORE THEY PLAY HARD TO GET...
...THE MORE FIRED UP I AM!
HISTORY'S GREATEST SUMO WRESTLER?
RAIDEN TAMEEMON!

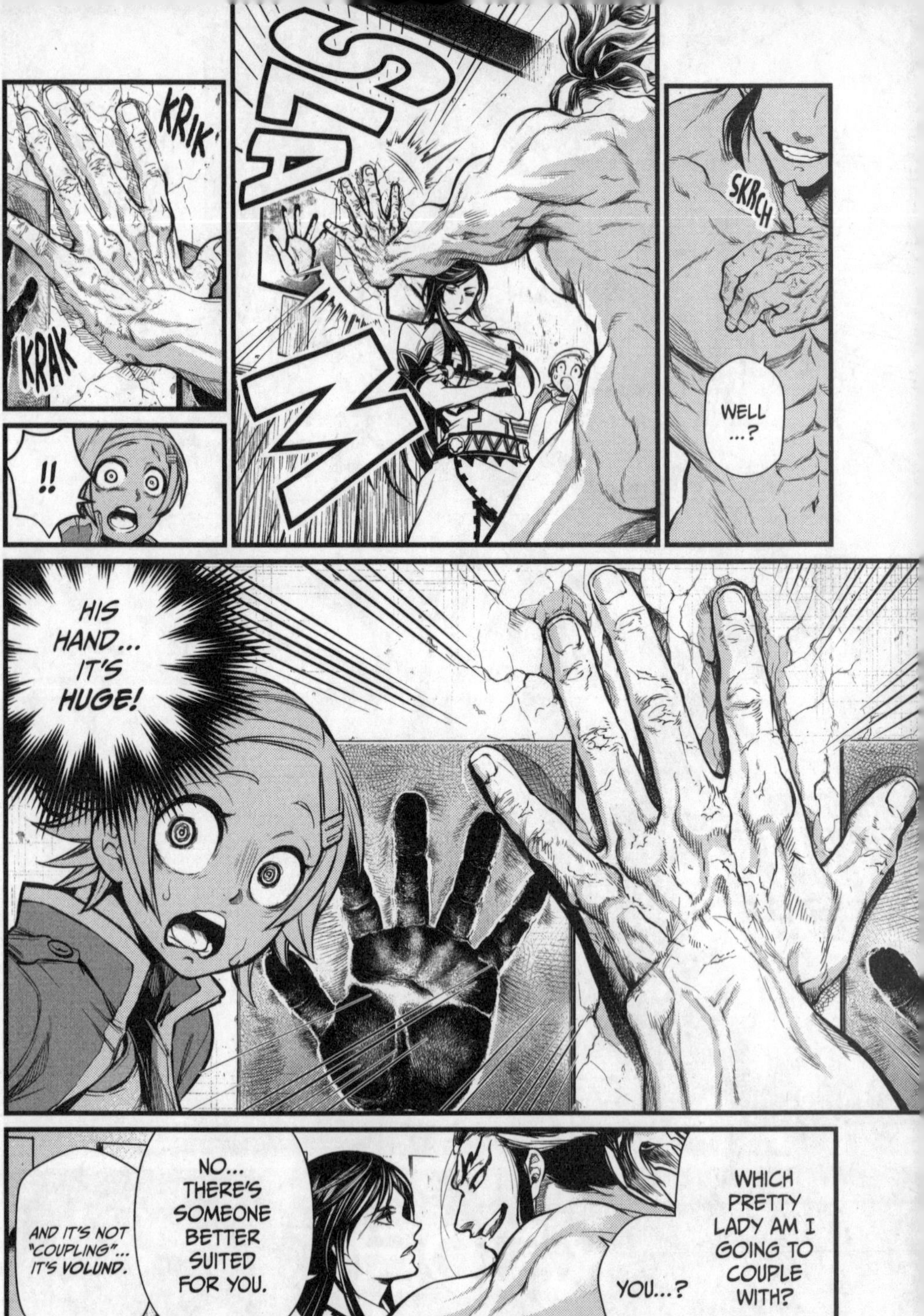
SKRCH
WELL ...?
SLAM
KRIK
KRAK
!!
HIS HAND... IT'S HUGE!
WHICH PRETTY LADY AM I GOING TO COUPLE WITH?
YOU...?
NO... THERE'S SOMEONE BETTER SUITED FOR YOU.
AND IT'S NOT "COUPLING"... IT'S VOLUND.

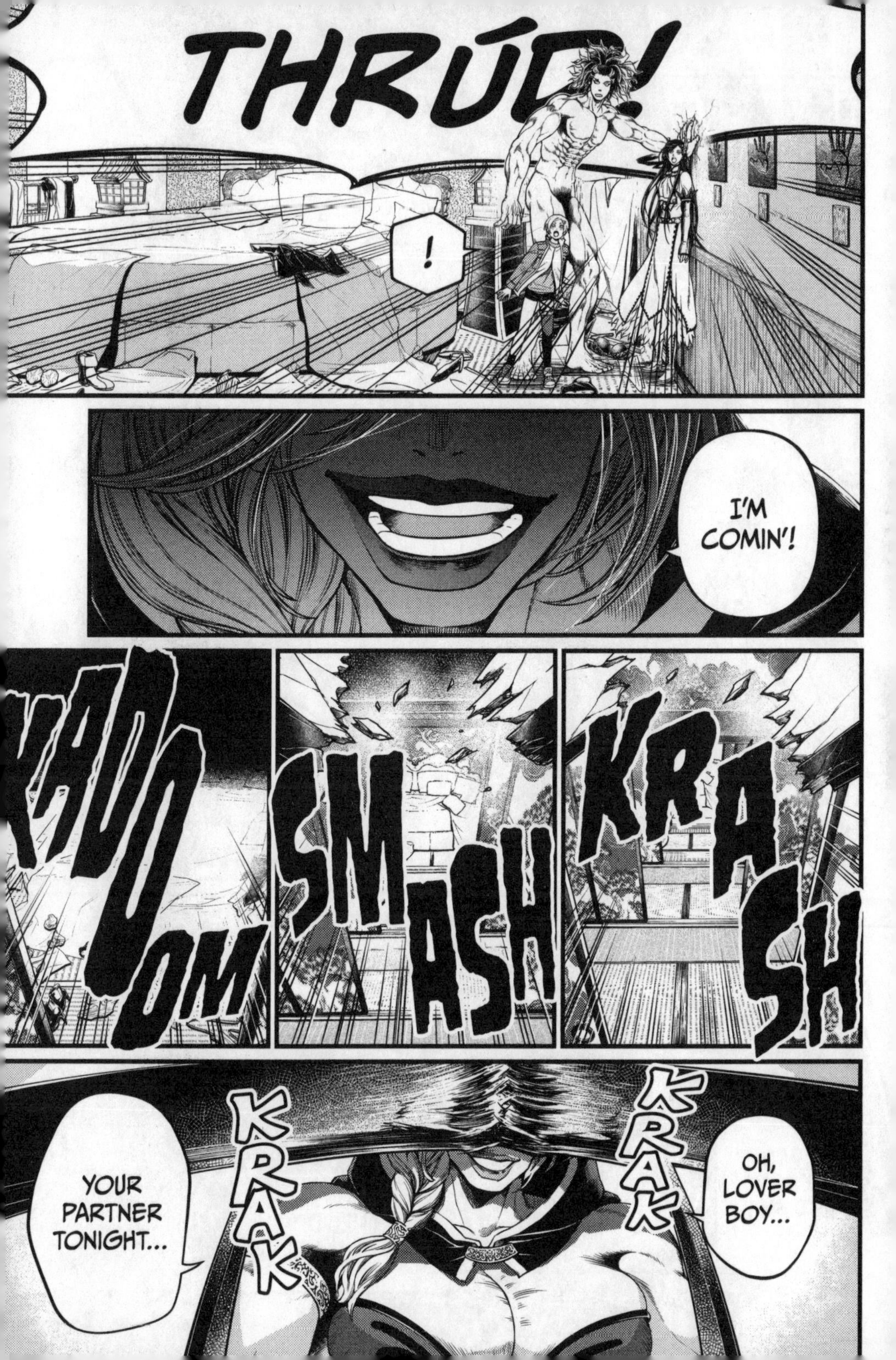
THRÚD!
!
I'M COMIN'!
KRASH
SMASH
OH, LOVER BOY...
KRAK
KRAK
YOUR PARTNER TONIGHT...

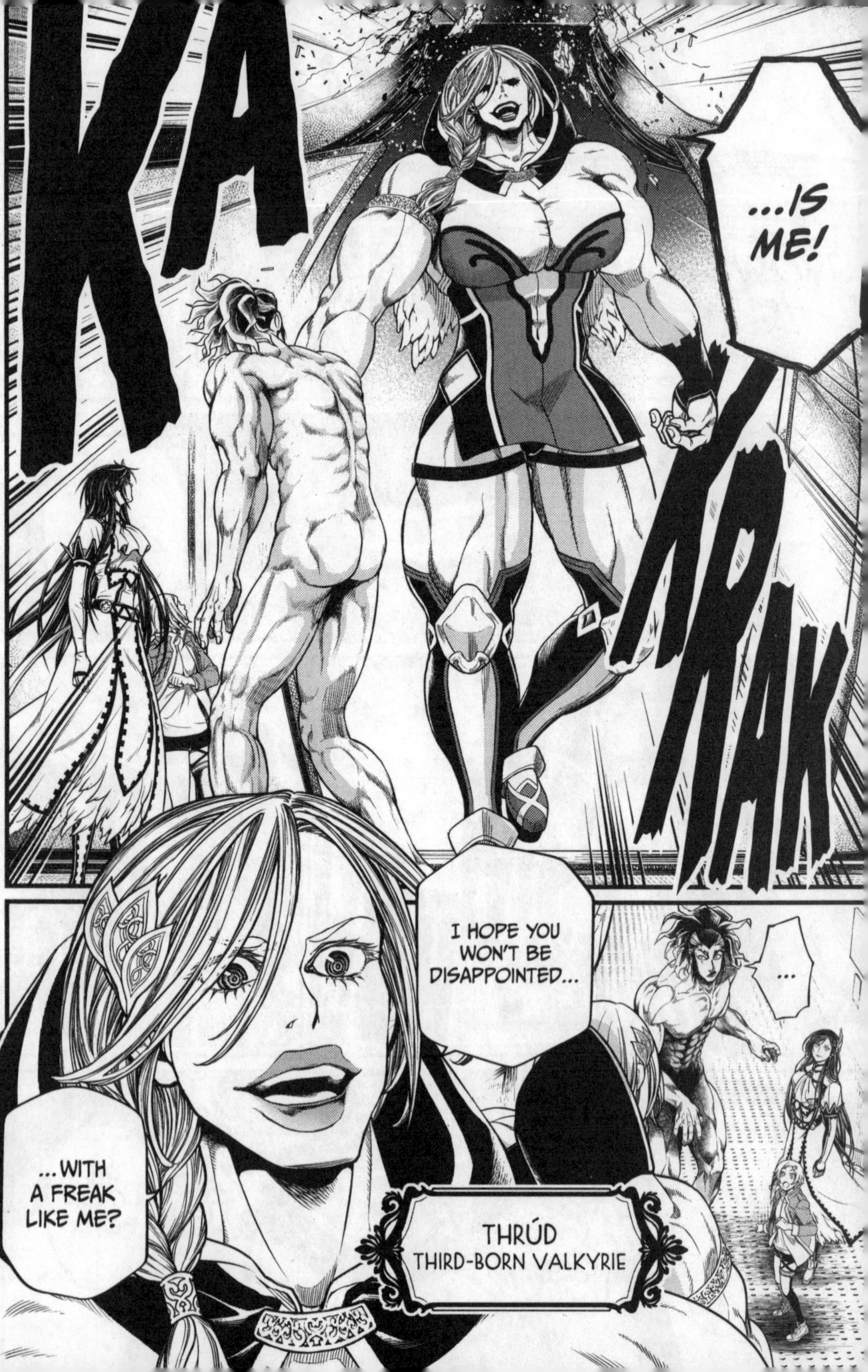
KA
...IS ME!
PAK
I HOPE YOU WON'T BE DISAPPOINTED...
...
...WITH A FREAK LIKE ME?
THRÚD
THIRD-BORN VALKYRIE

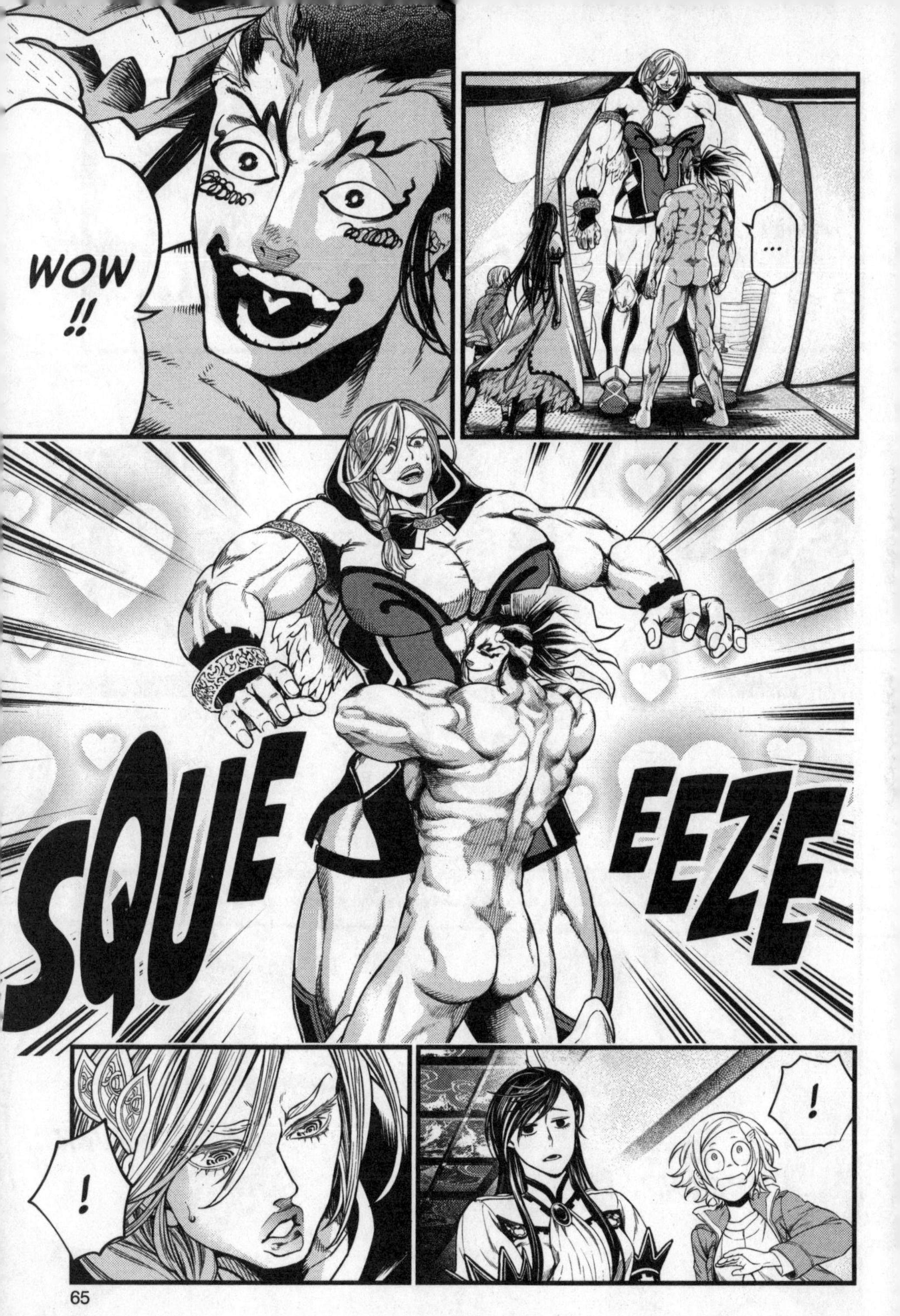
...
WOW !!
SQUE-EEZE
!
!

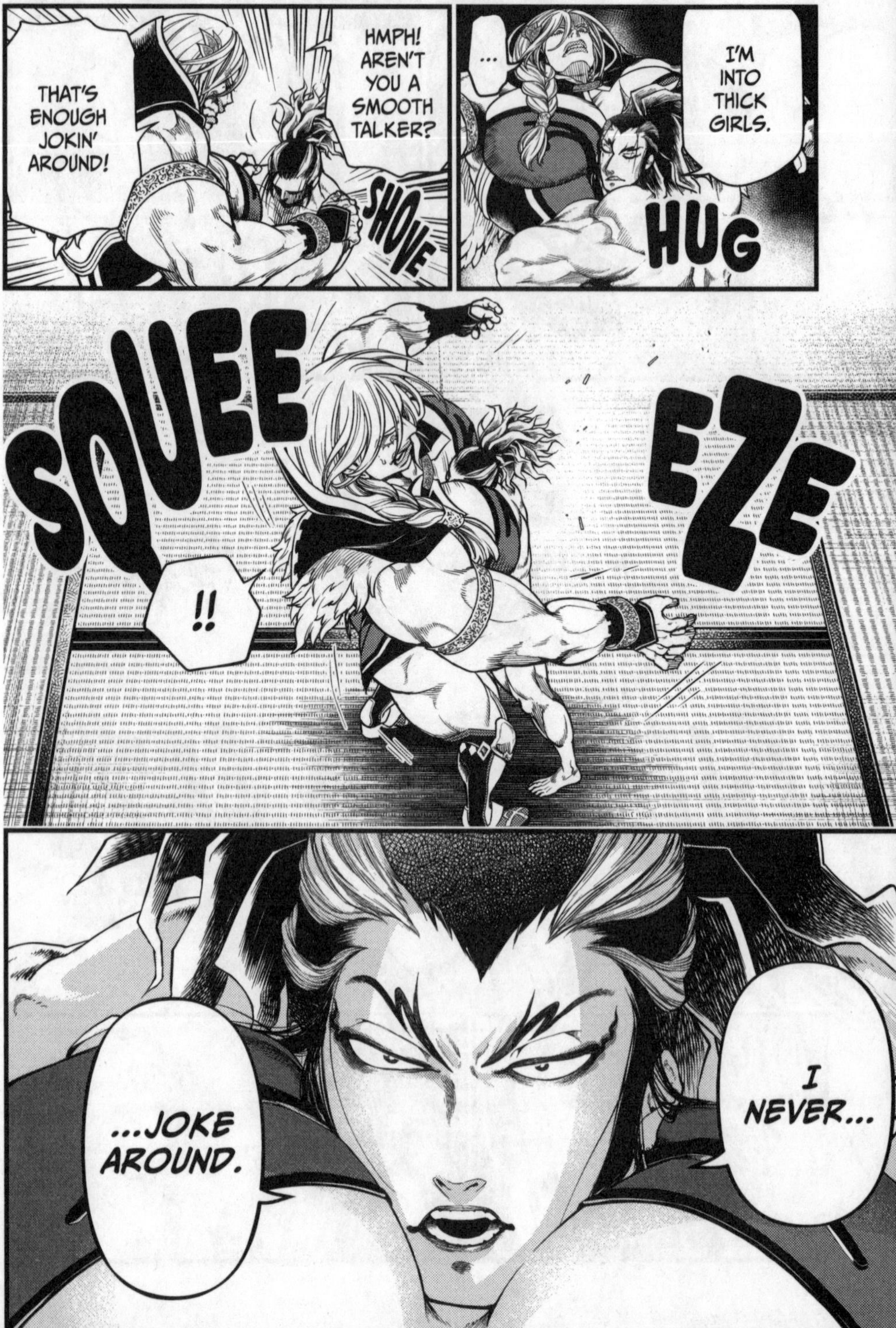
I'M INTO THICK GIRLS.
...
HUG
HMPH! AREN'T YOU A SMOOTH TALKER?
THAT'S ENOUGH JOKIN' AROUND!
SHOVE
SQUEE
EZE
!!
I NEVER...
...JOKE AROUND.

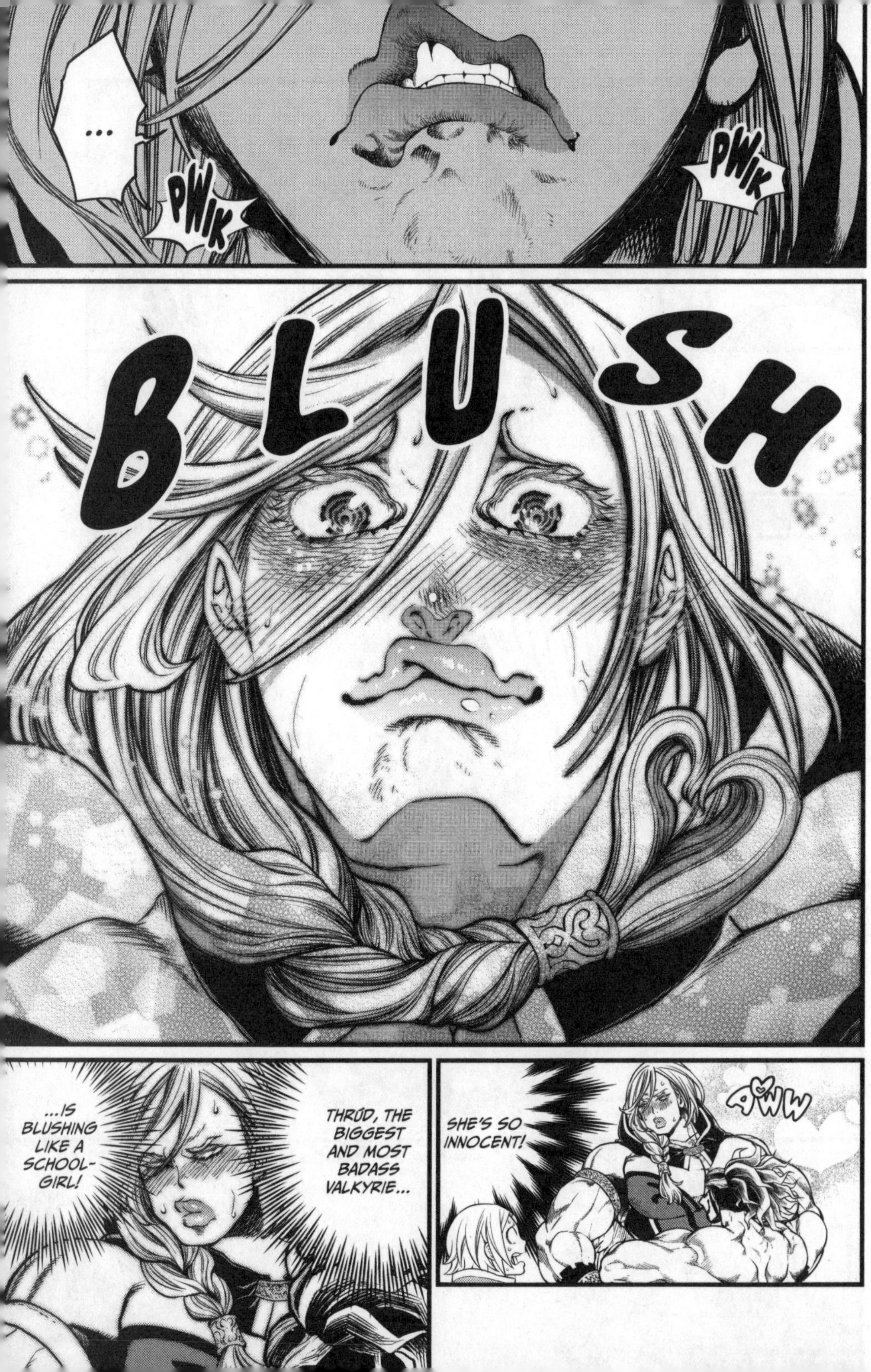
PWIK
...
PWIK
BLUSH
AWW
SHE'S SO INNOCENT!
THRÚD, THE BIGGEST AND MOST BADASS VALKYRIE...
...IS BLUSHING LIKE A SCHOOL-GIRL!

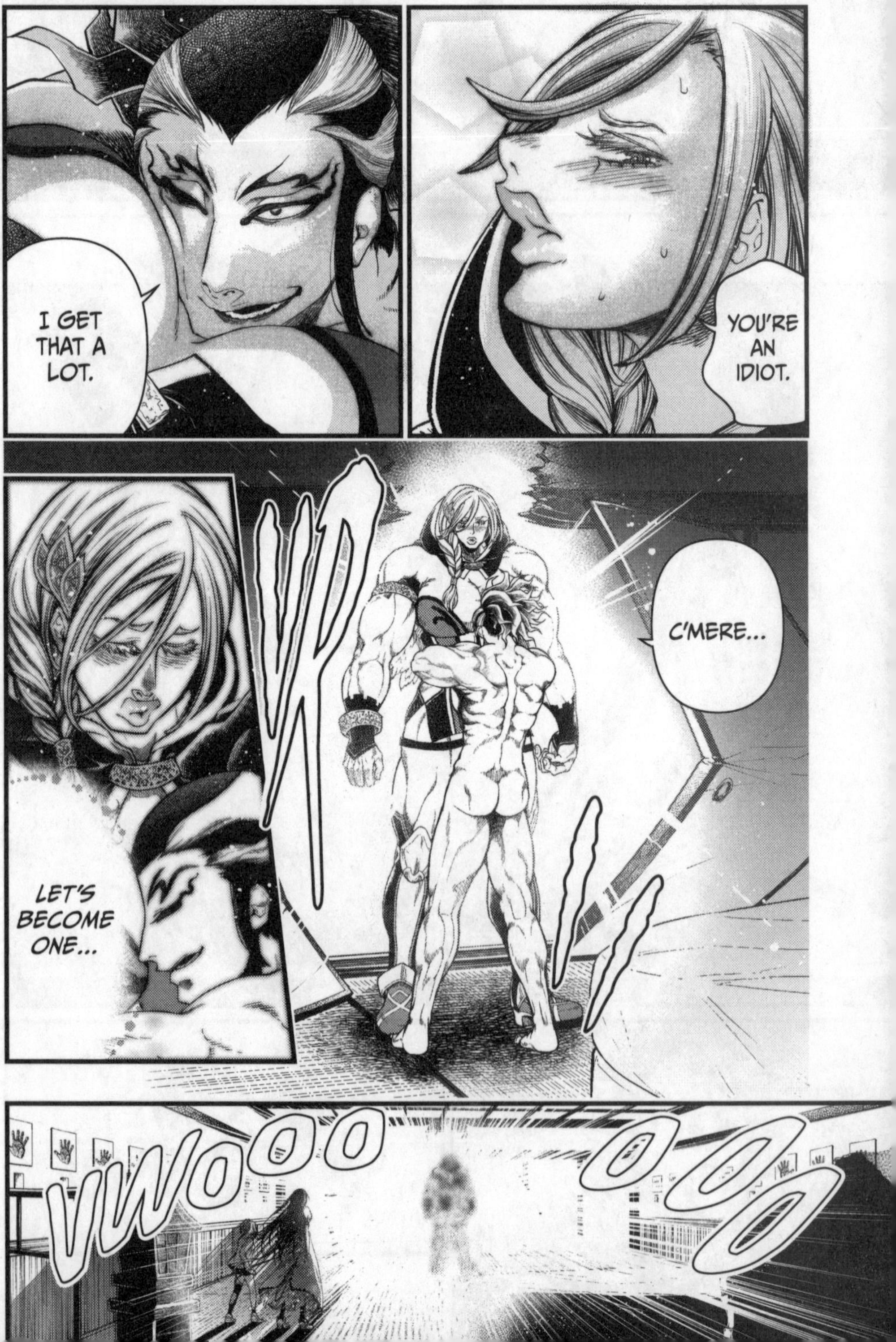
YOU'RE AN IDIOT.
I GET THAT A LOT.
C'MERE...
LET'S BECOME ONE...
VWOOOOOOO

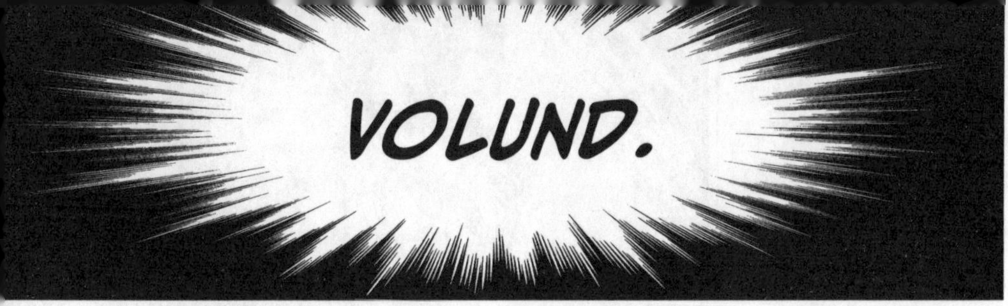
VOLUND.
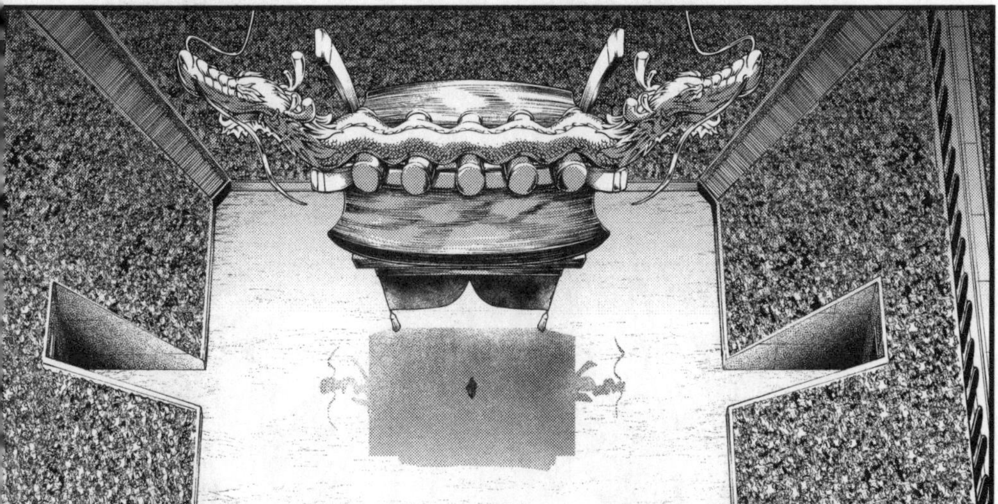
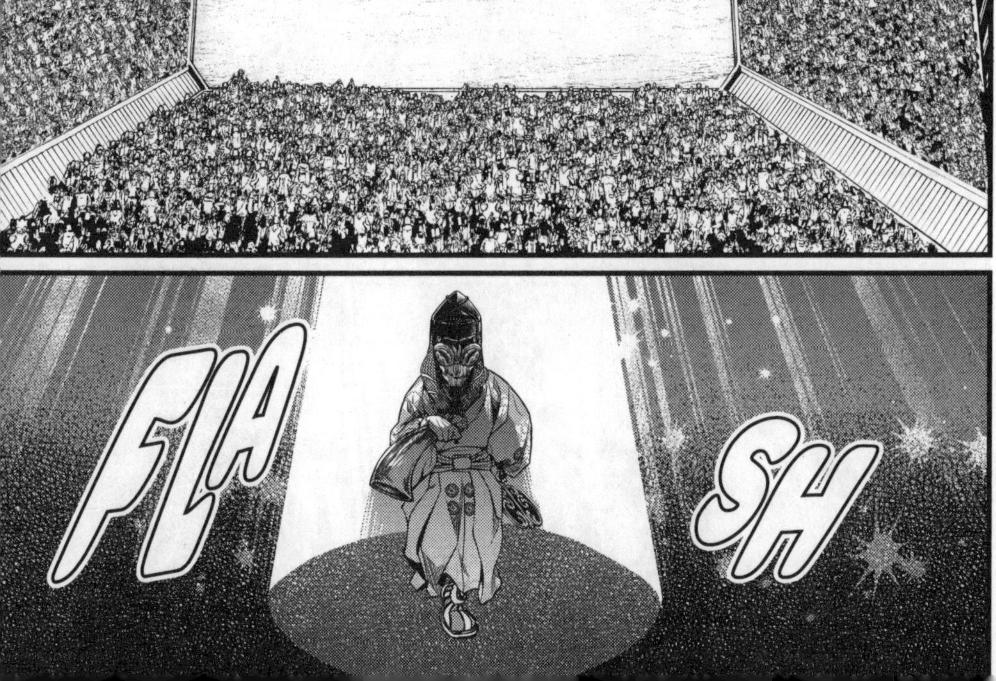
FLASH

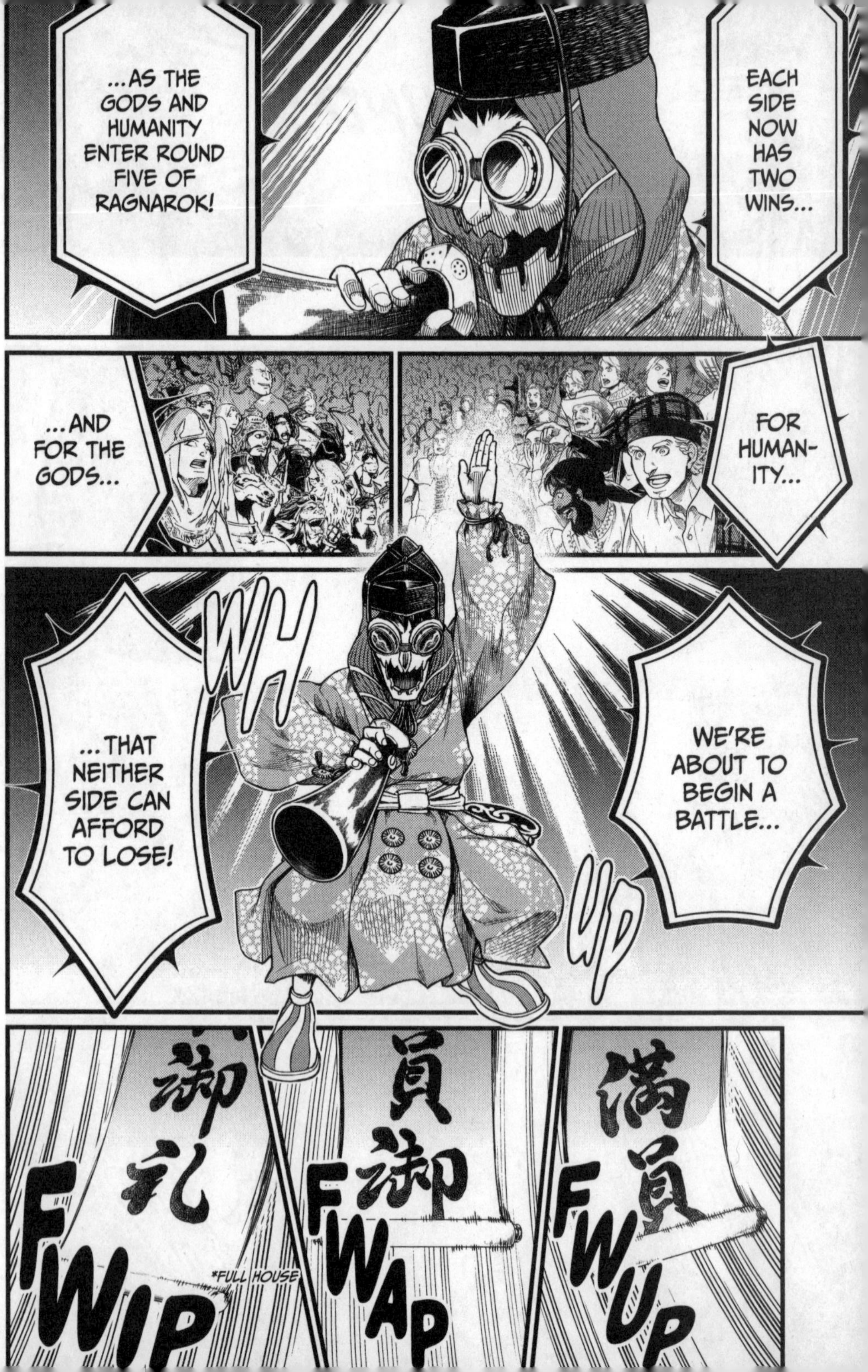
EACH SIDE NOW HAS TWO WINS...
...AS THE GODS AND HUMANITY ENTER ROUND FIVE OF RAGNAROK!
FOR HUMAN-ITY...
...AND FOR THE GODS...
WE'RE ABOUT TO BEGIN A BATTLE...
...THAT NEITHER SIDE CAN AFFORD TO LOSE!
WH
UP
FWUP
FWAP
FWIP
*FULL HOUSE

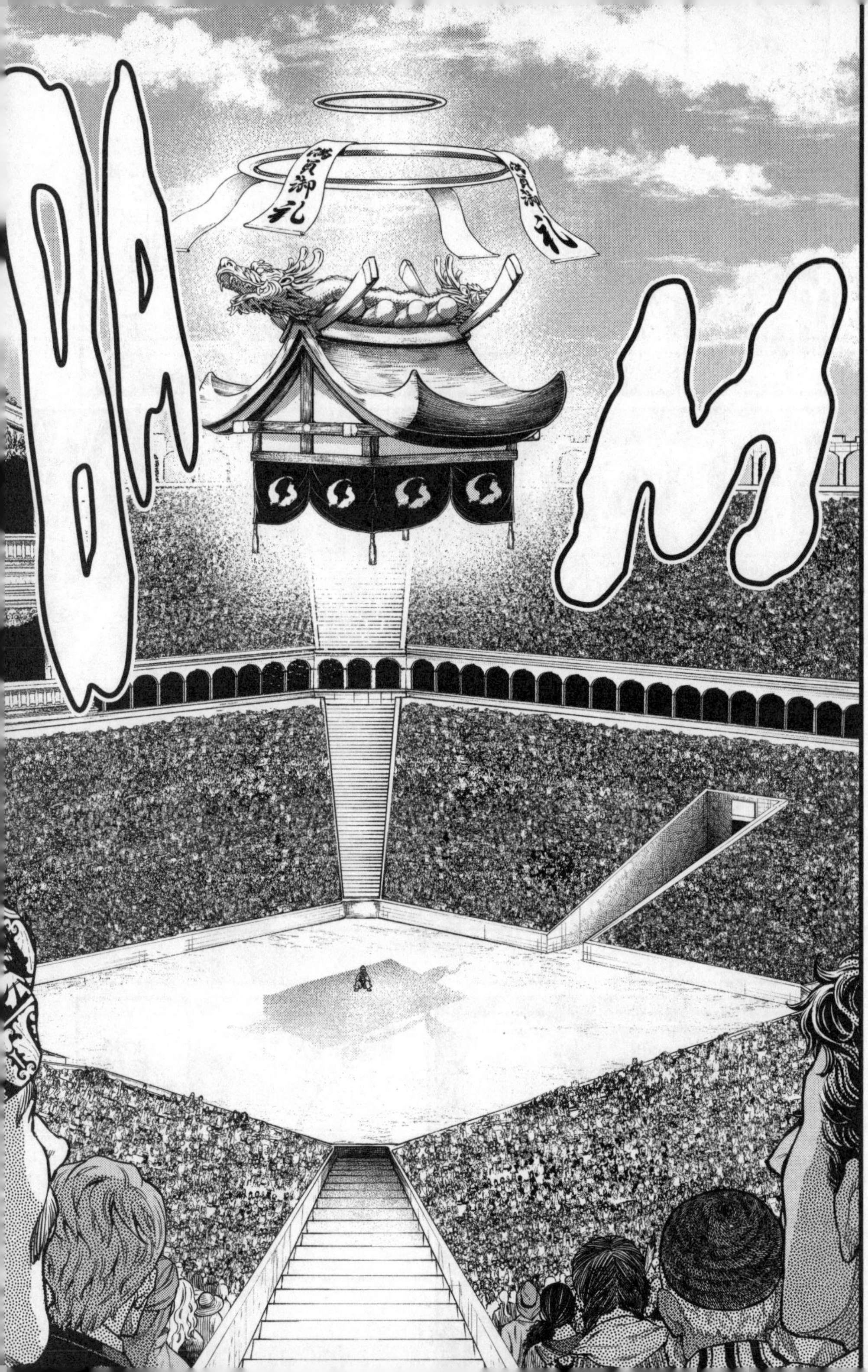
満員御礼
BAM

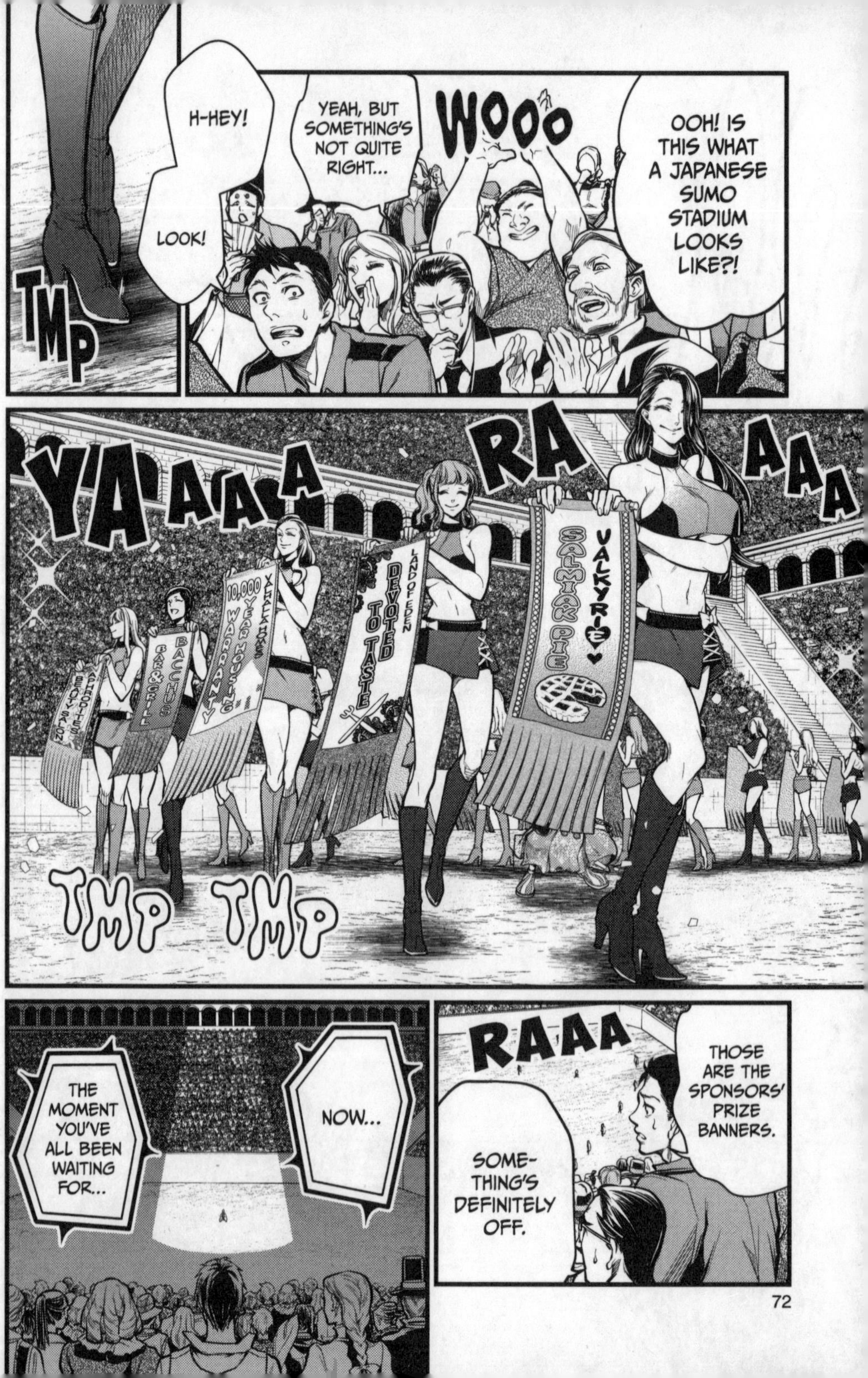
OOH! IS THIS WHAT A JAPANESE SUMO STADIUM LOOKS LIKE?!
WOOO
YEAH, BUT SOMETHING'S NOT QUITE RIGHT...
H-HEY!
LOOK!
TMP
AAA
RA
YAAAA
VALKYRIE♥
SALMIAK PIE
LAND OF EDEN
DEVOTED TO TASTE
VALHALLA HOMES
10,000 YEAR HOUSING WARRANTY
BACCHUS BAR & GRILL
APHRODITE'S BEAUTY SALON
TMP TMP
RAAA
THOSE ARE THE SPONSORS' PRIZE BANNERS.
SOME-THING'S DEFINITELY OFF.
NOW...
THE MOMENT YOU'VE ALL BEEN WAITING FOR...

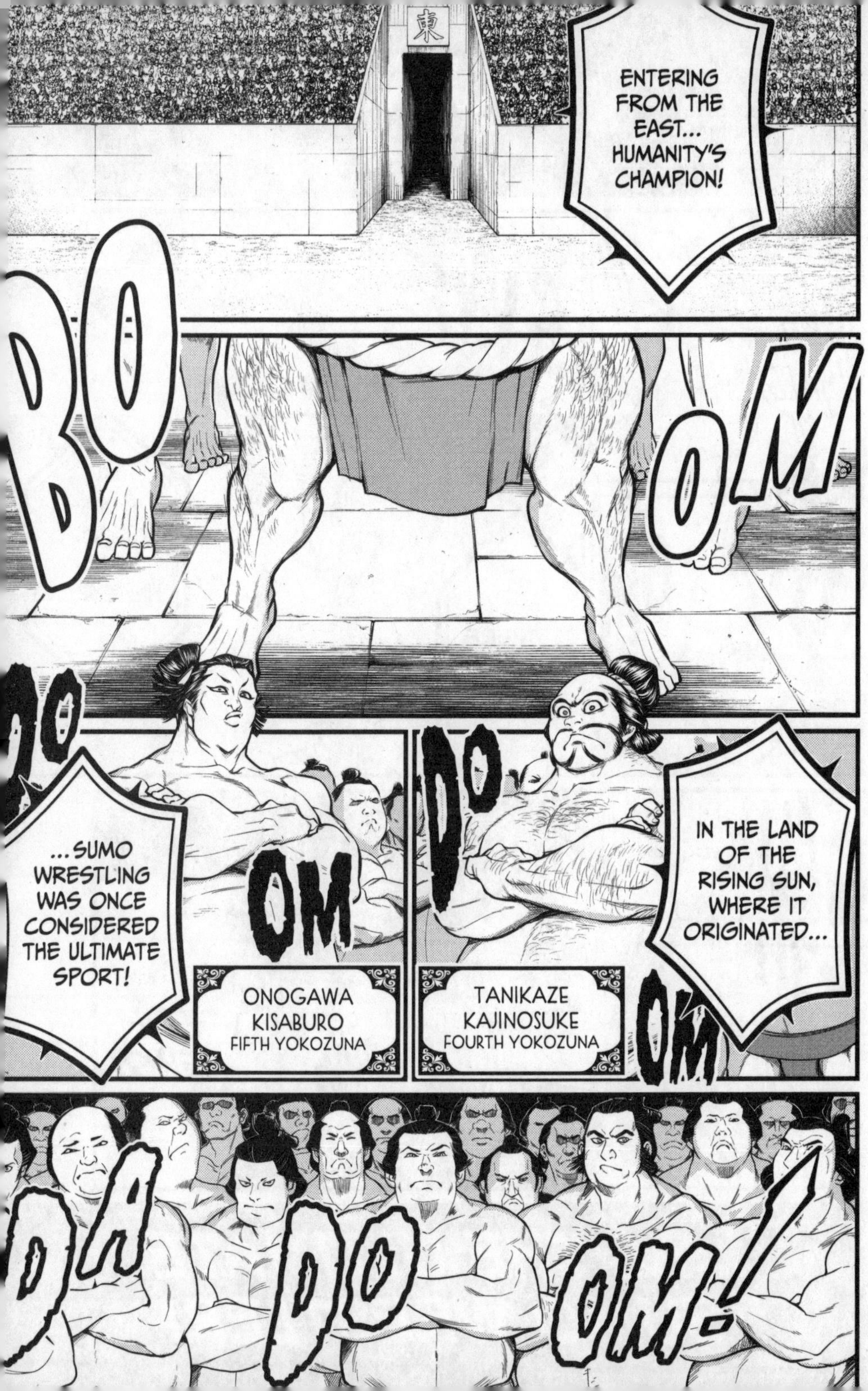
ENTERING FROM THE EAST... HUMANITY'S CHAMPION!
BOOM
DOOM
IN THE LAND OF THE RISING SUN, WHERE IT ORIGINATED...
TANIKAZE KAJINOSUKE
FOURTH YOKOZUNA
OM
DOOM
...SUMO WRESTLING WAS ONCE CONSIDERED THE ULTIMATE SPORT!
ONOGAWA KISABURO
FIFTH YOKOZUNA
DADOOM-!

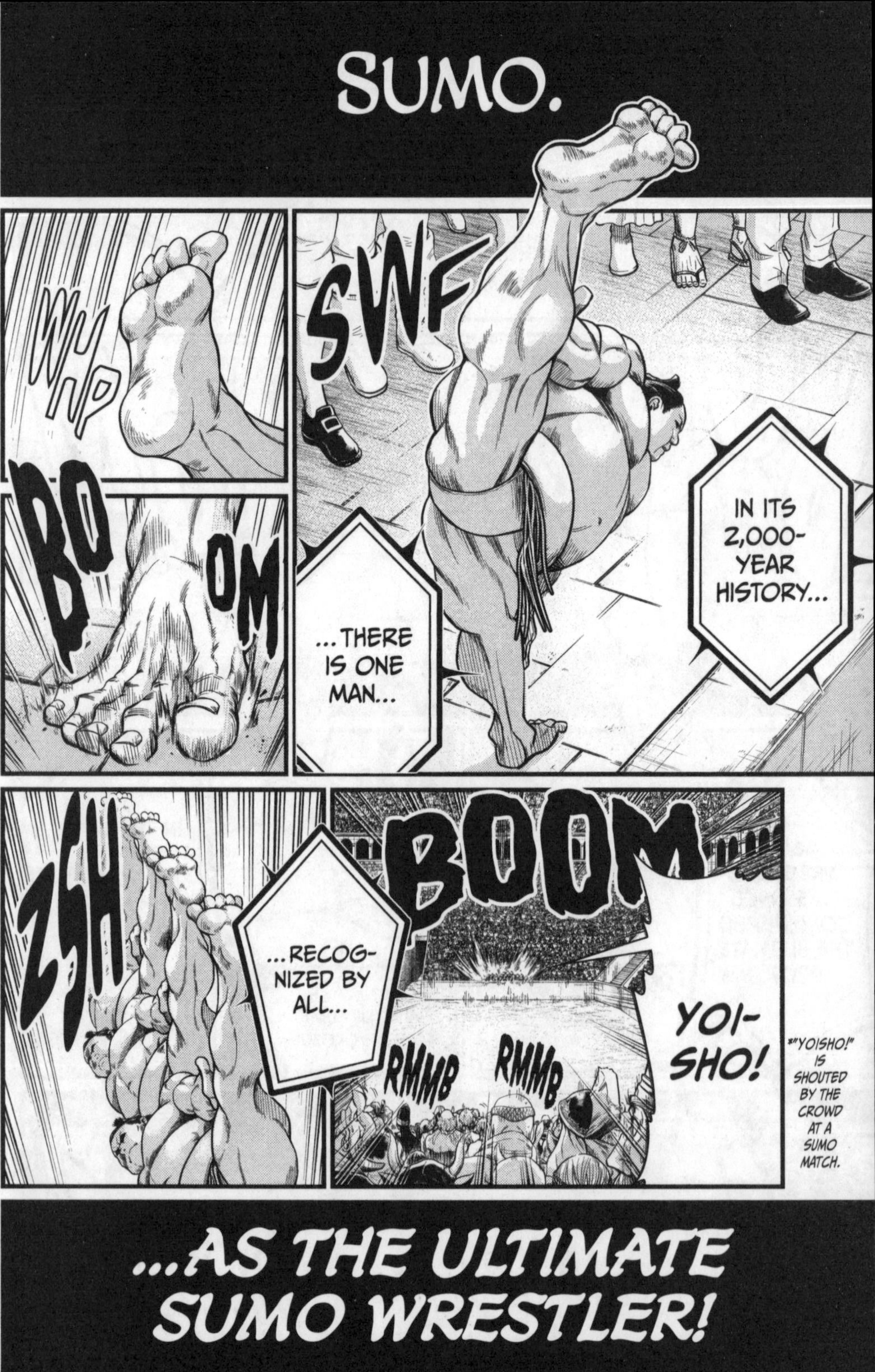
SUMO.
SWF
IN ITS 2,000-YEAR HISTORY...
...THERE IS ONE MAN...
WHP
BOOM
BOOM
...RECOGNIZED BY ALL...
YOI-SHO!
RMMB
RMMB
ZSH
...AS THE ULTIMATE SUMO WRESTLER!

*"YOISHO!" IS SHOUTED BY THE CROWD AT A SUMO MATCH.

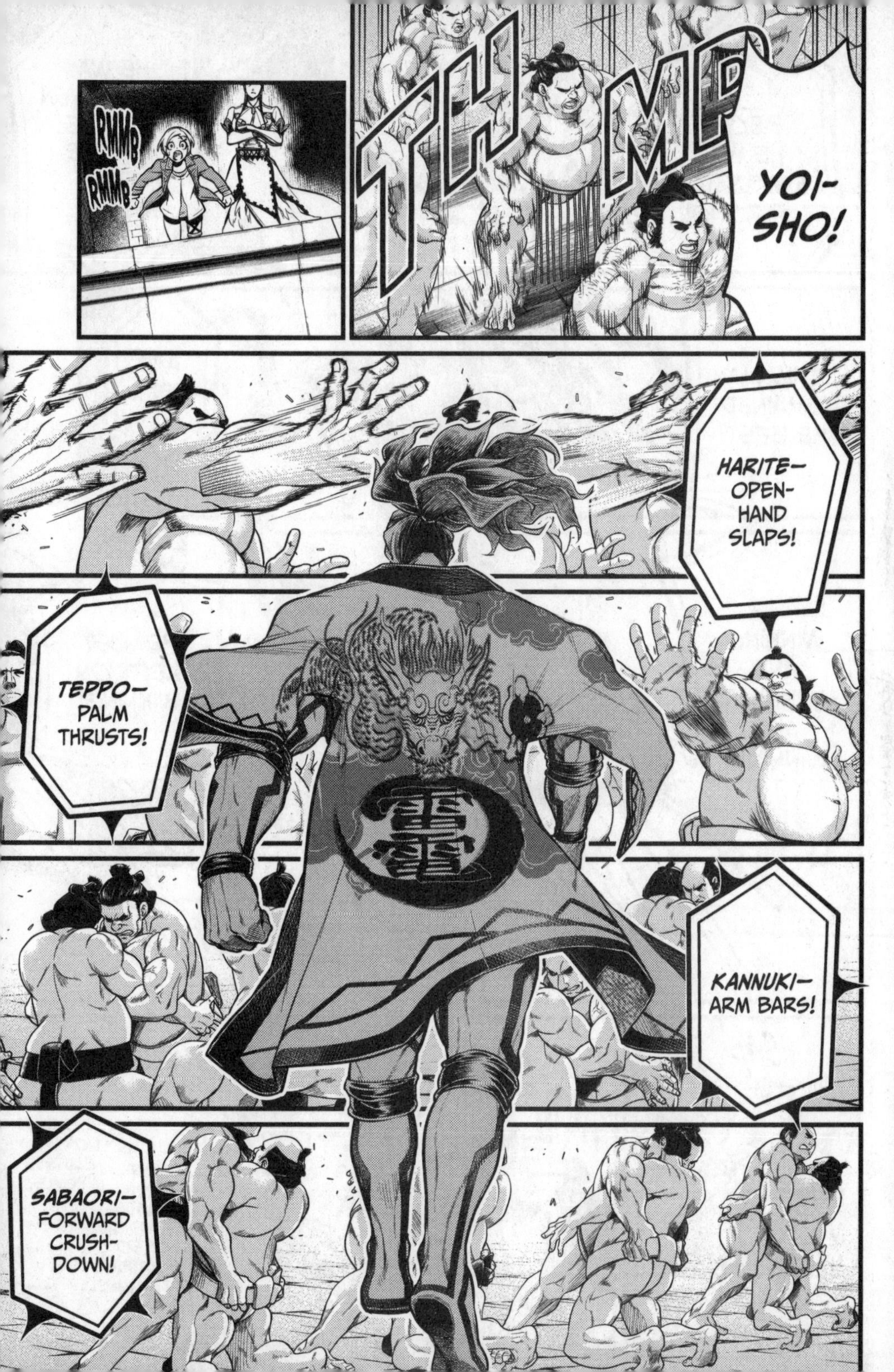
THMP
YOI-SHO!
RMMB RMMB
HARITE-OPEN-HAND SLAPS!
TEPPO-PALM THRUSTS!
KANNUKI-ARM BARS!
SABAORI-FORWARD CRUSH-DOWN!

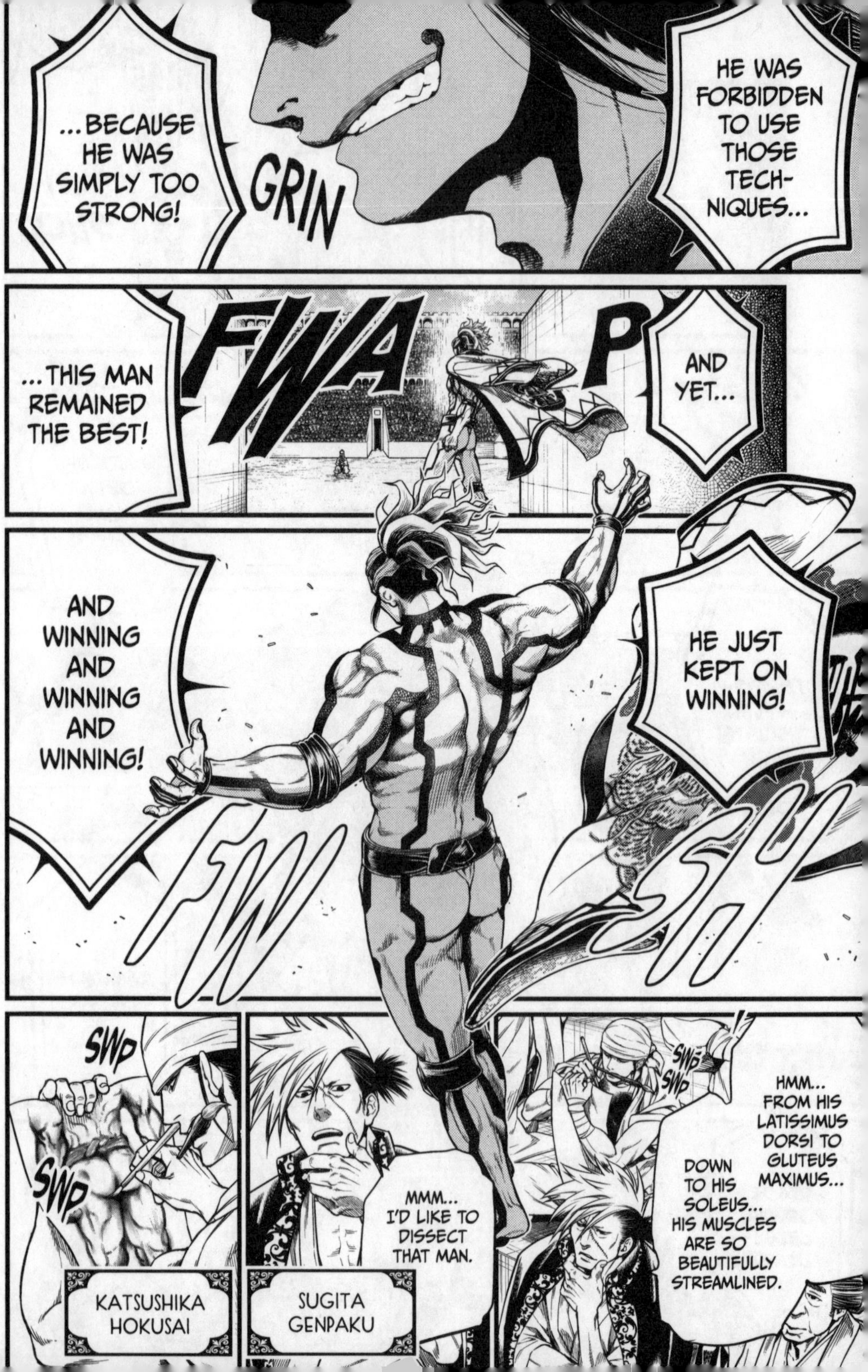
HE WAS FORBIDDEN TO USE THOSE TECH-NIQUES...
GRIN
...BECAUSE HE WAS SIMPLY TOO STRONG!
AND YET...
FWAP
...THIS MAN REMAINED THE BEST!
HE JUST KEPT ON WINNING!
AND WINNING AND WINNING AND WINNING!
FWSH
SWP SWP
HMM... FROM HIS LATISSIMUS DORSI TO GLUTEUS MAXIMUS...
DOWN TO HIS SOLEUS... HIS MUSCLES ARE SO BEAUTIFULLY STREAMLINED.
MMM... I'D LIKE TO DISSECT THAT MAN.
SUGITA GENPAKU
SWP
SWP
KATSUSHIKA HOKUSAI

YOISHO!

THE PEOPLE CALL THE MAN WHO REMAINED THE KING OF THE RING...

...FOR OVER 20 YEARS...

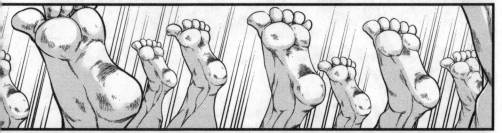

...THE UNRIVALED RIKISHI!*

*SUMO WRESTLER

YOISHO!!

RAI

HIS NAME IS...

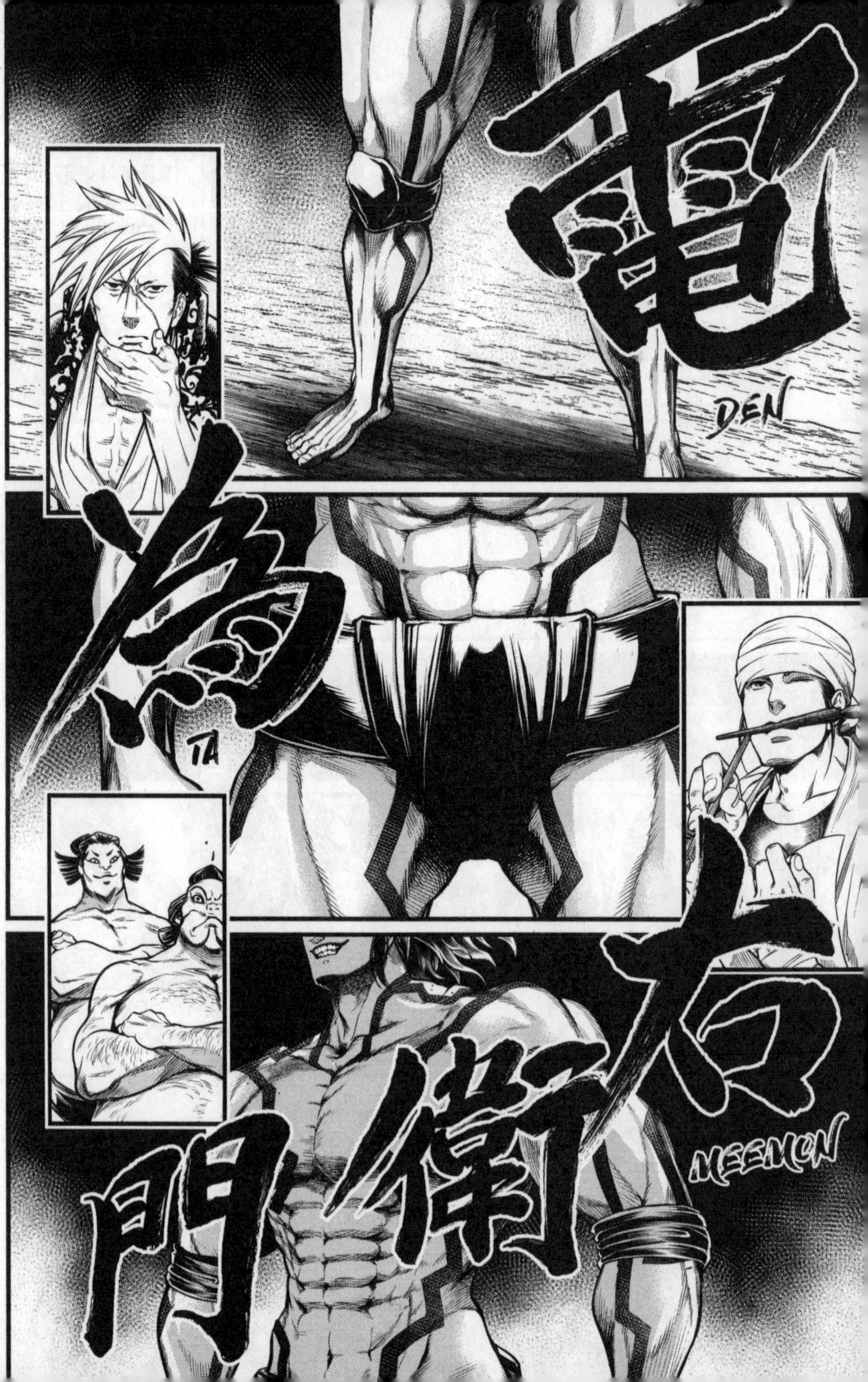
電
DEN
爲
TA
右衛門
MEEMON

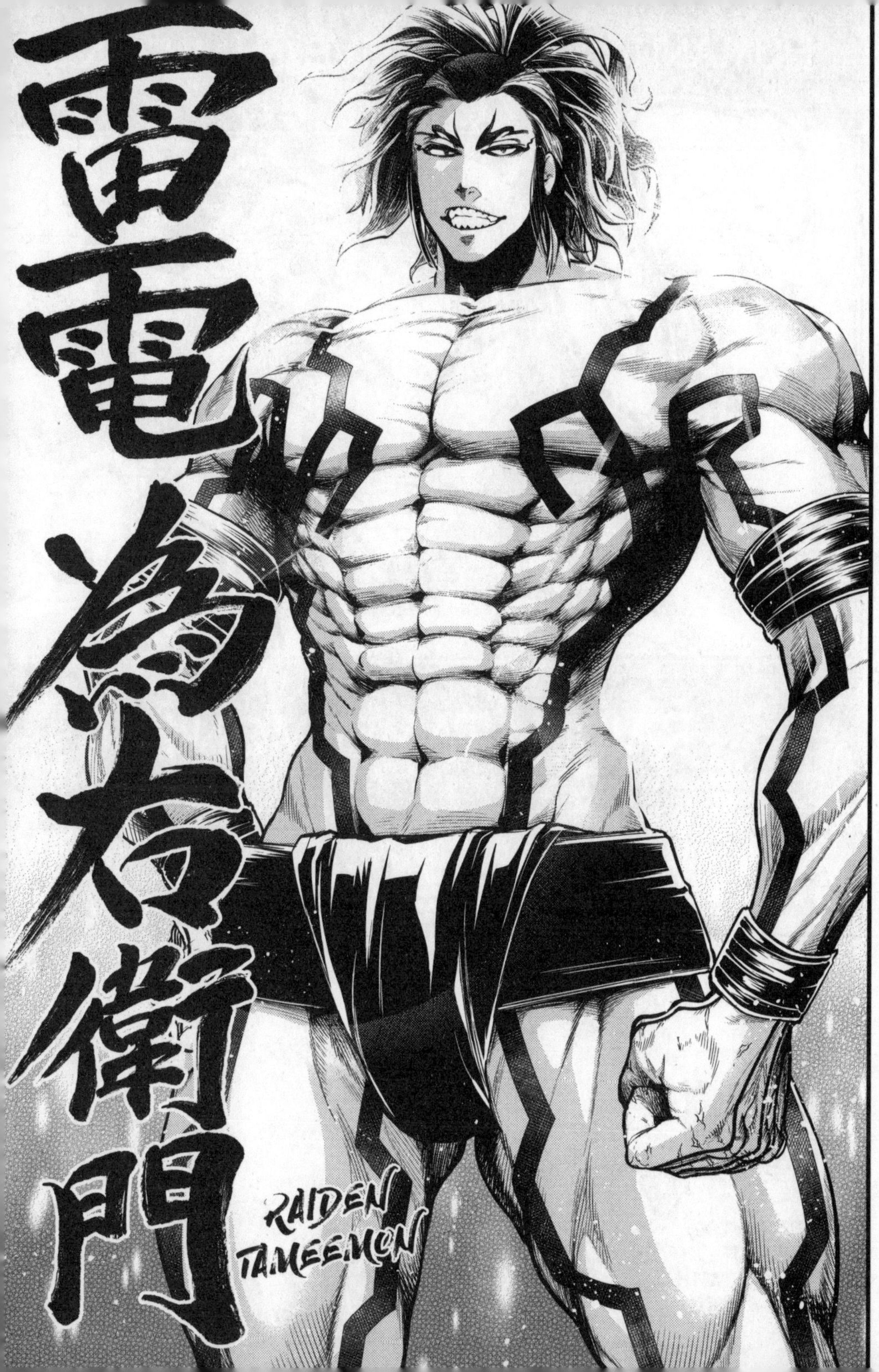
雷電爲右衛門
RAIDEN TAMEEMON

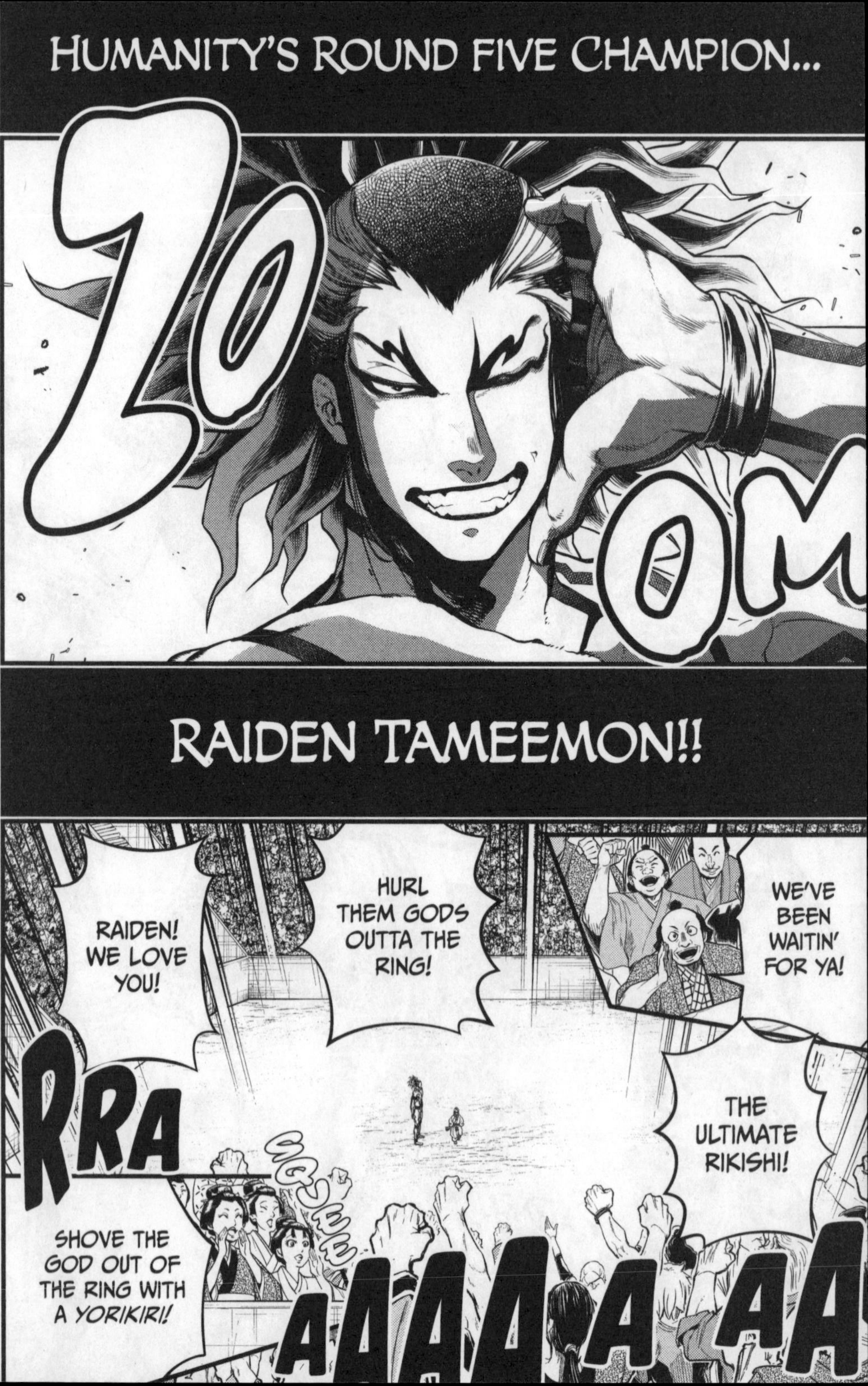
HUMANITY'S ROUND FIVE CHAMPION...
ZO
OM
RAIDEN TAMEEMON!!
WE'VE BEEN WAITIN' FOR YA!
HURL THEM GODS OUTTA THE RING!
RAIDEN! WE LOVE YOU!
THE ULTIMATE RIKISHI!
RRA
SHOVE THE GOD OUT OF THE RING WITH A *YORIKIRI!*
AAAAAAA

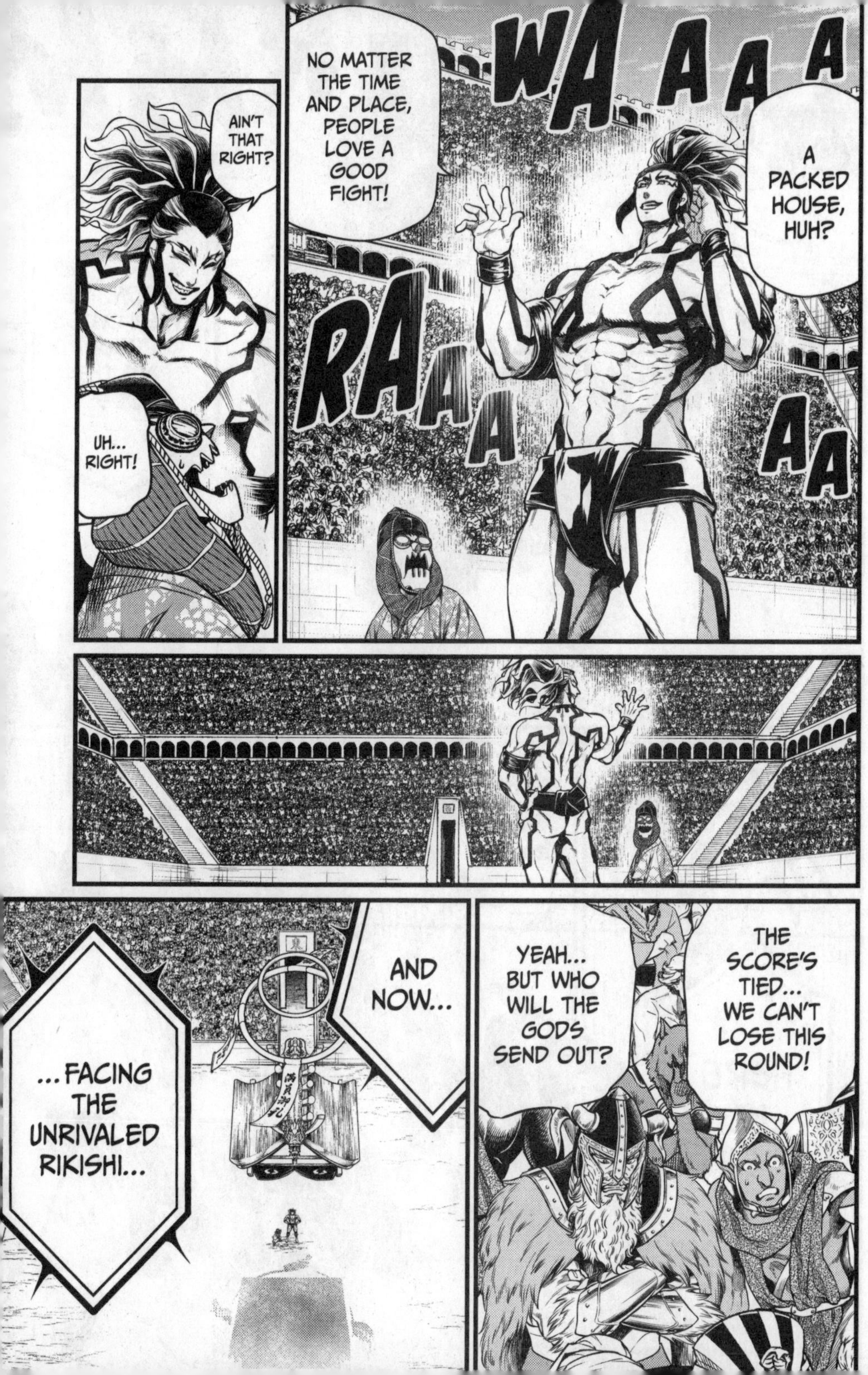
WAAAAA
A PACKED HOUSE, HUH?
NO MATTER THE TIME AND PLACE, PEOPLE LOVE A GOOD FIGHT!
RAAAA
AA
AIN'T THAT RIGHT?
UH... RIGHT!
THE SCORE'S TIED... WE CAN'T LOSE THIS ROUND!
YEAH... BUT WHO WILL THE GODS SEND OUT?
AND NOW...
...FACING THE UNRIVALED RIKISHI...

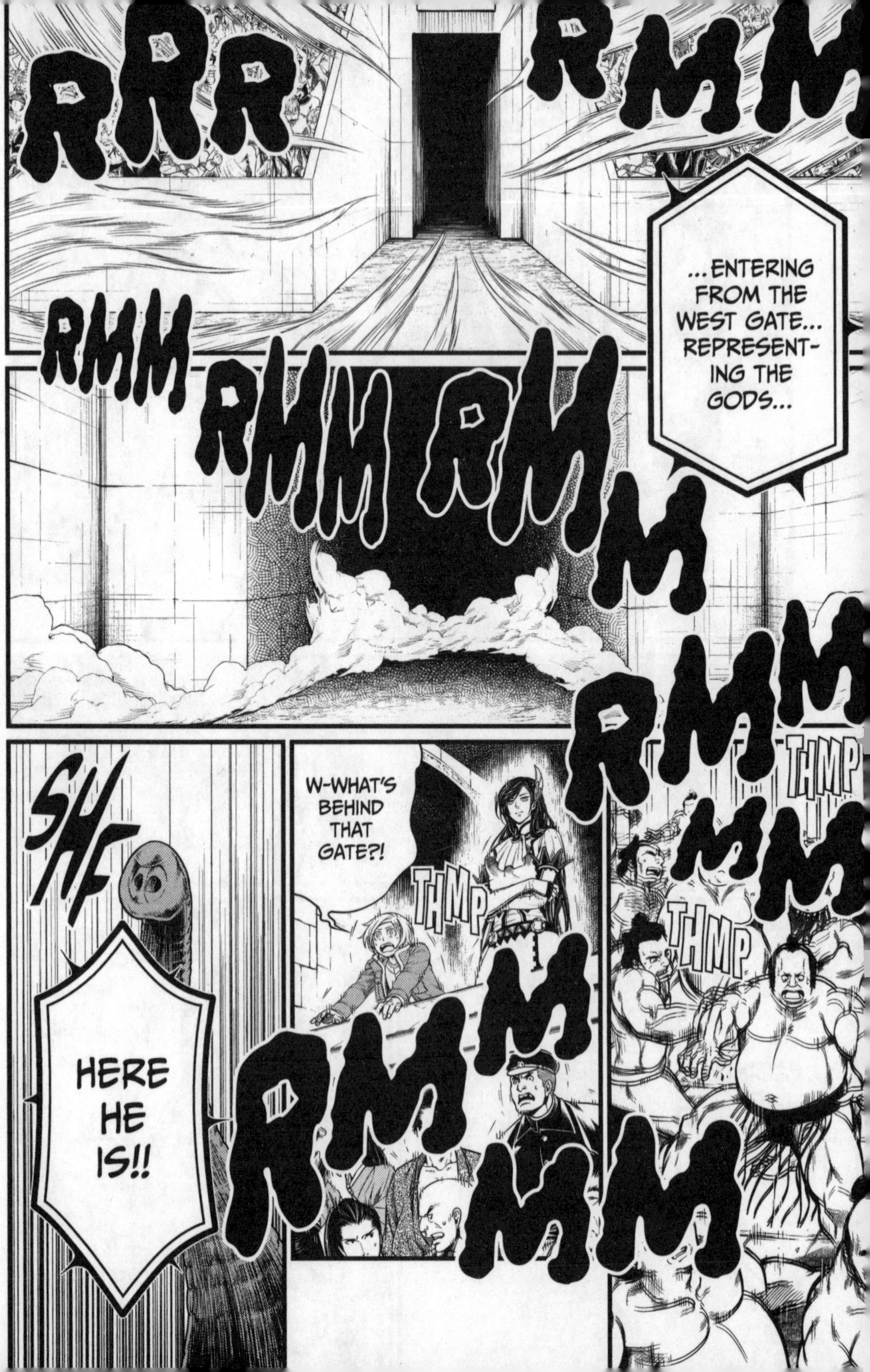
RRR RMM
...ENTERING FROM THE WEST GATE... REPRESENTING THE GODS...
RMM RMM RMM RMM
RMM RMM
THMP
W-WHAT'S BEHIND THAT GATE?!
THMP
THMP
RMM MMM
SHF
HERE HE IS!!

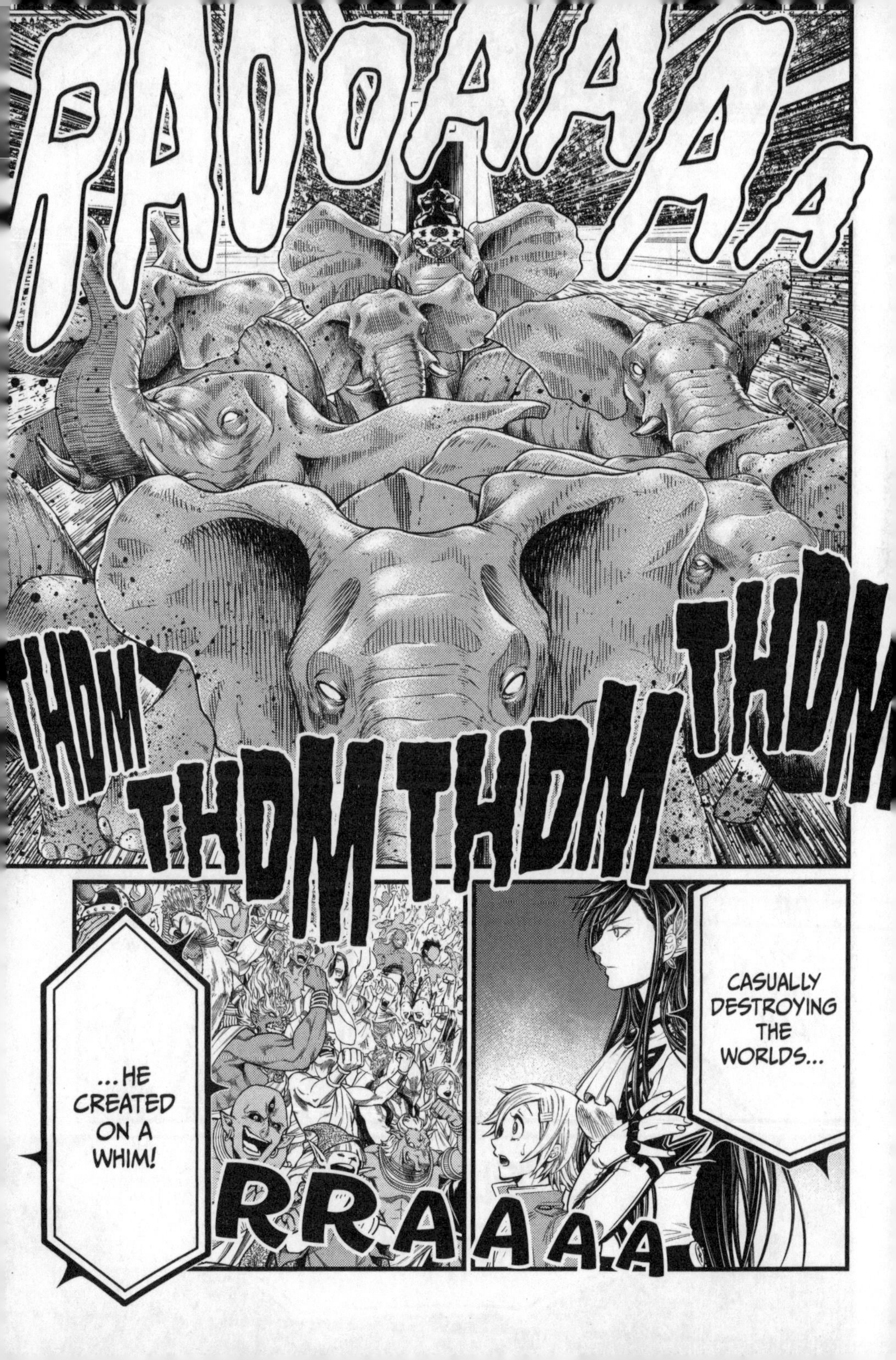
RAOOAAA
THOM THOM THOM THOM
CASUALLY DESTROYING THE WORLDS...
...HE CREATED ON A WHIM!
RRAAAAA

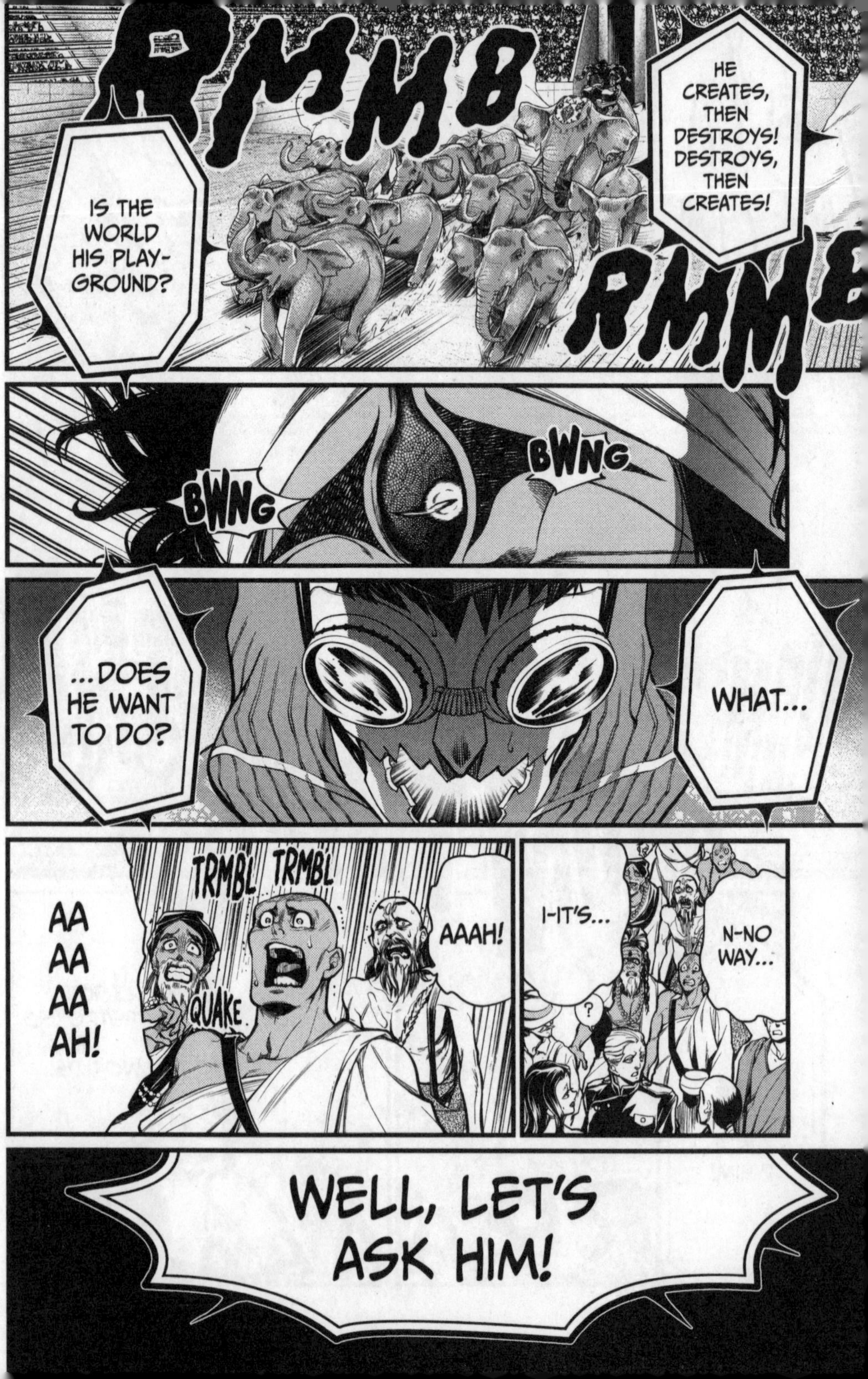
HE CREATES, THEN DESTROYS! DESTROYS, THEN CREATES!
RMMB
RMMB
IS THE WORLD HIS PLAY-GROUND?
BWNG
BWNG
WHAT...
...DOES HE WANT TO DO?
N-NO WAY...
I-IT'S...
?
AAAH!
TRMBL TRMBL
QUAKE
AA AA AA AH!
WELL, LET'S ASK HIM!

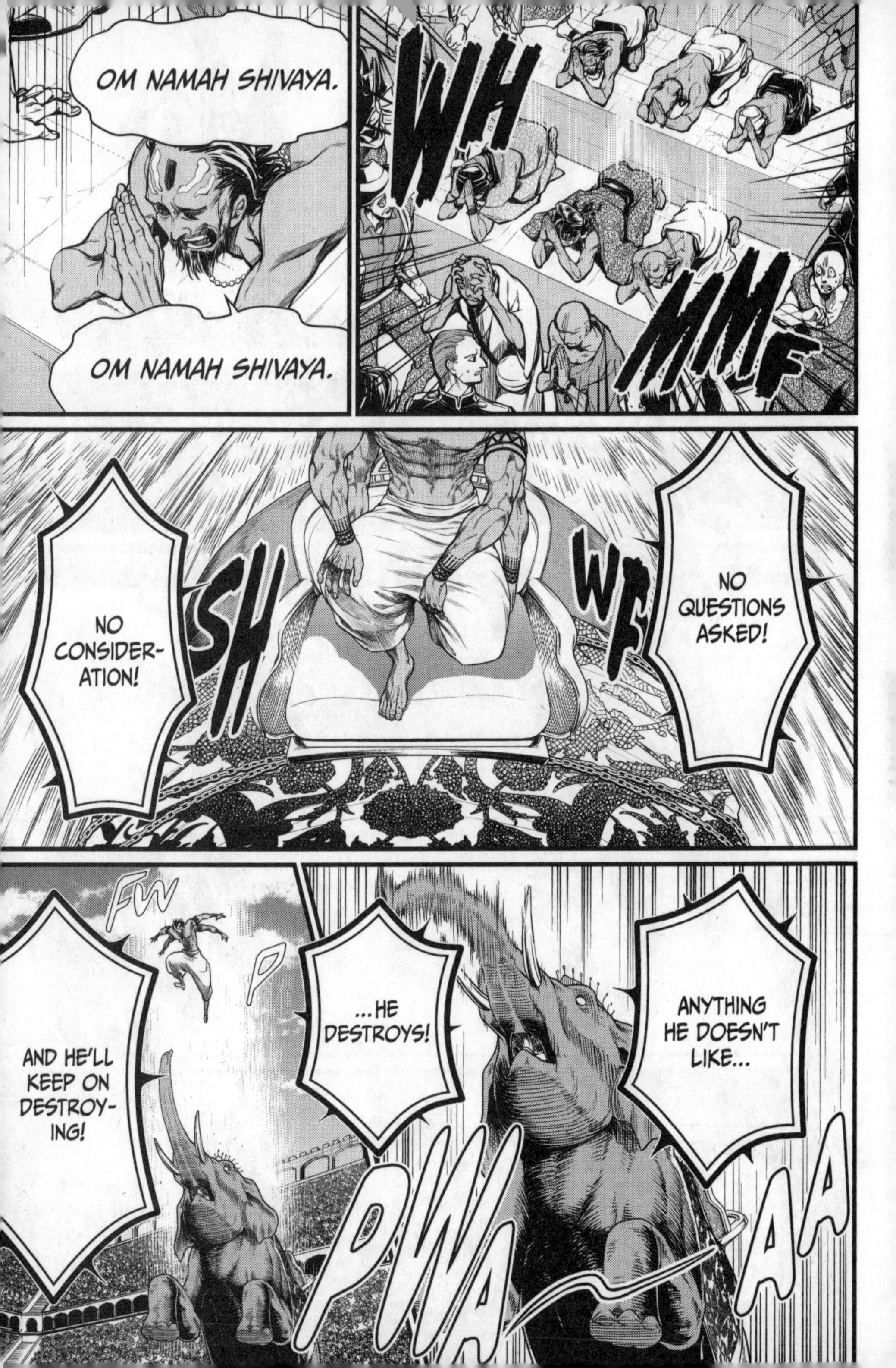
WH
MMF
OM NAMAH SHIVAYA.
OM NAMAH SHIVAYA.
NO QUESTIONS ASKED!
WF
SH
NO CONSIDER-ATION!
ANYTHING HE DOESN'T LIKE...
...HE DESTROYS!
P
FW
AND HE'LL KEEP ON DESTROY-ING!
PWAAA

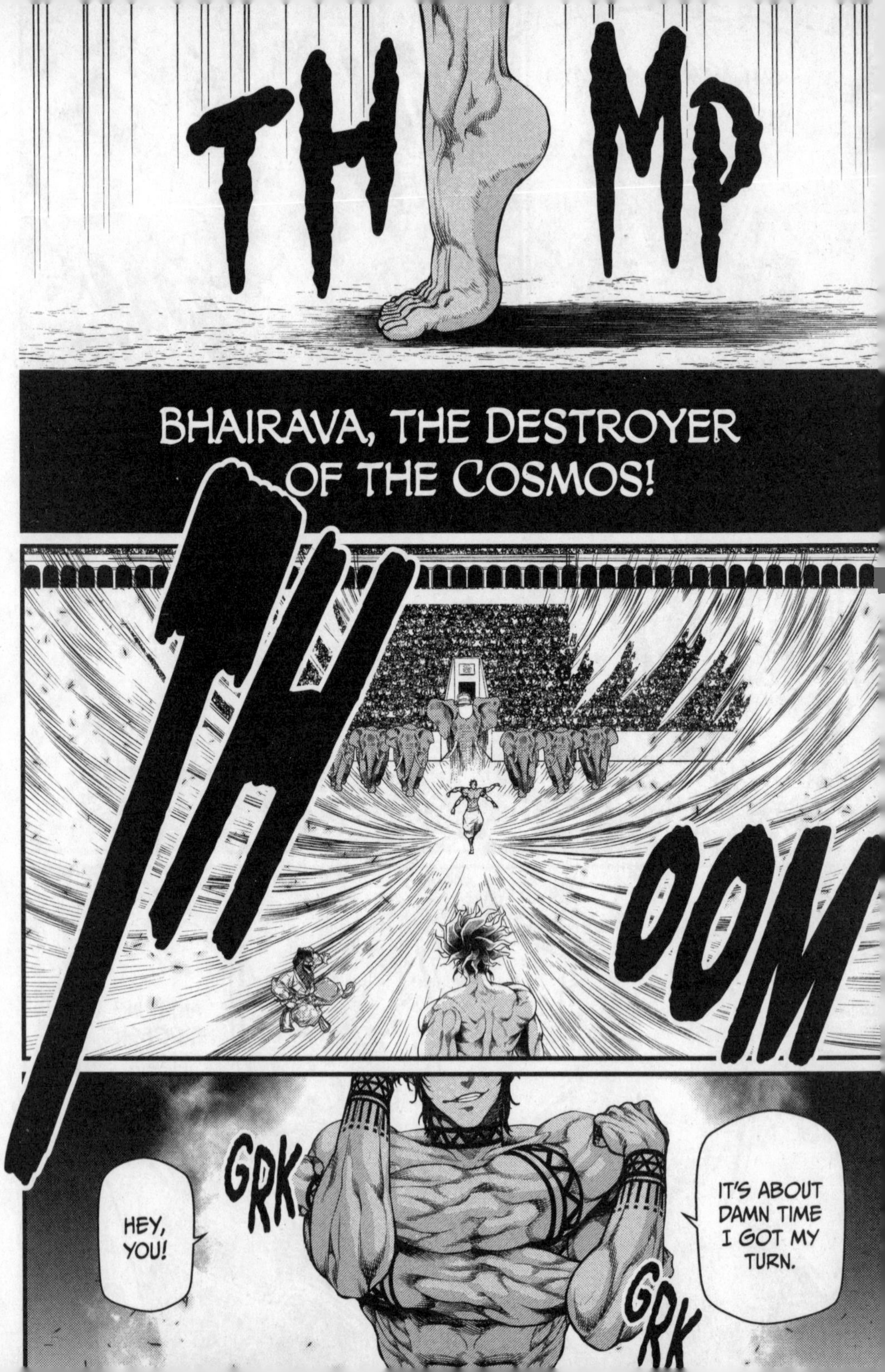
THUMP
BHAIRAVA, THE DESTROYER OF THE COSMOS!
VROOOM
IT'S ABOUT DAMN TIME I GOT MY TURN.
GRK
GRK
HEY, YOU!

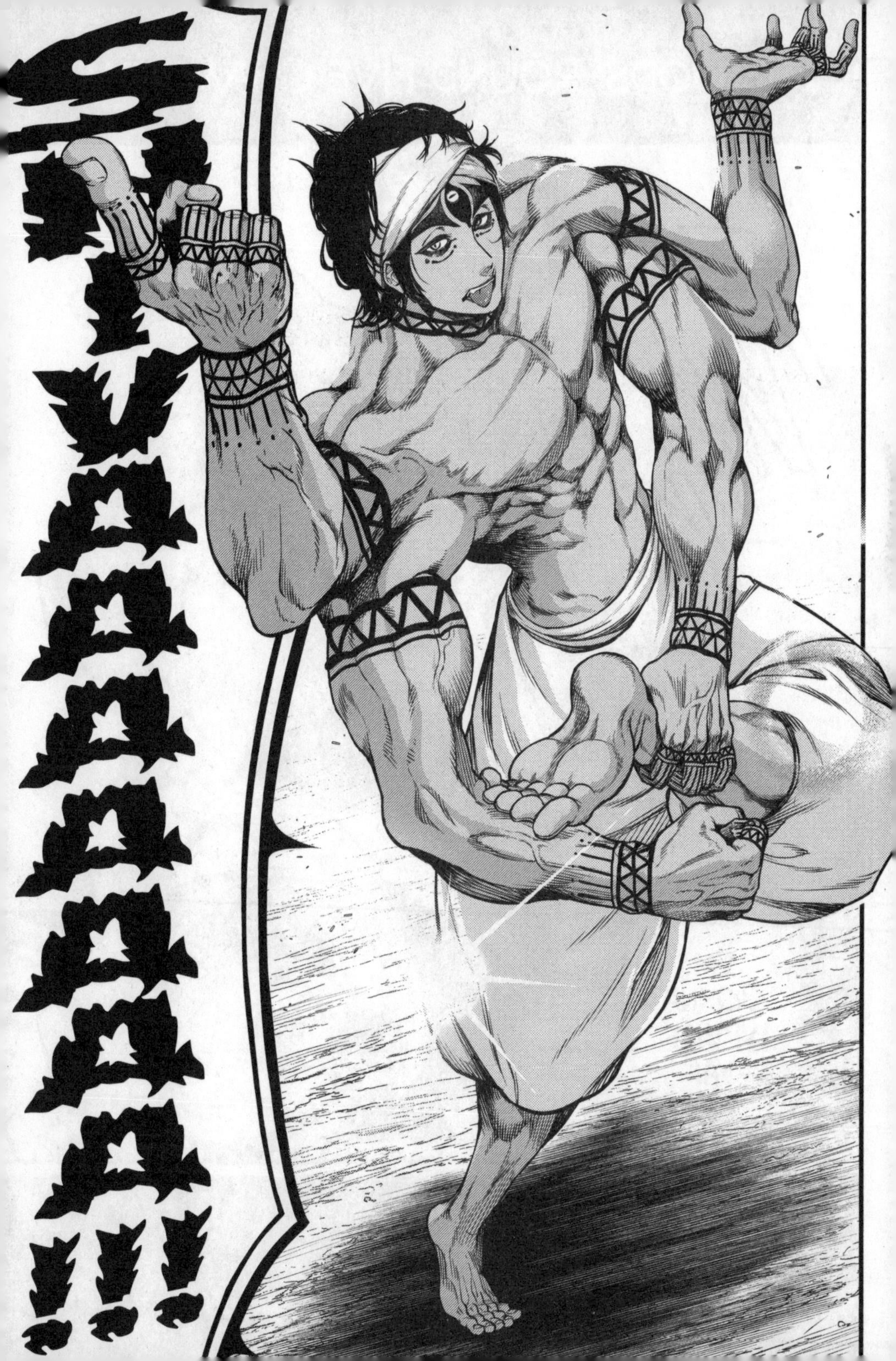
SHWAAAAAAAA!!

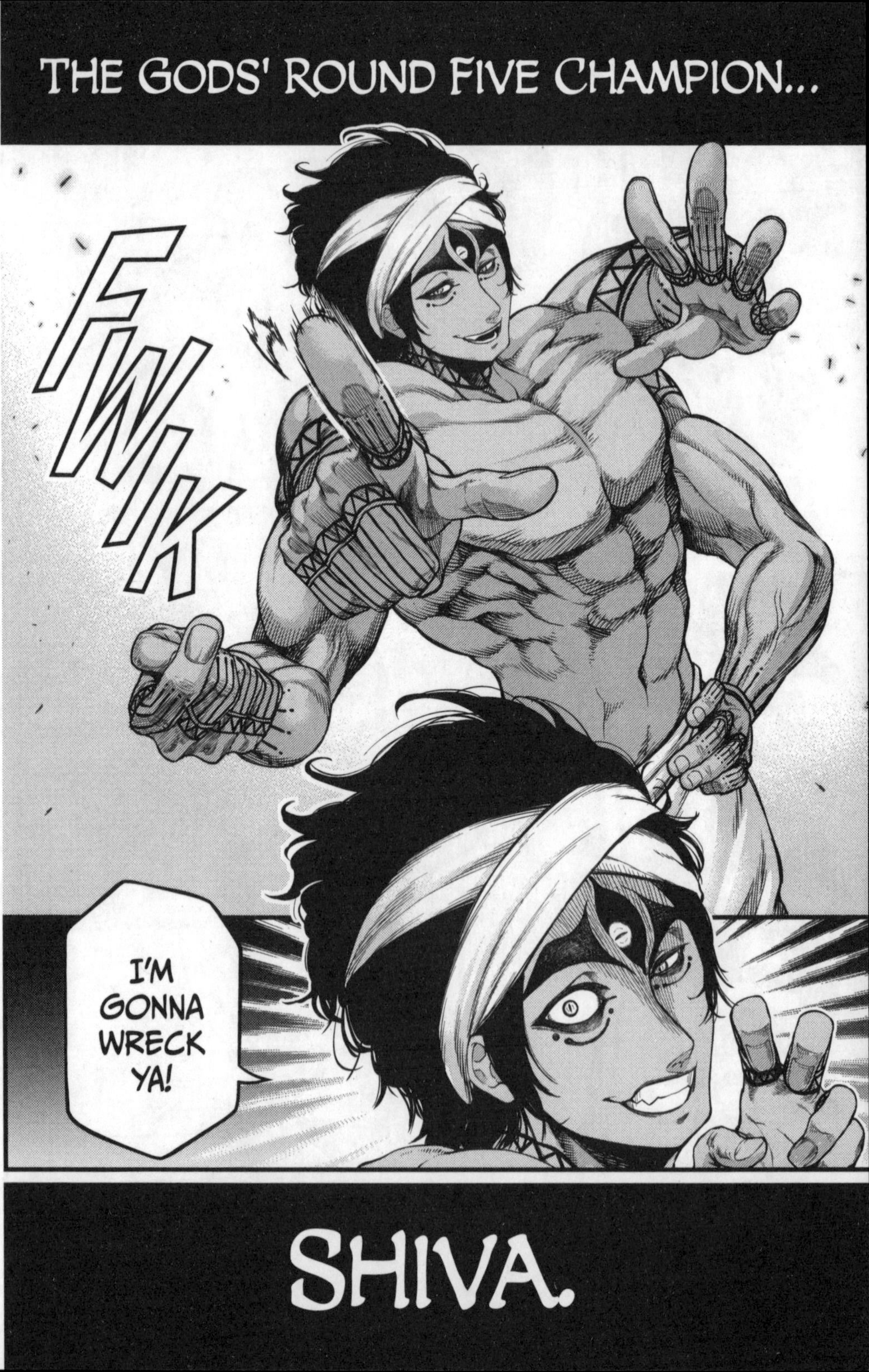
THE GODS' ROUND FIVE CHAMPION...
FWIK
I'M GONNA WRECK YA!
SHIVA.

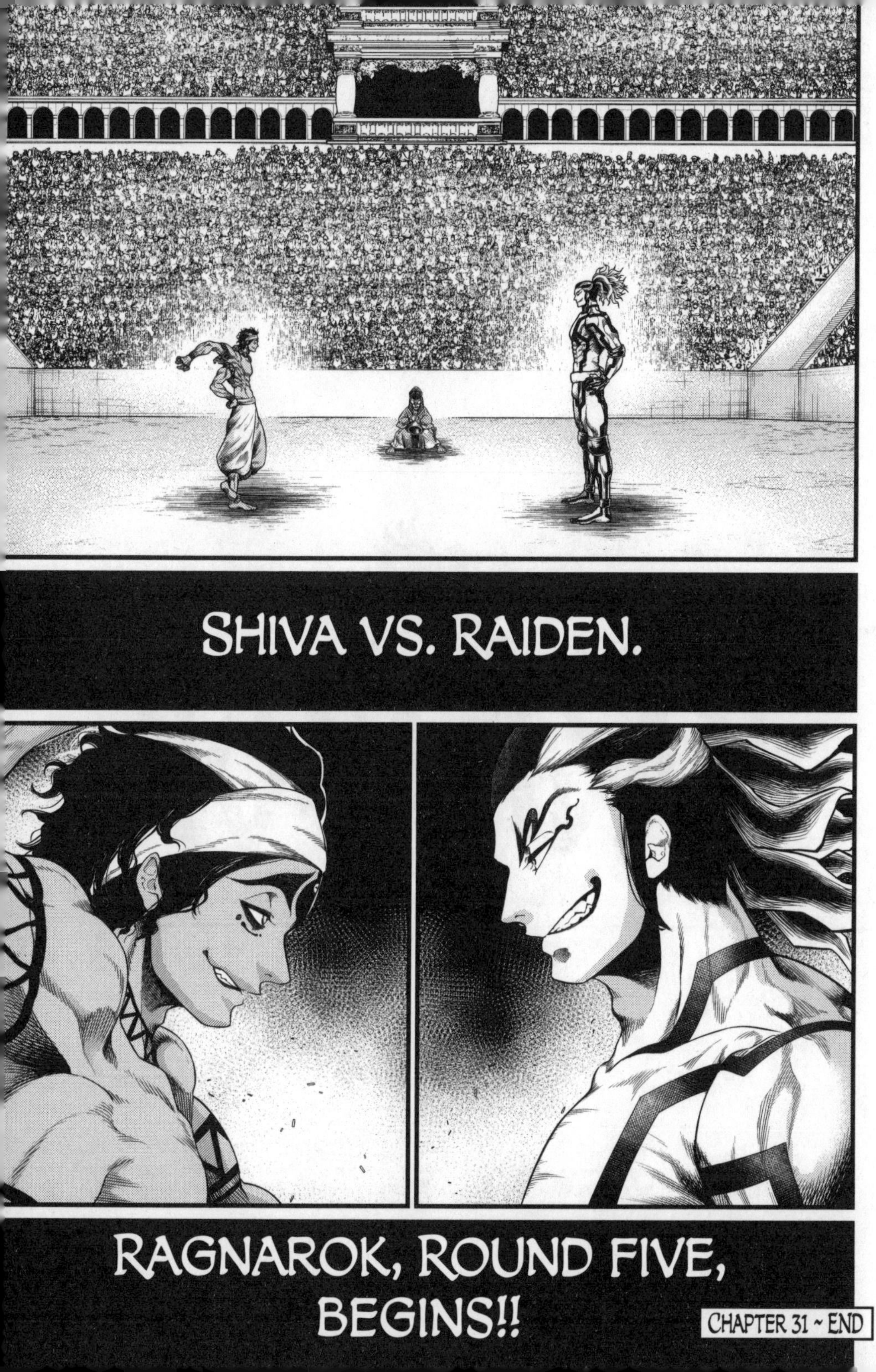
SHIVA VS. RAIDEN.
RAGNAROK, ROUND FIVE, BEGINS!!
CHAPTER 31 ~ END

RECORD OF RAGNAROK

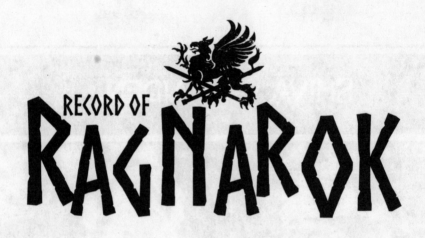

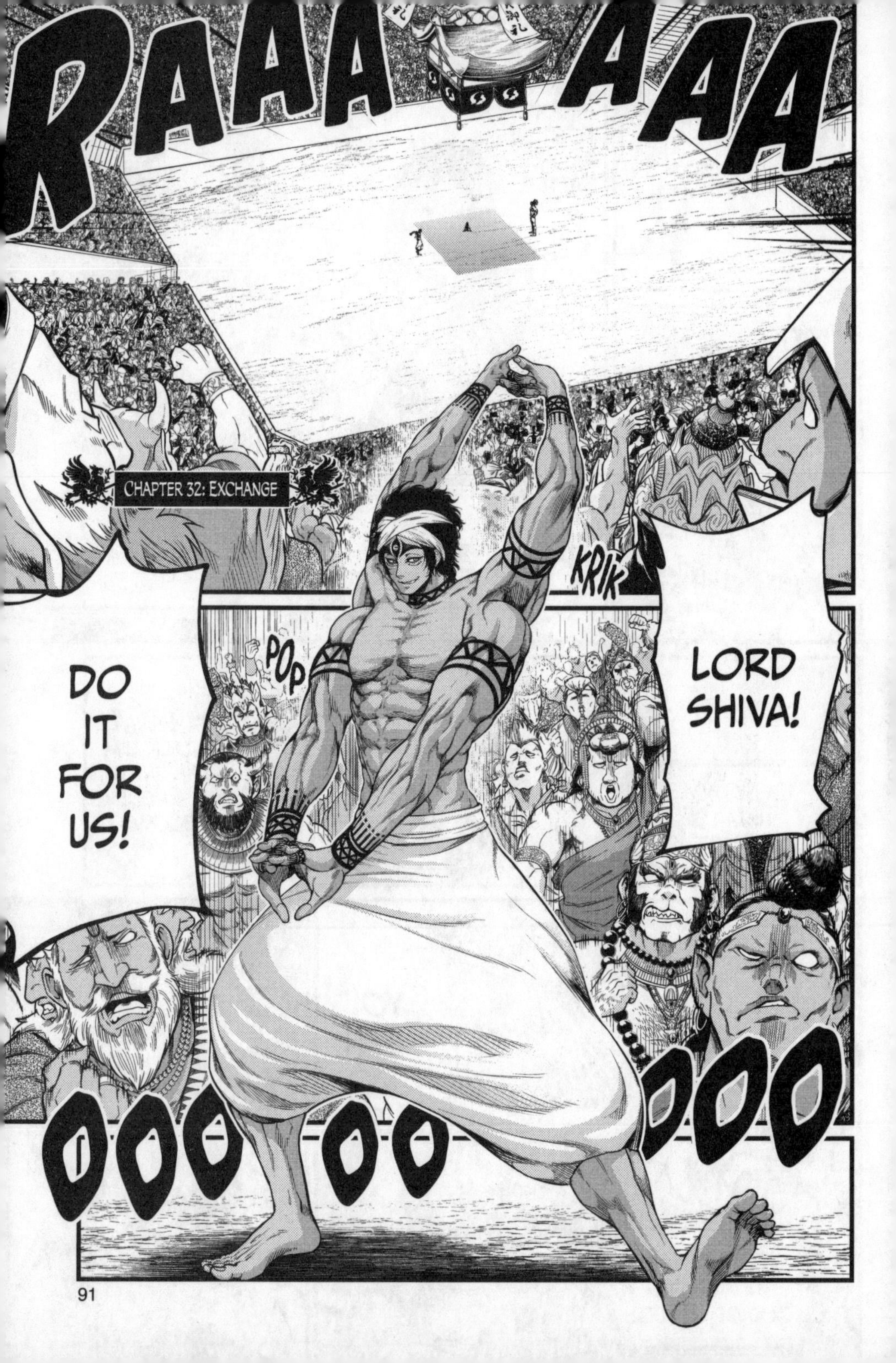
RAAAAAAA
CHAPTER 32: EXCHANGE
KRIK
LORD SHIVA!
POP
DO IT FOR US!
OOOOOOOOOO

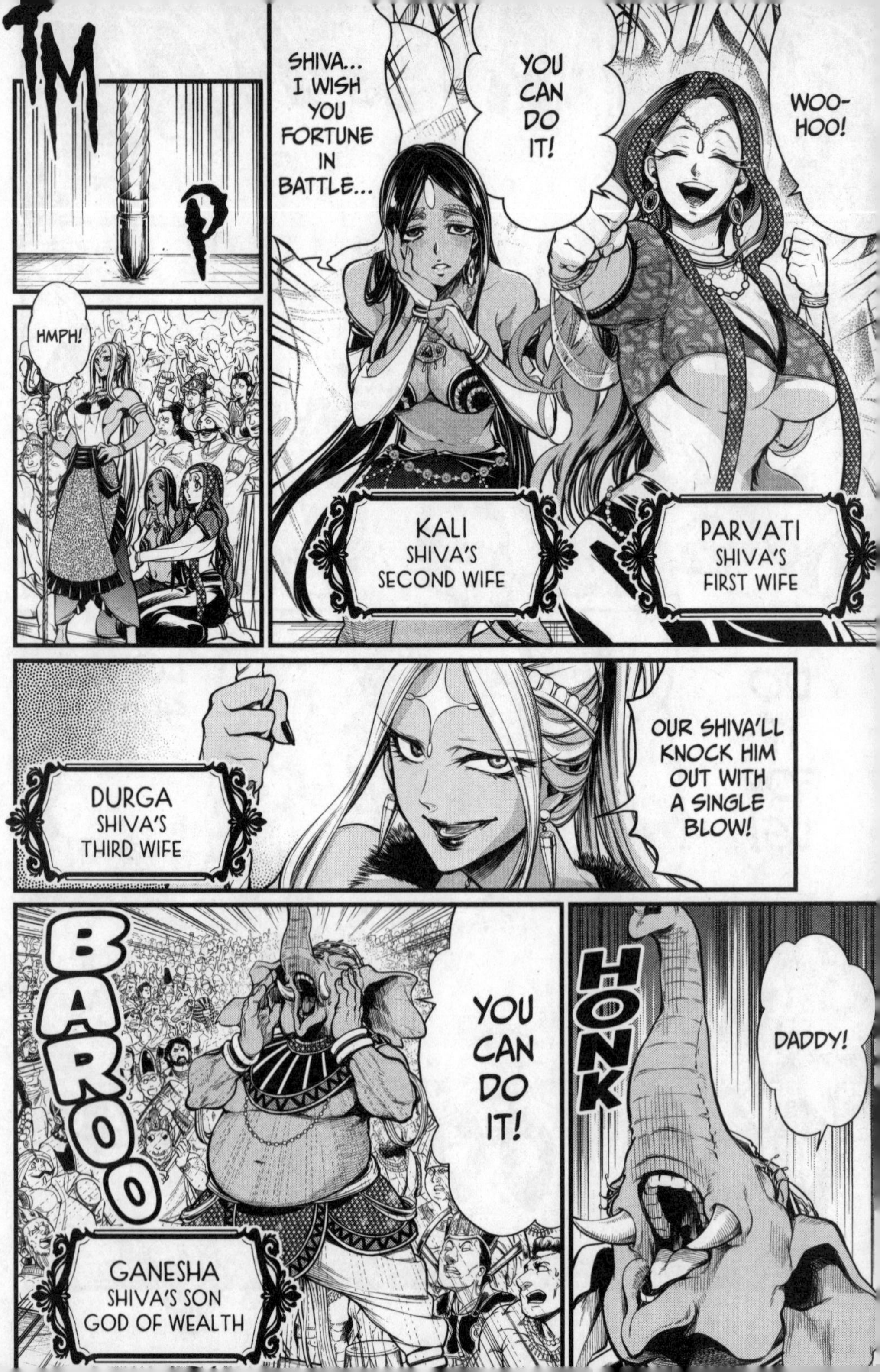
WOO-HOO!
YOU CAN DO IT!
SHIVA... I WISH YOU FORTUNE IN BATTLE...
PARVATI SHIVA'S FIRST WIFE
KALI SHIVA'S SECOND WIFE
TMP
HMPH!
OUR SHIVA'LL KNOCK HIM OUT WITH A SINGLE BLOW!
DURGA SHIVA'S THIRD WIFE
DADDY!
HONK
YOU CAN DO IT!
BAROO
GANESHA SHIVA'S SON GOD OF WEALTH

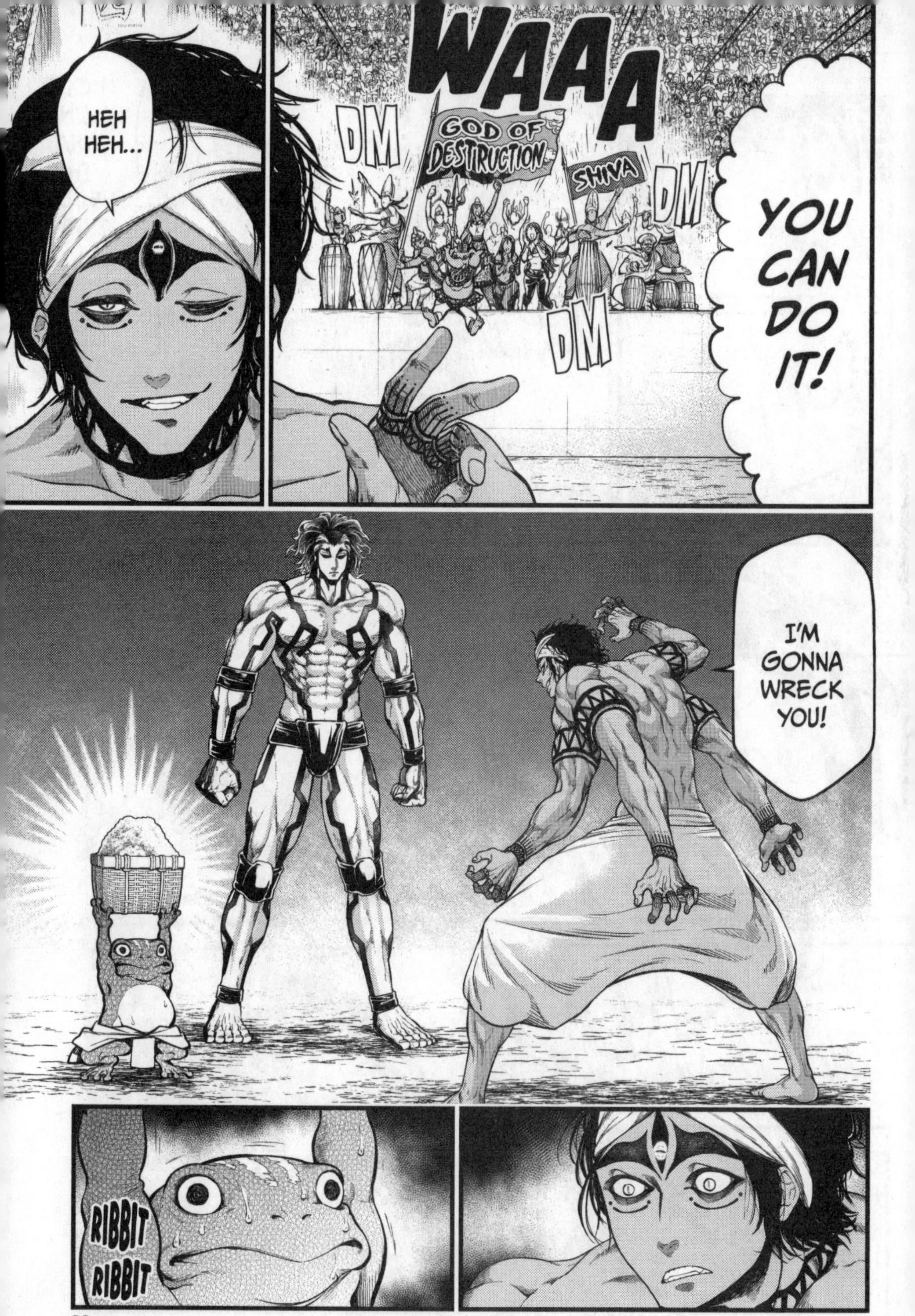
WAAA
DM
GOD OF DESTRUCTION
SHIVA
DM
DM
YOU CAN DO IT!
HEH HEH...
I'M GONNA WRECK YOU!
RIBBIT RIBBIT

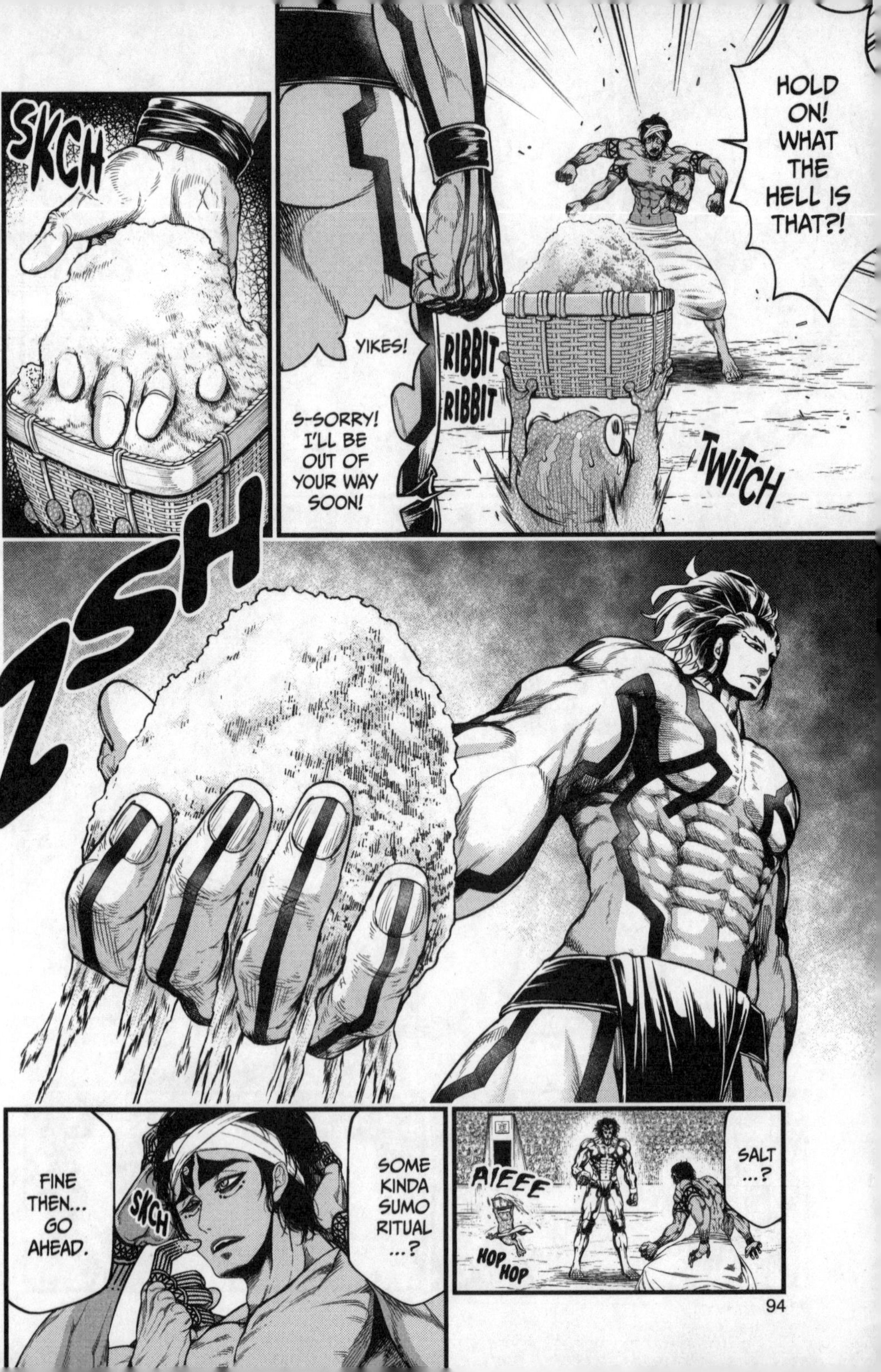
HOLD ON! WHAT THE HELL IS THAT?!
TWITCH
RIBBIT RIBBIT
YIKES!
S-SORRY! I'LL BE OUT OF YOUR WAY SOON!
SKCH
ZSH
SALT ...?
AIEEE
HOP HOP
SOME KINDA SUMO RITUAL ...?
SKCH
FINE THEN... GO AHEAD.

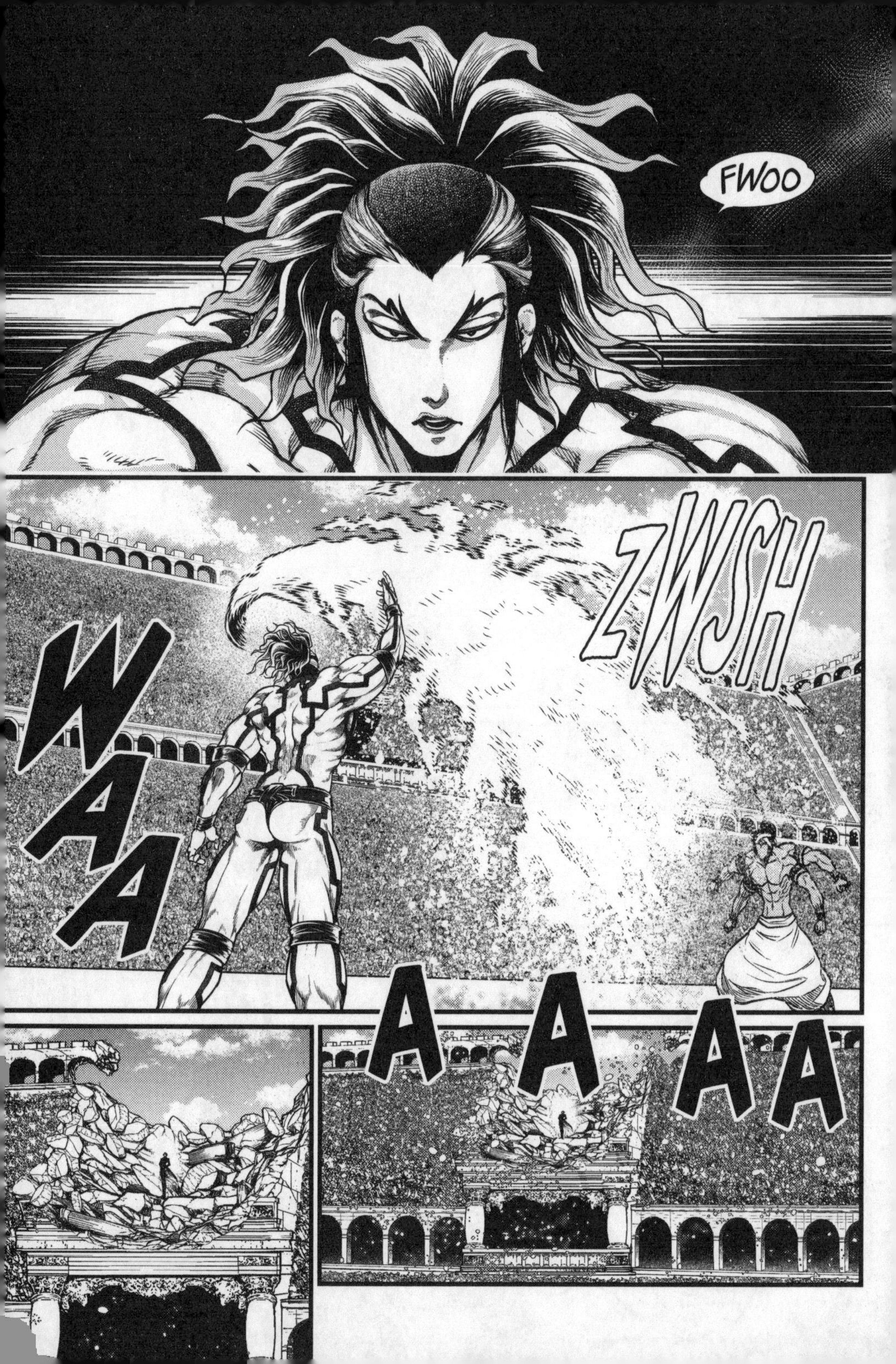
FWOO
ZWSH
WAAA
A A A AA

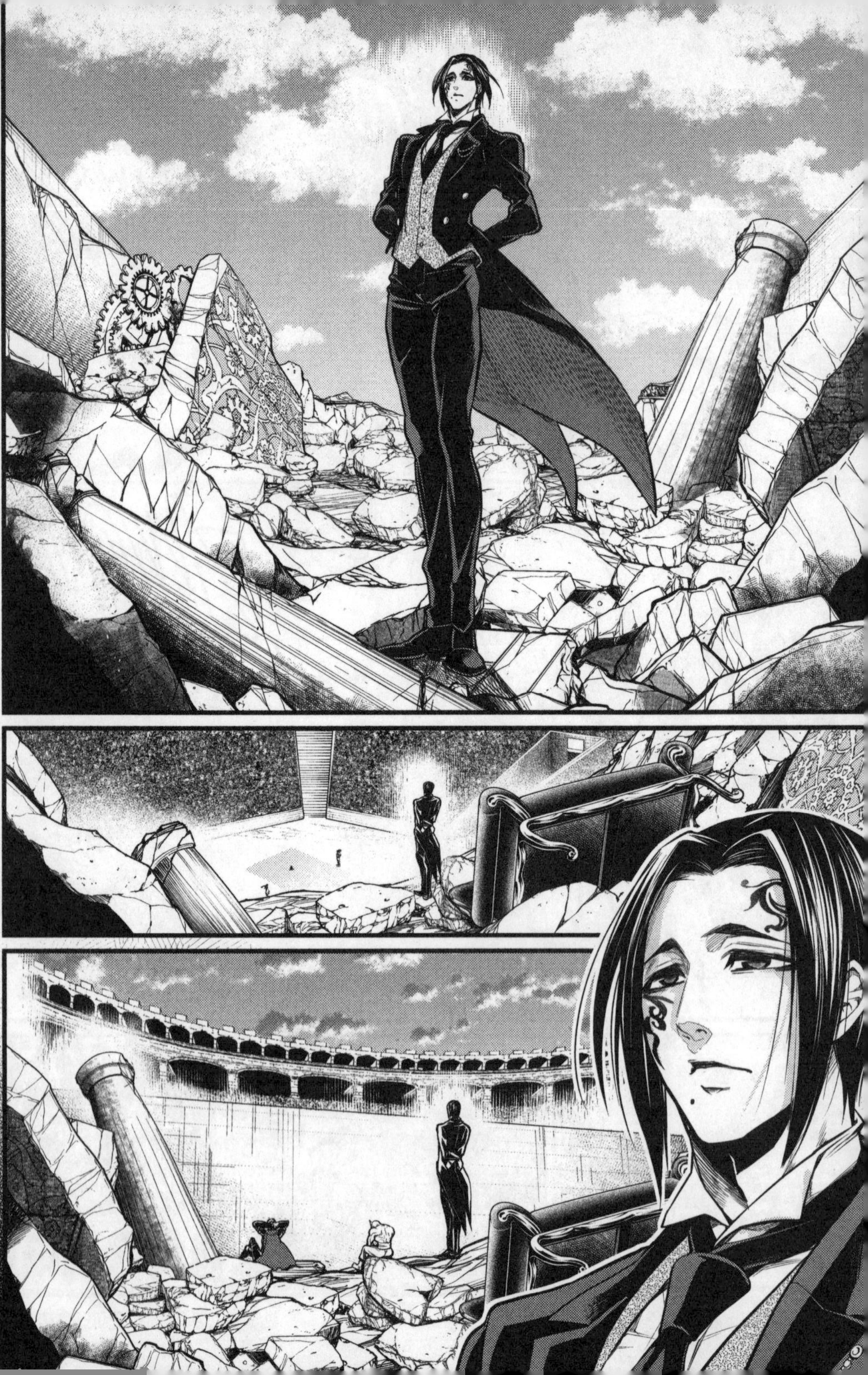

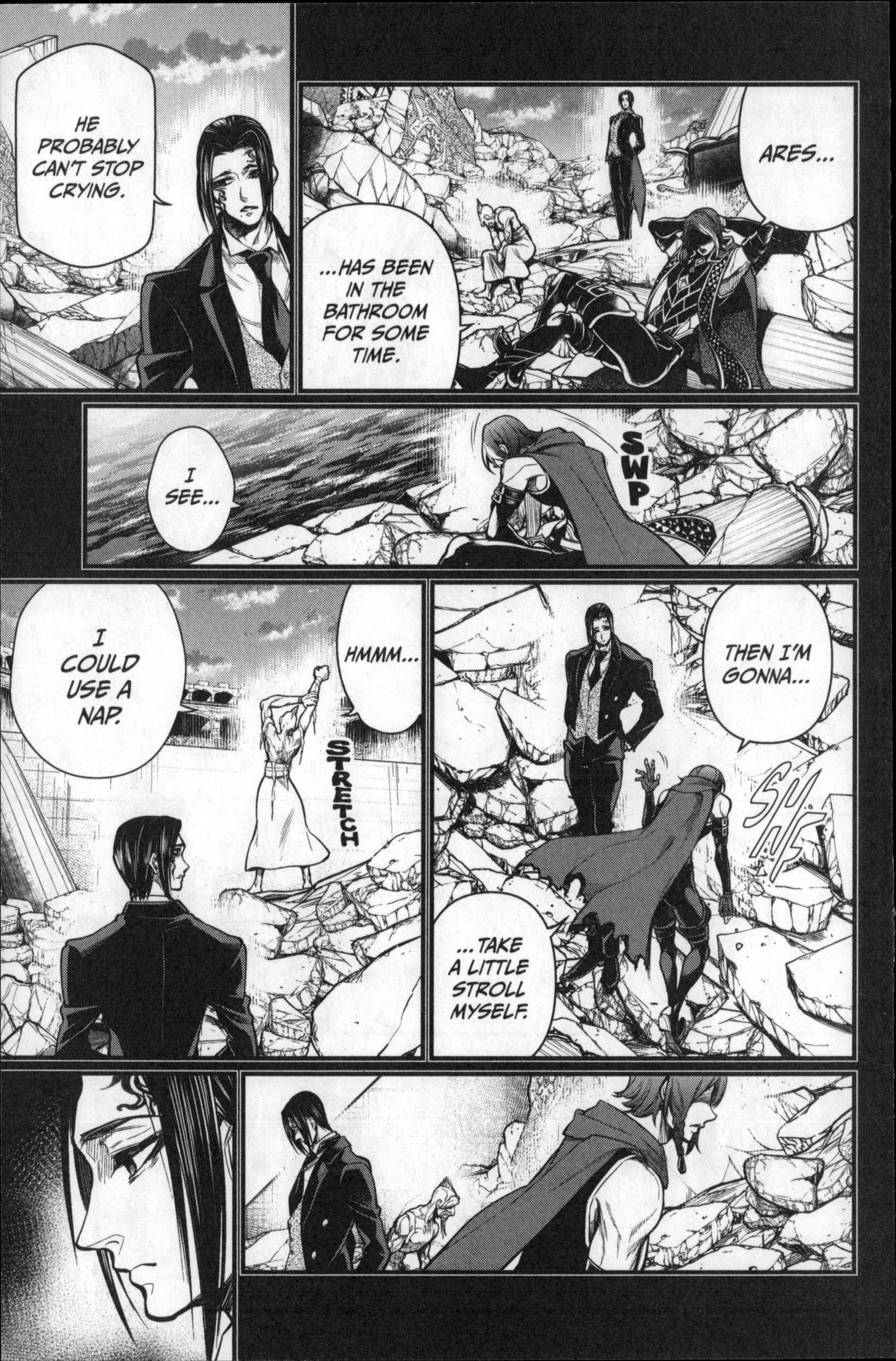
ARES...
...HAS BEEN IN THE BATHROOM FOR SOME TIME.
HE PROBABLY CAN'T STOP CRYING.
SWP
I SEE...
THEN I'M GONNA...
...TAKE A LITTLE STROLL MYSELF.
HMMM...
STRETCH
I COULD USE A NAP.

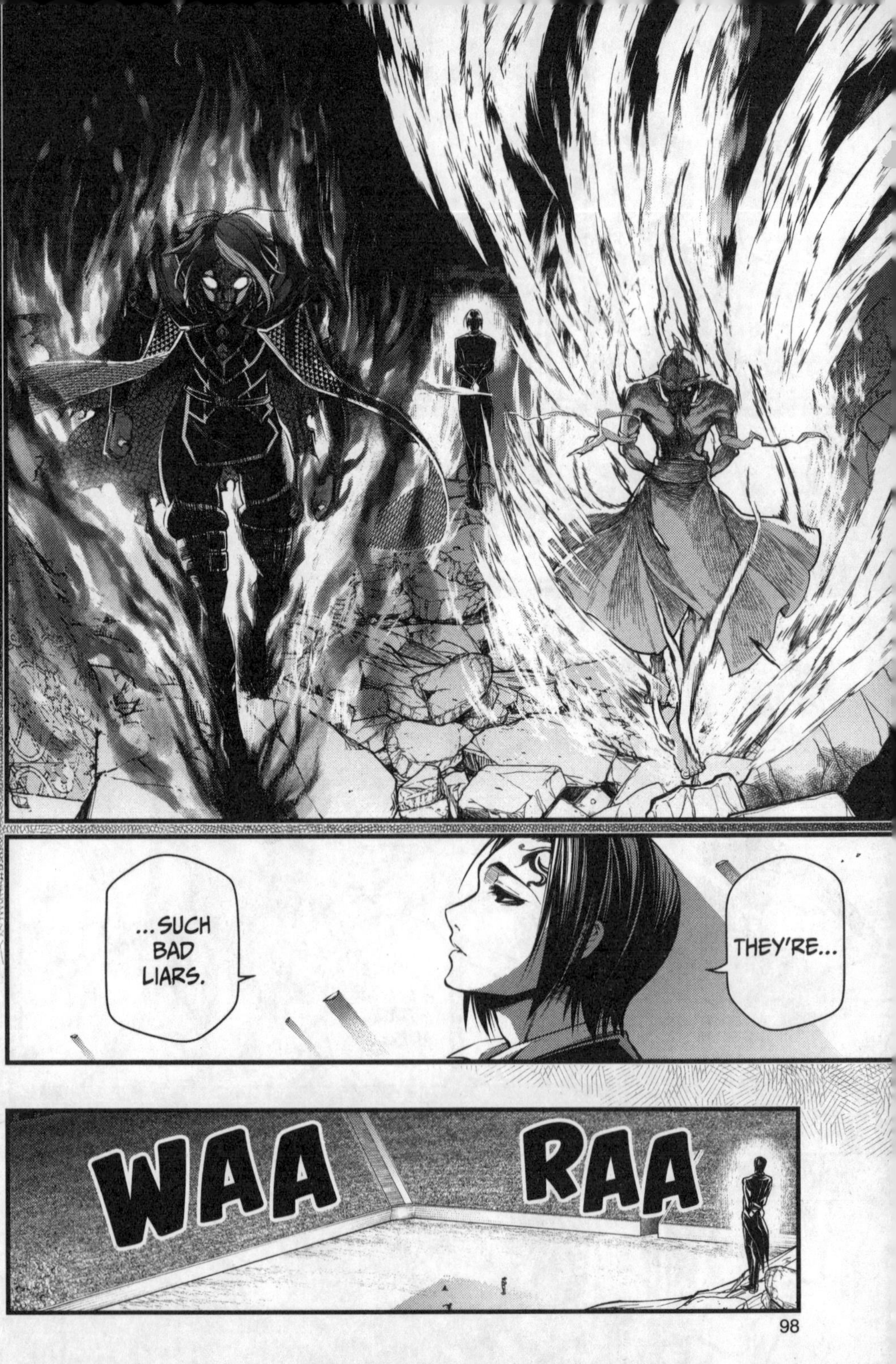
THEY'RE...
...SUCH BAD LIARS.
WAA RAA

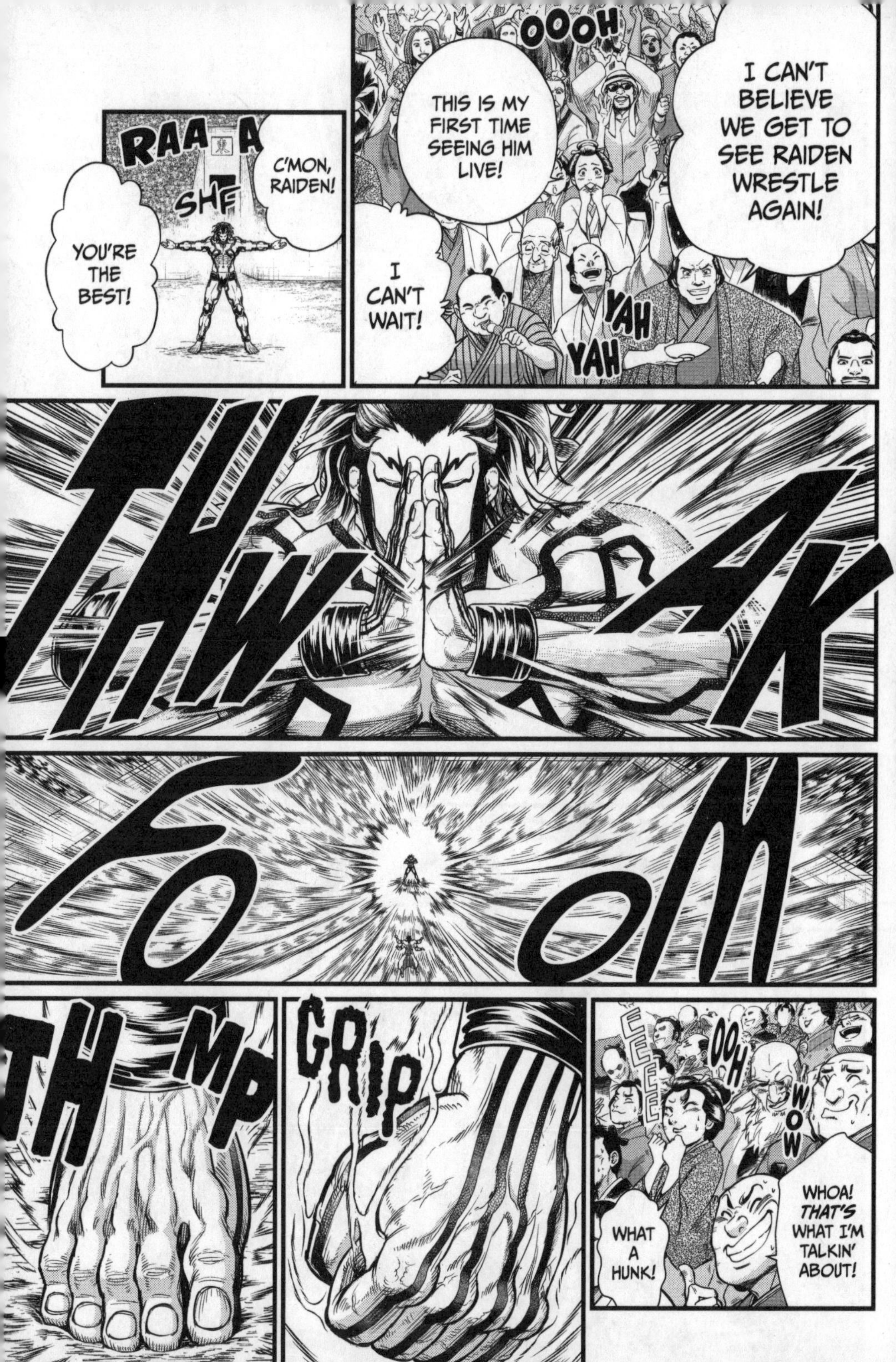
OOOH
I CAN'T BELIEVE WE GET TO SEE RAIDEN WRESTLE AGAIN!
THIS IS MY FIRST TIME SEEING HIM LIVE!
I CAN'T WAIT!
YAH
YAH
C'MON, RAIDEN!
RAA A
SHF
YOU'RE THE BEST!
THWAK
FOOM
OOH
EEEE
WOW
WHOA! THAT'S WHAT I'M TALKIN' ABOUT!
WHAT A HUNK!
GRIP
THMP

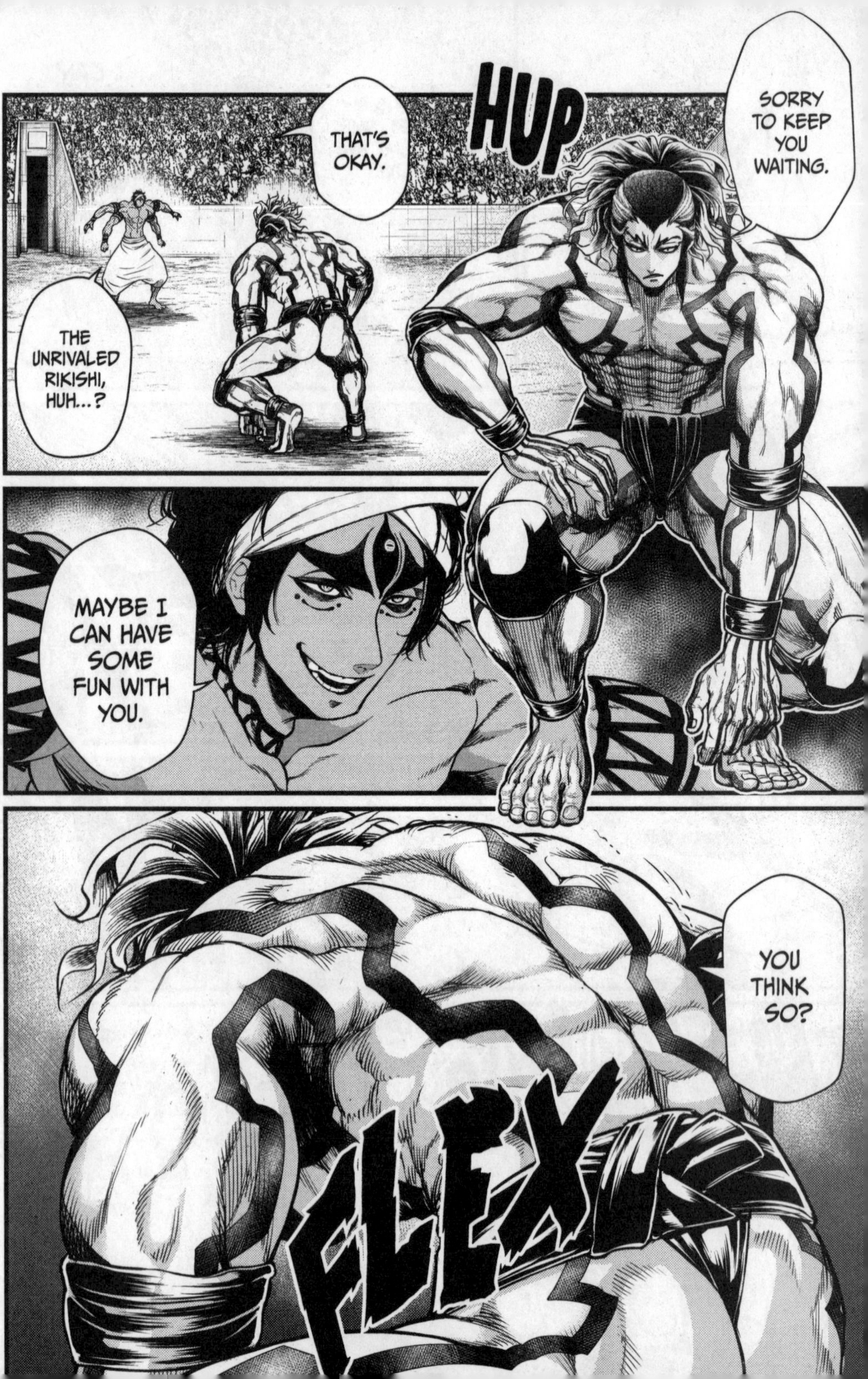
SORRY TO KEEP YOU WAITING.
HUP
THAT'S OKAY.
THE UNRIVALED RIKISHI, HUH...?
MAYBE I CAN HAVE SOME FUN WITH YOU.
YOU THINK SO?
FLEX

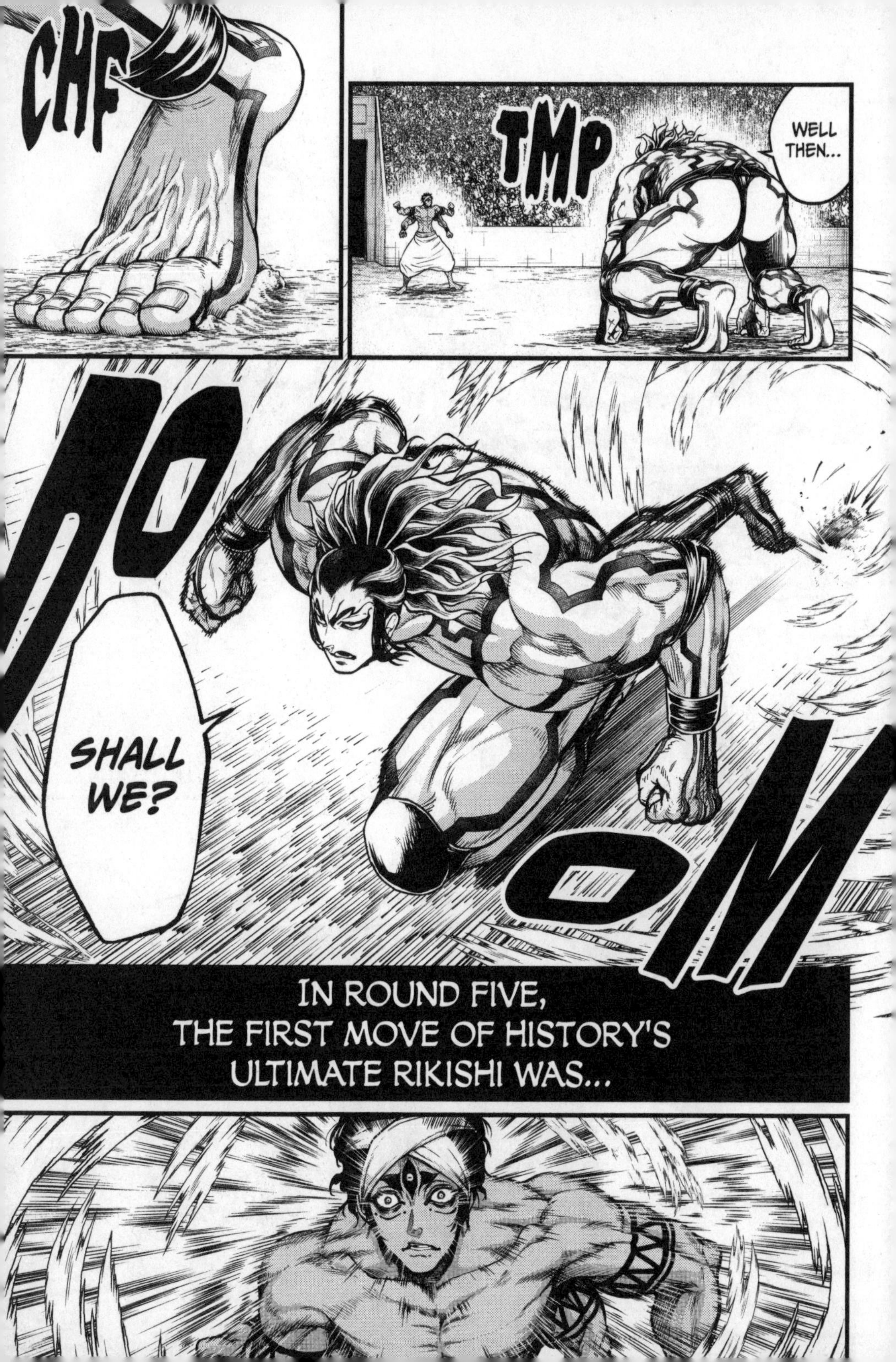
TMP
WELL THEN...
CHF
SHALL WE?
IN ROUND FIVE, THE FIRST MOVE OF HISTORY'S ULTIMATE RIKISHI WAS...

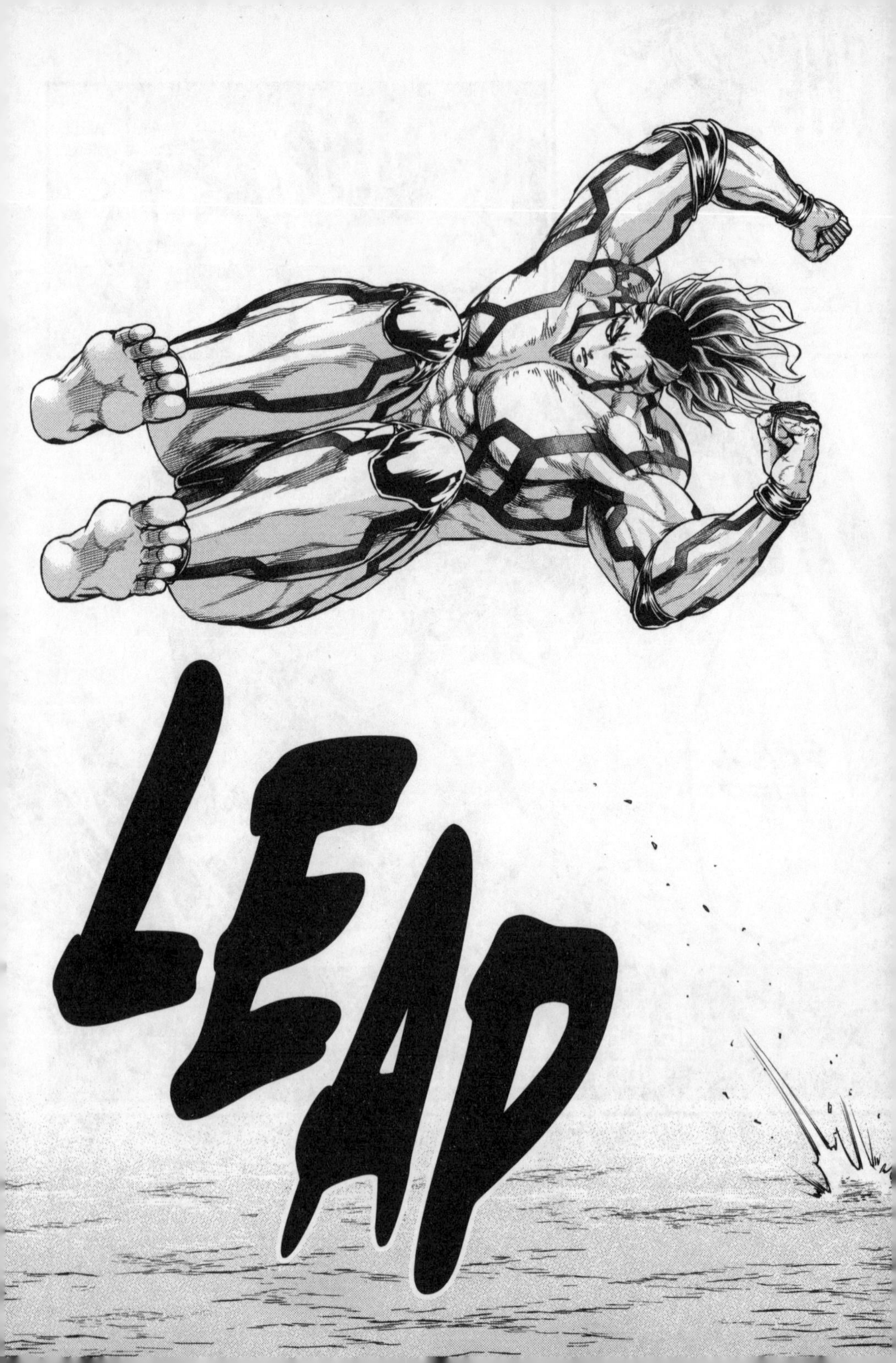
LEAP

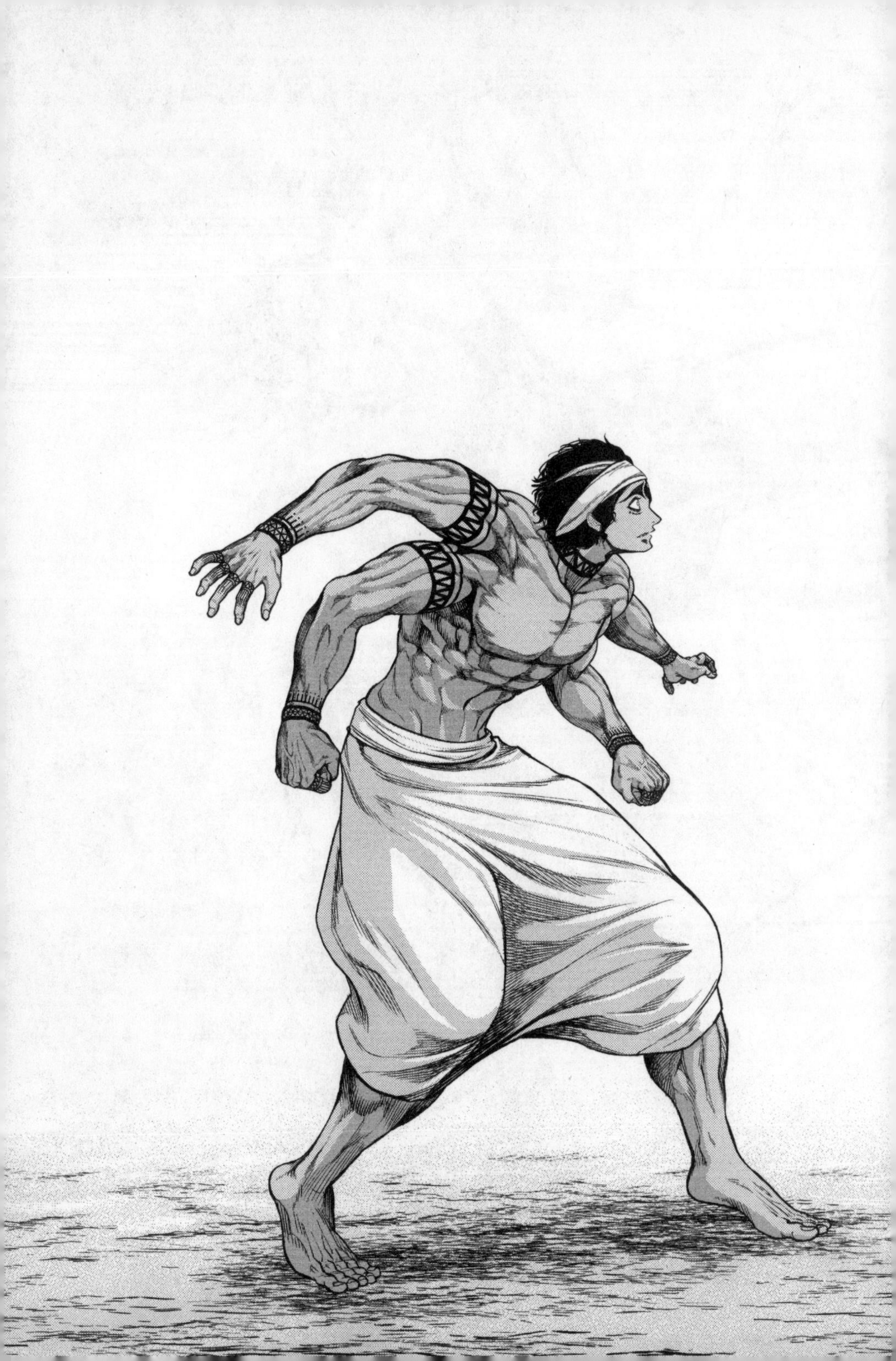

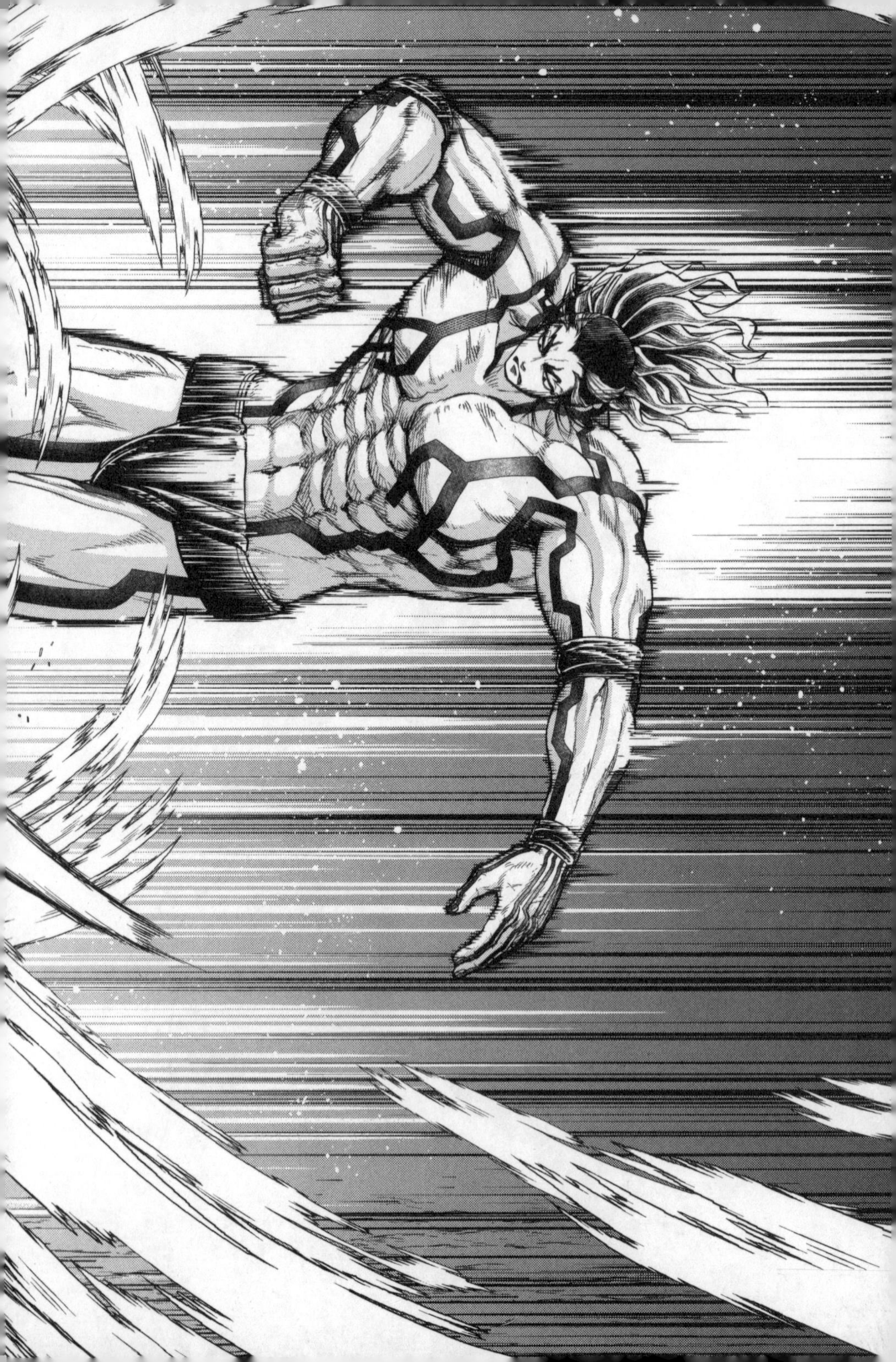

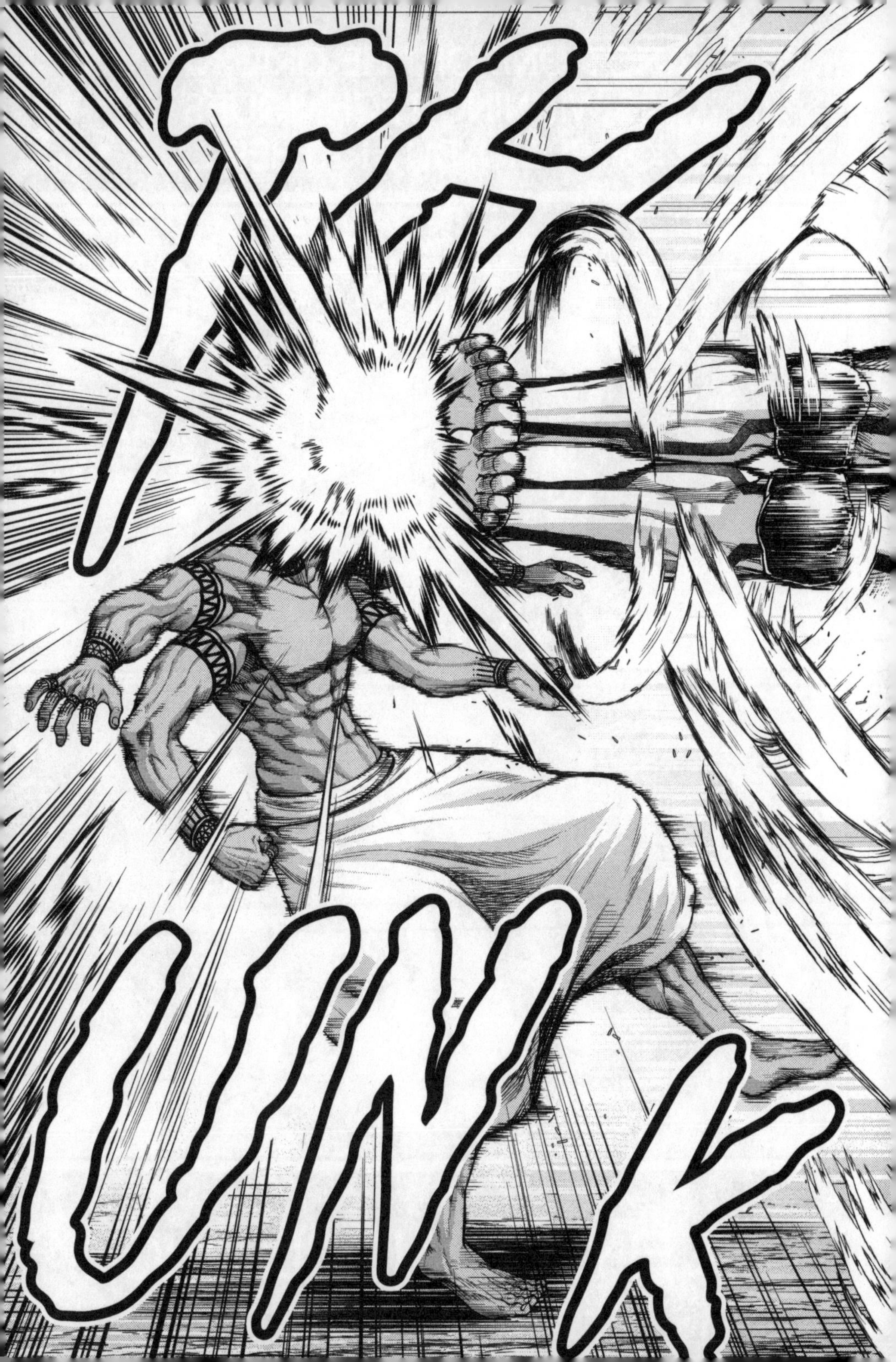
THUNK

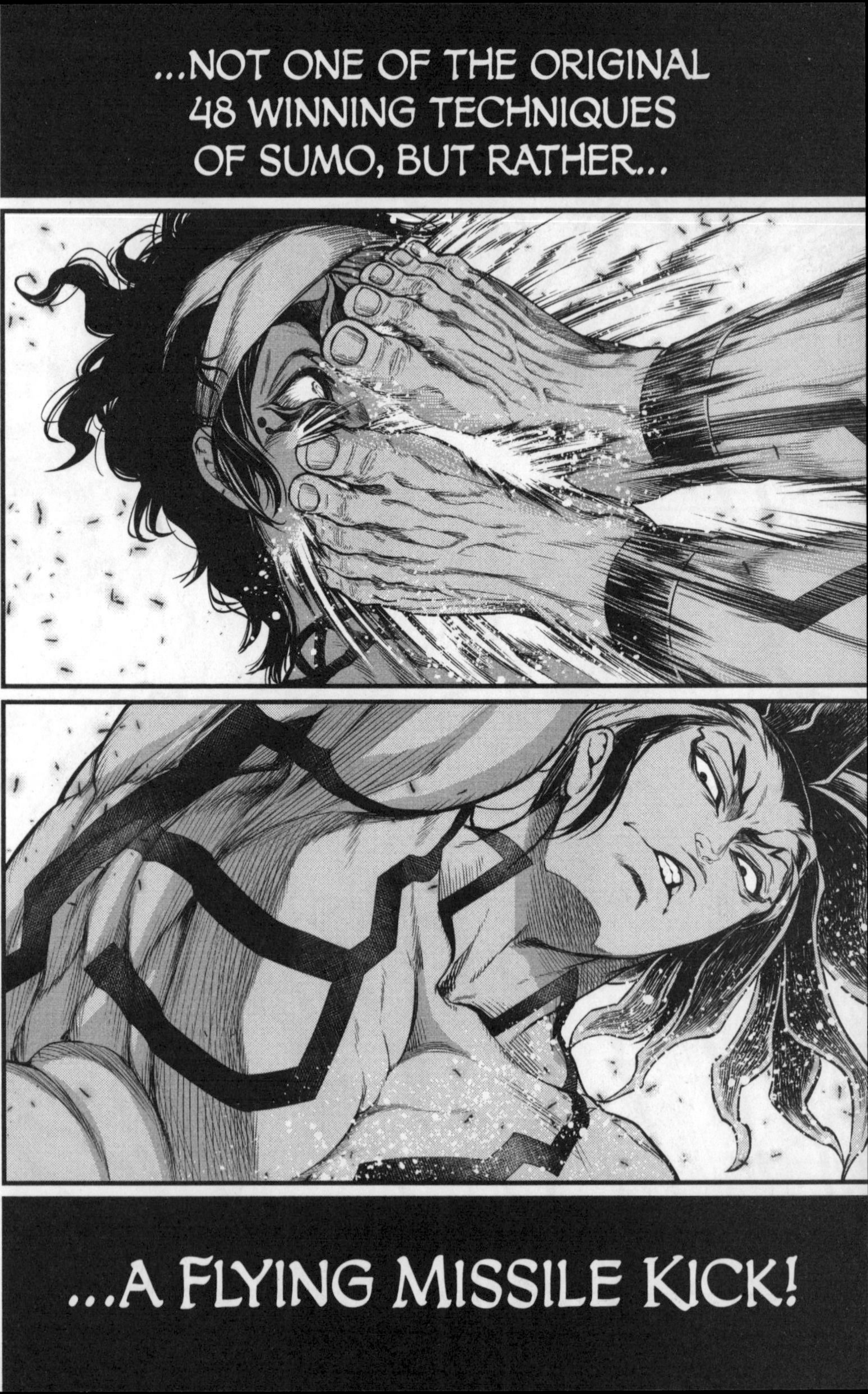
...NOT ONE OF THE ORIGINAL 48 WINNING TECHNIQUES OF SUMO, BUT RATHER...
...A FLYING MISSILE KICK!

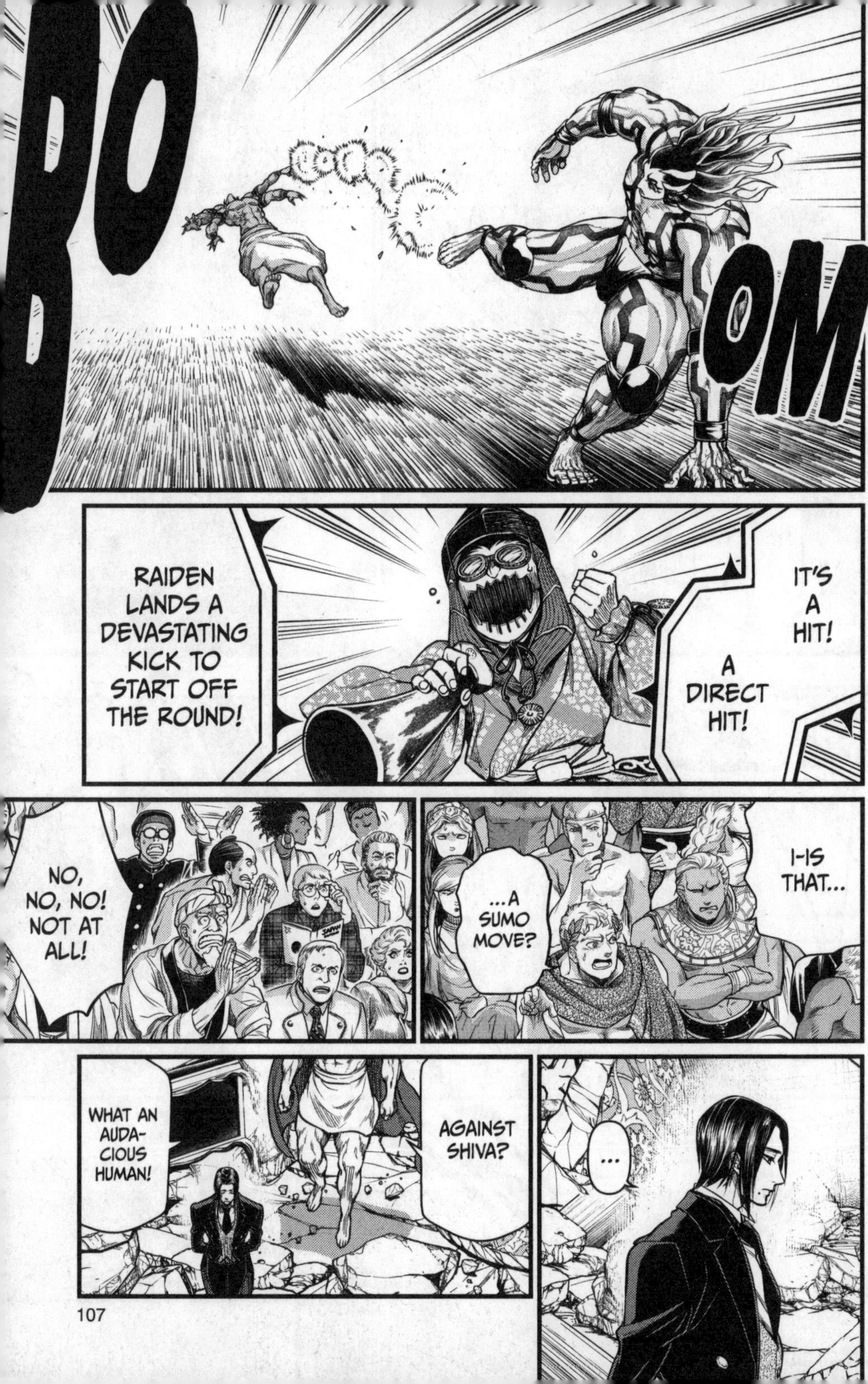
BOOM
IT'S A HIT!
A DIRECT HIT!
RAIDEN LANDS A DEVASTATING KICK TO START OFF THE ROUND!
I-IS THAT...
...A SUMO MOVE?
NO, NO, NO! NOT AT ALL!
...
AGAINST SHIVA?
WHAT AN AUDACIOUS HUMAN!

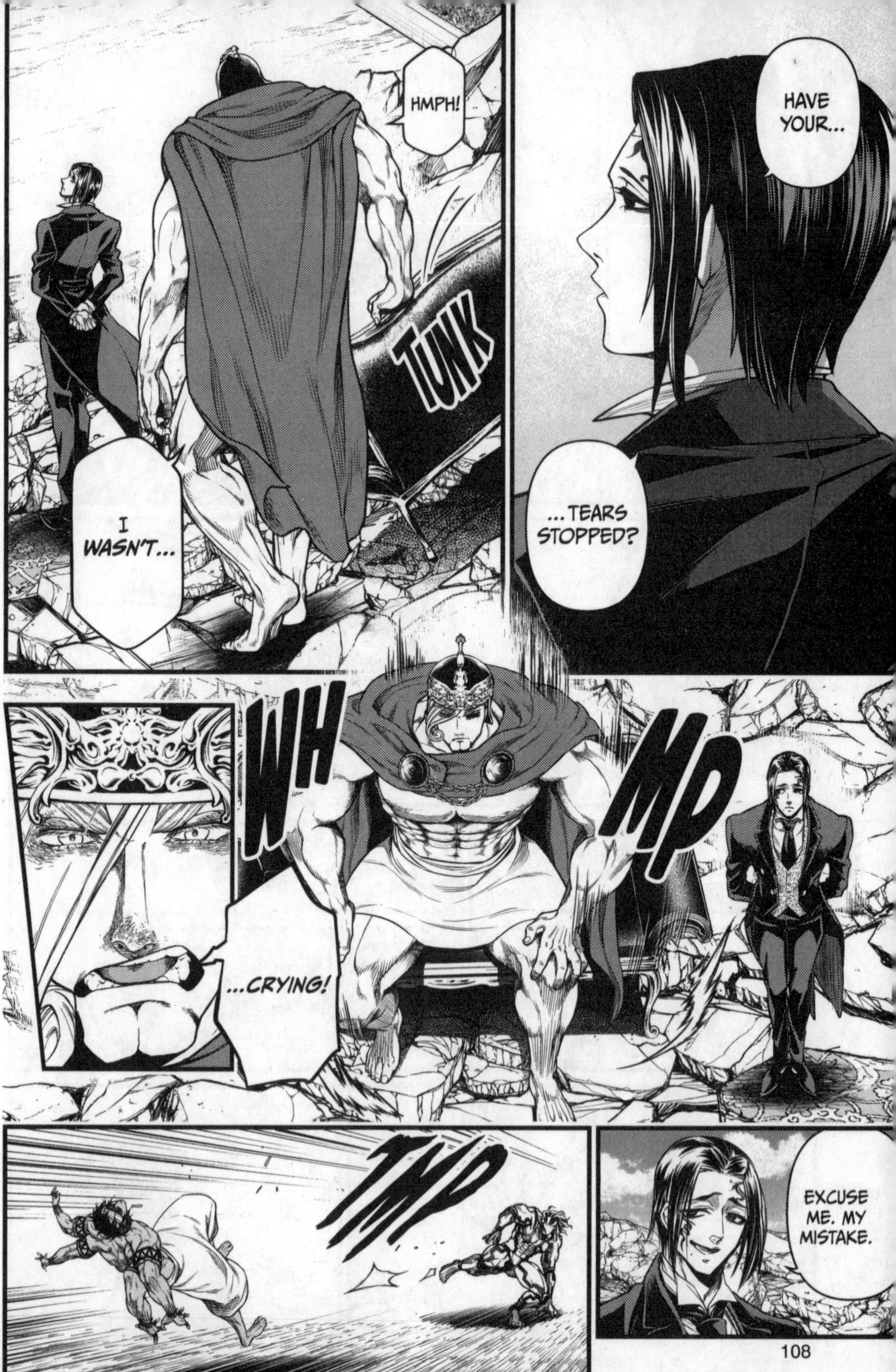
HAVE YOUR...
...TEARS STOPPED?
HMPH!
TUNK
I WASN'T...
WHMP
...CRYING!
EXCUSE ME. MY MISTAKE.
TMP

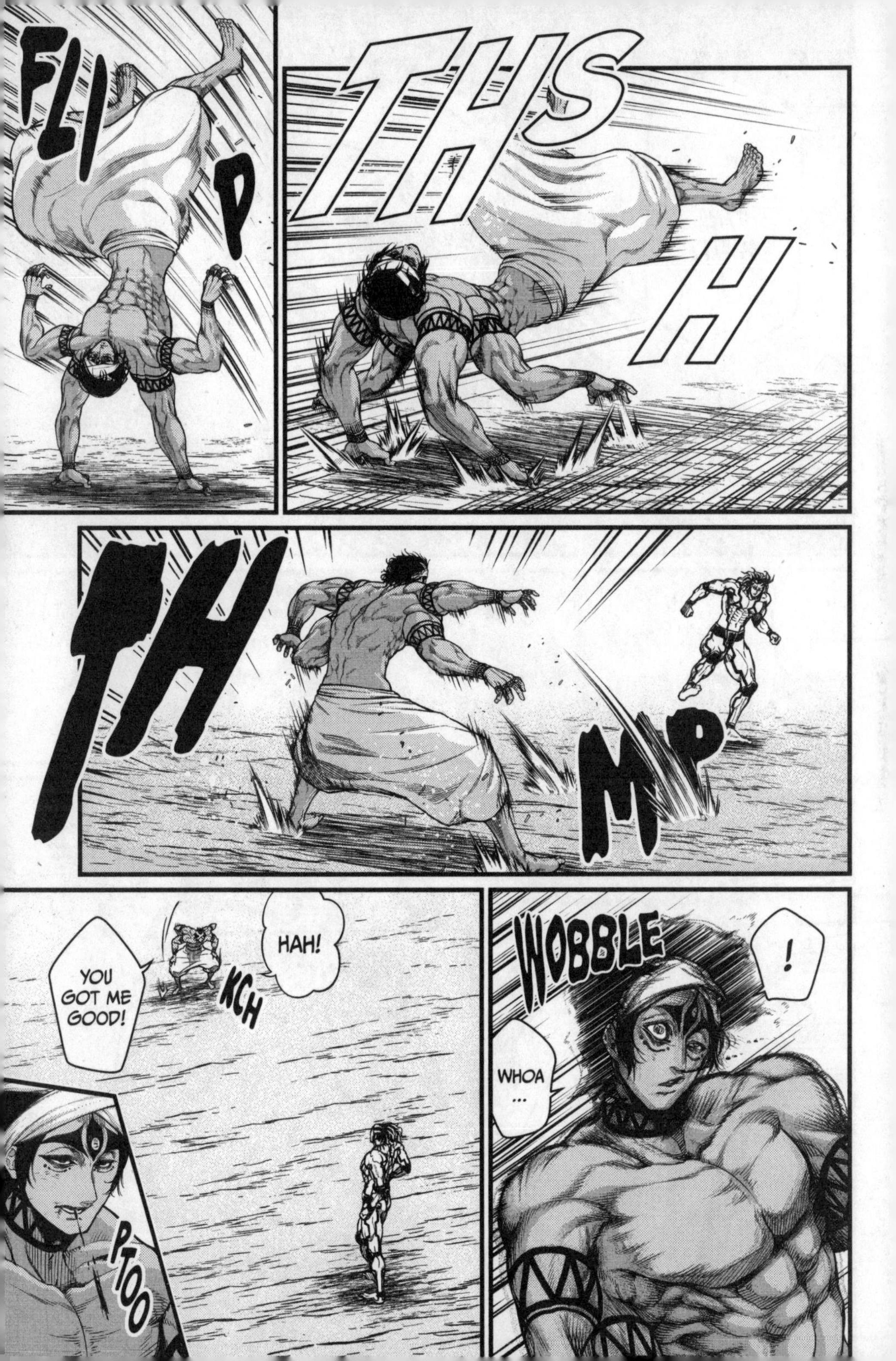
THSH
FLIP
THMP
WOBBLE
!
WHOA ...
HAH!
KCH
YOU GOT ME GOOD!
PTOO

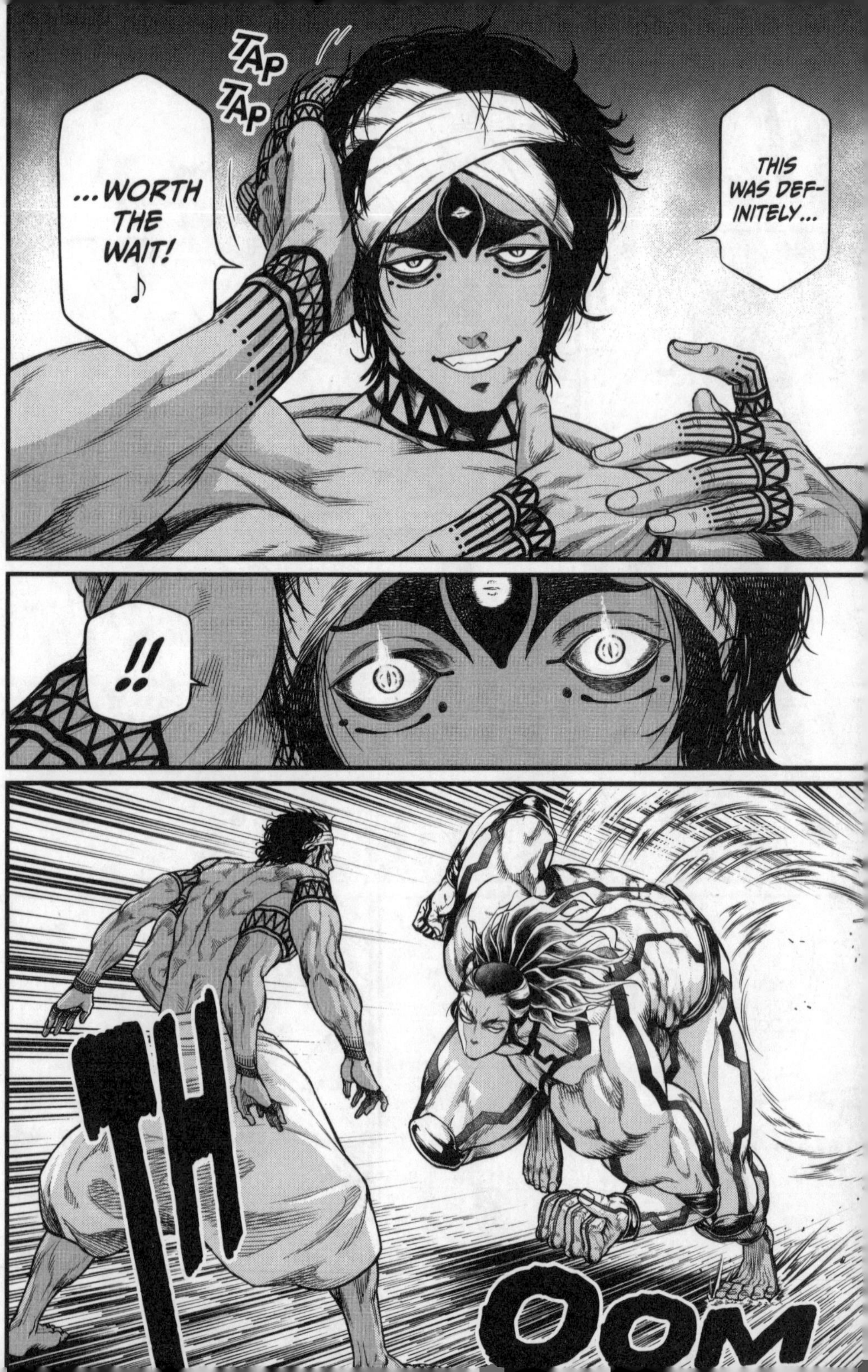
THIS WAS DEF-INITELY...
TAP TAP
...WORTH THE WAIT! ♪
!!
TH
OOM

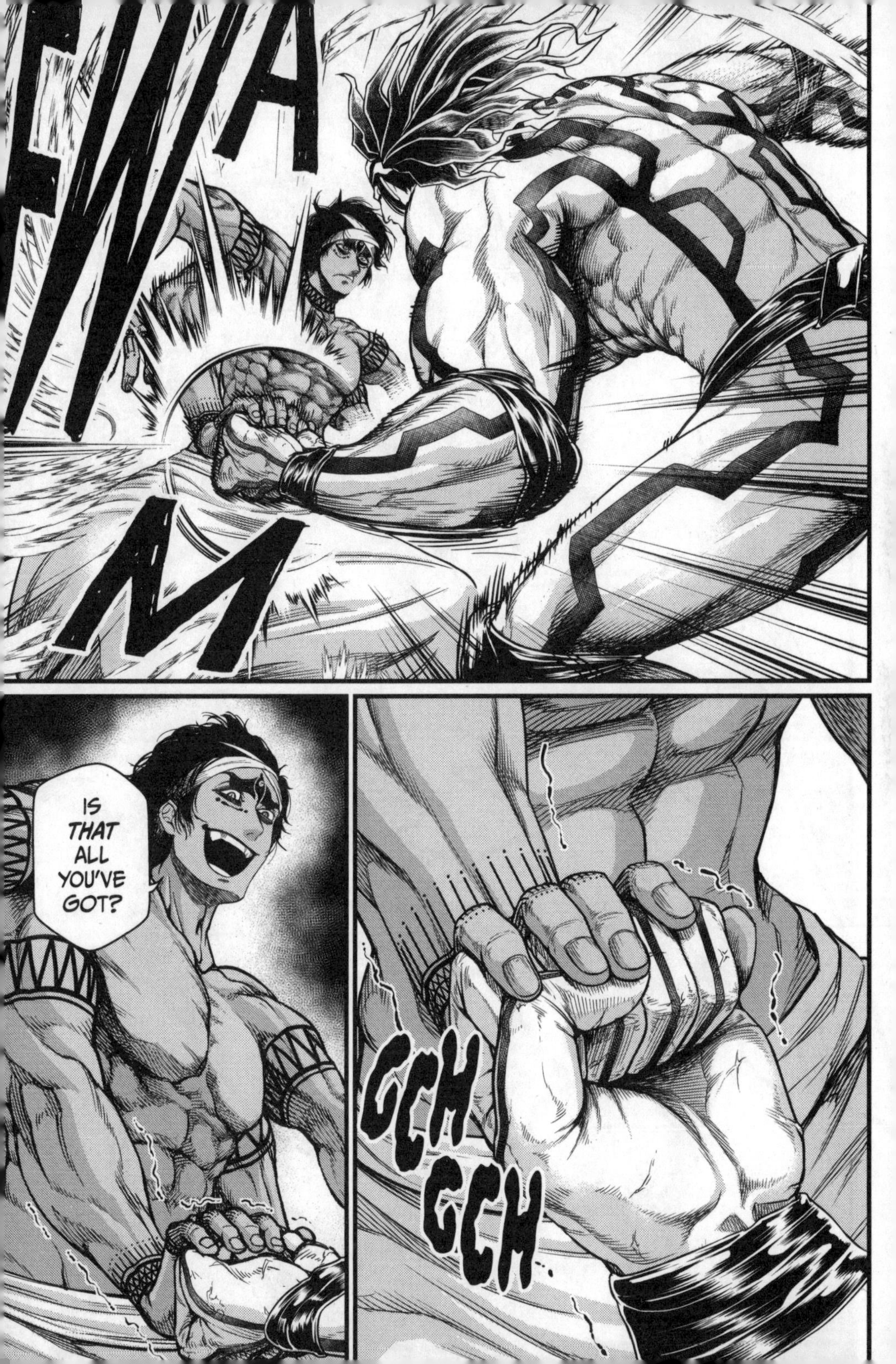
FWAM
GCH GCH
IS THAT ALL YOU'VE GOT?

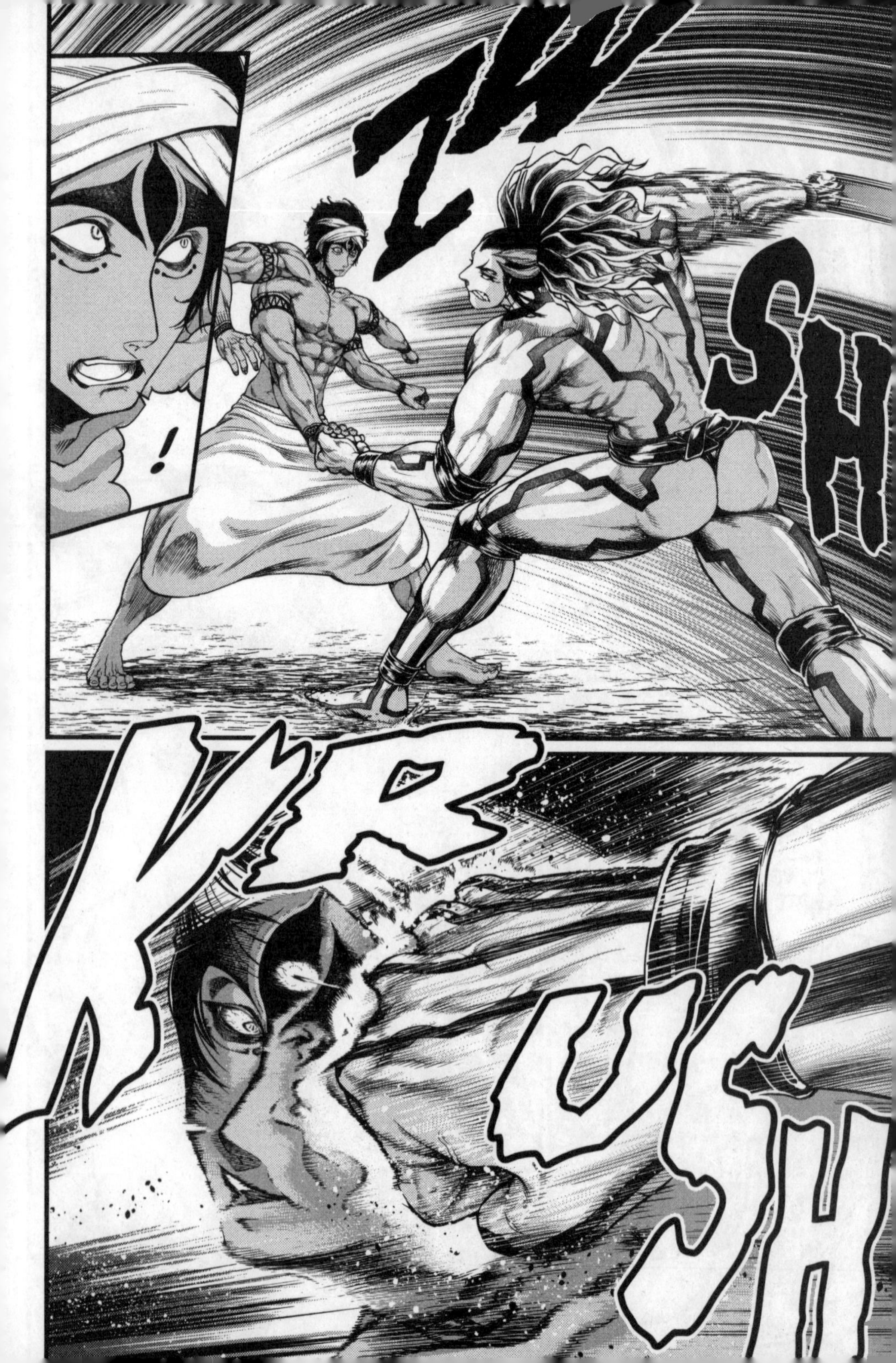
ZWI
SH
!
KRUSH

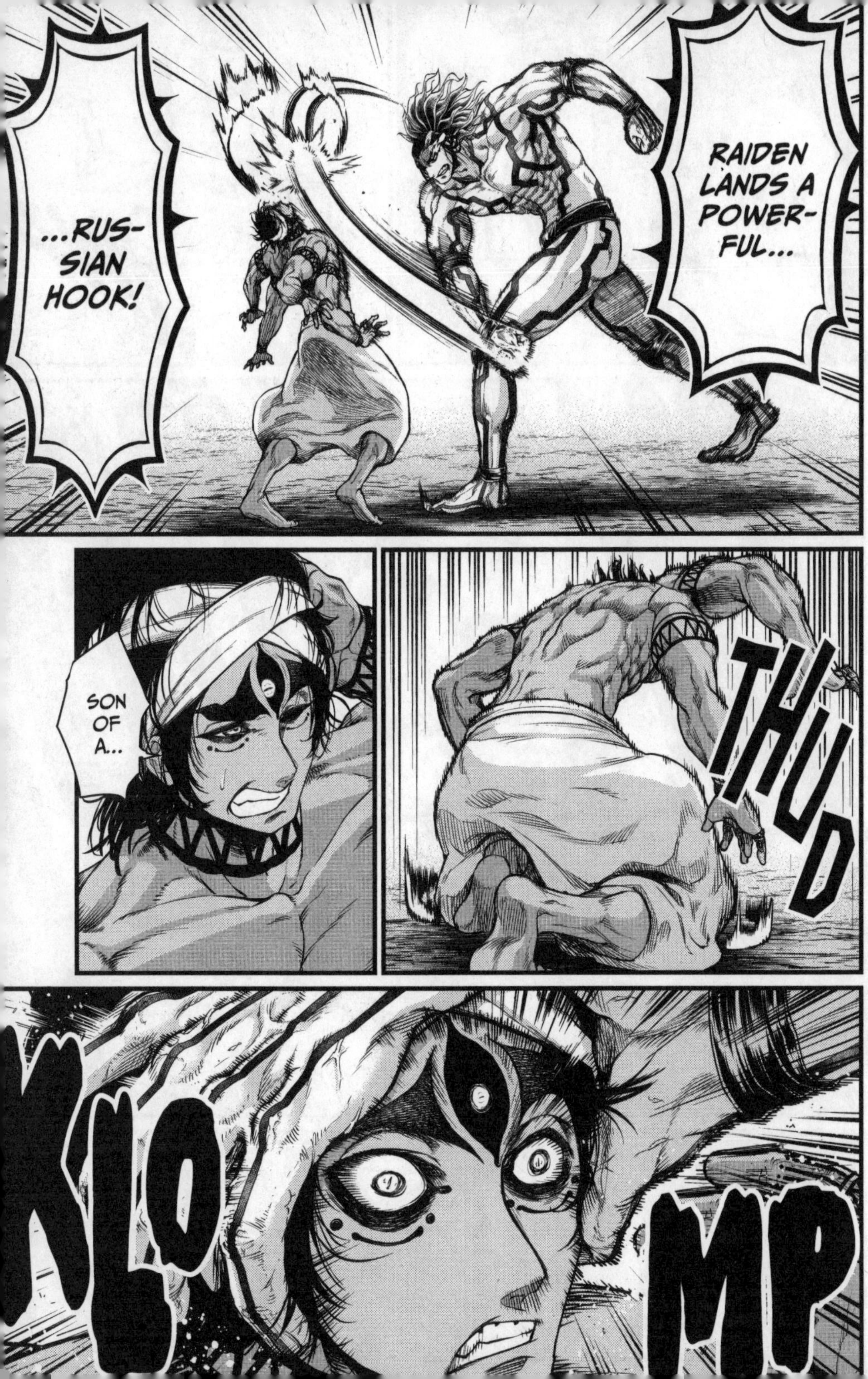
RAIDEN LANDS A POWER-FUL...
...RUS-SIAN HOOK!
THUD
SON OF A...
KLOMP

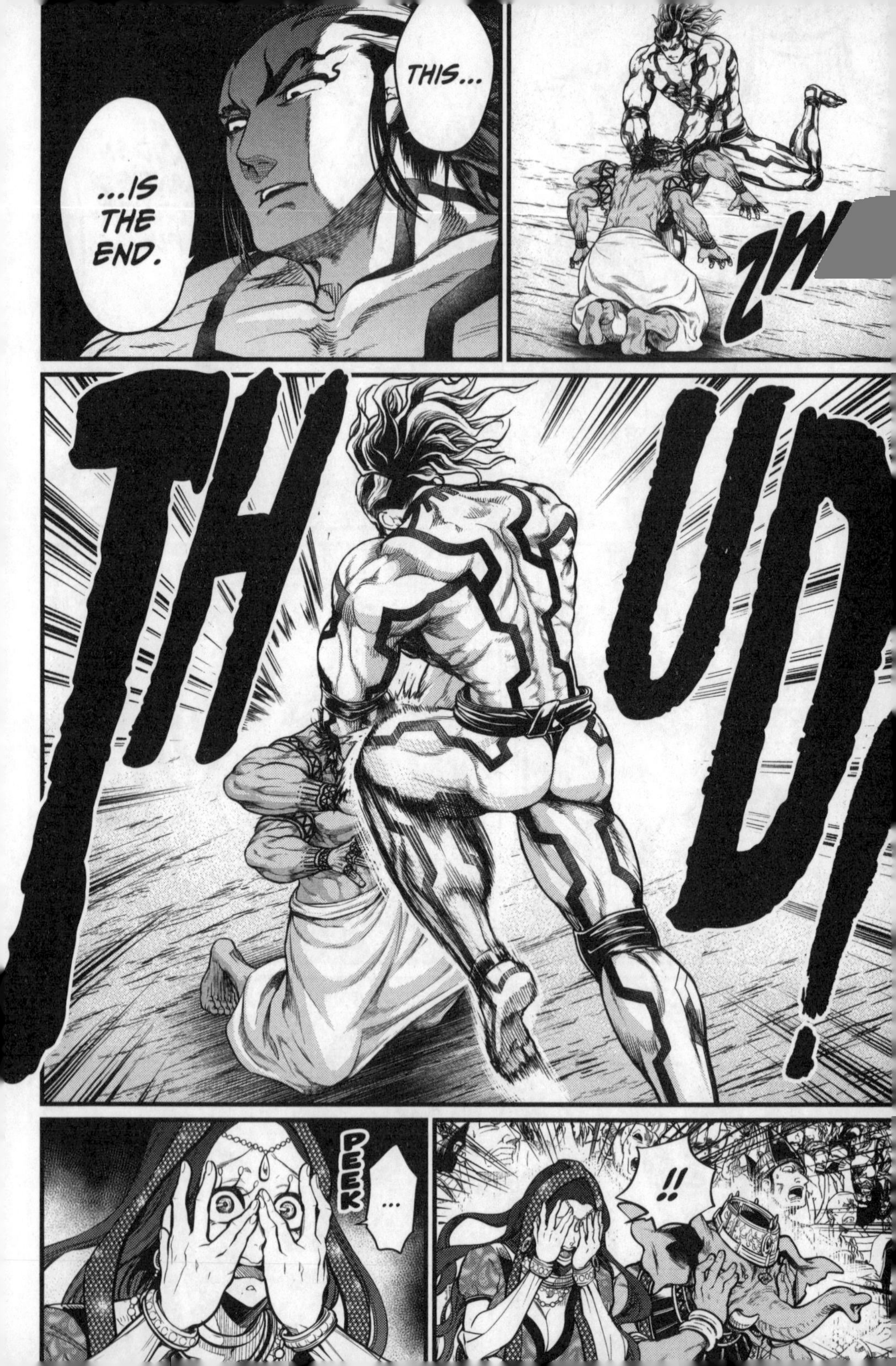
ZW
THIS...
...IS THE END.
THUD!
!!
PEEK
...

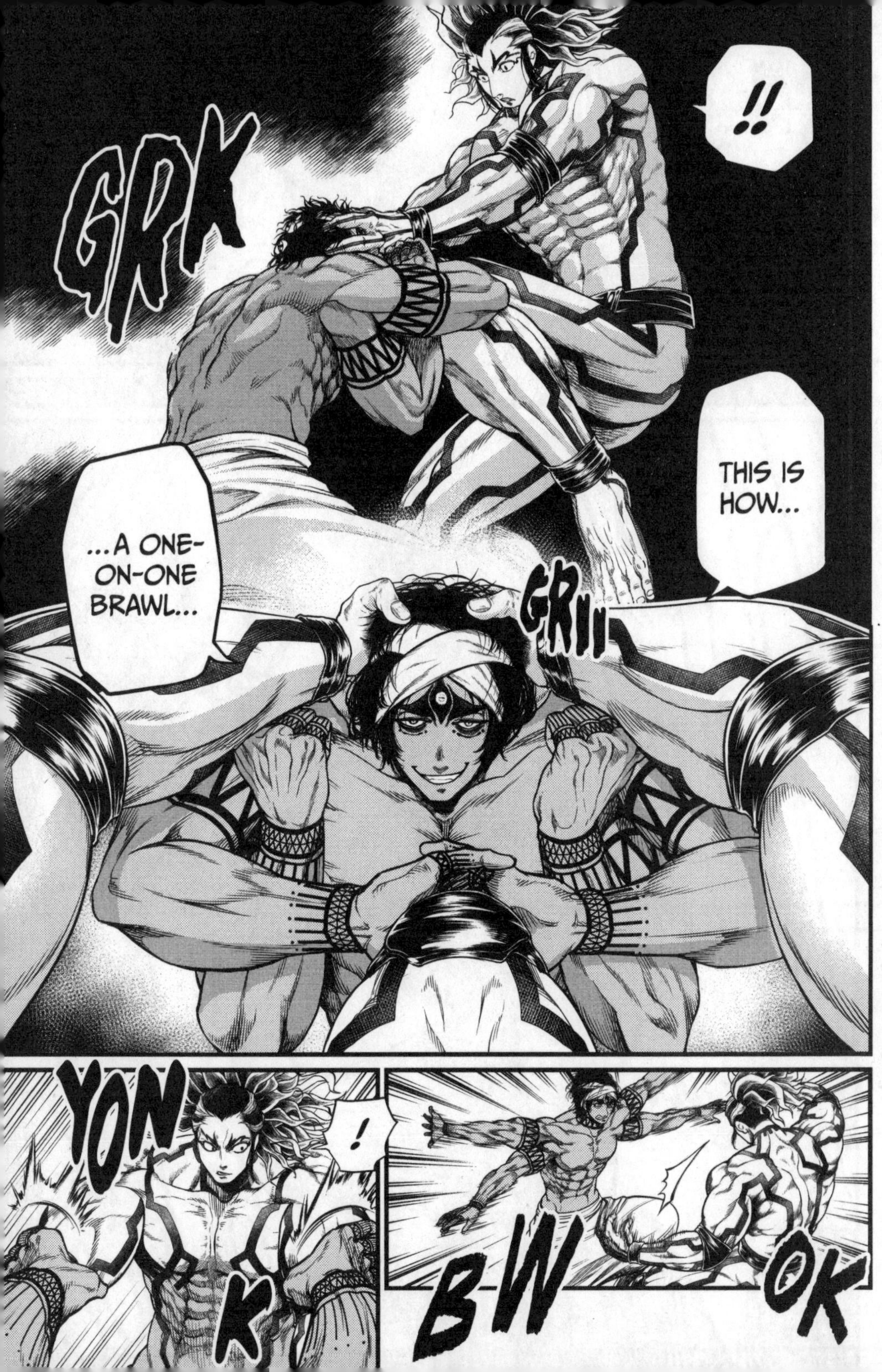
!!
GRK
THIS IS HOW...
...A ONE-ON-ONE BRAWL...
GRIII
BWOK
YONK
!

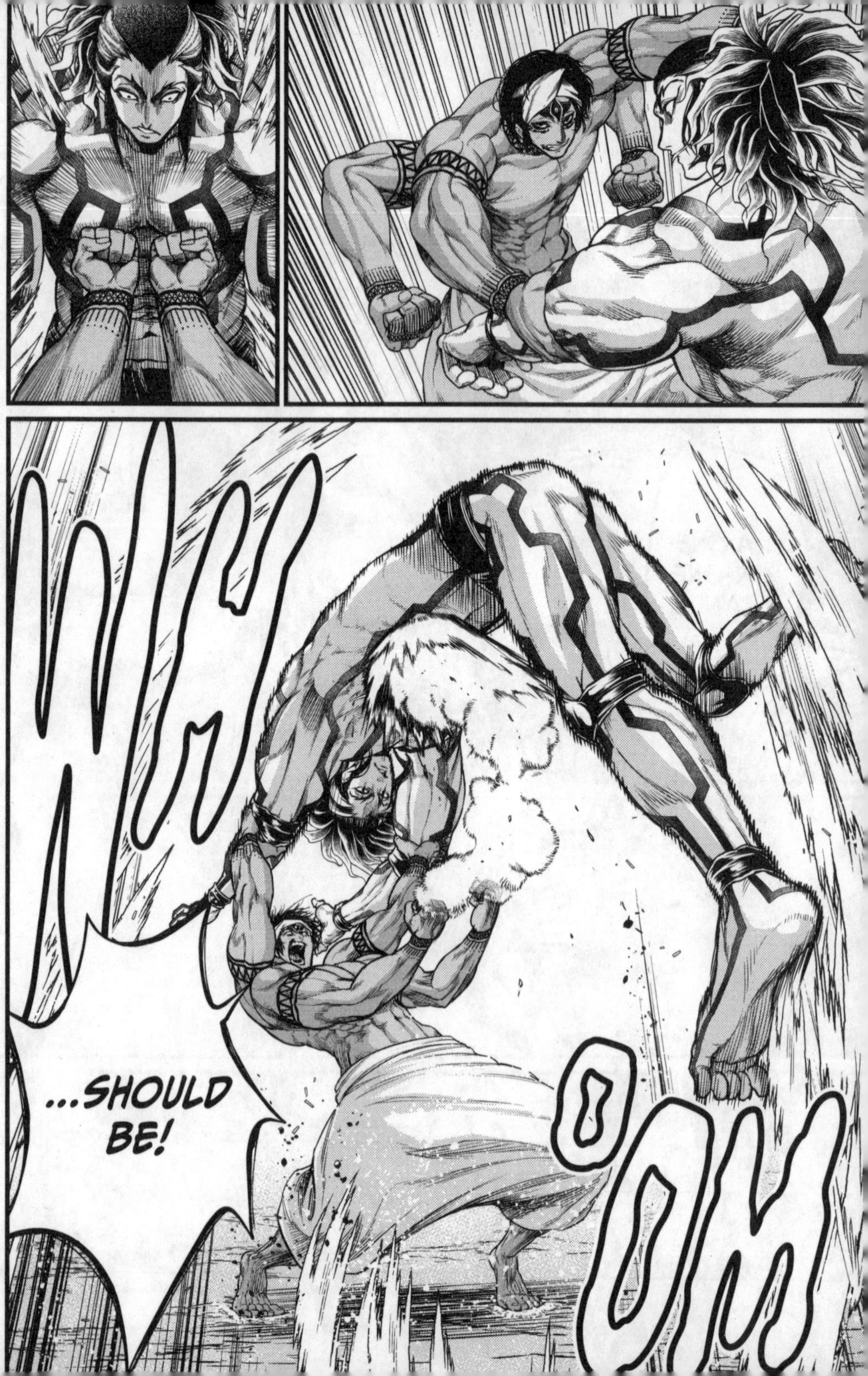
...SHOULD BE!

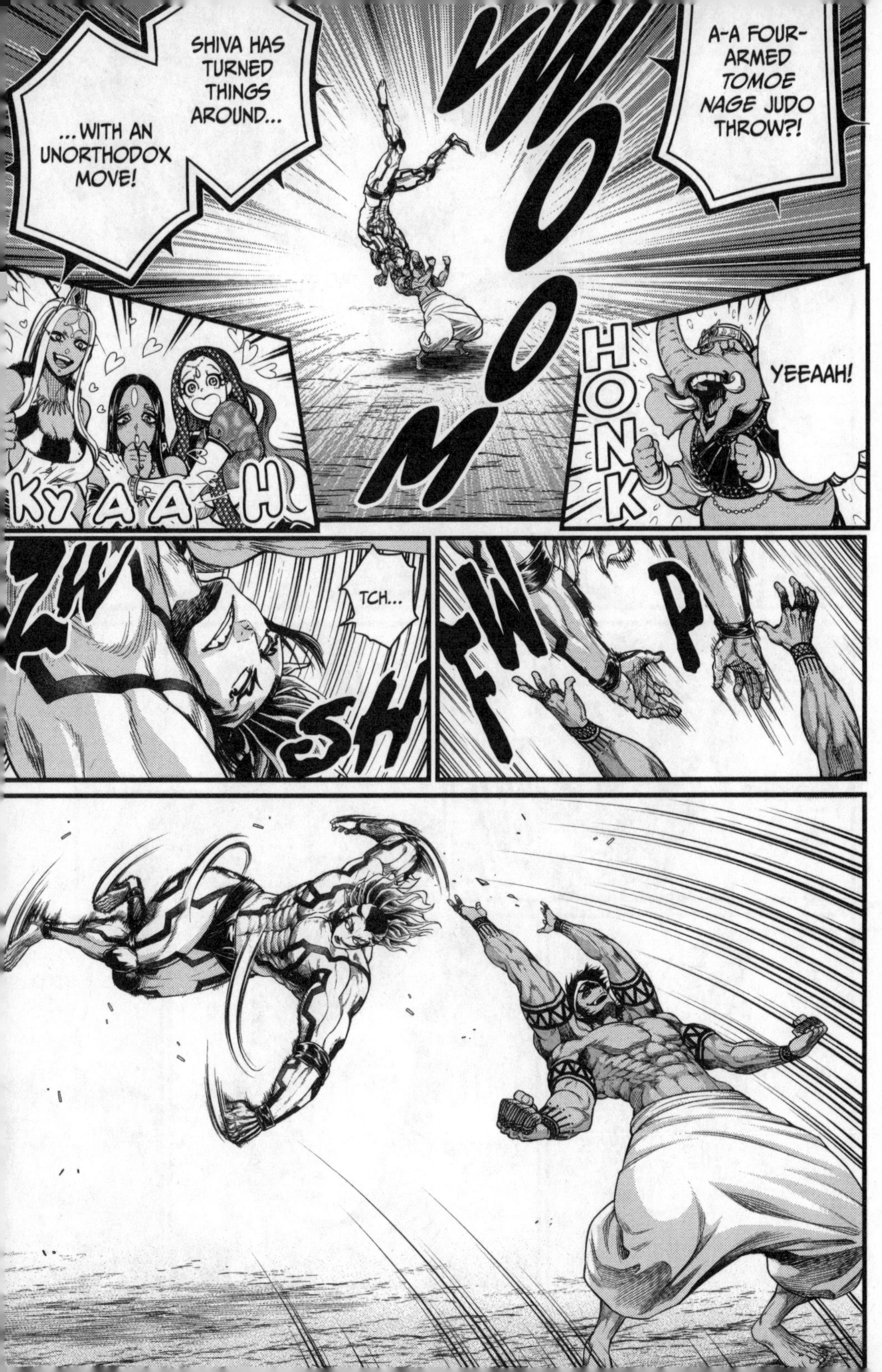
A-A FOUR-ARMED TOMOE NAGE JUDO THROW?!
WOOOM
SHIVA HAS TURNED THINGS AROUND...
...WITH AN UNORTHODOX MOVE!
HONK
YEEAAH!
KYAAH
FWP
TCH...
ZW
SH

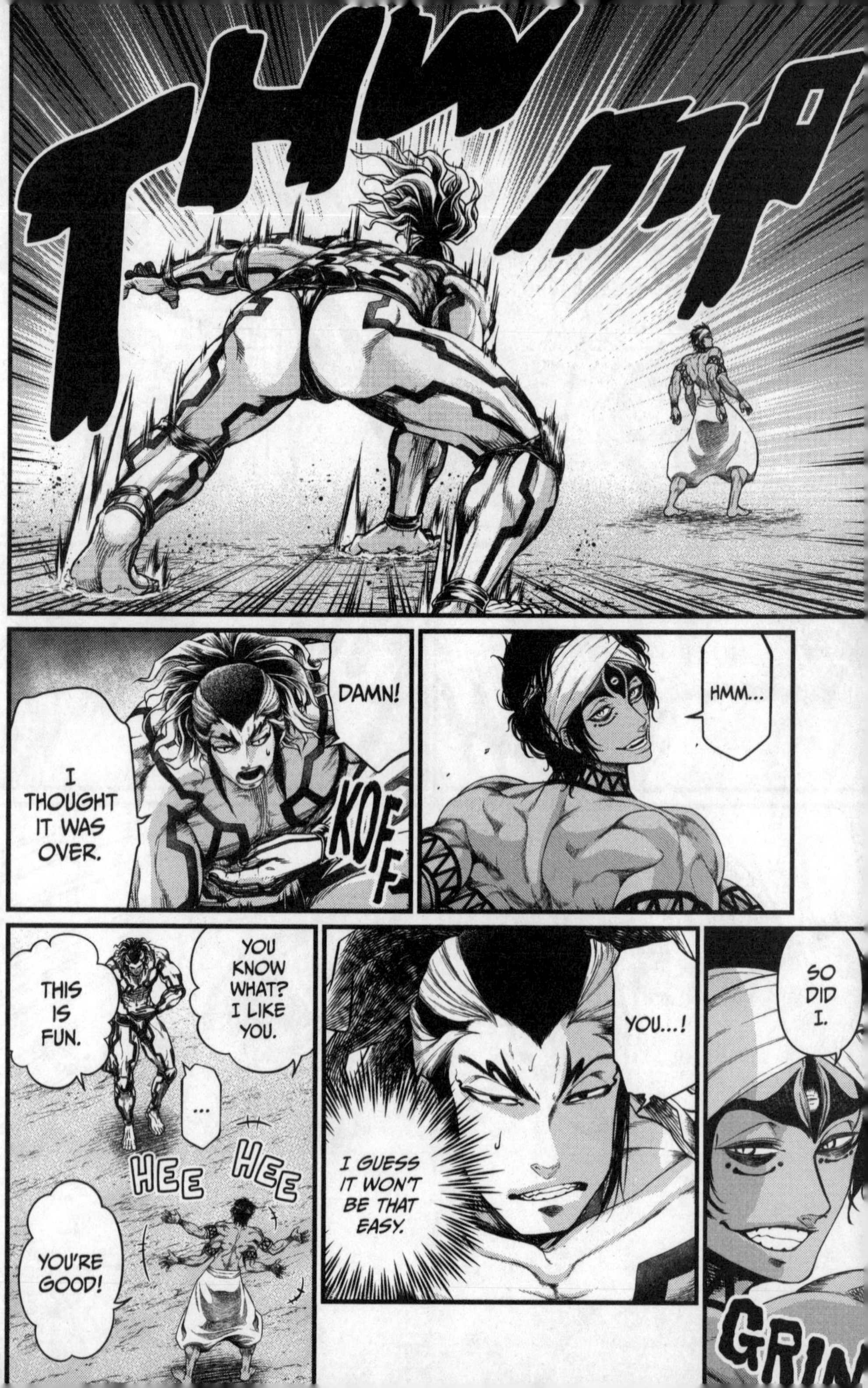
THWAP
HMM...
DAMN!
I THOUGHT IT WAS OVER.
KOFF
SO DID I.
GRIN
YOU...!
I GUESS IT WON'T BE THAT EASY.
YOU KNOW WHAT? I LIKE YOU.
THIS IS FUN.
...
HEE HEE
YOU'RE GOOD!

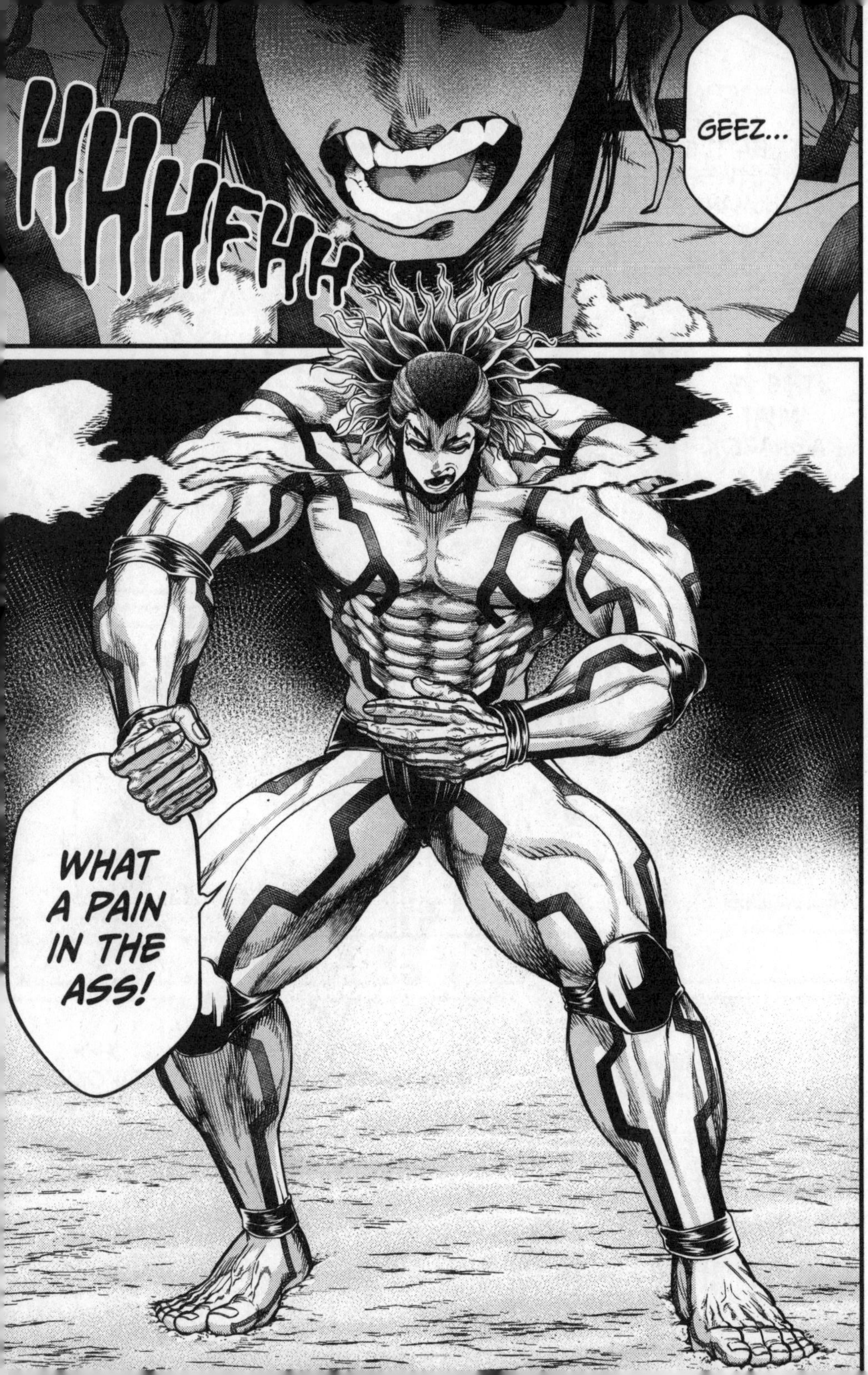
GEEZ...
HHHFHH
WHAT A PAIN IN THE ASS!

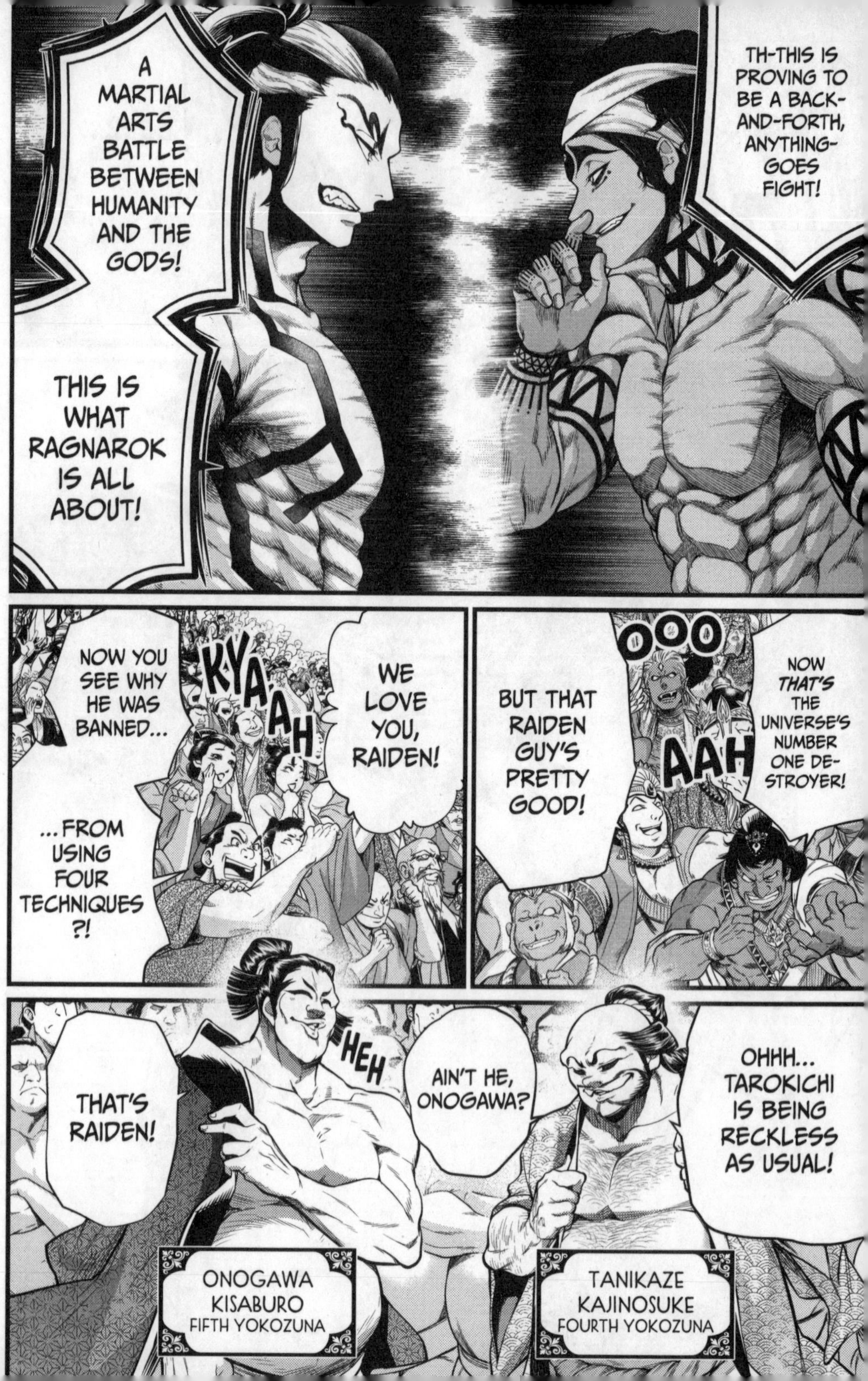
TH-THIS IS PROVING TO BE A BACK-AND-FORTH, ANYTHING-GOES FIGHT!
A MARTIAL ARTS BATTLE BETWEEN HUMANITY AND THE GODS!
THIS IS WHAT RAGNAROK IS ALL ABOUT!
OOO
NOW *THAT'S* THE UNIVERSE'S NUMBER ONE DE-STROYER!
AAH
BUT THAT RAIDEN GUY'S PRETTY GOOD!
WE LOVE YOU, RAIDEN!
KYAAAH
NOW YOU SEE WHY HE WAS BANNED...
...FROM USING FOUR TECHNIQUES?!
OHHH... TAROKICHI IS BEING RECKLESS AS USUAL!
AIN'T HE, ONOGAWA?
TANIKAZE KAJINOSUKE FOURTH YOKOZUNA
HEH
THAT'S RAIDEN!
ONOGAWA KISABURO FIFTH YOKOZUNA

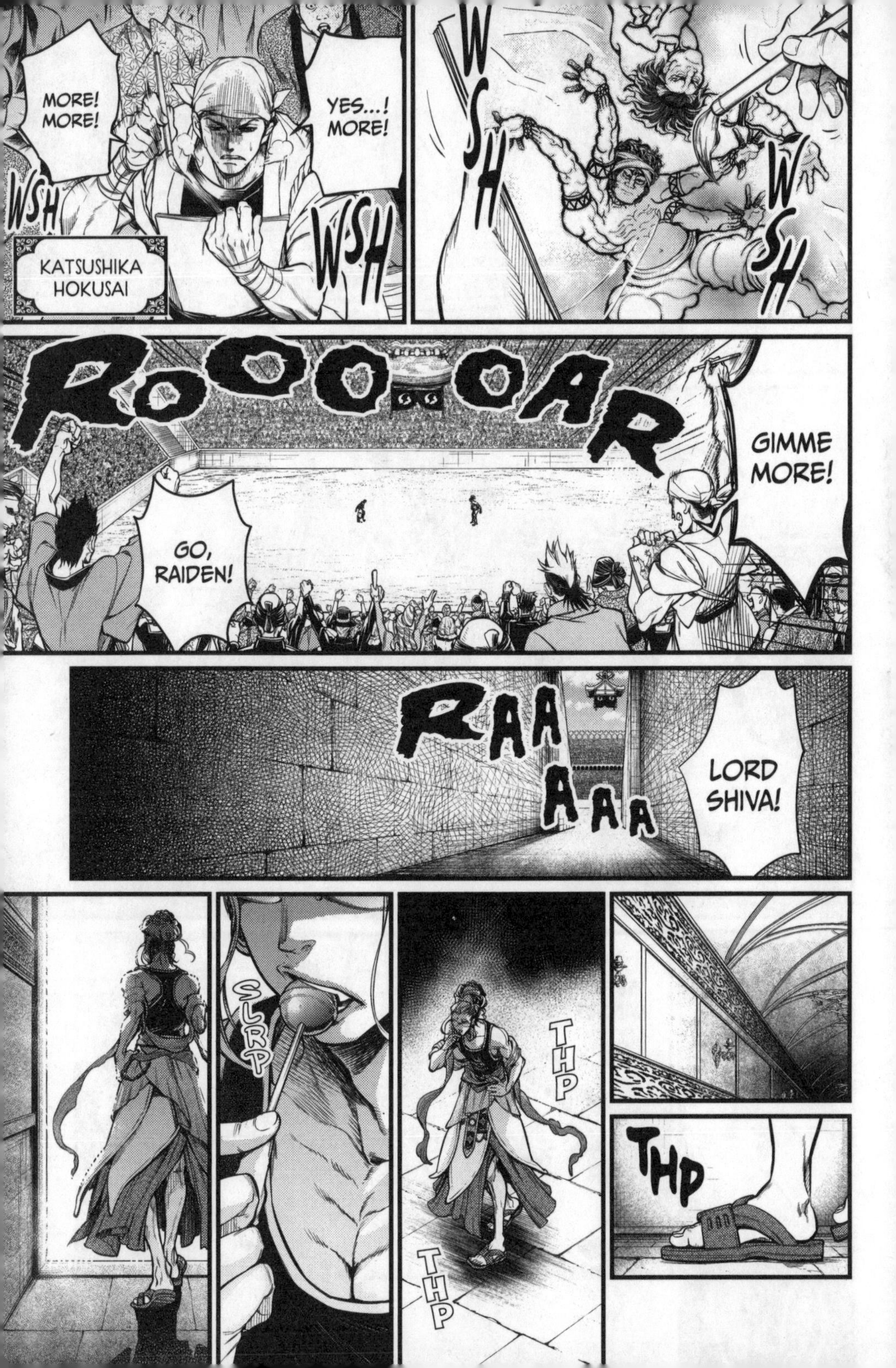
WSH
WSH
YES...! MORE!
MORE! MORE!
WSH
WSH
KATSUSHIKA HOKUSAI
ROOOOAR
GIMME MORE!
GO, RAIDEN!
RAAAAA
LORD SHIVA!
THP
THP
THP
SLRP

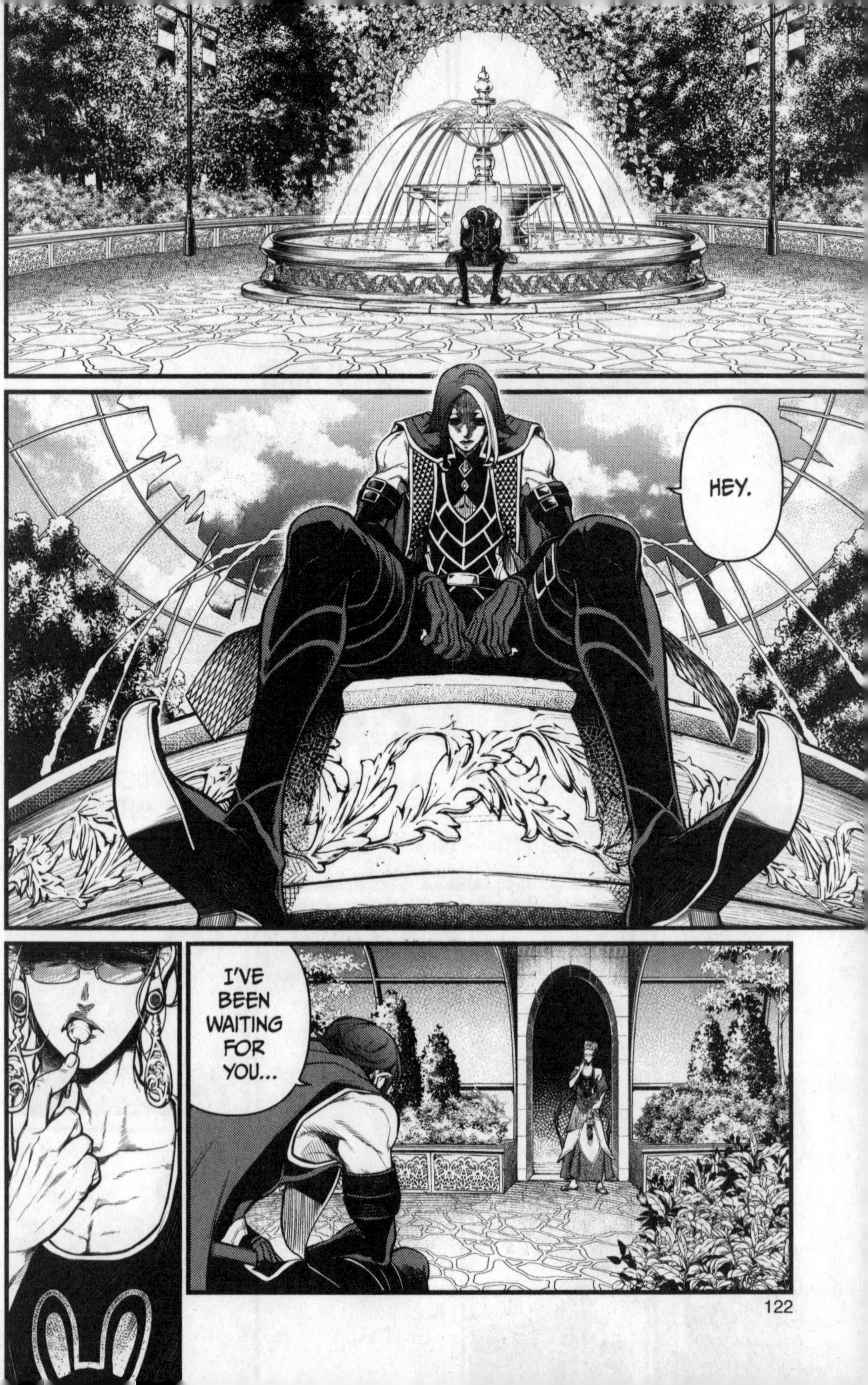
HEY.
I'VE BEEN WAITING FOR YOU...

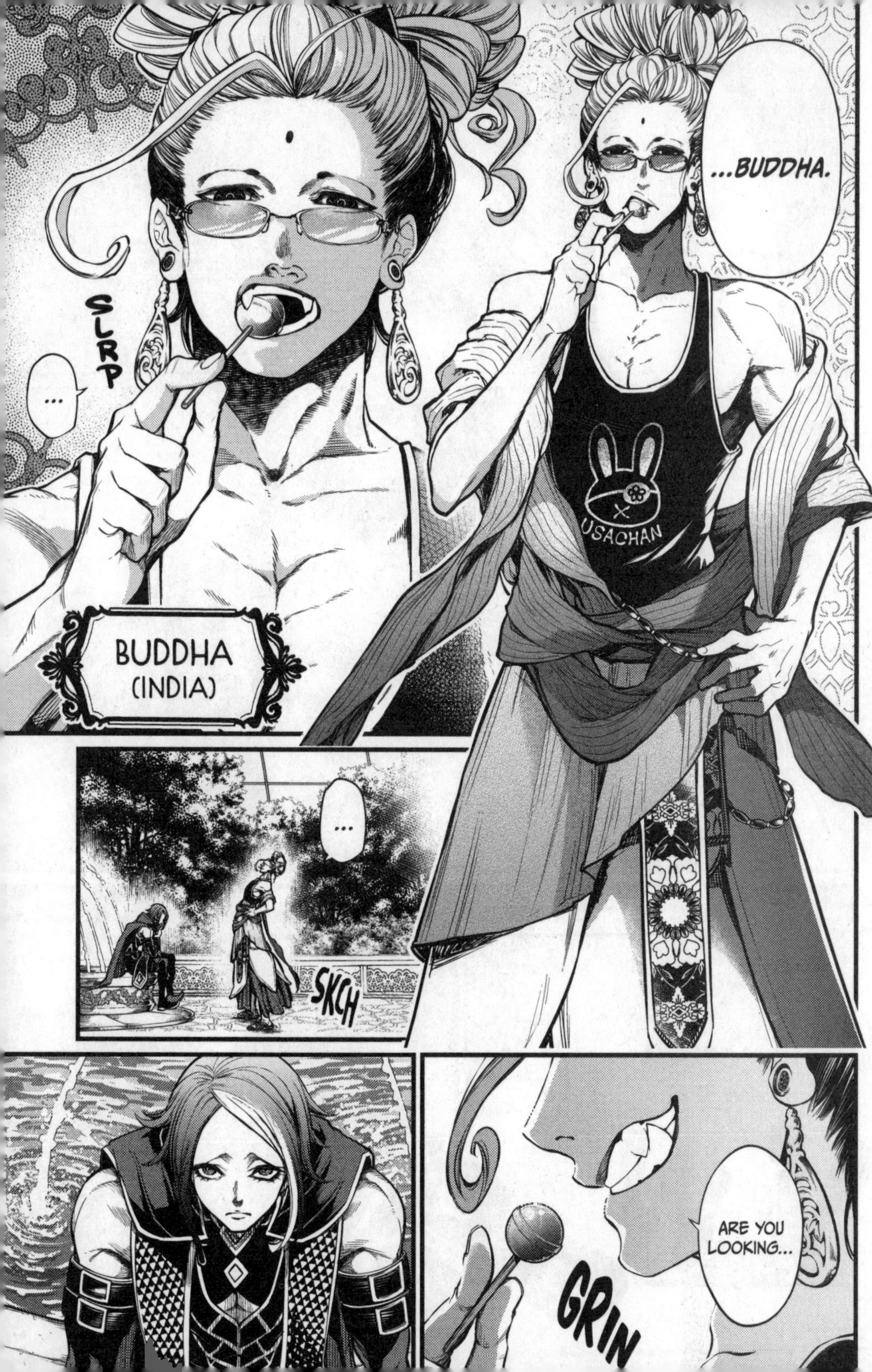
...BUDDHA.
SLRP
...
BUDDHA (INDIA)
...
SKCH
ARE YOU LOOKING...
GRIN

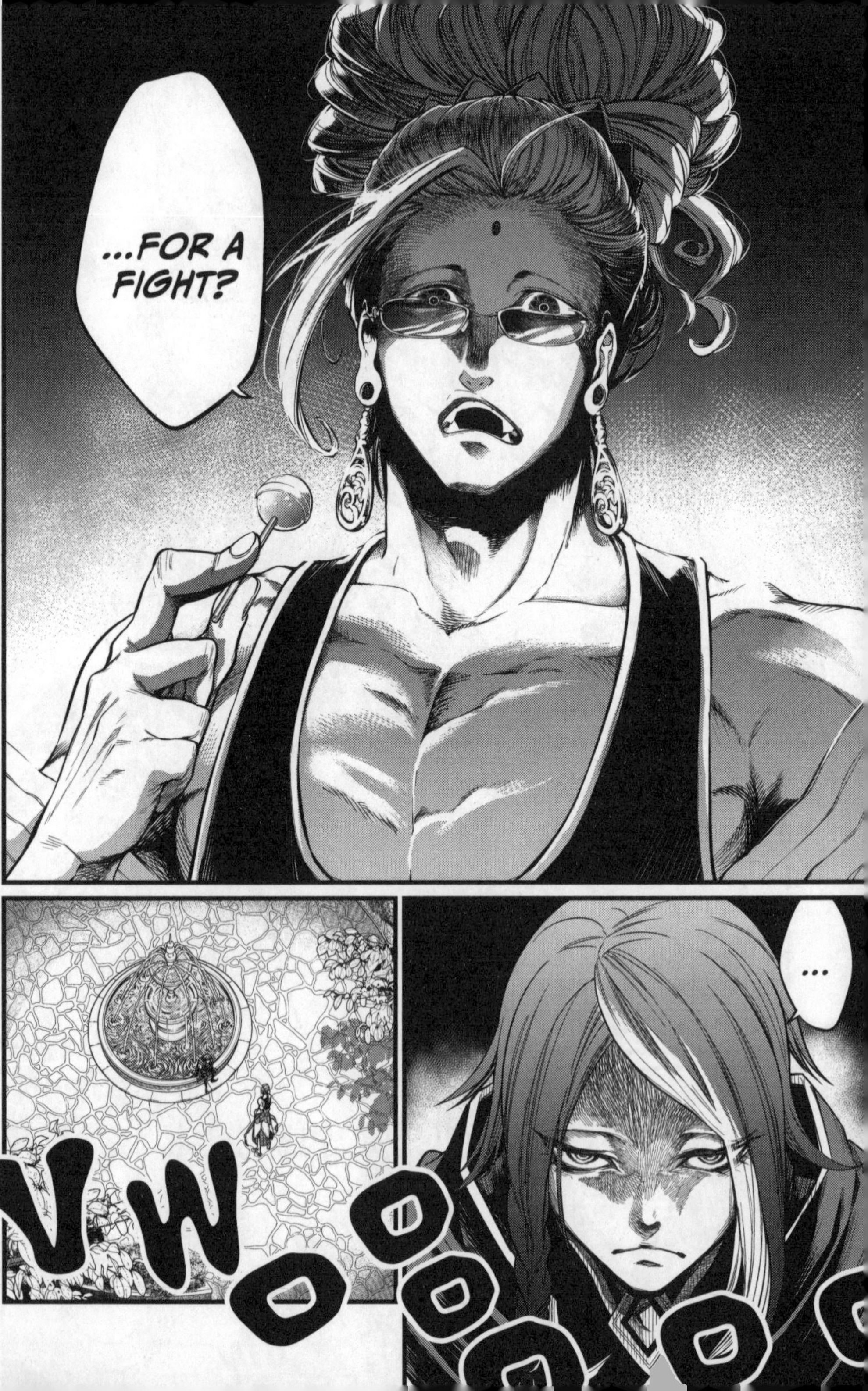
...FOR A FIGHT?
...
VWOOOOOOOO

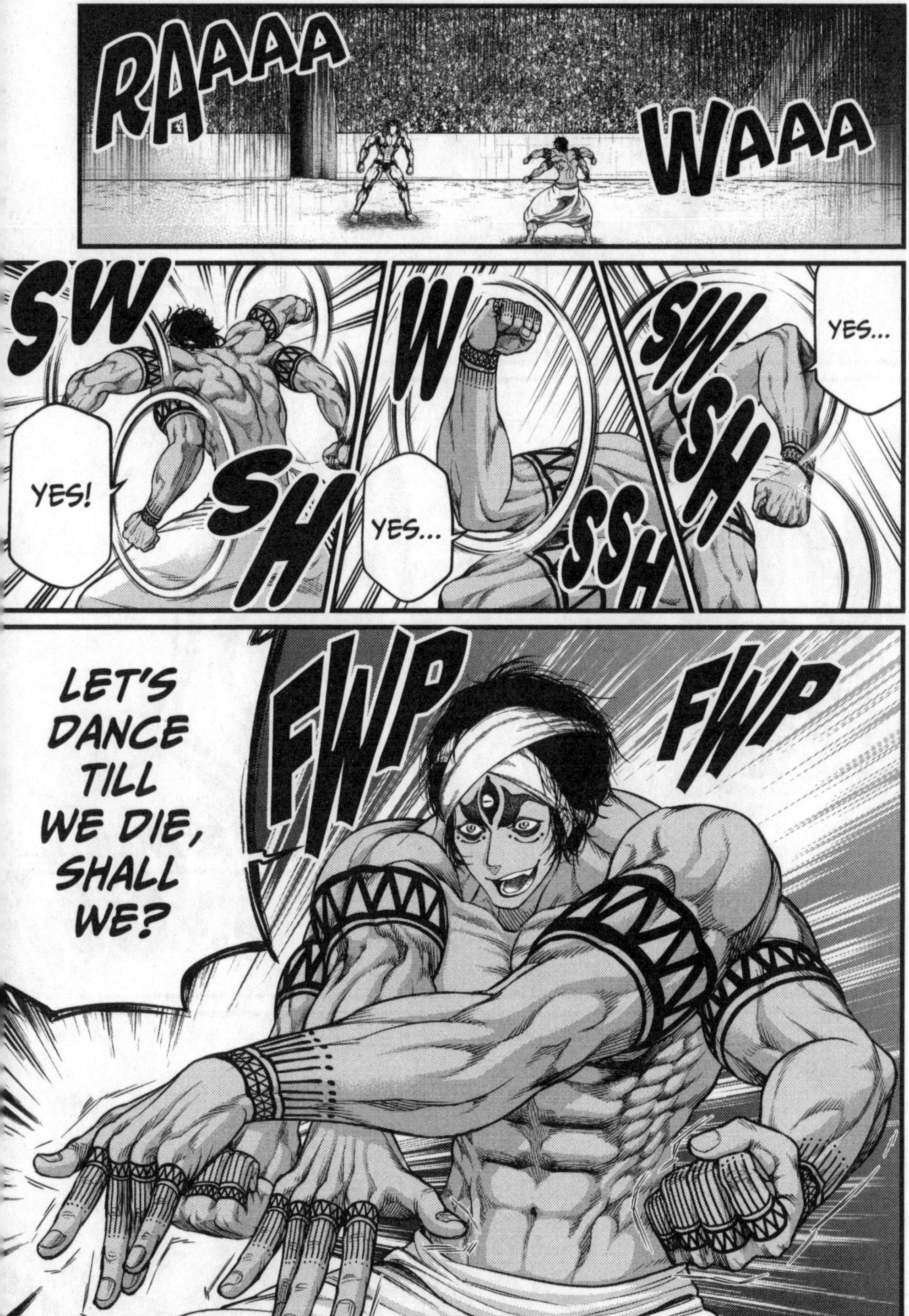
RAAAA
WAAAA
YES...
SWSH
SSH
W
YES...
SW
YES!
SH
FWP
FWP
LET'S DANCE TILL WE DIE, SHALL WE?

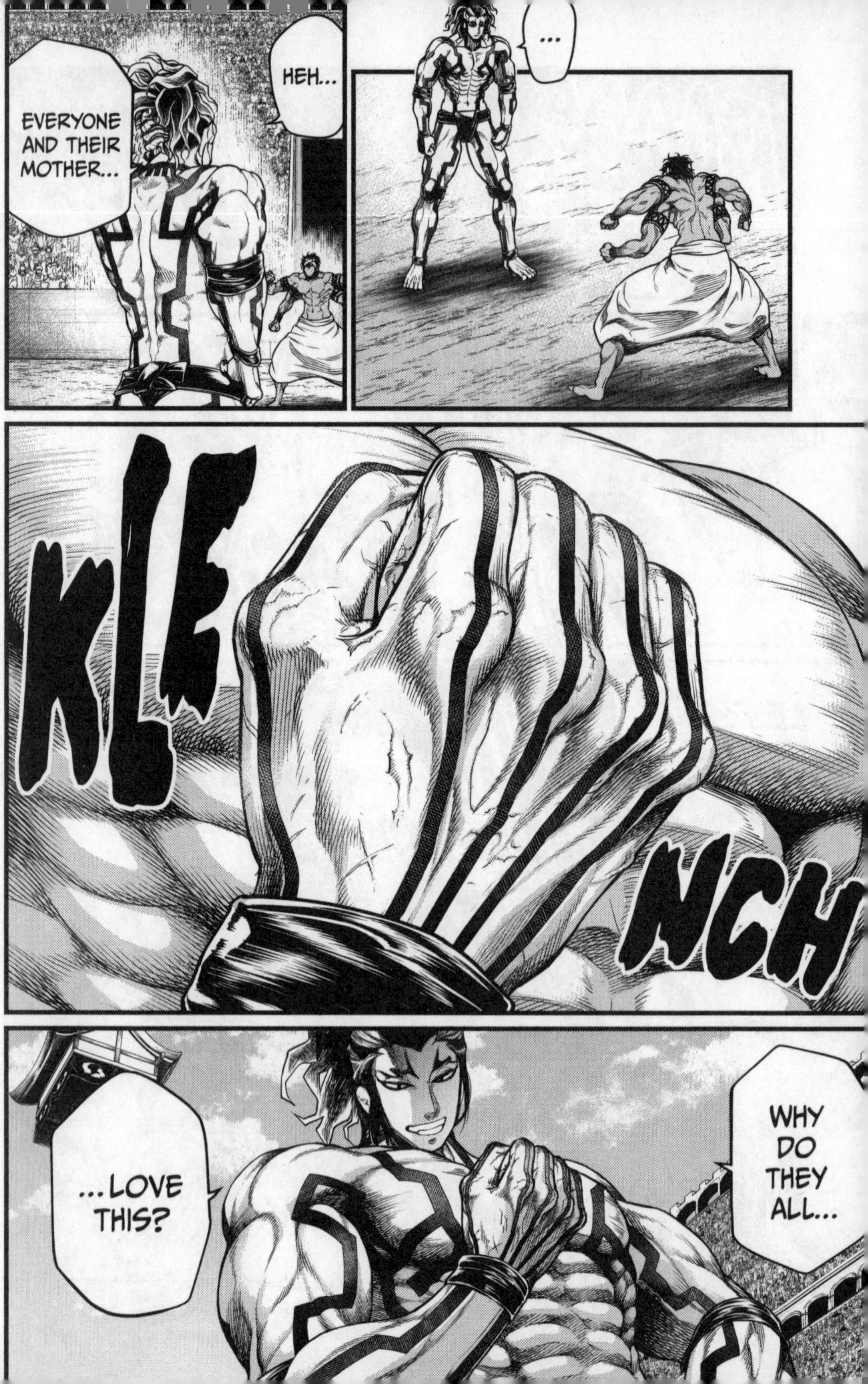
...
HEH...
EVERYONE AND THEIR MOTHER...
KLENCH
WHY DO THEY ALL...
...LOVE THIS?

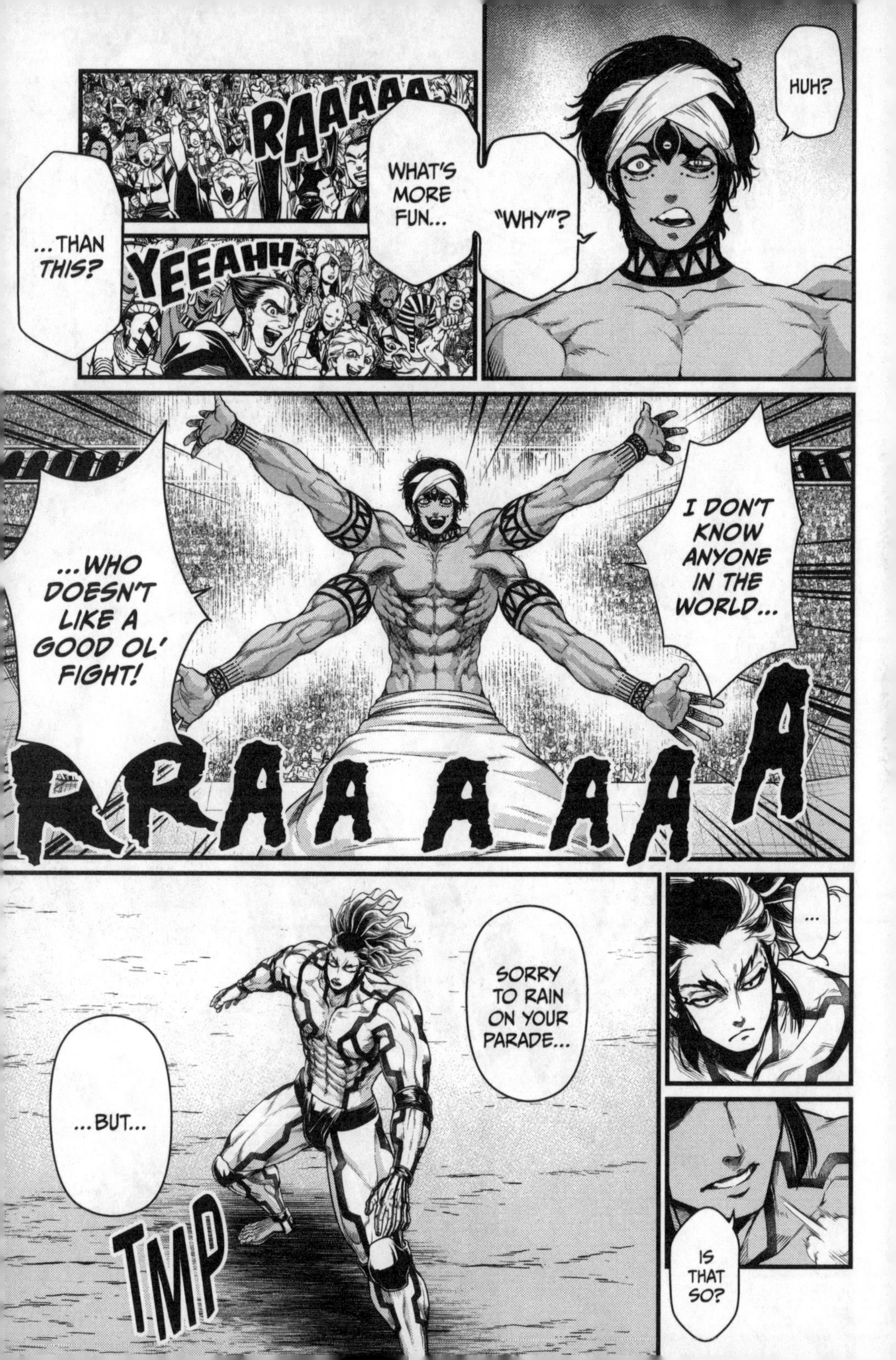
HUH?
"WHY"?
WHAT'S MORE FUN...
RAAAAA
...THAN THIS?
YEEAHH
I DON'T KNOW ANYONE IN THE WORLD...
...WHO DOESN'T LIKE A GOOD OL' FIGHT!
RRAAAAA
...
IS THAT SO?
SORRY TO RAIN ON YOUR PARADE...
...BUT...
TMP

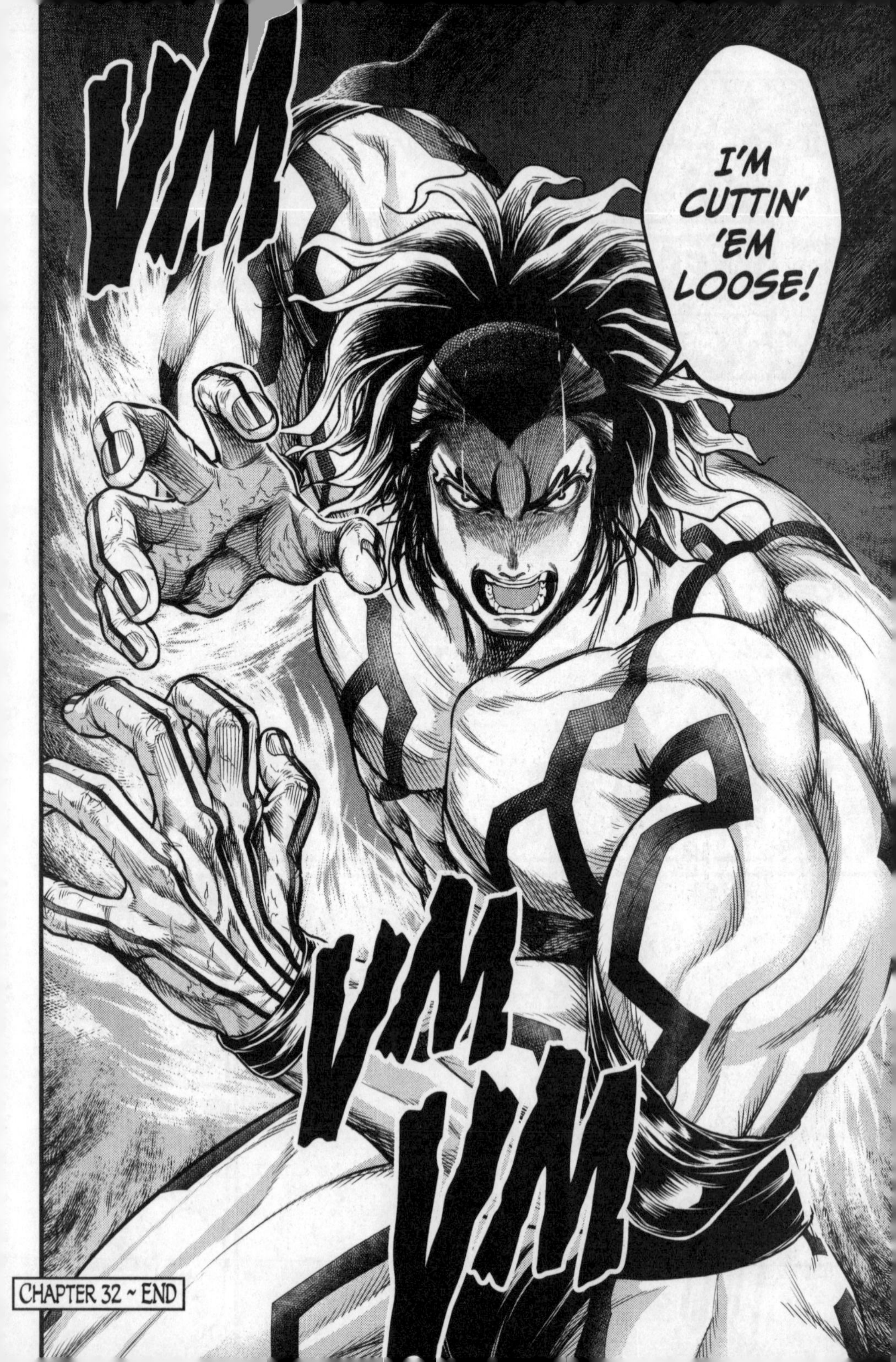
VM
I'M CUTTIN' 'EM LOOSE!
VM VM VM
CHAPTER 32 ~ END

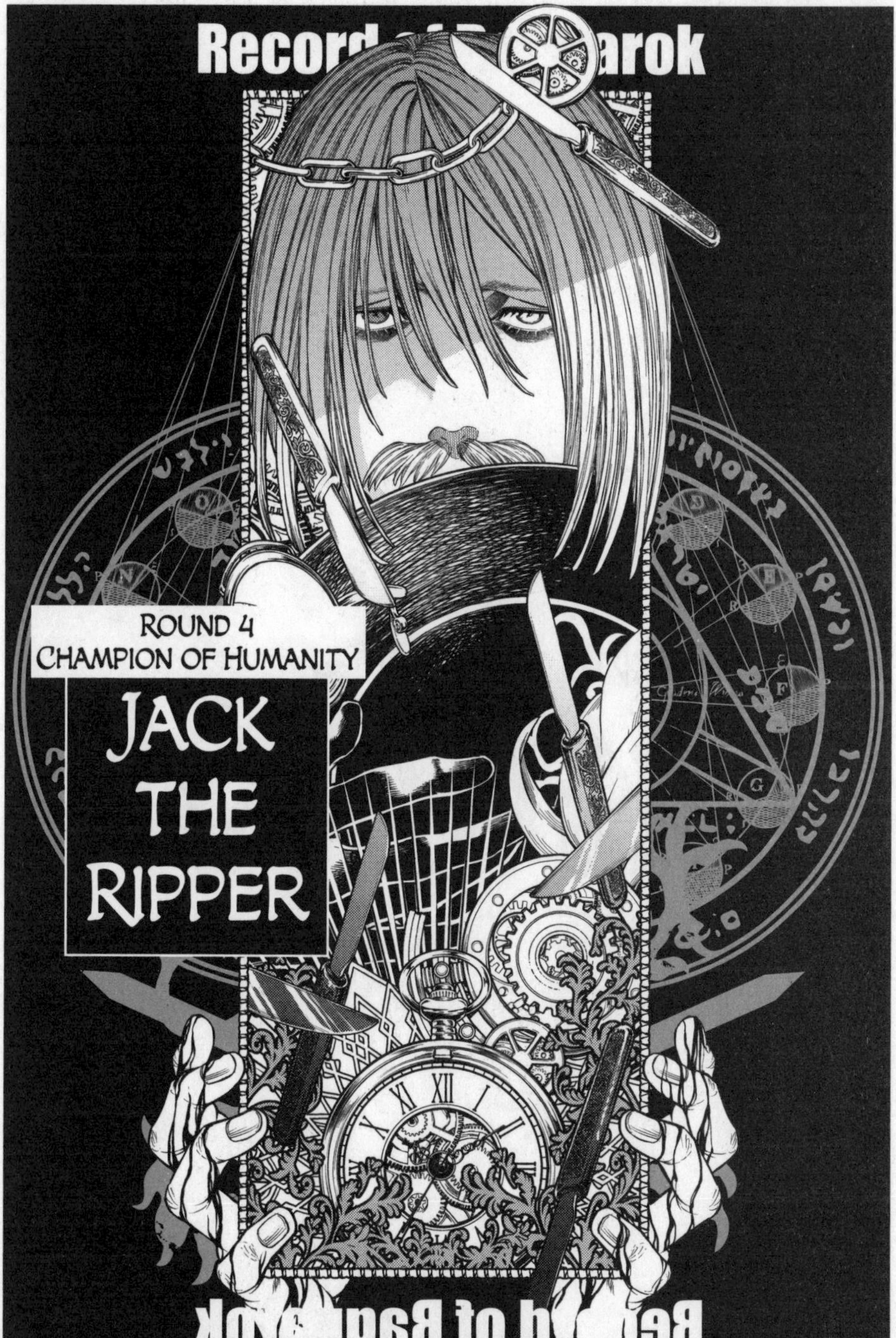
ROUND 4
CHAMPION OF HUMANITY
JACK THE RIPPER

RECORD OF
RAGNAROK

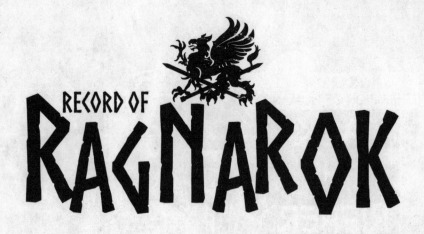

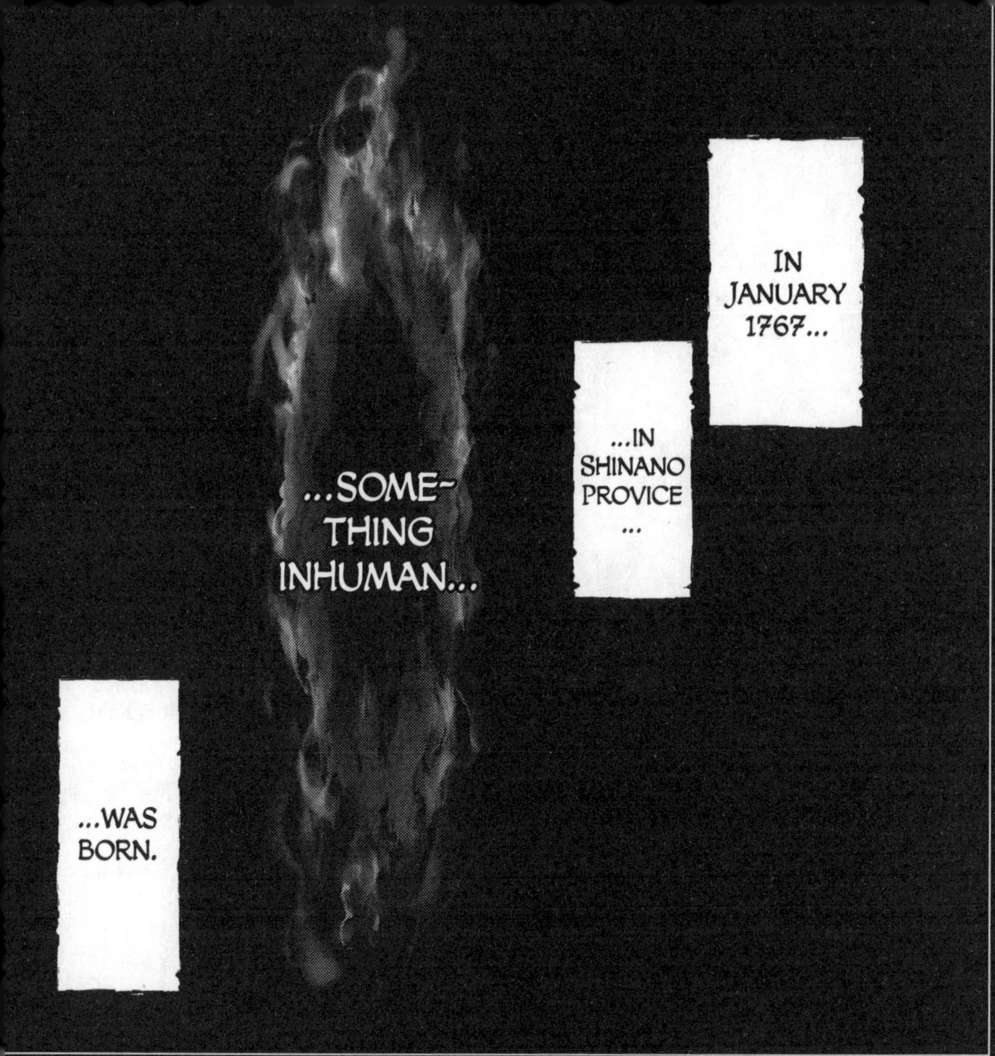
IN JANUARY 1767...
...IN SHINANO PROVICE ...
...SOME-THING INHUMAN...
...WAS BORN.
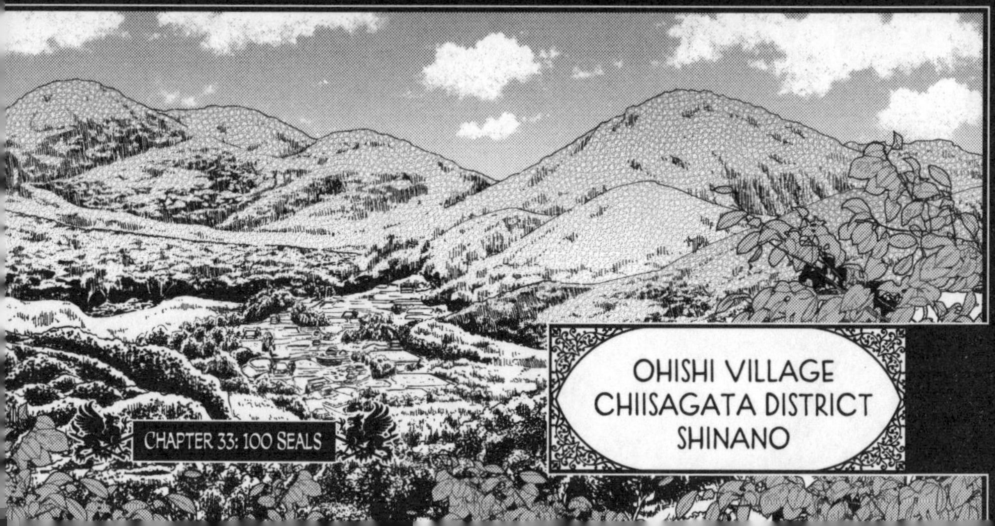
OHISHI VILLAGE CHIISAGATA DISTRICT SHINANO
CHAPTER 33: 100 SEALS

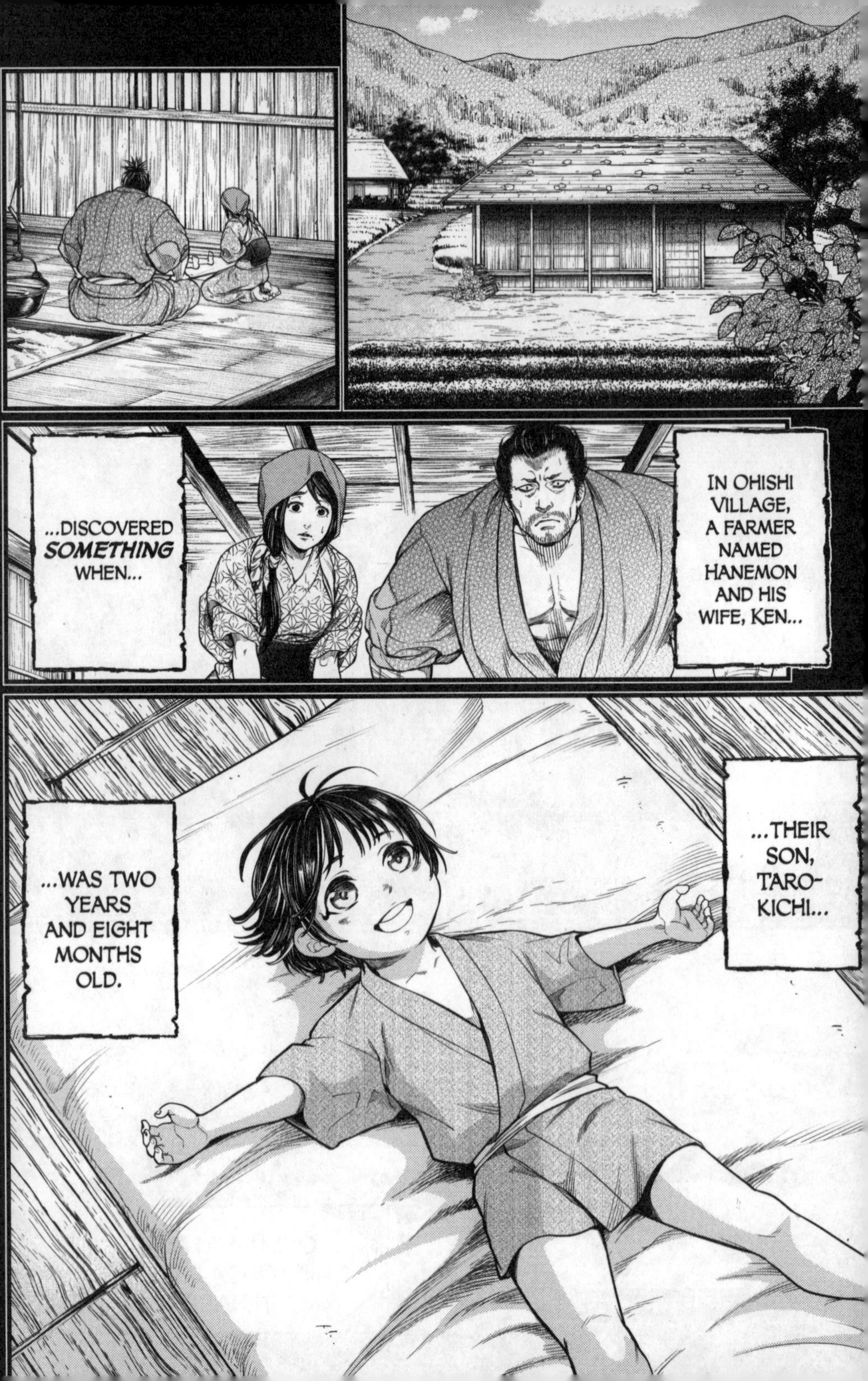
IN OHISHI VILLAGE, A FARMER NAMED HANEMON AND HIS WIFE, KEN...
...DISCOVERED *SOMETHING* WHEN...
...THEIR SON, TARO-KICHI...
...WAS TWO YEARS AND EIGHT MONTHS OLD.

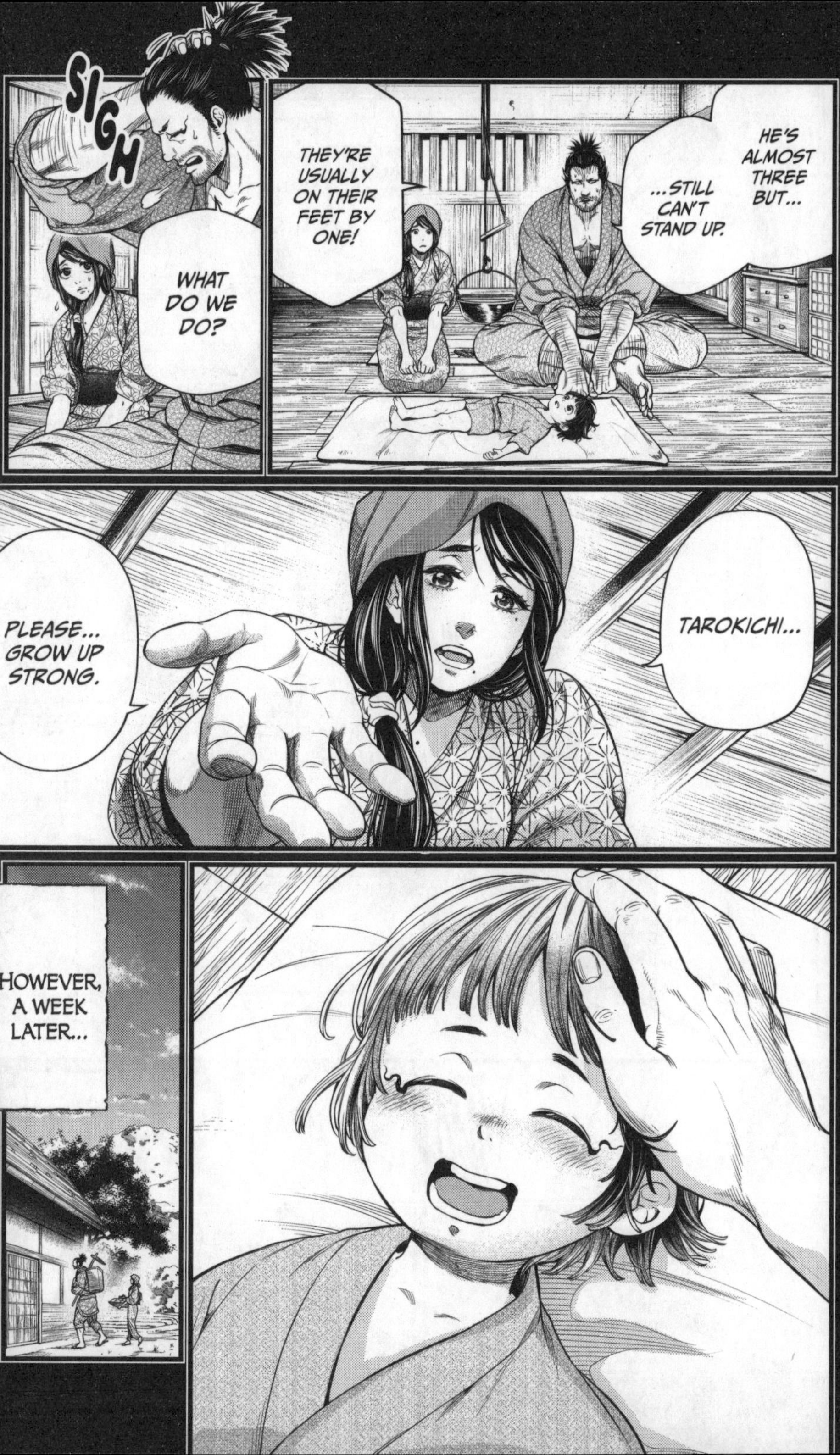
HE'S ALMOST THREE BUT...
...STILL CAN'T STAND UP.
THEY'RE USUALLY ON THEIR FEET BY ONE!
SIGH
WHAT DO WE DO?
TAROKICHI...
PLEASE... GROW UP STRONG.
HOWEVER, A WEEK LATER...

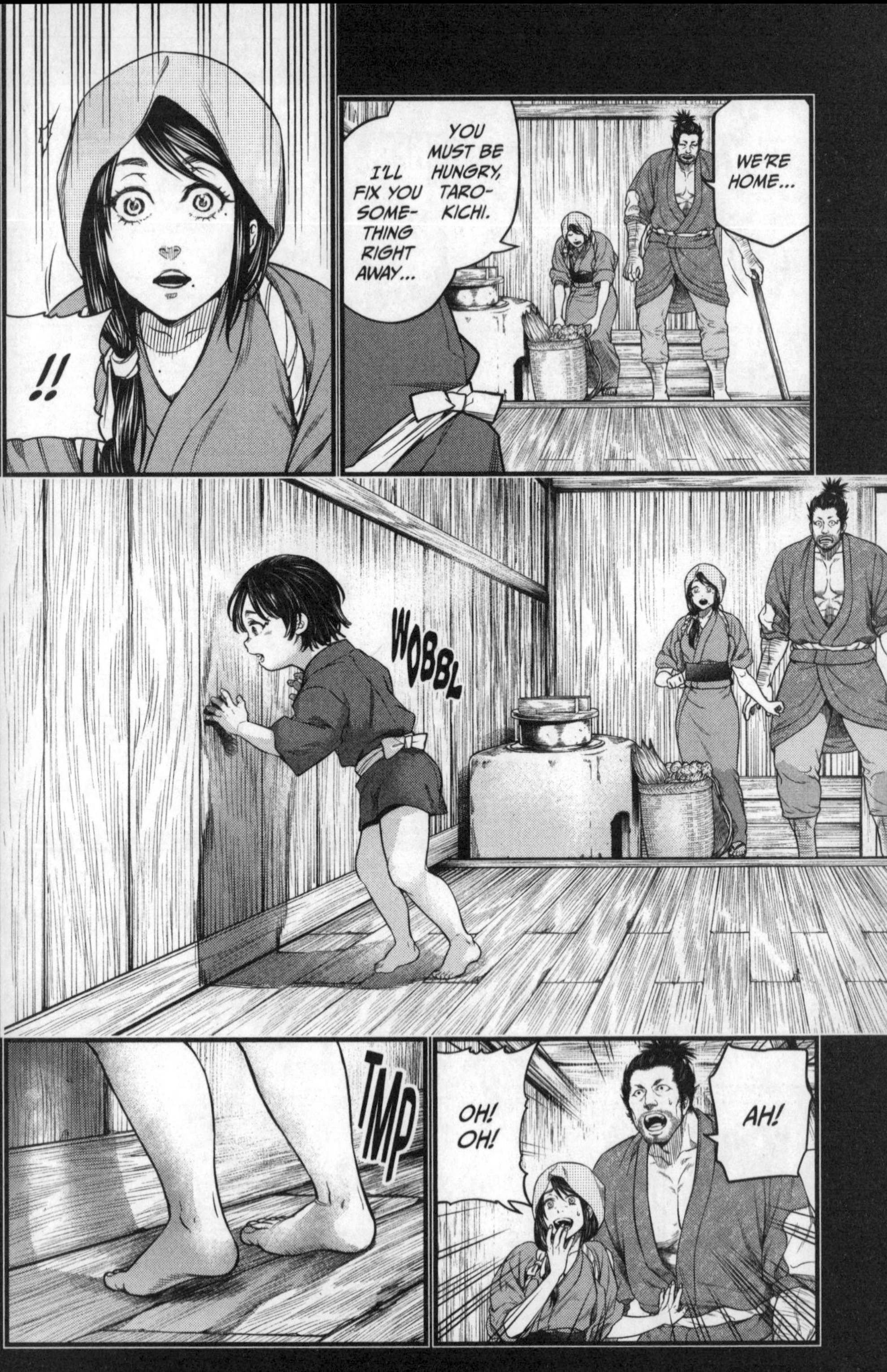
WE'RE HOME...
YOU MUST BE HUNGRY, TARO-KICHI.
I'LL FIX YOU SOME-THING RIGHT AWAY...
!!
WOBBL
AH!
OH! OH!
TMP

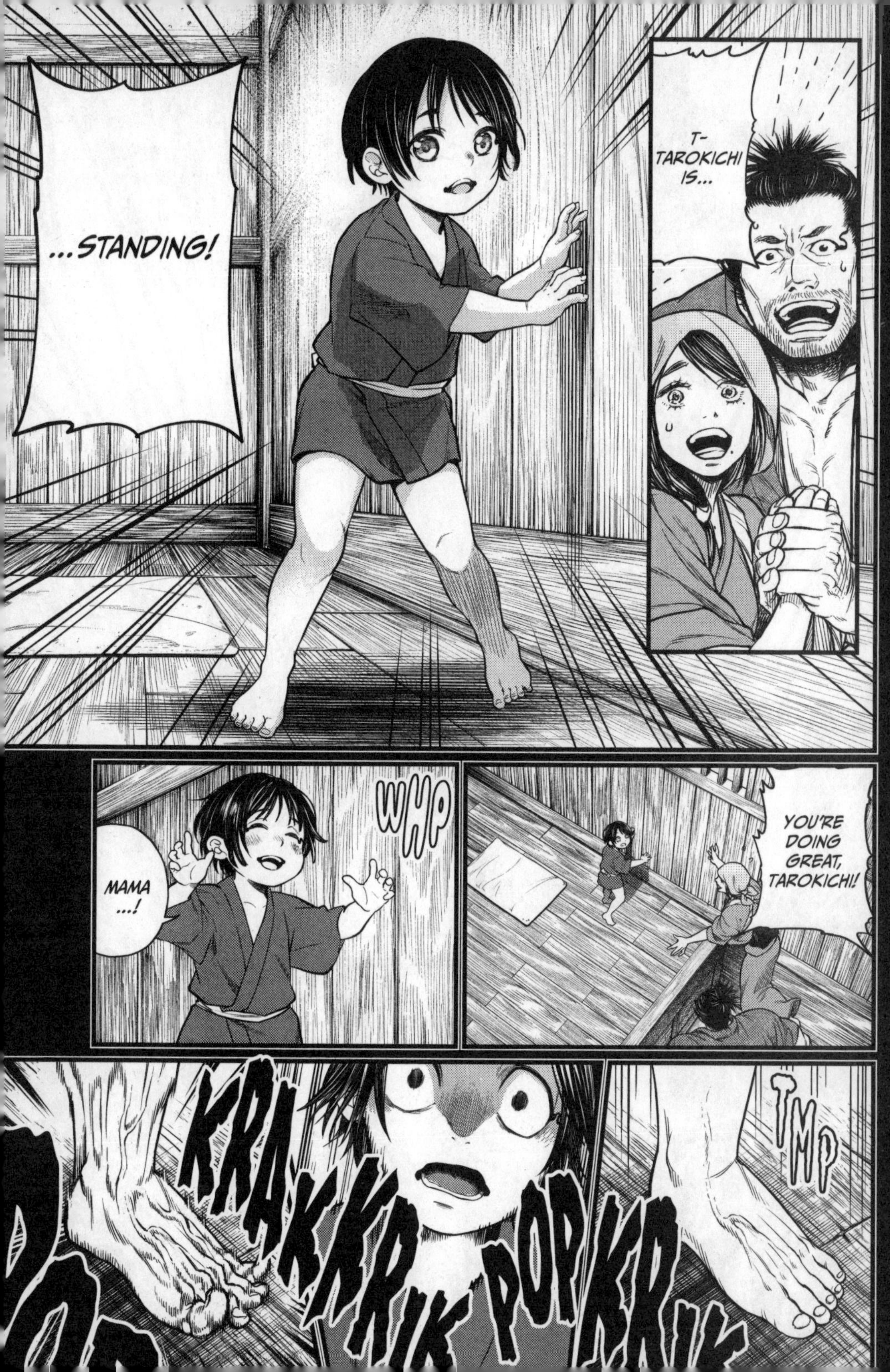
T-TAROKICHI IS...
...STANDING!
YOU'RE DOING GREAT, TAROKICHI!
WHP
MAMA ...!
TMP
KRAKKRIK
POPKR

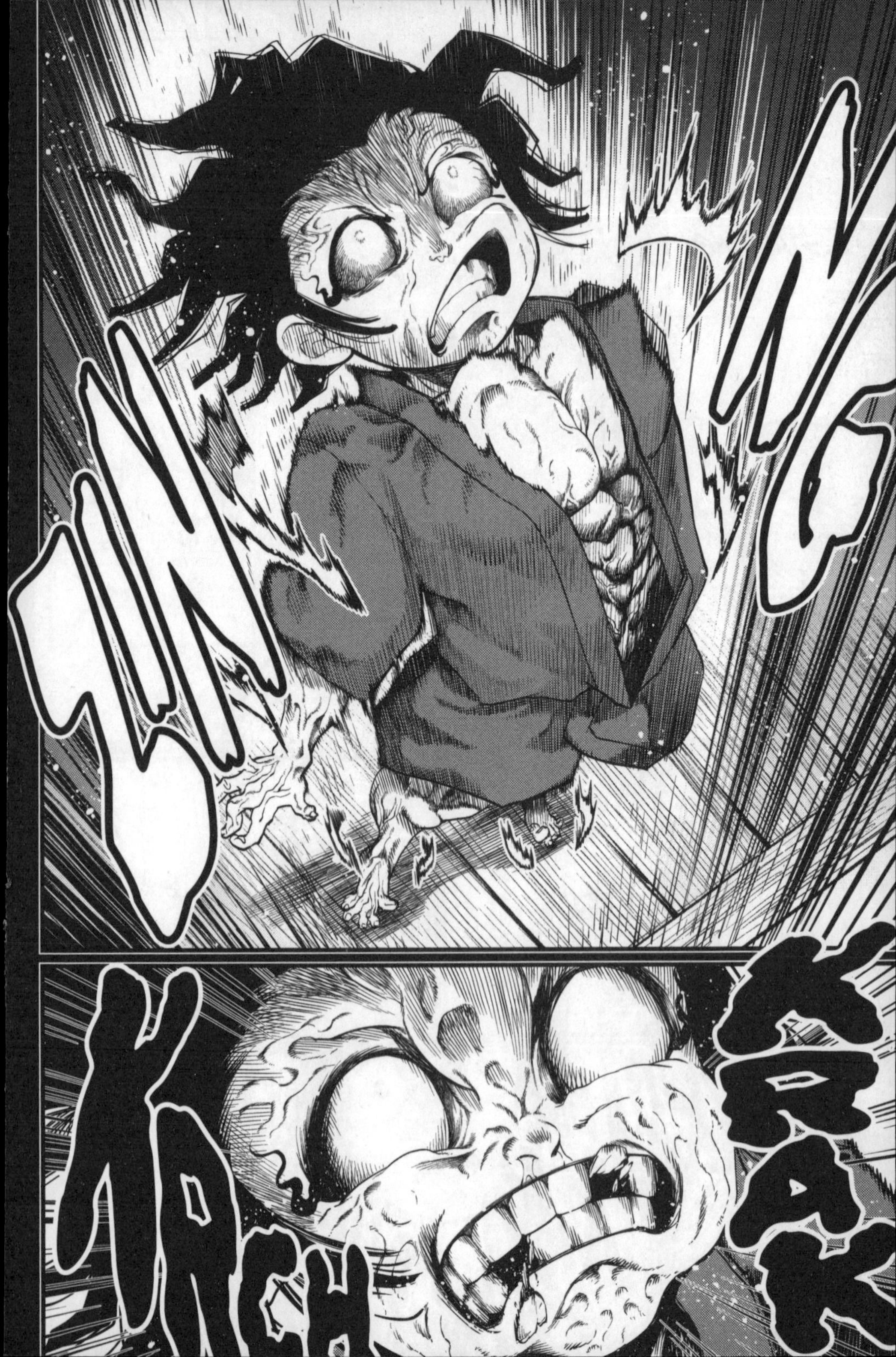

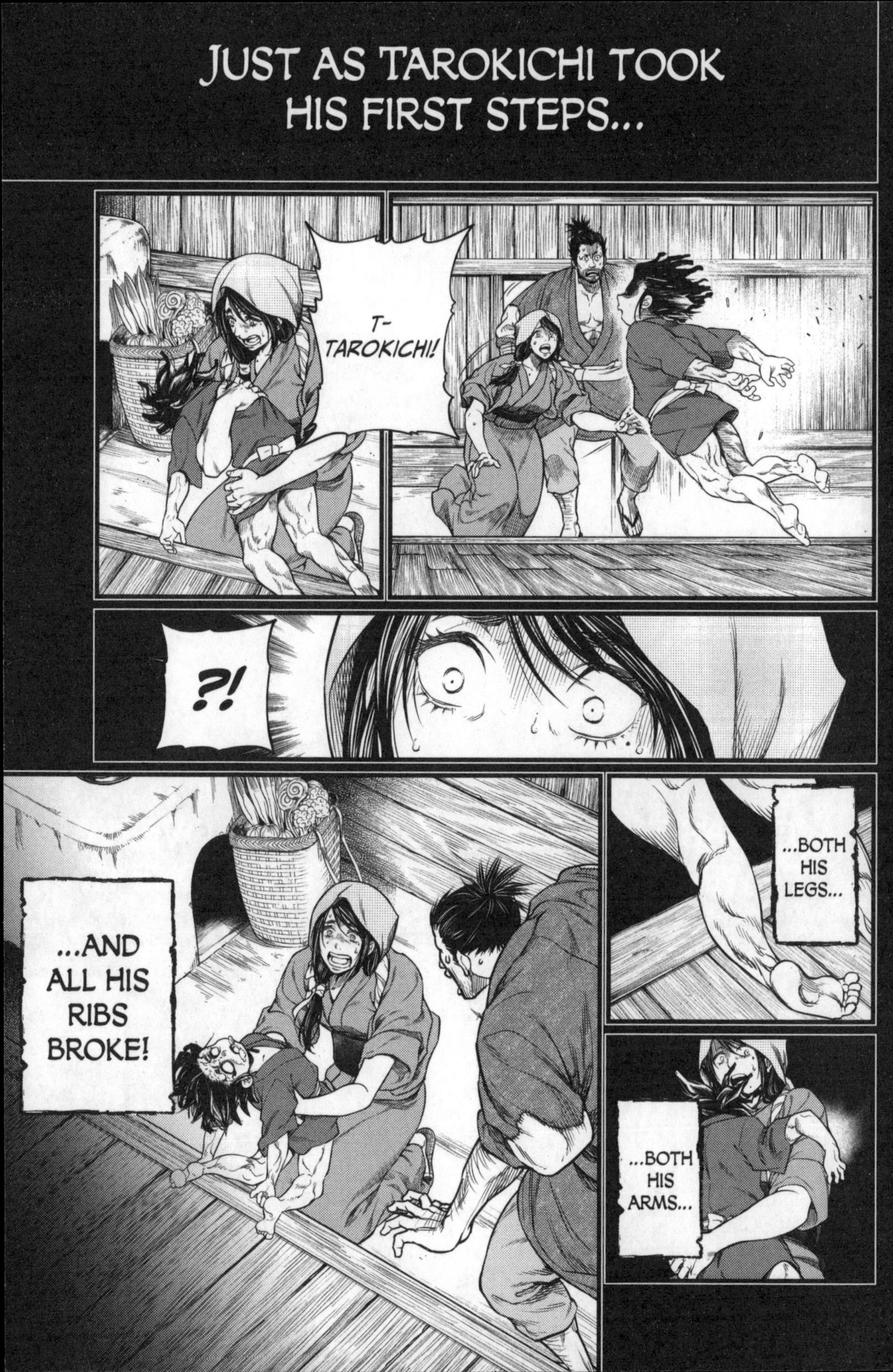
JUST AS TAROKICHI TOOK HIS FIRST STEPS...
T-TAROKICHI!
?!
...BOTH HIS LEGS...
...BOTH HIS ARMS...
...AND ALL HIS RIBS BROKE!

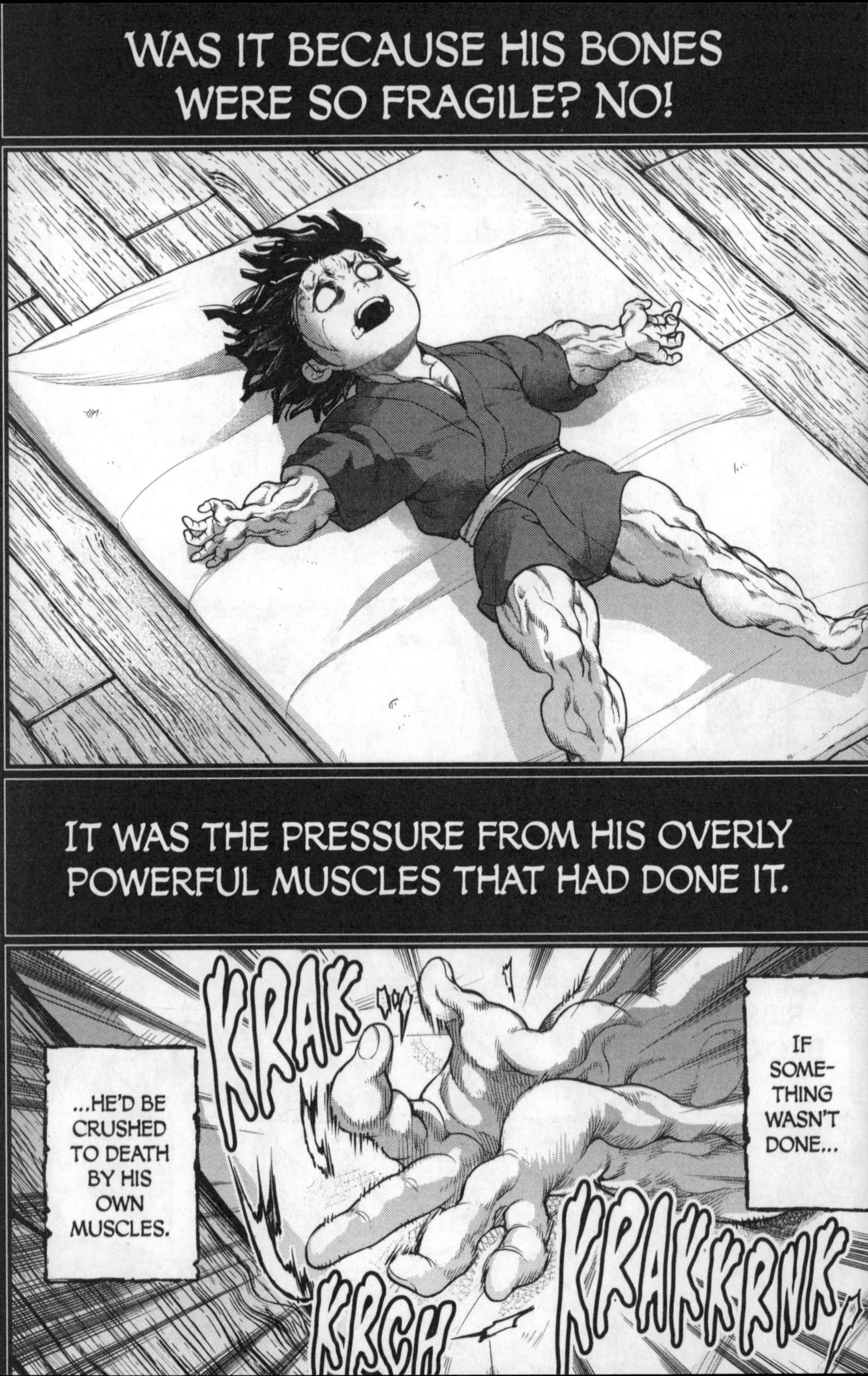
WAS IT BECAUSE HIS BONES WERE SO FRAGILE? NO!
IT WAS THE PRESSURE FROM HIS OVERLY POWERFUL MUSCLES THAT HAD DONE IT.
IF SOMETHING WASN'T DONE...
KRAK
...HE'D BE CRUSHED TO DEATH BY HIS OWN MUSCLES.
KRAKKRNK
KRCH

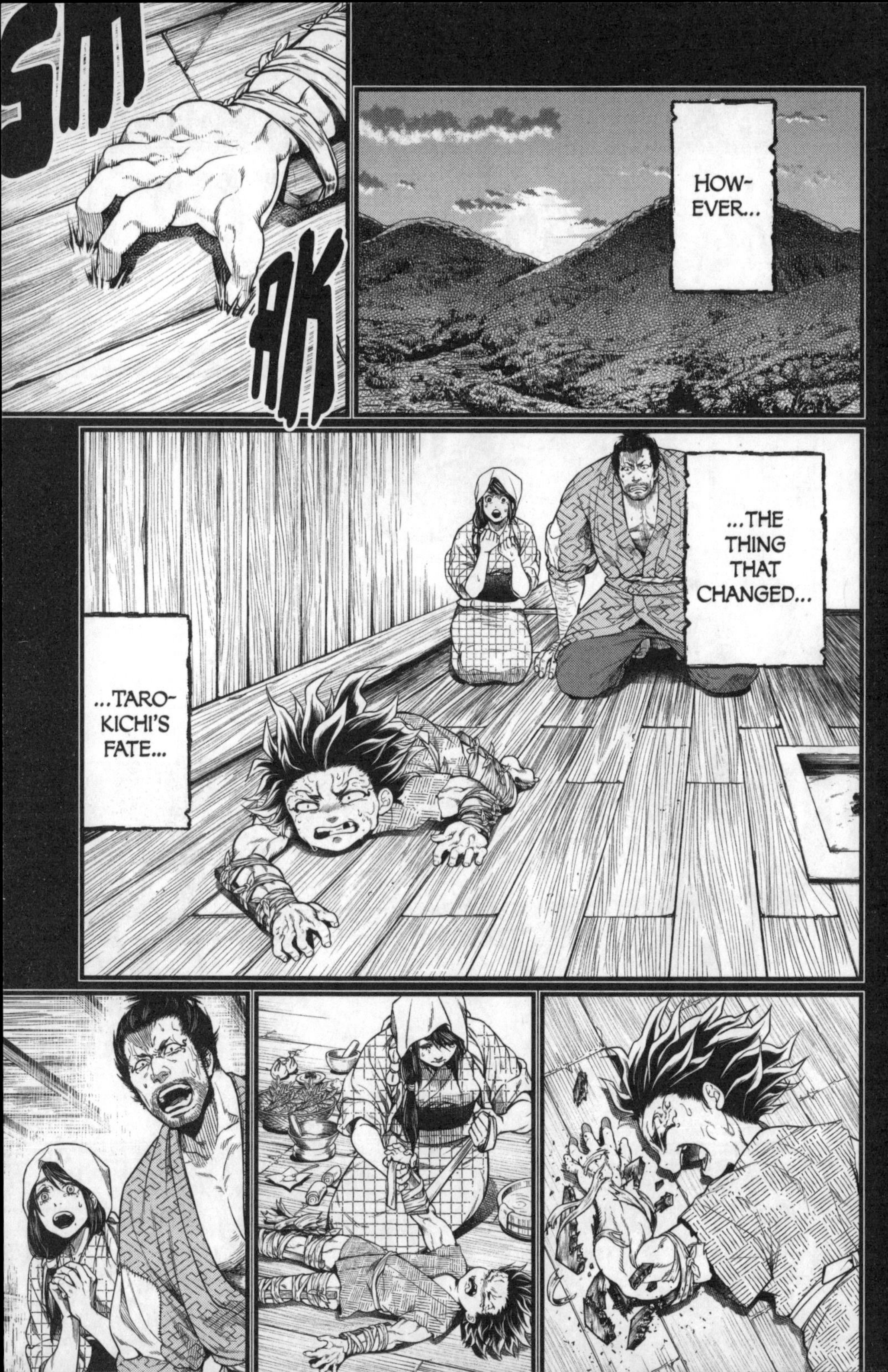
HOW-EVER...
AK
...THE THING THAT CHANGED...
...TARO-KICHI'S FATE...

...WAS ALSO...

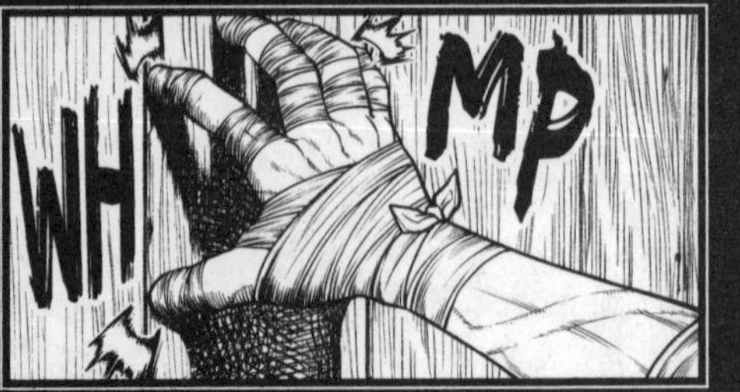
WH MP

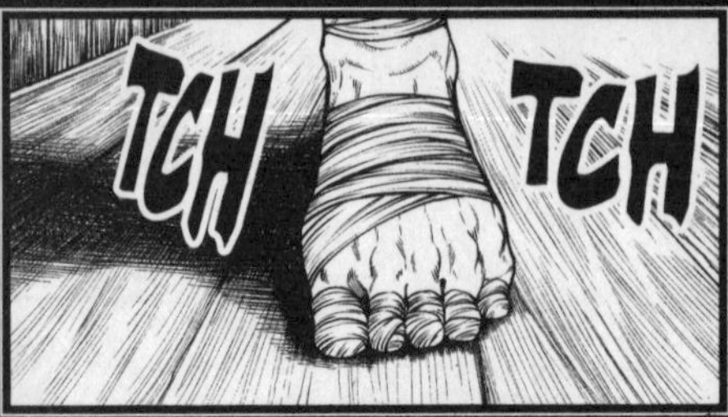
TCH
TCH

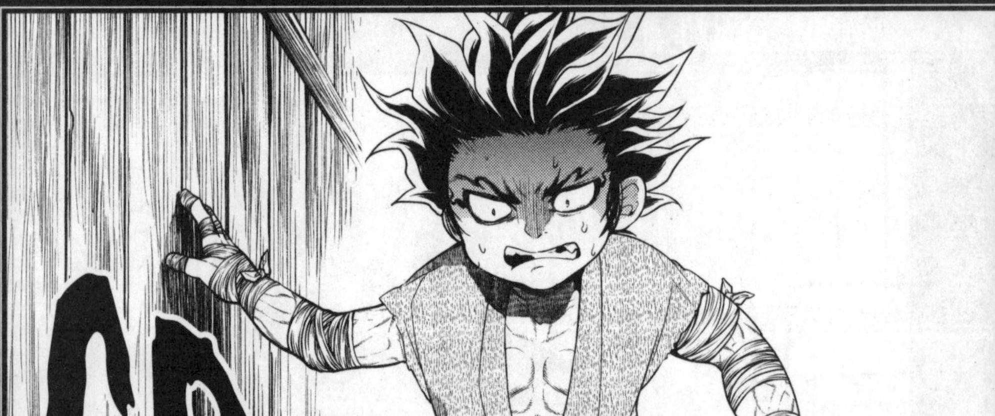
GR
SH

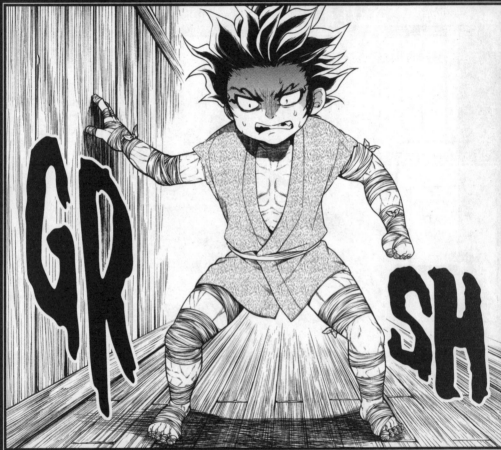

...HIS MUSCLES.

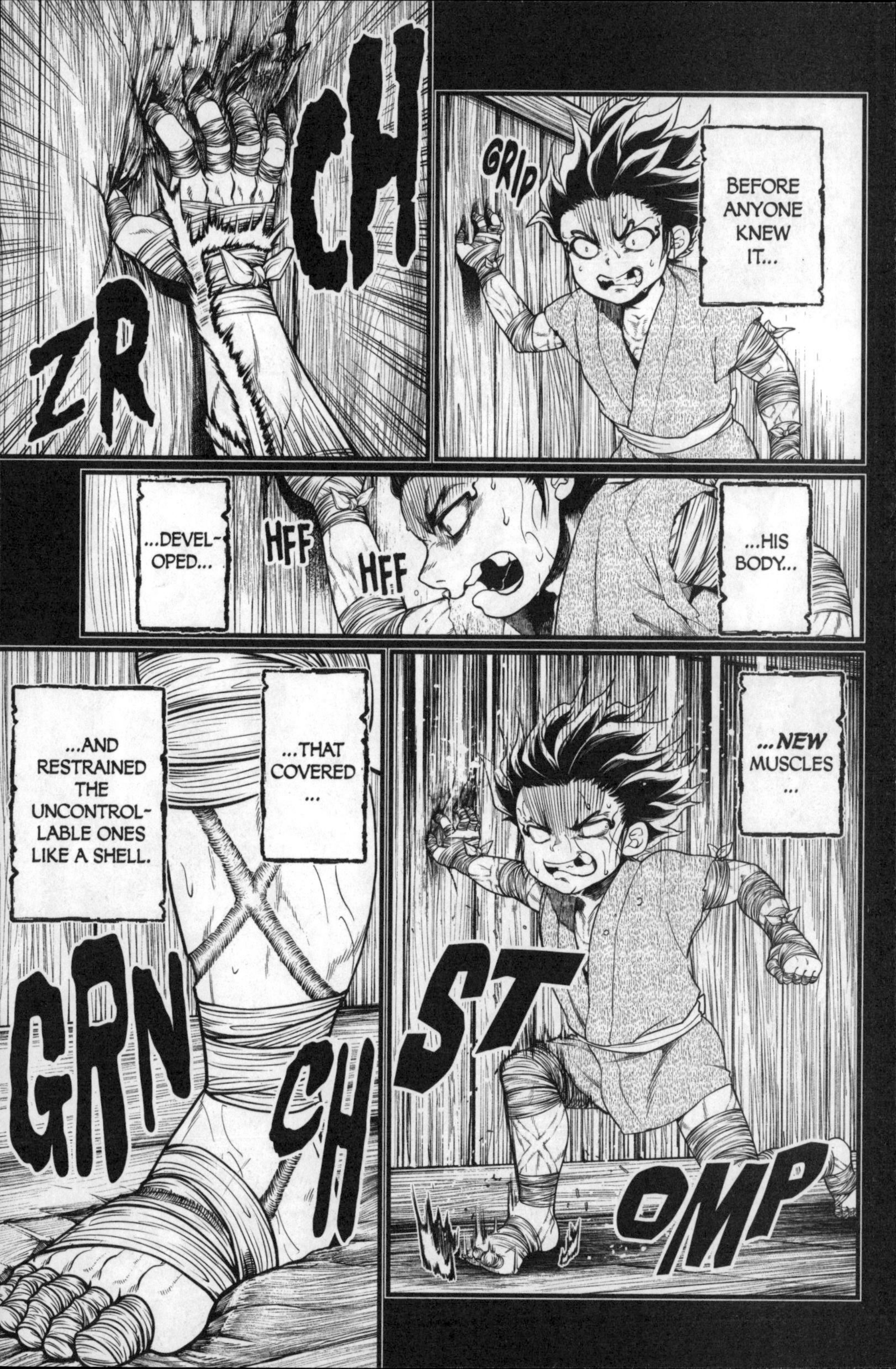
GRIP
BEFORE ANYONE KNEW IT...
ZR
CH
...HIS BODY...
HFF
HFF
...DEVEL-OPED...
...NEW MUSCLES ...
ST
OMP
...THAT COVERED ...
...AND RESTRAINED THE UNCONTROL-LABLE ONES LIKE A SHELL.
GRN
CH

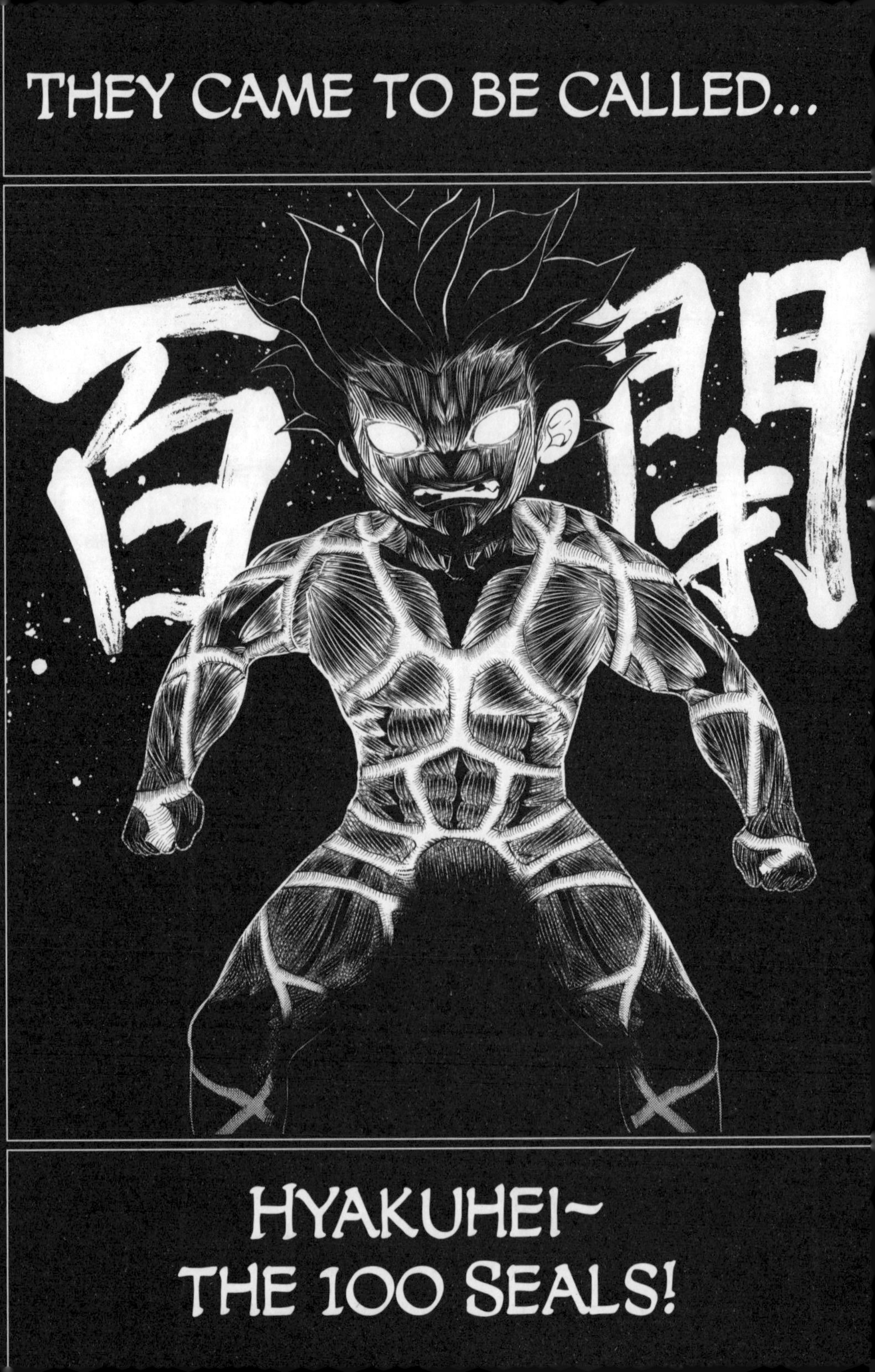
THEY CAME TO BE CALLED...
百閉
HYAKUHEI~
THE 100 SEALS!

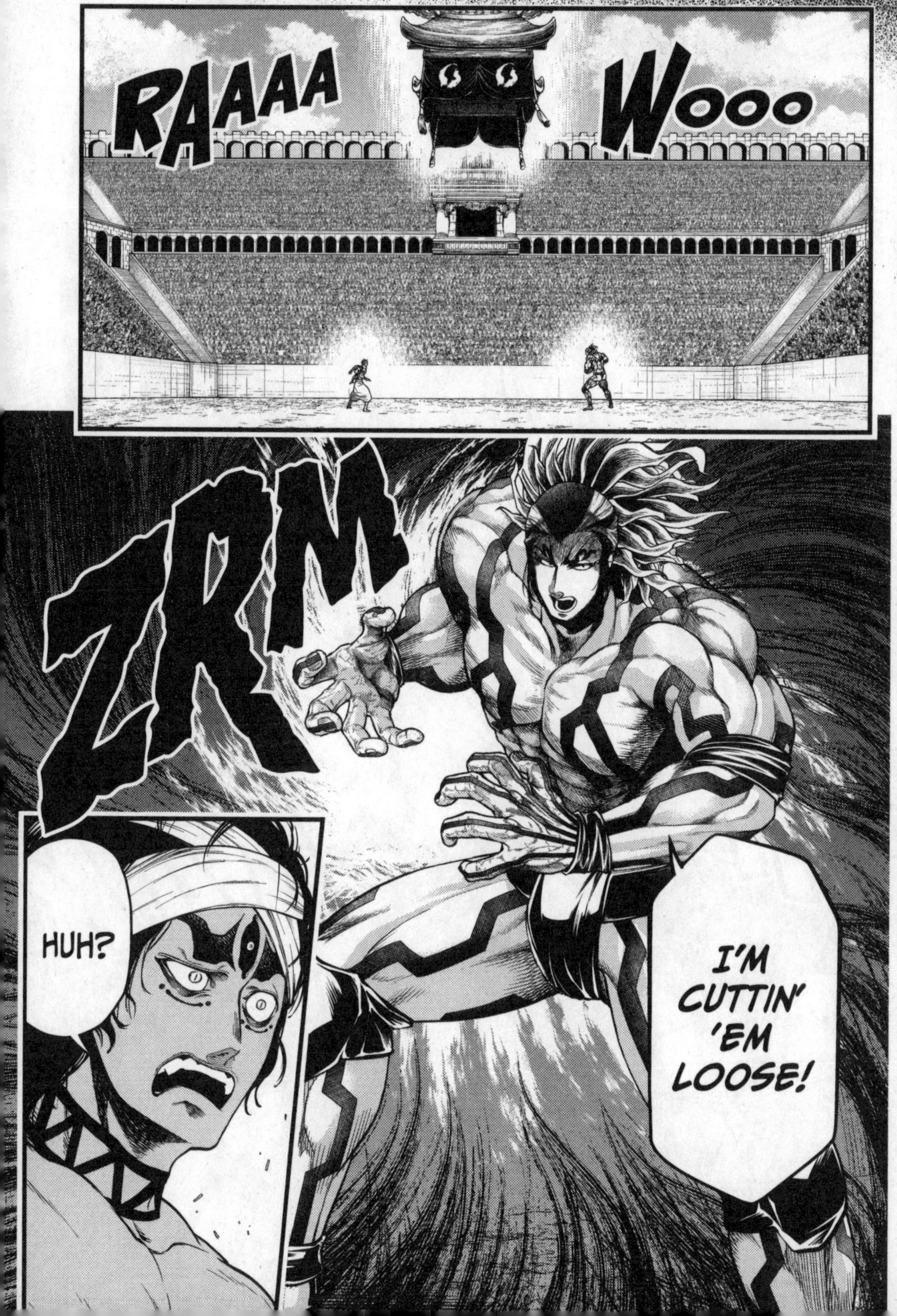
RAAAA WOOO
ZRM
I'M CUTTIN' 'EM LOOSE!
HUH?

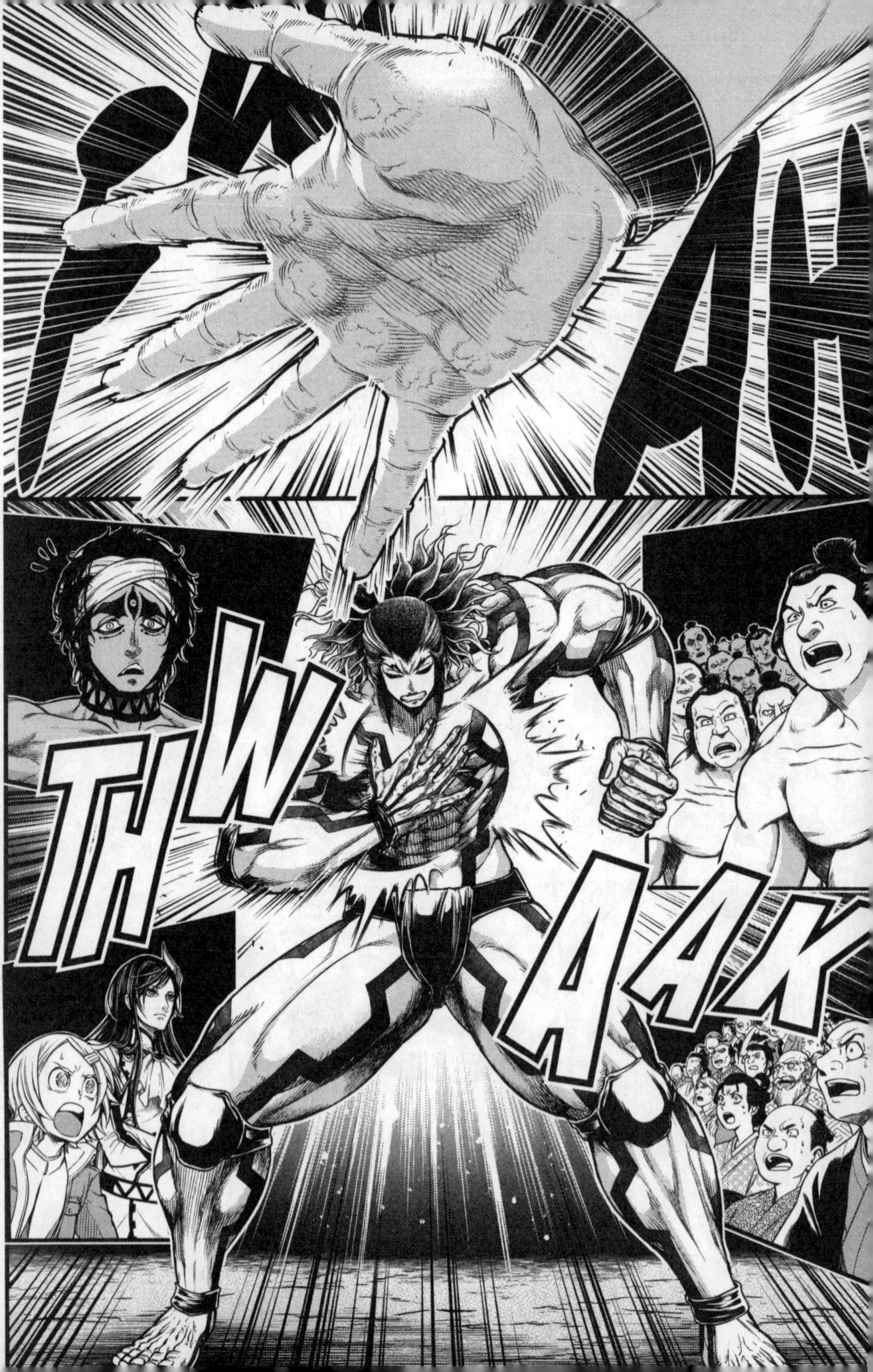
THWAAK

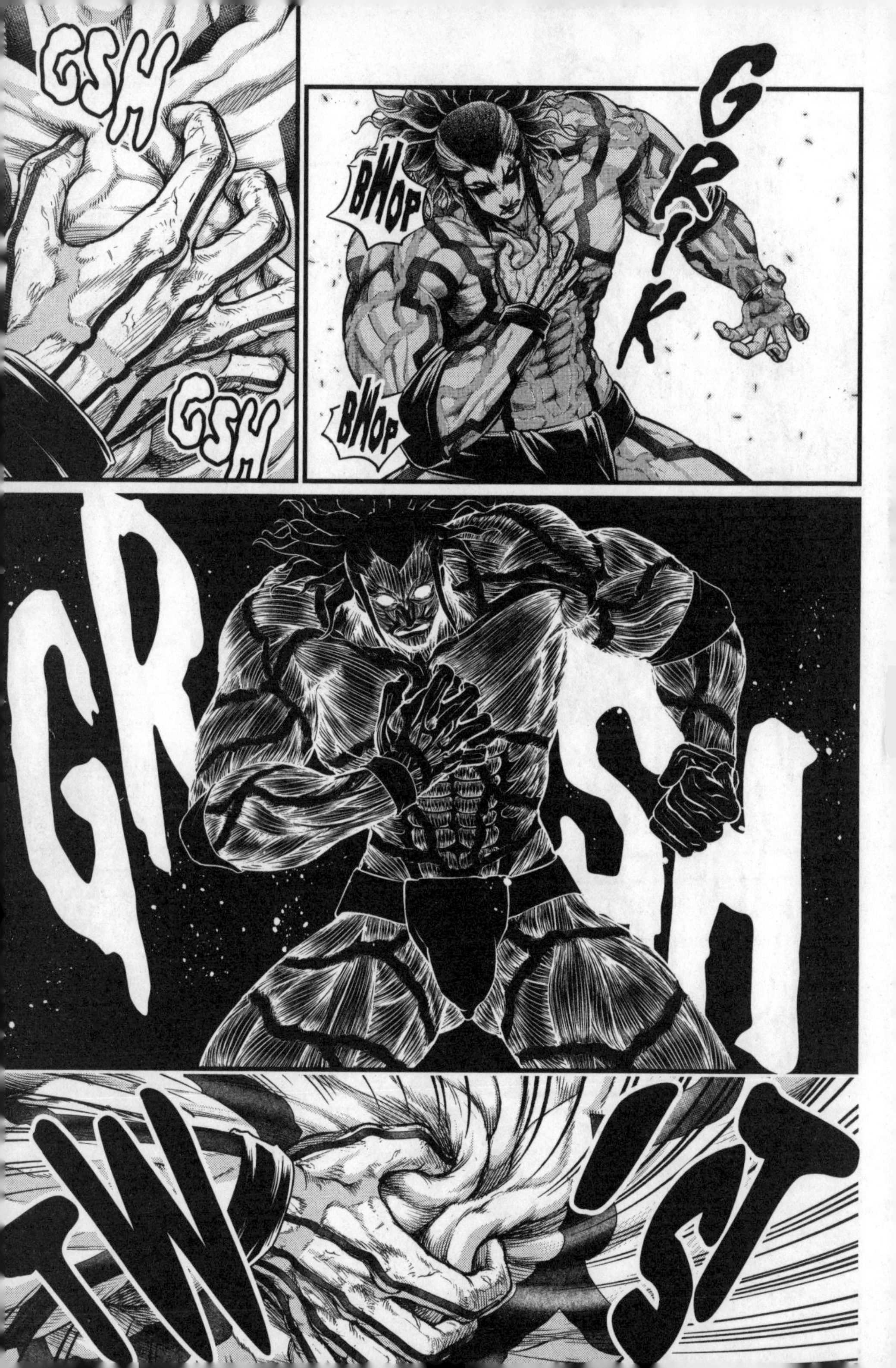
GRIK
BWOP
BWOP
GSH
GSH
GRSH
TWIST

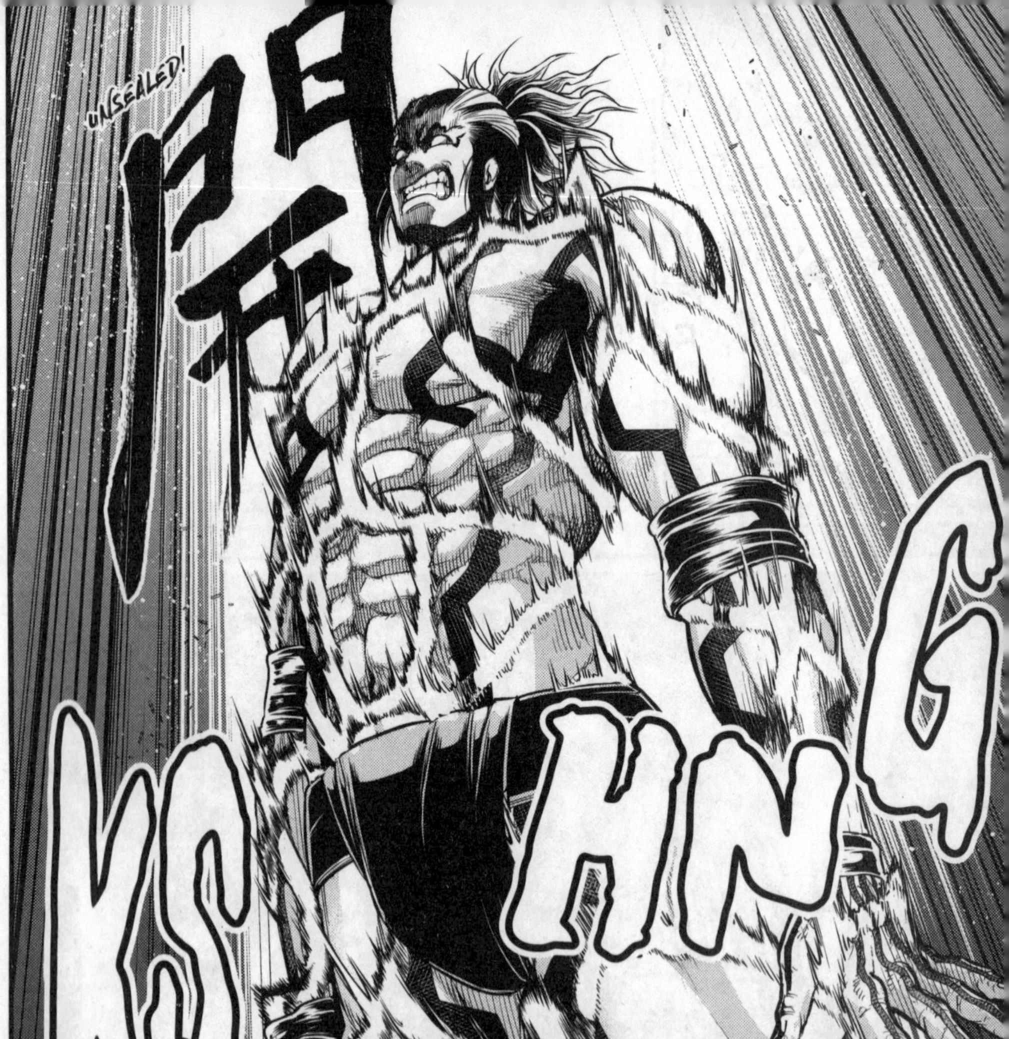
UNSEALED!
KSHHNG
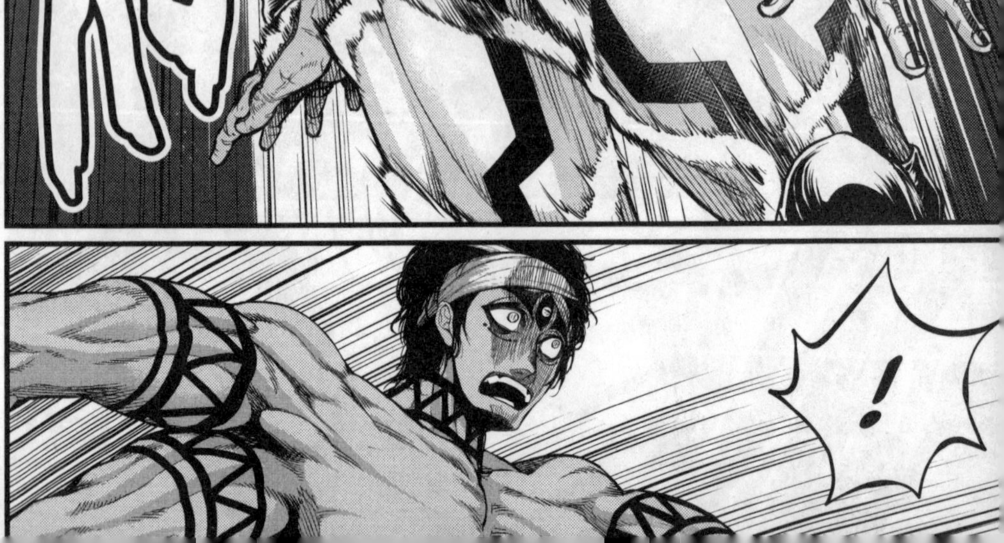
!

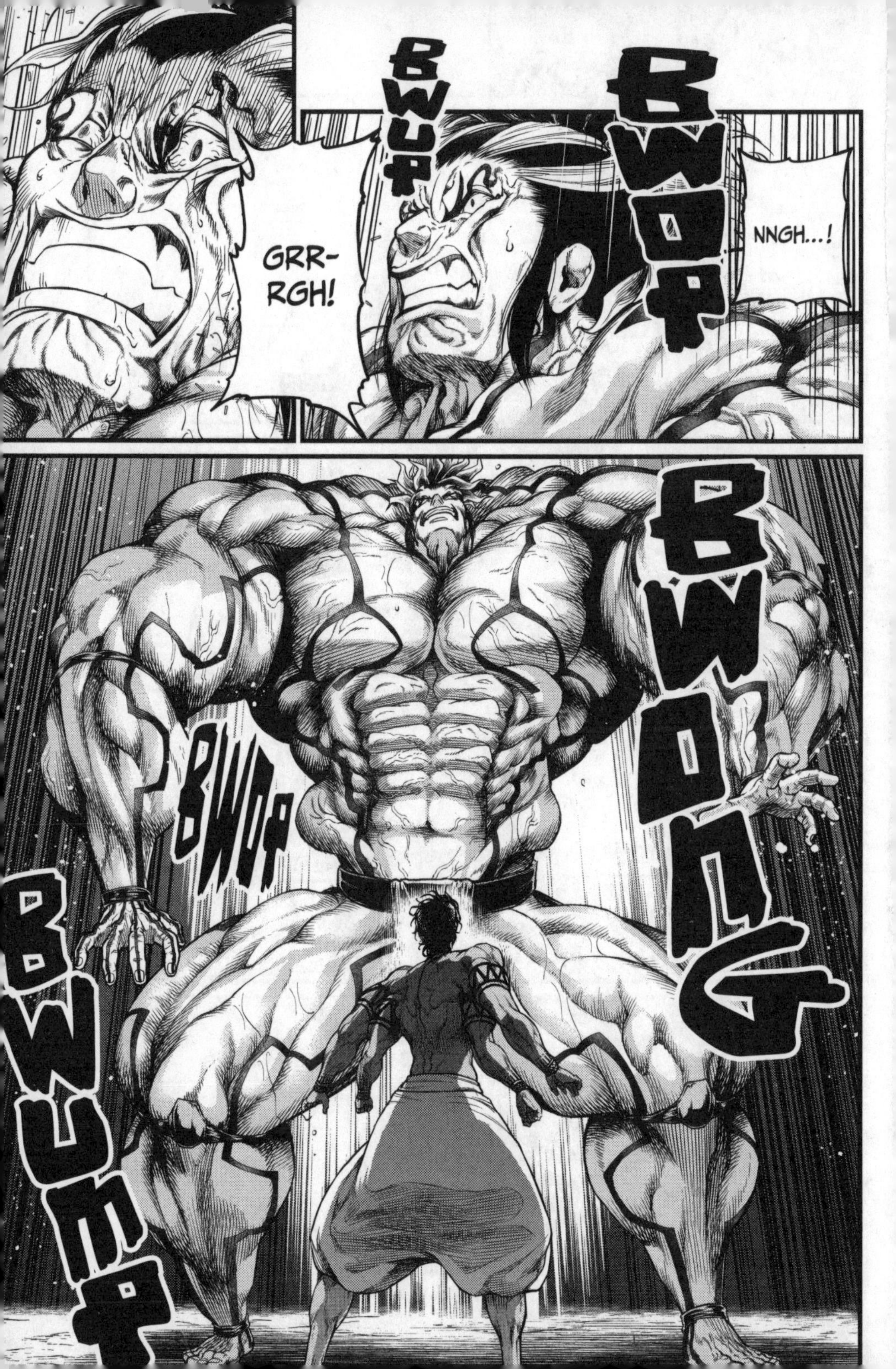
BWOP
NNGH...!
BWUP
GRR-RGH!
BWONG
BWOP
BWUMP

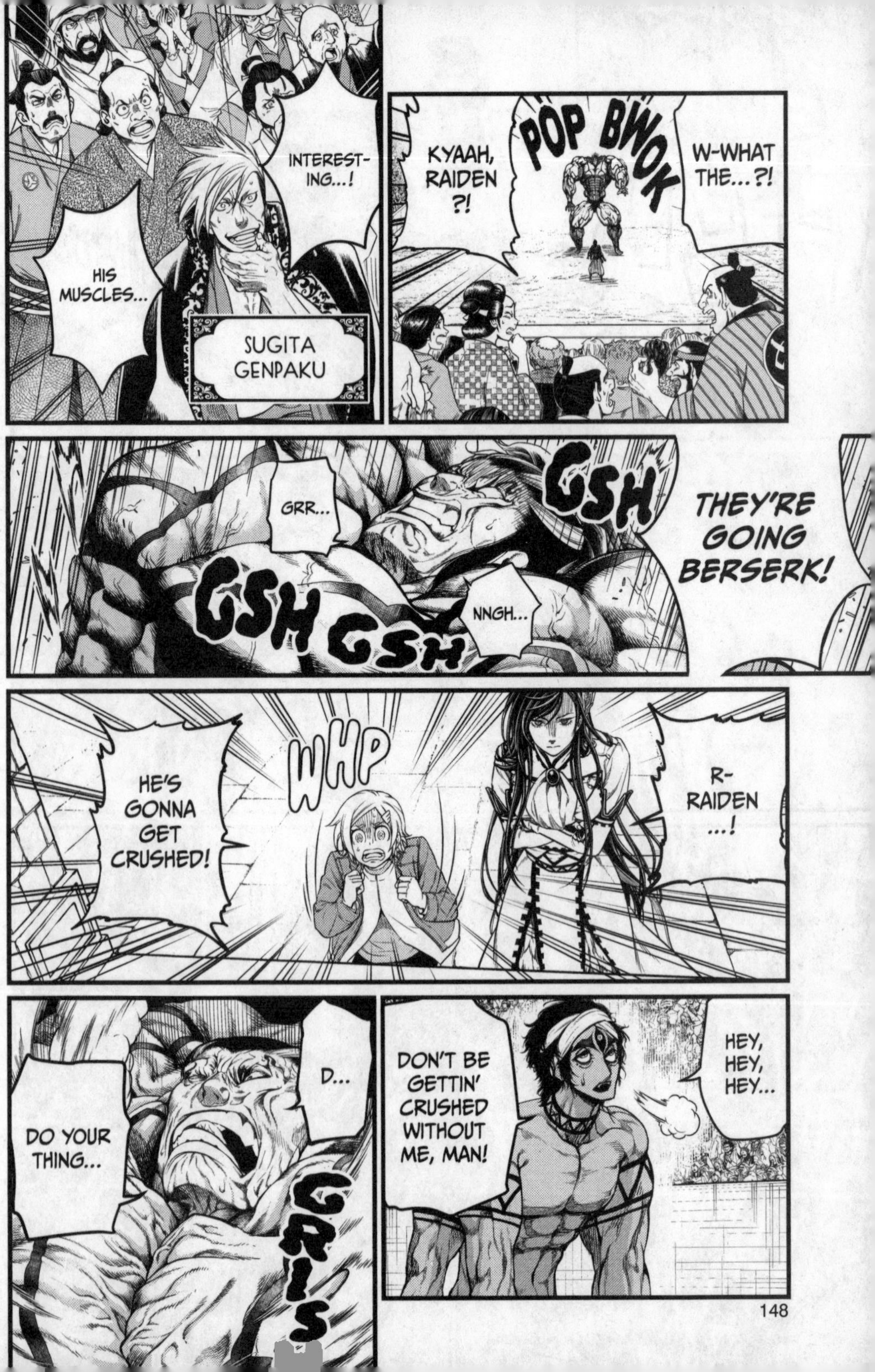
W-WHAT THE...?!
POP BWOK
KYAAH, RAIDEN ?!
INTEREST-ING...!
HIS MUSCLES...
SUGITA GENPAKU
THEY'RE GOING BERSERK!
GSH
GRR...
NNGH...
GSH GSH
R-RAIDEN ...!
WHP
HE'S GONNA GET CRUSHED!
HEY, HEY, HEY...
DON'T BE GETTIN' CRUSHED WITHOUT ME, MAN!
D...
DO YOUR THING...
GRIS

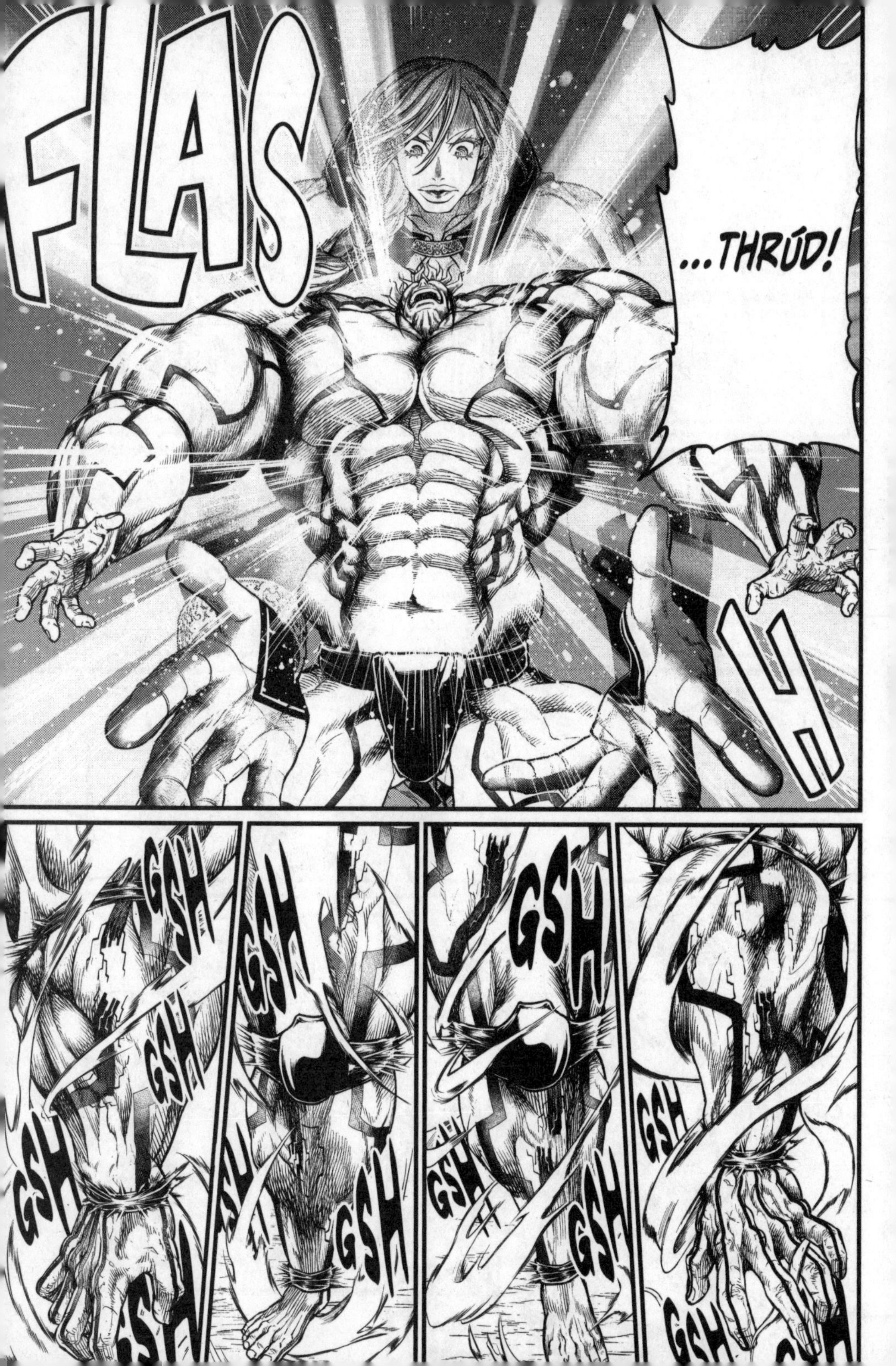
...THRÚD!
FLASH
GSH
GSH
GSH
GSH
GSH
GSH
GSH
GSH
GSH
GSH
GSH
GSH

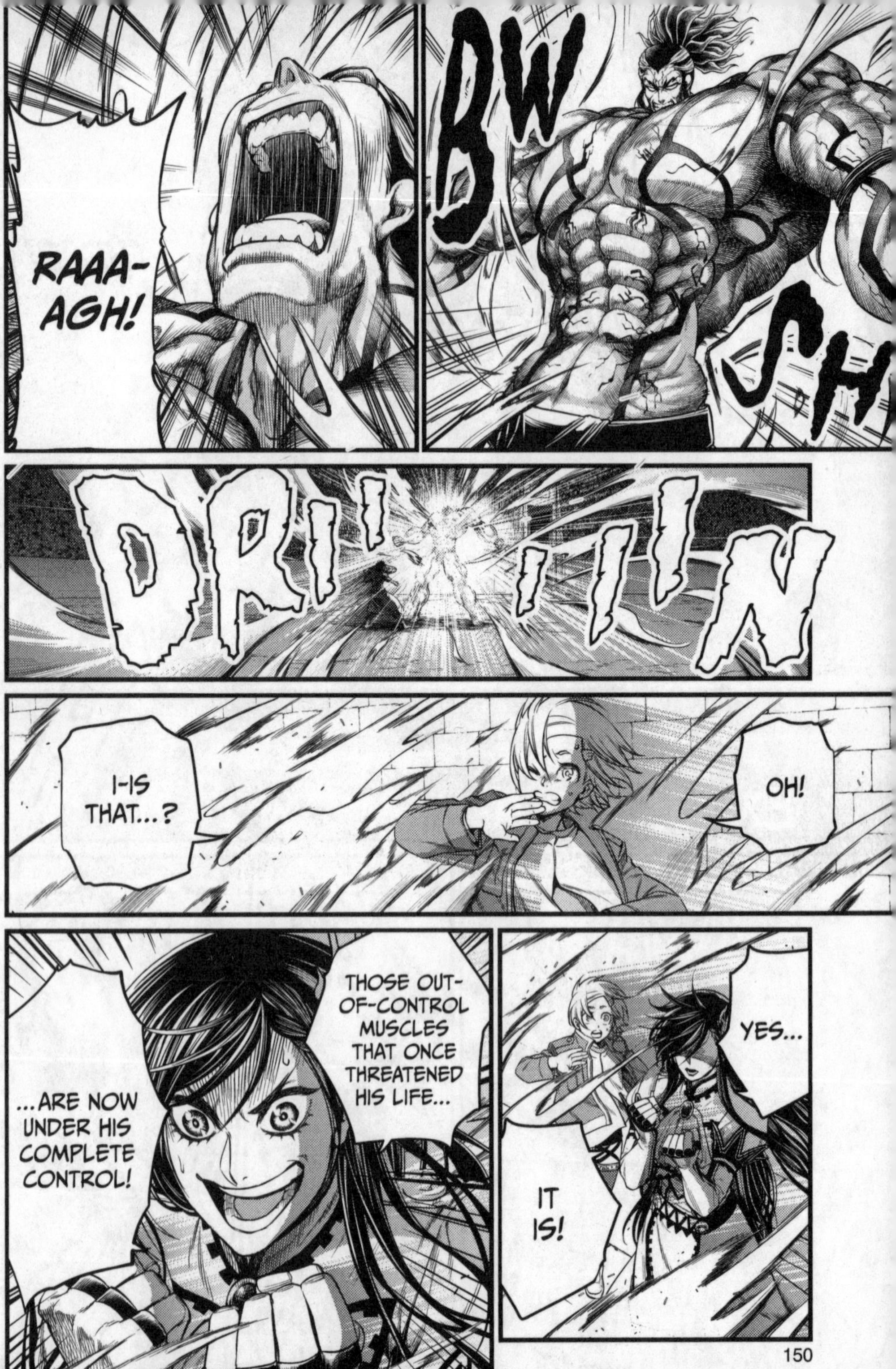
BW
SH
RAAA-AGH!
DRIIIIN
OH!
I-IS THAT...?
YES...
IT IS!
THOSE OUT-OF-CONTROL MUSCLES THAT ONCE THREATENED HIS LIFE...
...ARE NOW UNDER HIS COMPLETE CONTROL!

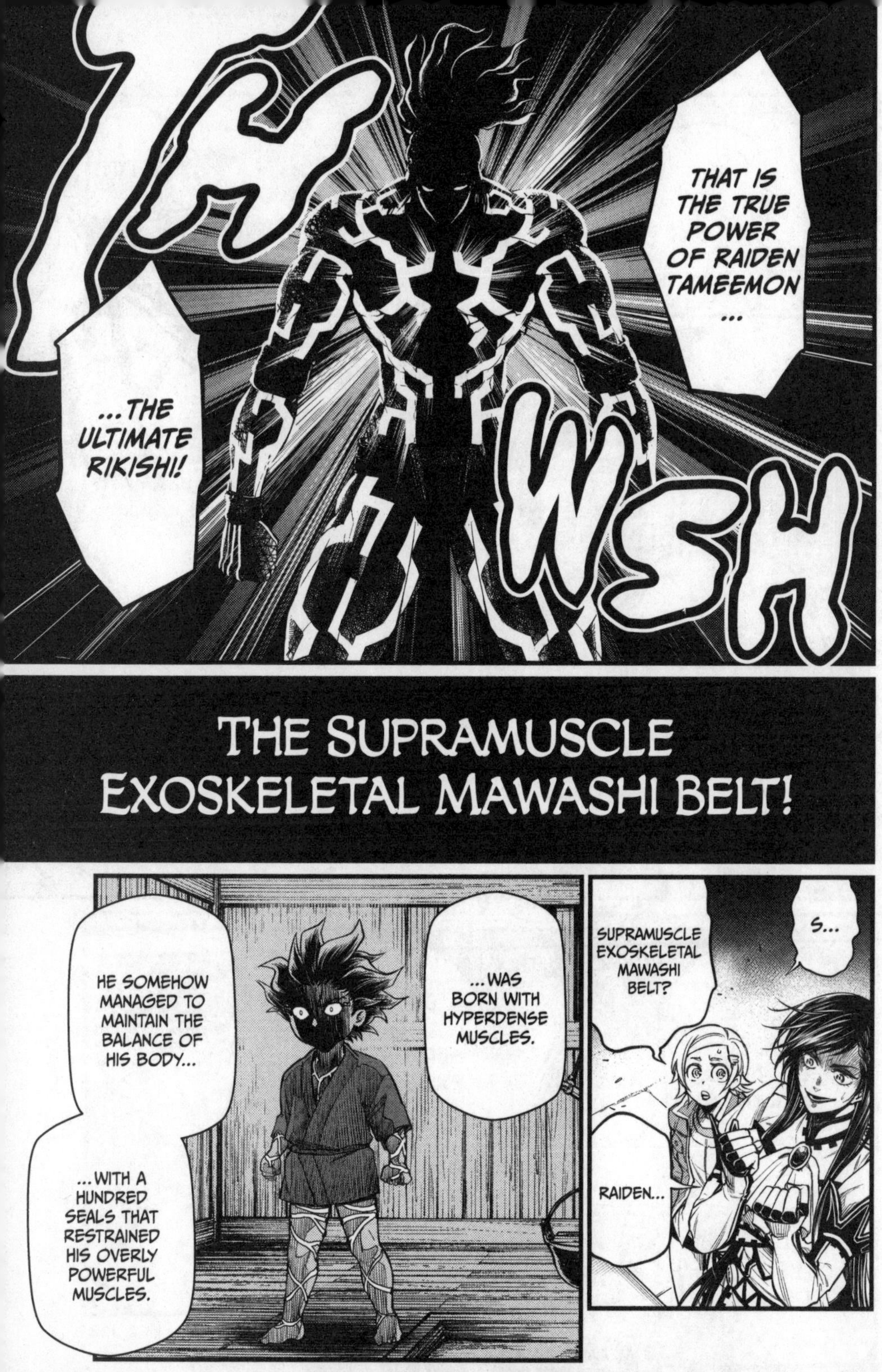
THAT IS THE TRUE POWER OF RAIDEN TAMEEMON ...
...THE ULTIMATE RIKISHI!
WSH
THE SUPRAMUSCLE EXOSKELETAL MAWASHI BELT!
S...
SUPRAMUSCLE EXOSKELETAL MAWASHI BELT?
RAIDEN...
...WAS BORN WITH HYPERDENSE MUSCLES.
HE SOMEHOW MANAGED TO MAINTAIN THE BALANCE OF HIS BODY...
...WITH A HUNDRED SEALS THAT RESTRAINED HIS OVERLY POWERFUL MUSCLES.

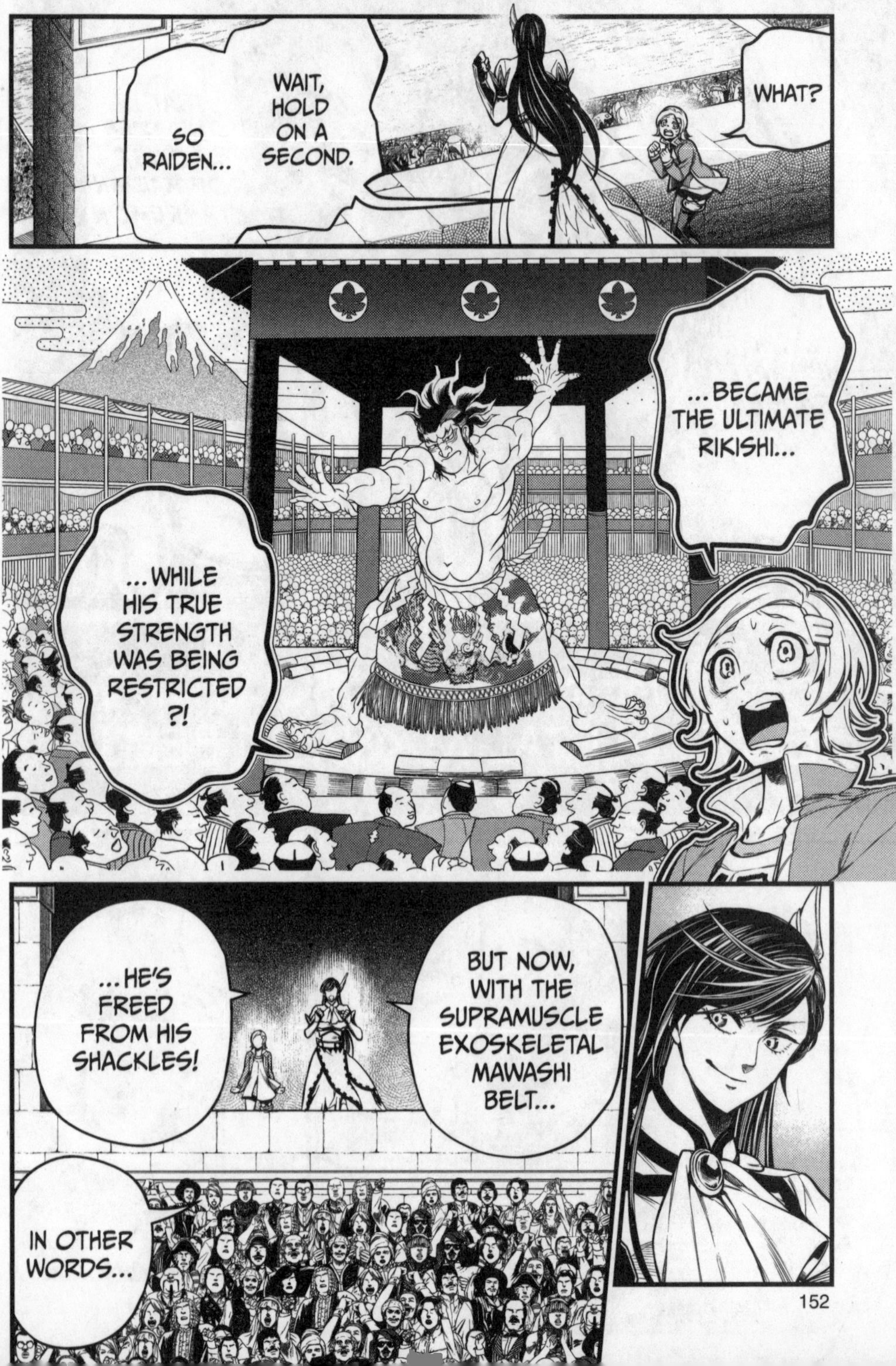
WHAT?
WAIT, HOLD ON A SECOND.
SO RAIDEN...
...BECAME THE ULTIMATE RIKISHI...
...WHILE HIS TRUE STRENGTH WAS BEING RESTRICTED ?!
BUT NOW, WITH THE SUPRAMUSCLE EXOSKELETAL MAWASHI BELT...
...HE'S FREED FROM HIS SHACKLES!
IN OTHER WORDS...

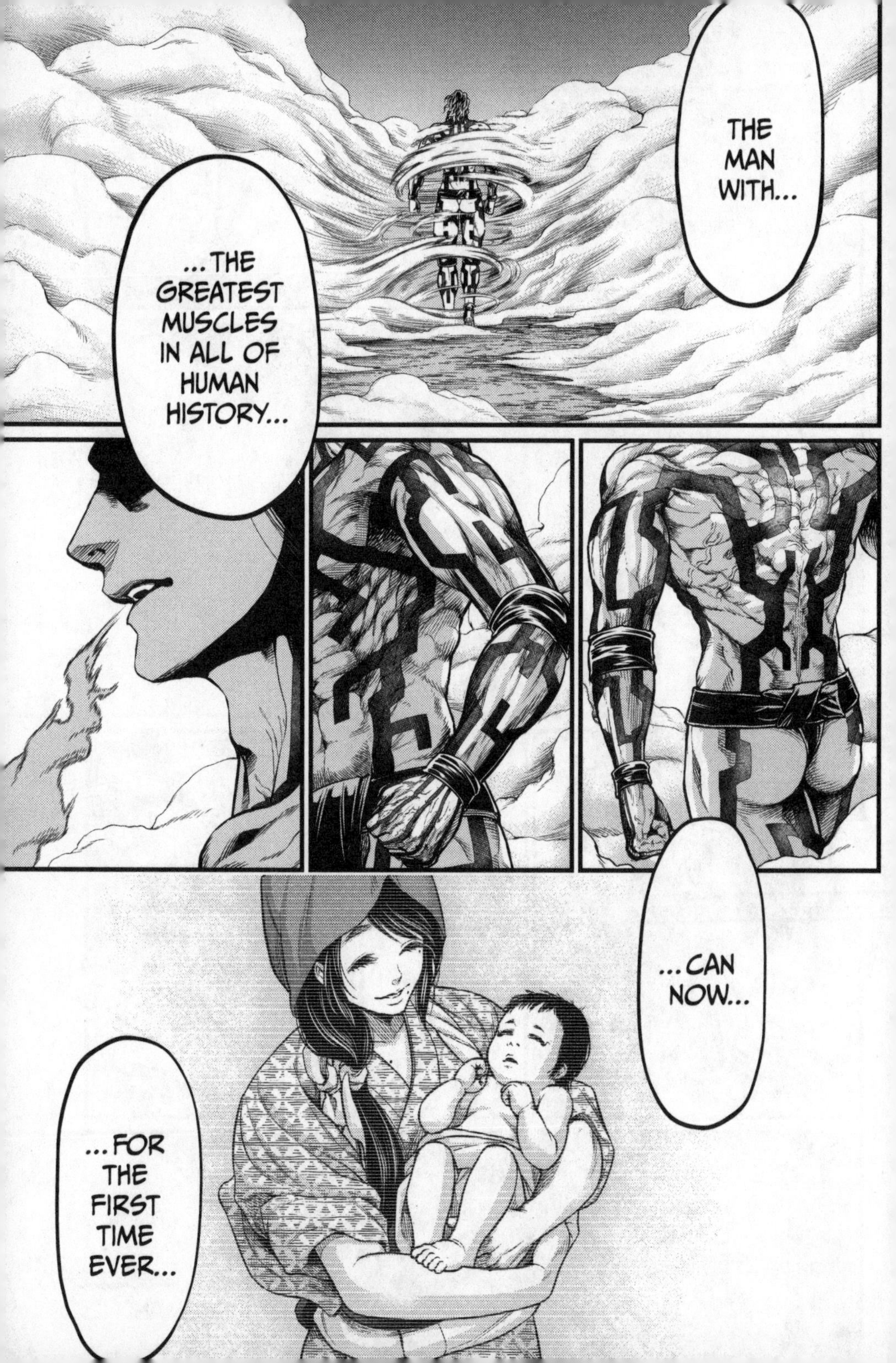
THE MAN WITH...
...THE GREATEST MUSCLES IN ALL OF HUMAN HISTORY...
...CAN NOW...
...FOR THE FIRST TIME EVER...

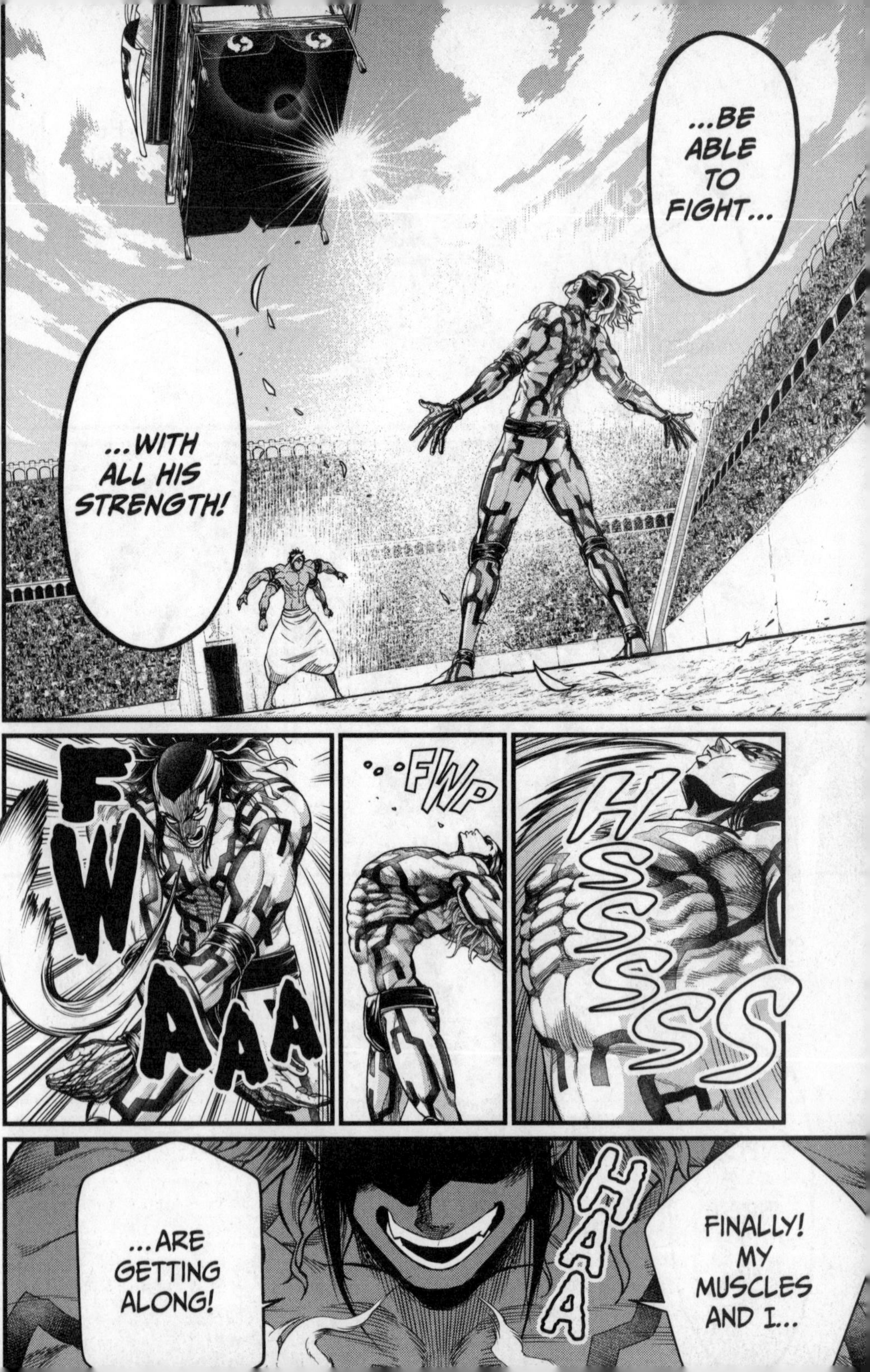
...BE ABLE TO FIGHT...
...WITH ALL HIS STRENGTH!
HSSSSSS
FWP
FWAAA
FINALLY! MY MUSCLES AND I...
HAA
...ARE GETTING ALONG!

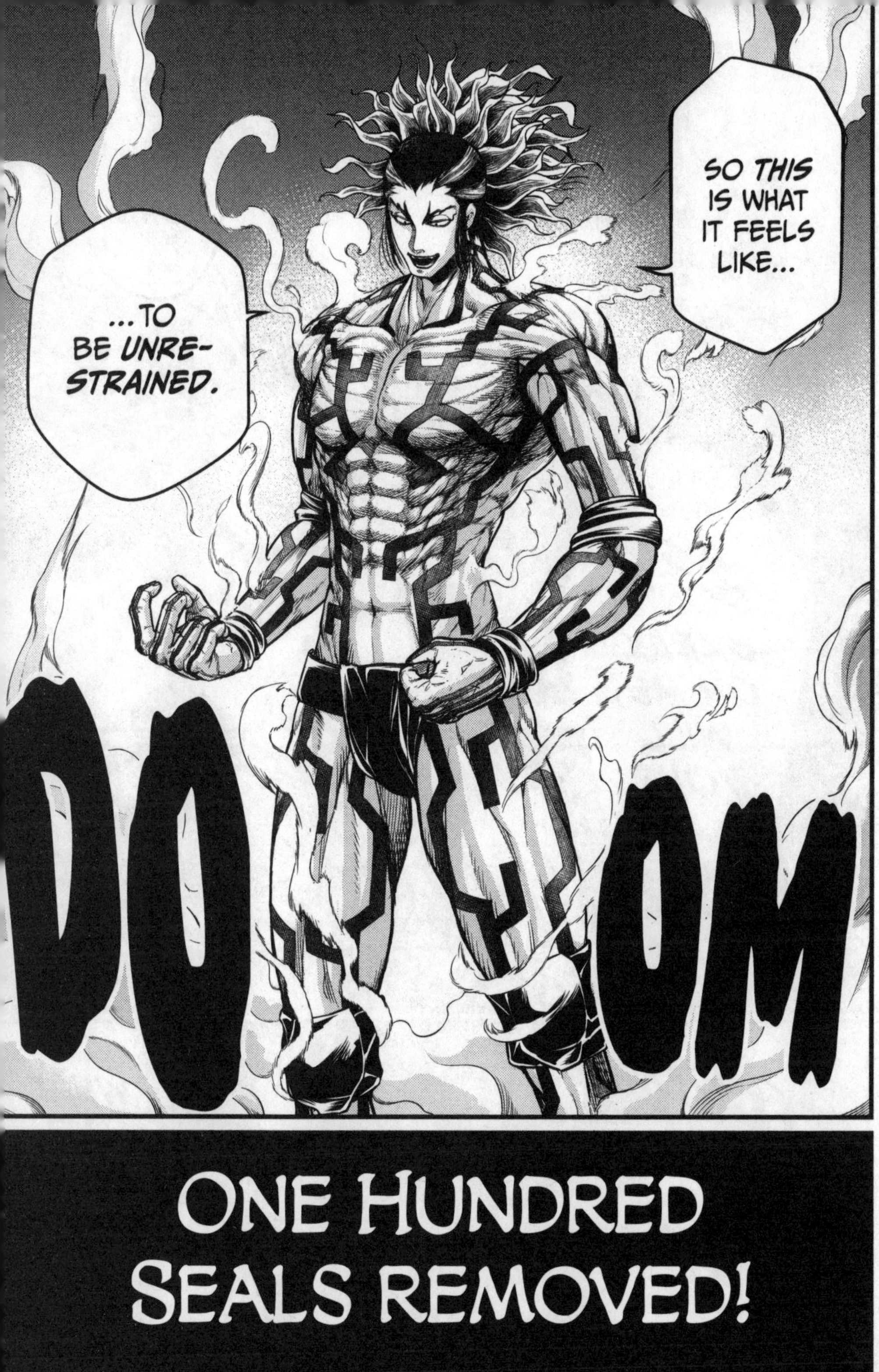
SO THIS IS WHAT IT FEELS LIKE...
...TO BE UNRE-STRAINED.
DOOM
ONE HUNDRED SEALS REMOVED!

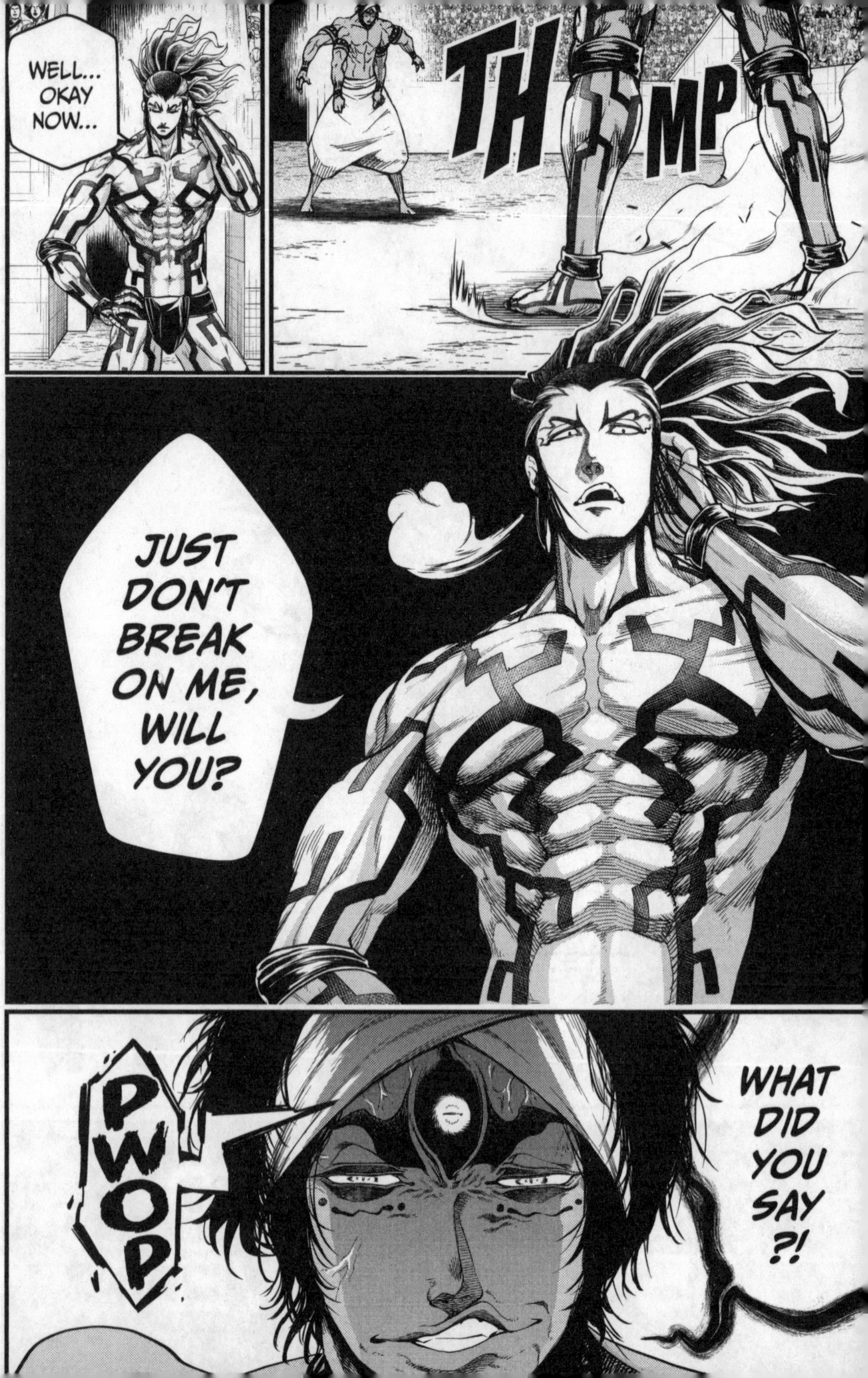
THMP
WELL... OKAY NOW...
JUST DON'T BREAK ON ME, WILL YOU?
WHAT DID YOU SAY ?!
PWOP

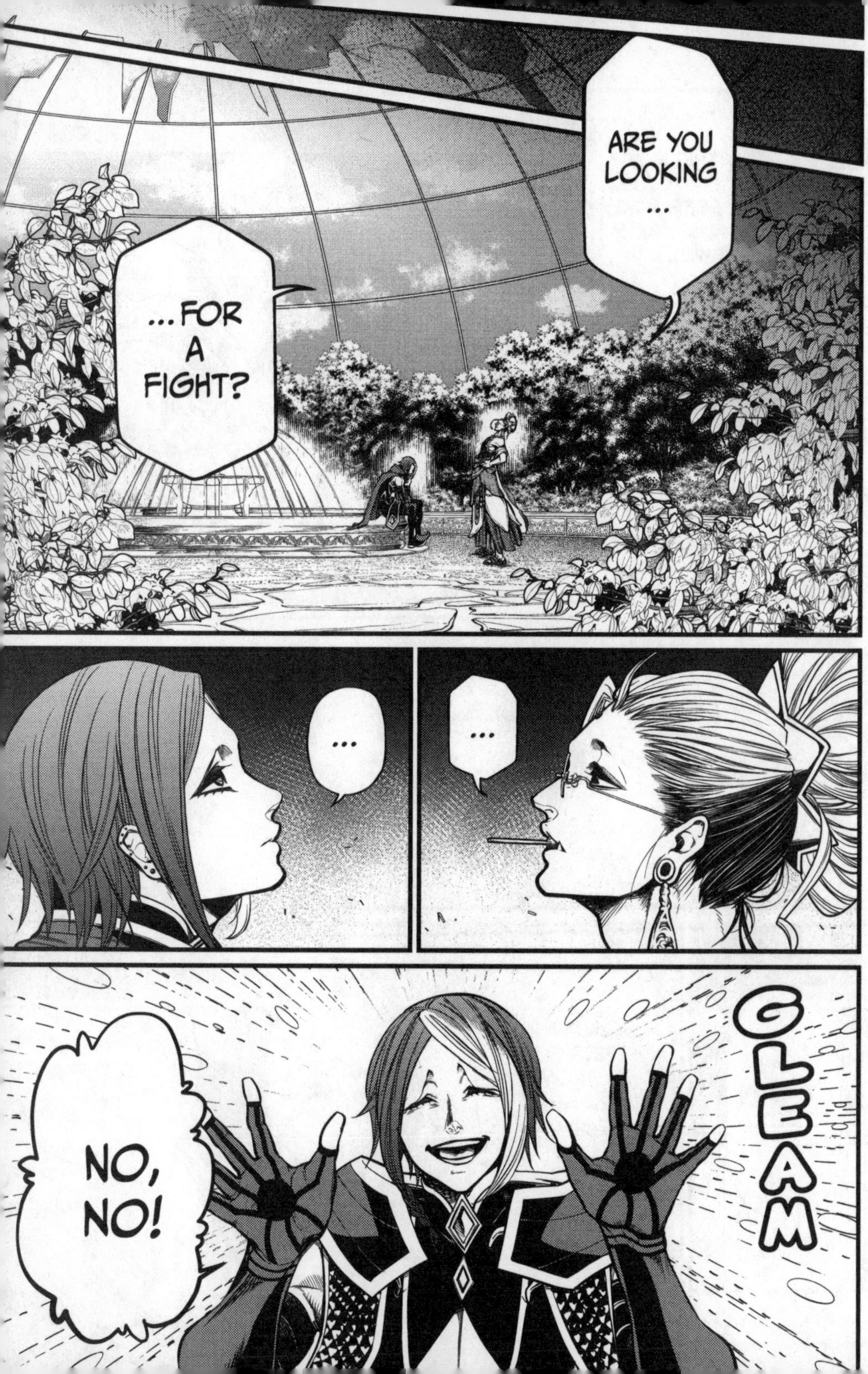
ARE YOU LOOKING ...
...FOR A FIGHT?
...
...
GLEAM
NO, NO!

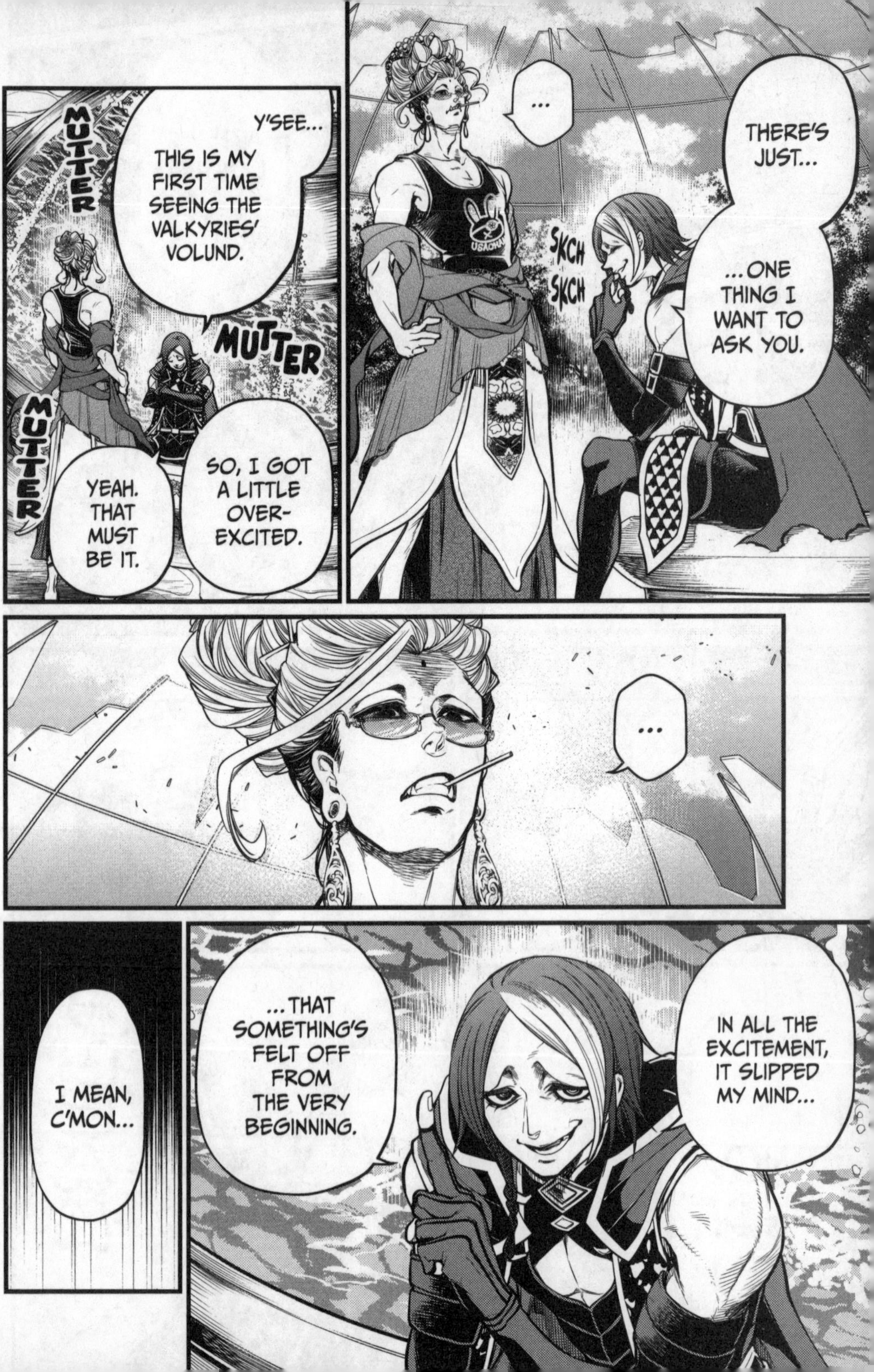
THERE'S JUST...
...ONE THING I WANT TO ASK YOU.
...
SKCH SKCH
Y'SEE...
THIS IS MY FIRST TIME SEEING THE VALKYRIES' VOLUND.
MUTTER
MUTTER
SO, I GOT A LITTLE OVER-EXCITED.
MUTTER
YEAH. THAT MUST BE IT.
...
IN ALL THE EXCITEMENT, IT SLIPPED MY MIND...
...THAT SOMETHING'S FELT OFF FROM THE VERY BEGINNING.
I MEAN, C'MON...

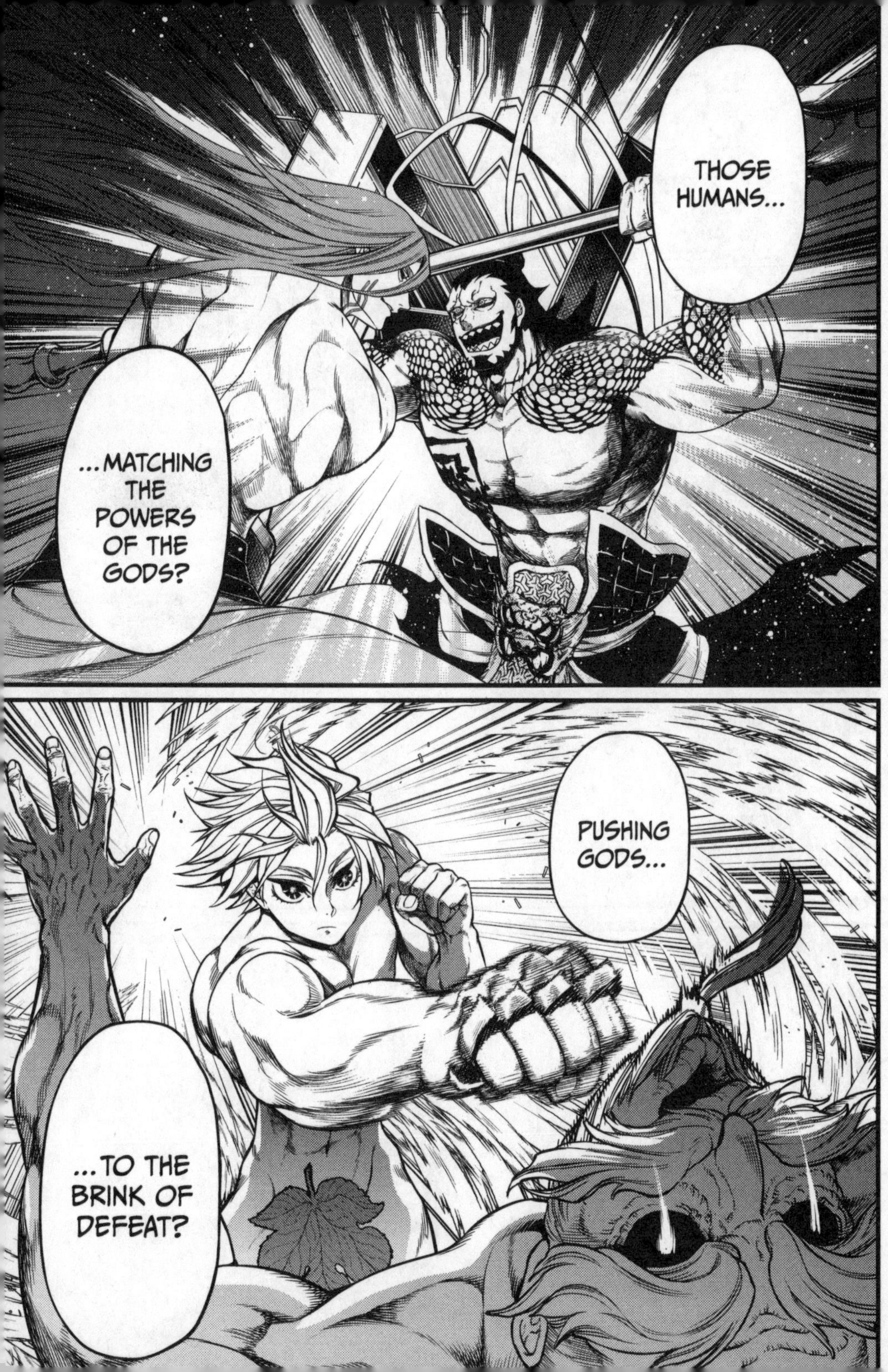
THOSE HUMANS...
...MATCHING THE POWERS OF THE GODS?
PUSHING GODS...
...TO THE BRINK OF DEFEAT?

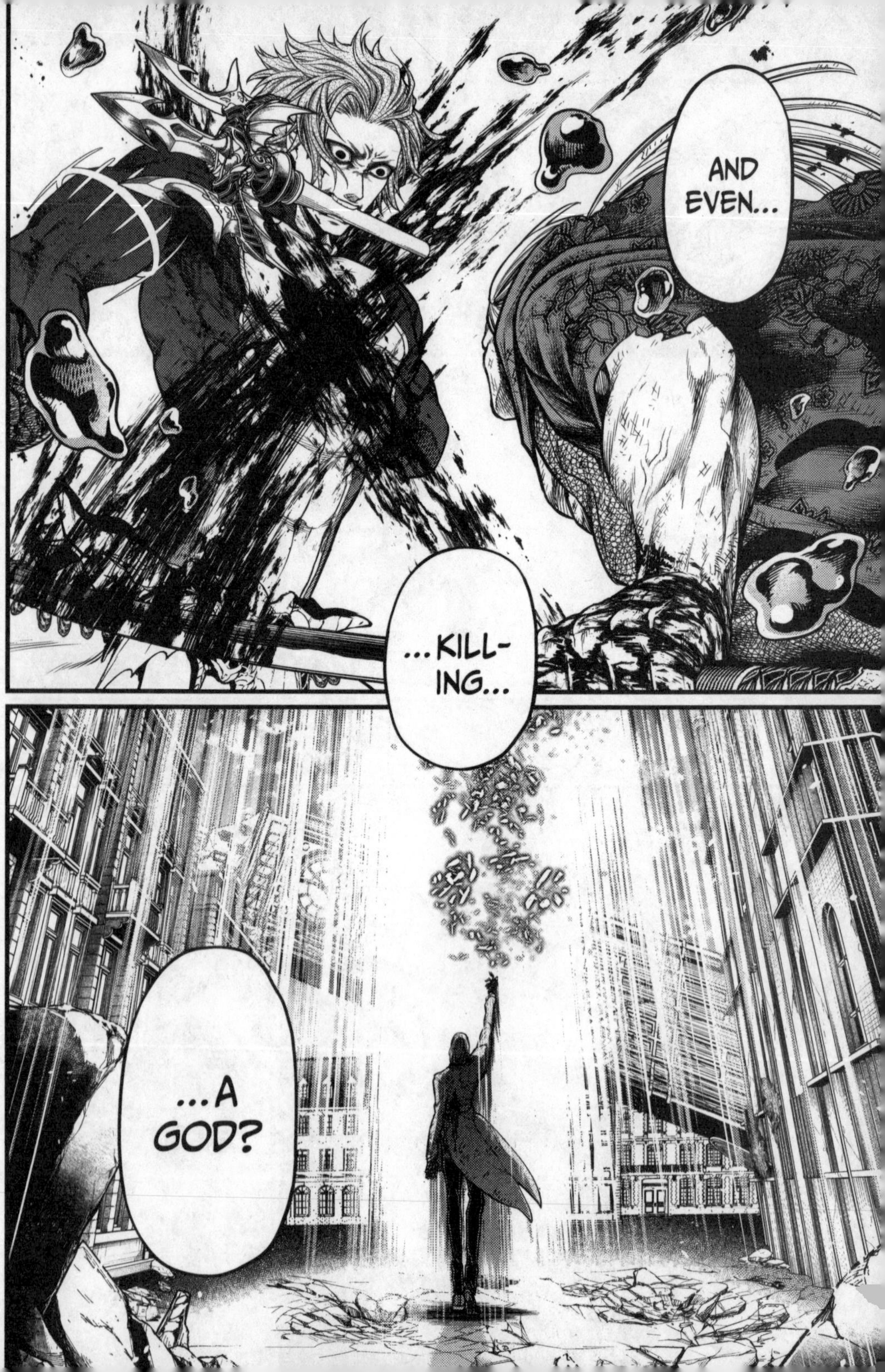
AND EVEN...
...KILL-ING...
...A GOD?

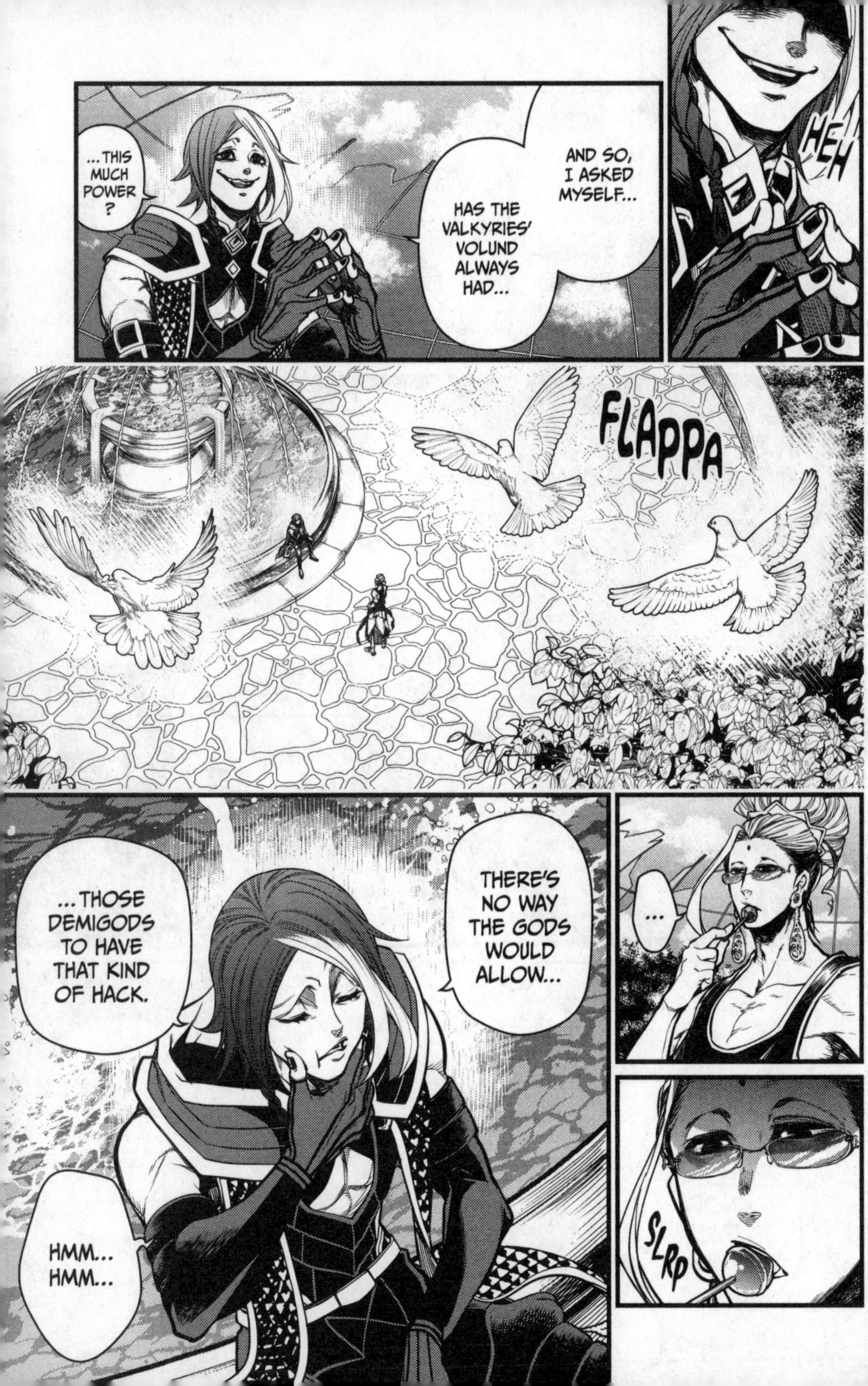
HEH
AND SO, I ASKED MYSELF...
HAS THE VALKYRIES' VOLUND ALWAYS HAD...
...THIS MUCH POWER?
FLAPPA
...
SLRP
THERE'S NO WAY THE GODS WOULD ALLOW...
...THOSE DEMIGODS TO HAVE THAT KIND OF HACK.
HMM... HMM...

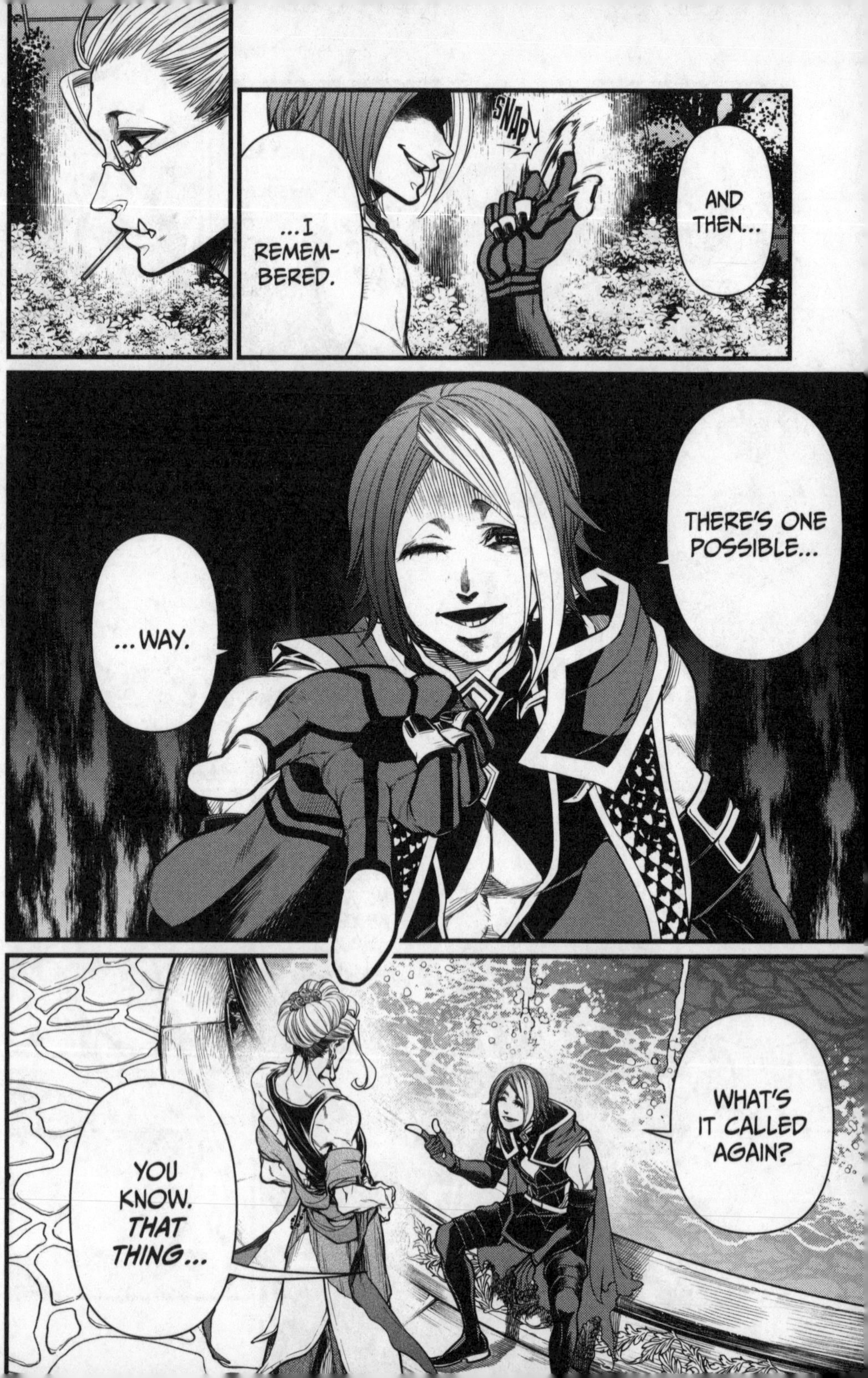
AND THEN...
SNAP
...I REMEMBERED.
THERE'S ONE POSSIBLE...
...WAY.
WHAT'S IT CALLED AGAIN?
YOU KNOW. *THAT* THING...

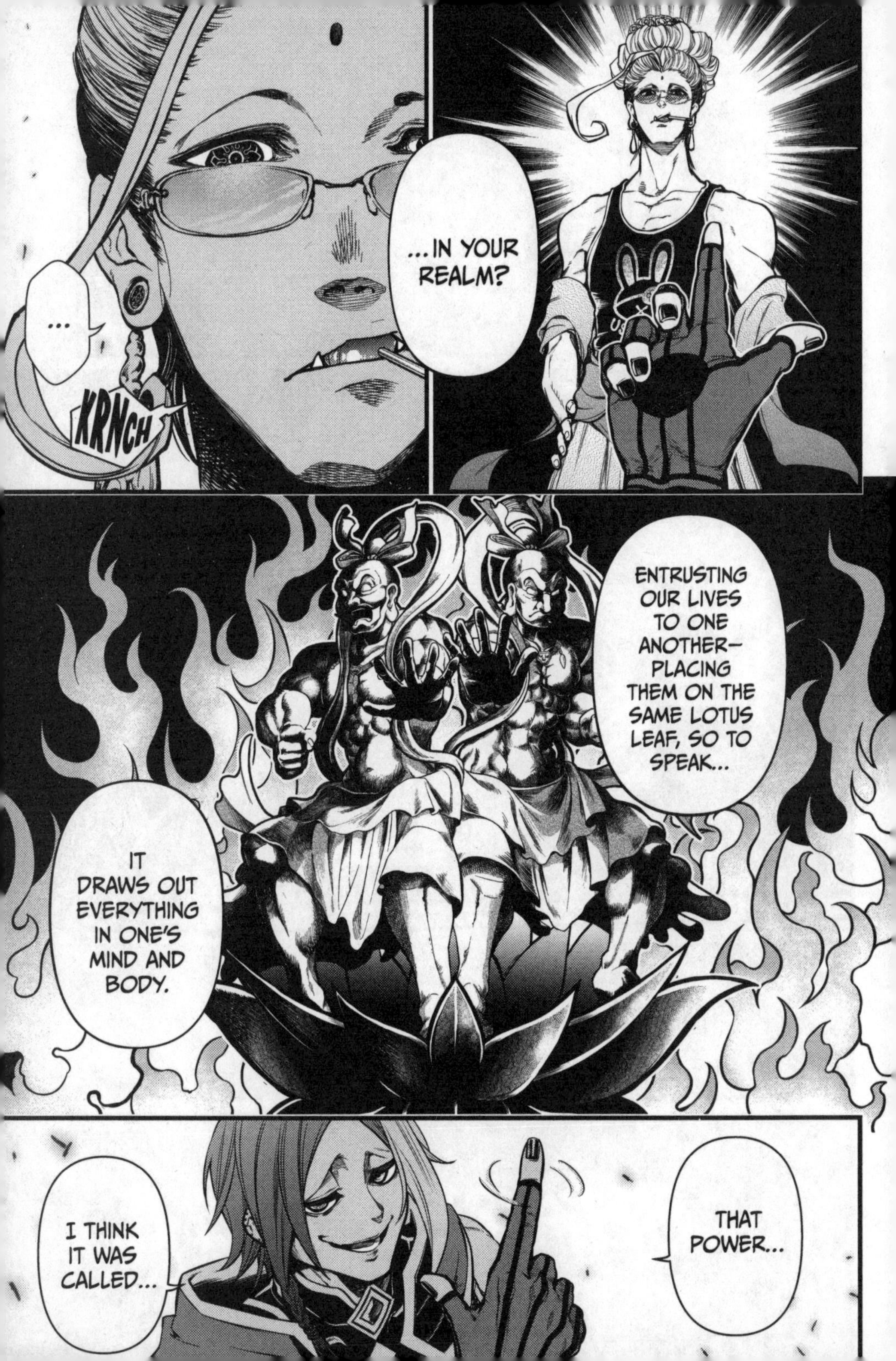
...IN YOUR REALM?
...
KRNCH
ENTRUSTING OUR LIVES TO ONE ANOTHER—PLACING THEM ON THE SAME LOTUS LEAF, SO TO SPEAK...
IT DRAWS OUT EVERYTHING IN ONE'S MIND AND BODY.
THAT POWER...
I THINK IT WAS CALLED...

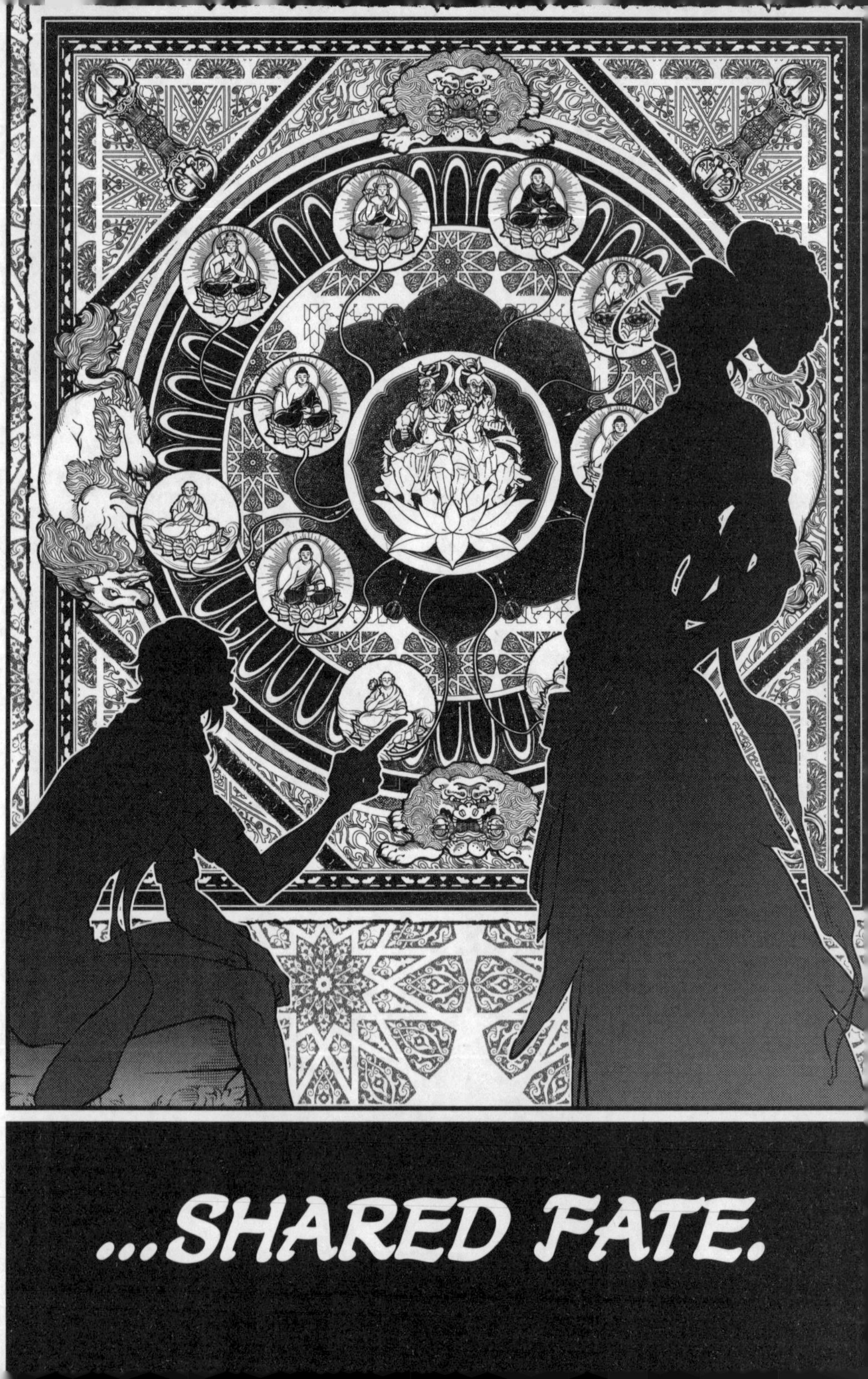
...SHARED FATE.

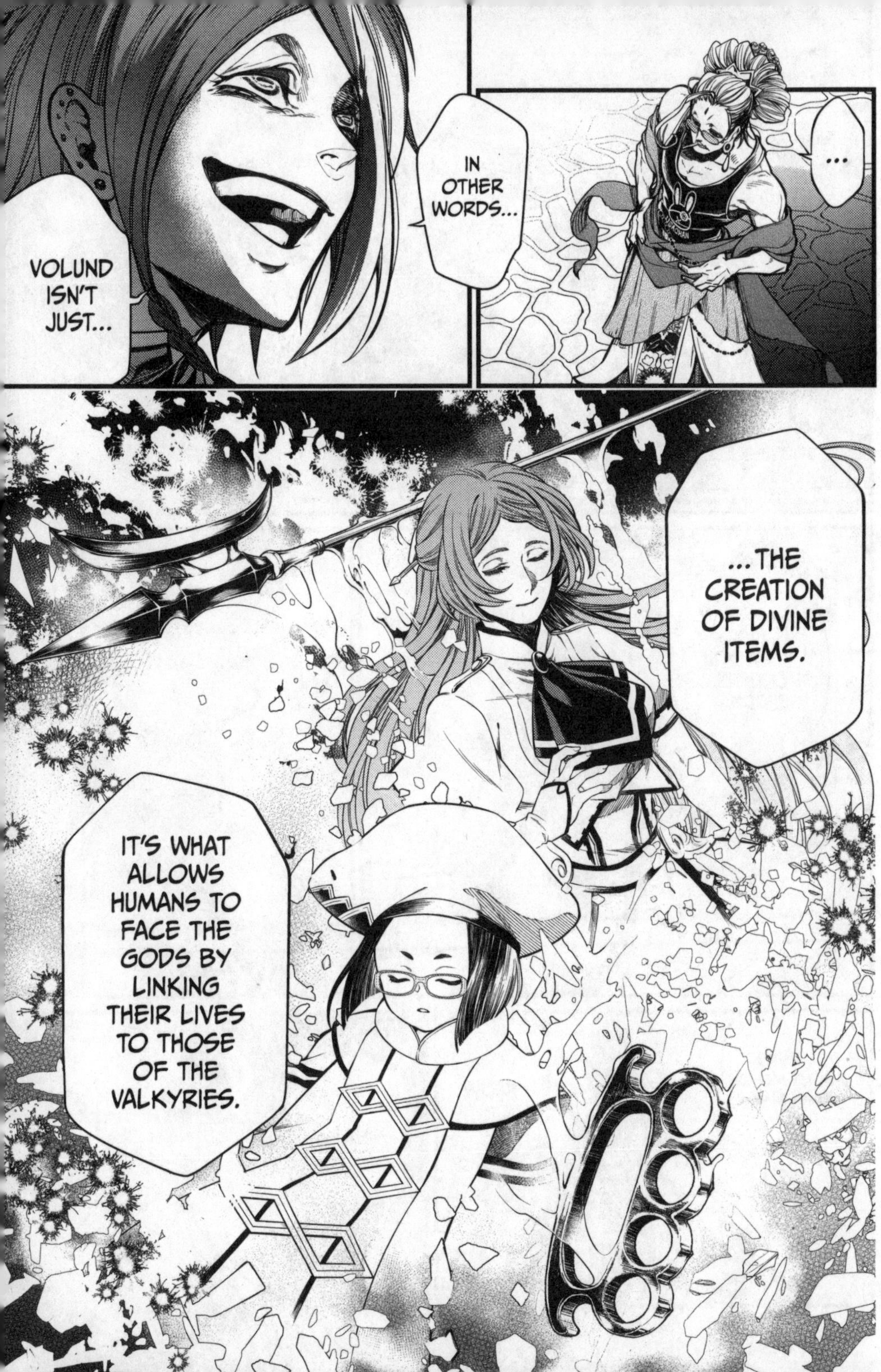
...
IN OTHER WORDS...
VOLUND ISN'T JUST...
...THE CREATION OF DIVINE ITEMS.
IT'S WHAT ALLOWS HUMANS TO FACE THE GODS BY LINKING THEIR LIVES TO THOSE OF THE VALKYRIES.

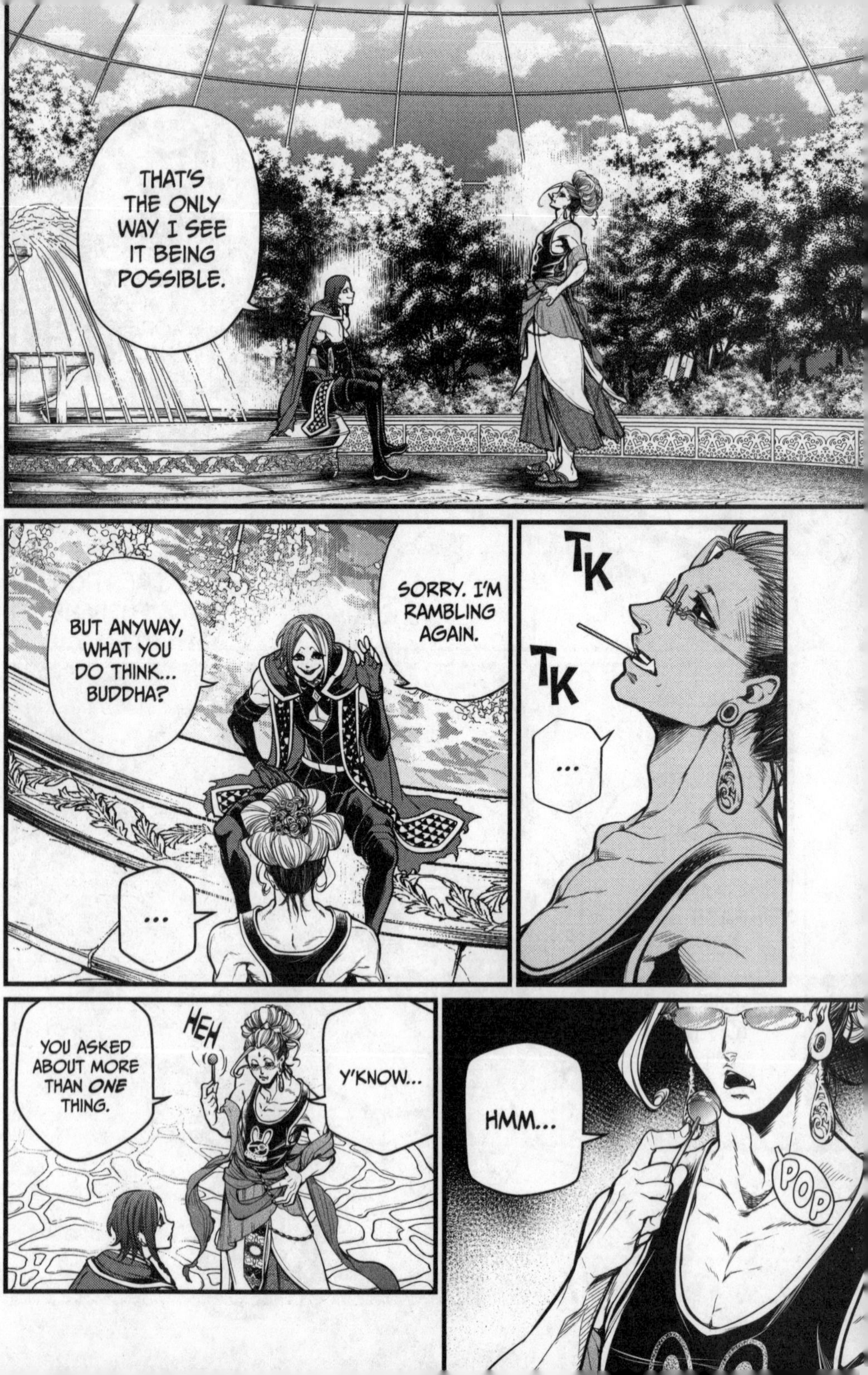
THAT'S THE ONLY WAY I SEE IT BEING POSSIBLE.
TK
TK
...
SORRY. I'M RAMBLING AGAIN.
BUT ANYWAY, WHAT YOU DO THINK... BUDDHA?
...
HMM...
POP
Y'KNOW...
YOU ASKED ABOUT MORE THAN *ONE* THING.
HEH

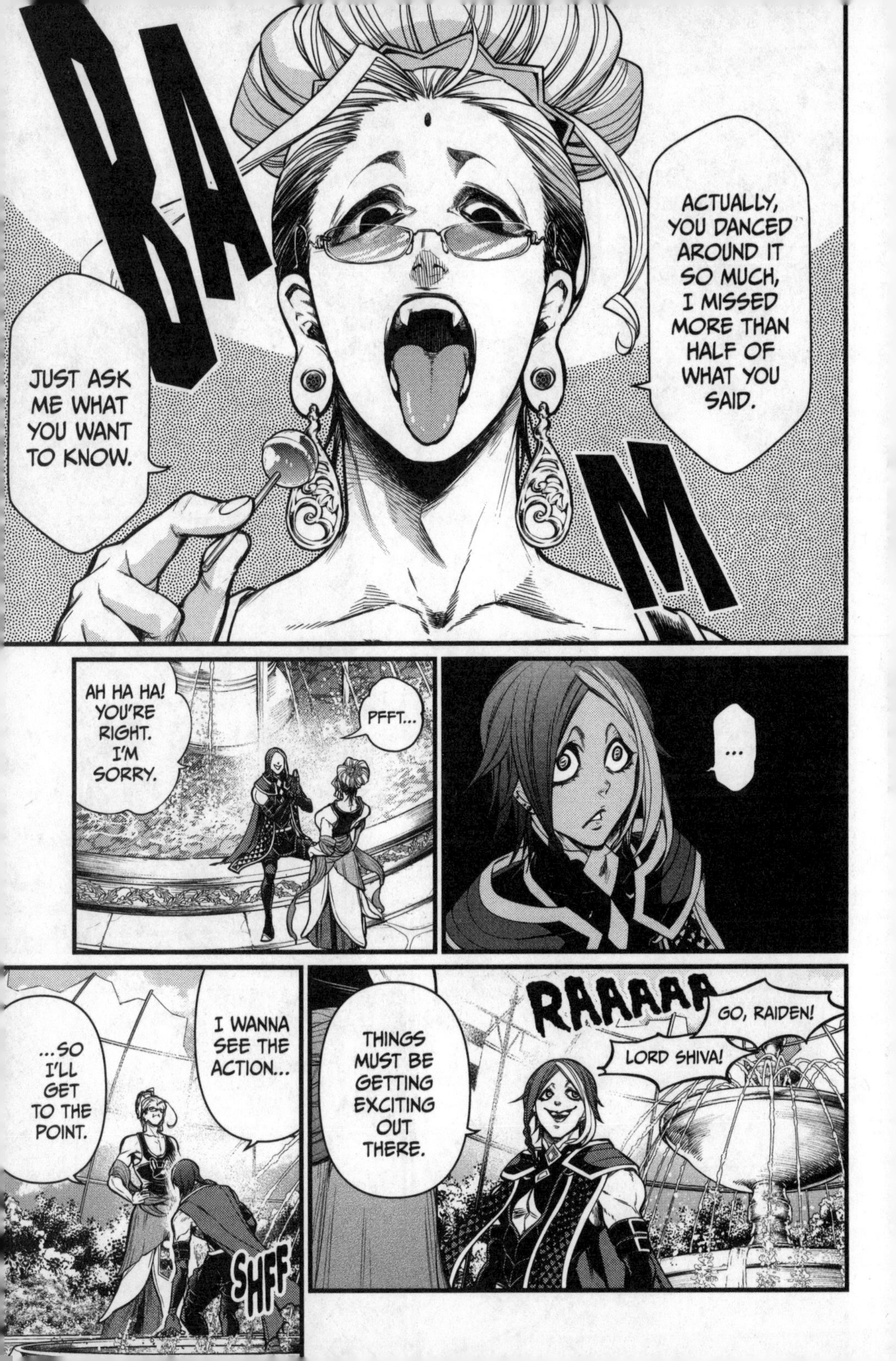
RAM
ACTUALLY, YOU DANCED AROUND IT SO MUCH, I MISSED MORE THAN HALF OF WHAT YOU SAID.
JUST ASK ME WHAT YOU WANT TO KNOW.
...
PFFT...
AH HA HA! YOU'RE RIGHT. I'M SORRY.
RAAAAA
GO, RAIDEN!
LORD SHIVA!
THINGS MUST BE GETTING EXCITING OUT THERE.
I WANNA SEE THE ACTION...
...SO I'LL GET TO THE POINT.
SHFF

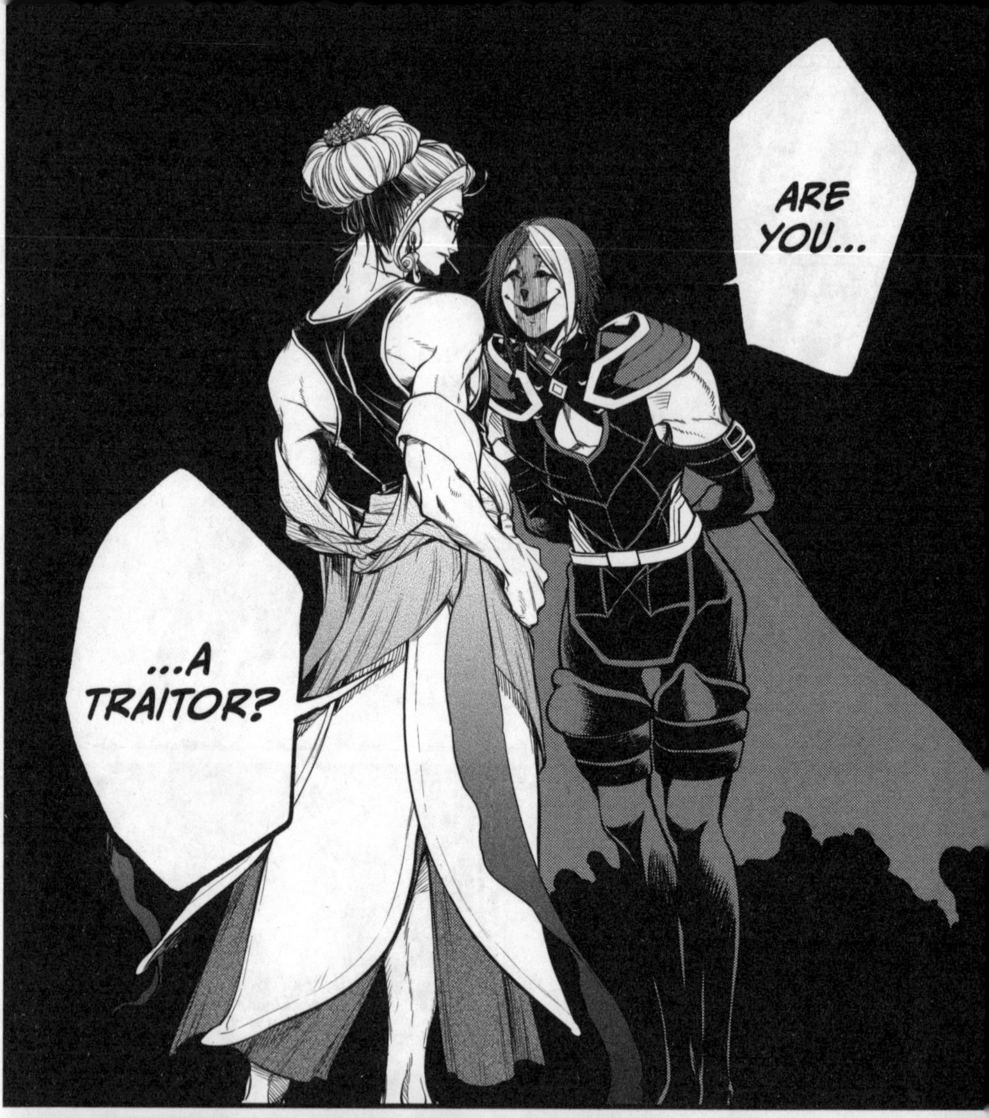
ARE YOU...
...A TRAITOR?
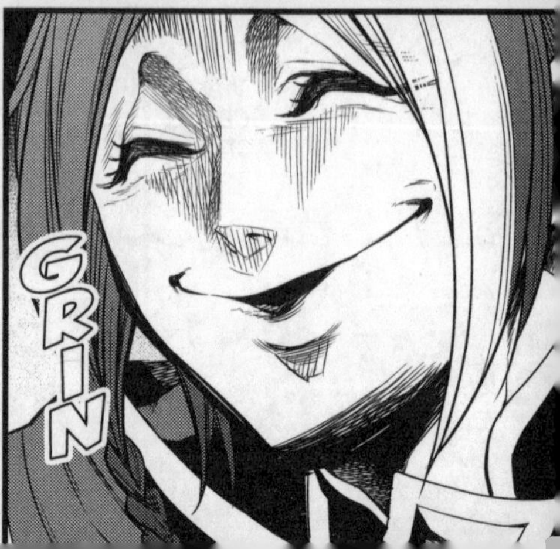
GRIN
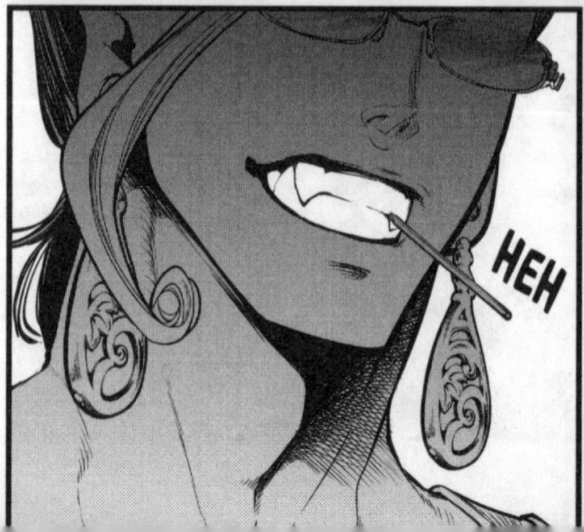
HEH

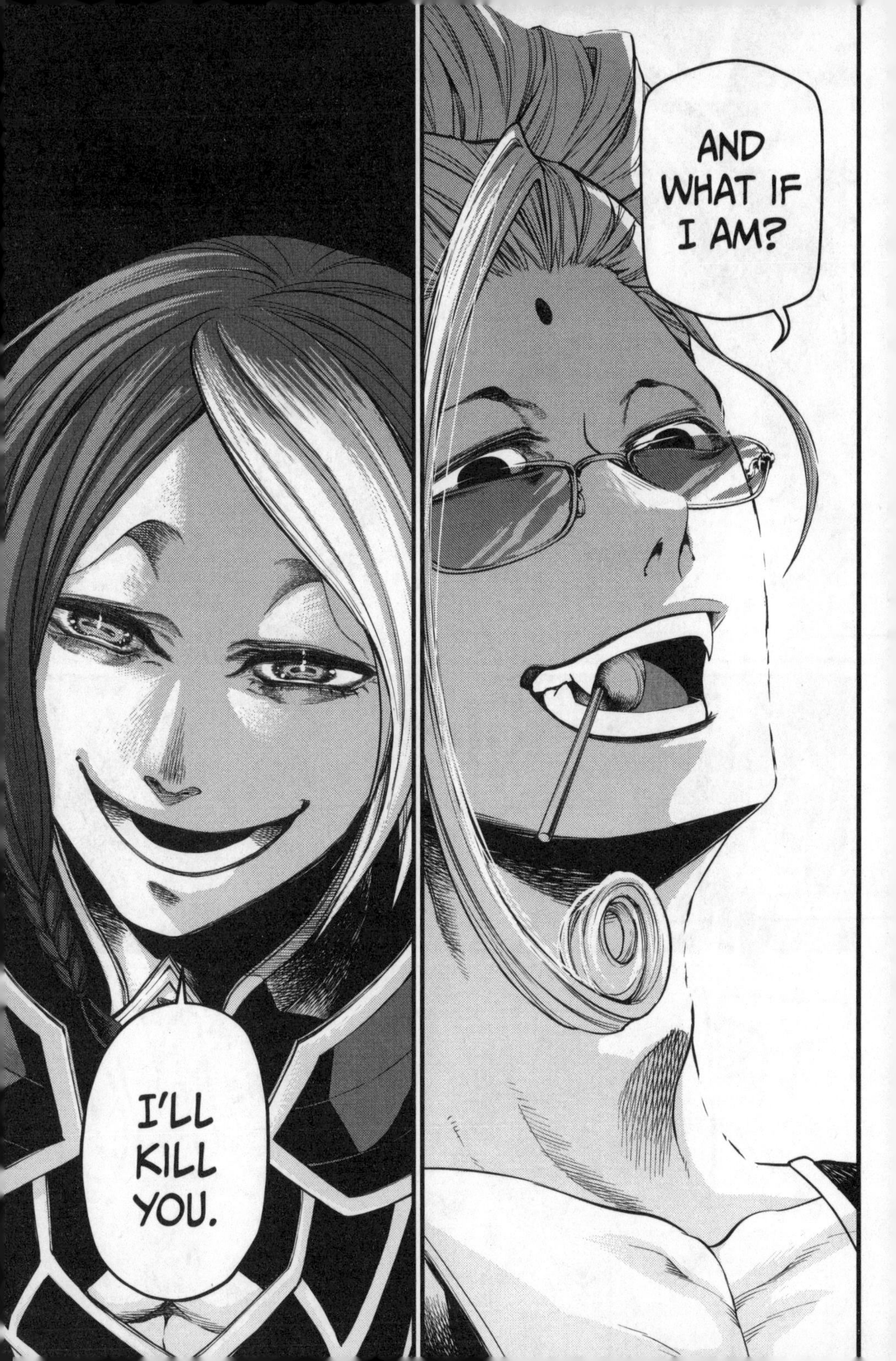
AND WHAT IF I AM?
I'LL KILL YOU.

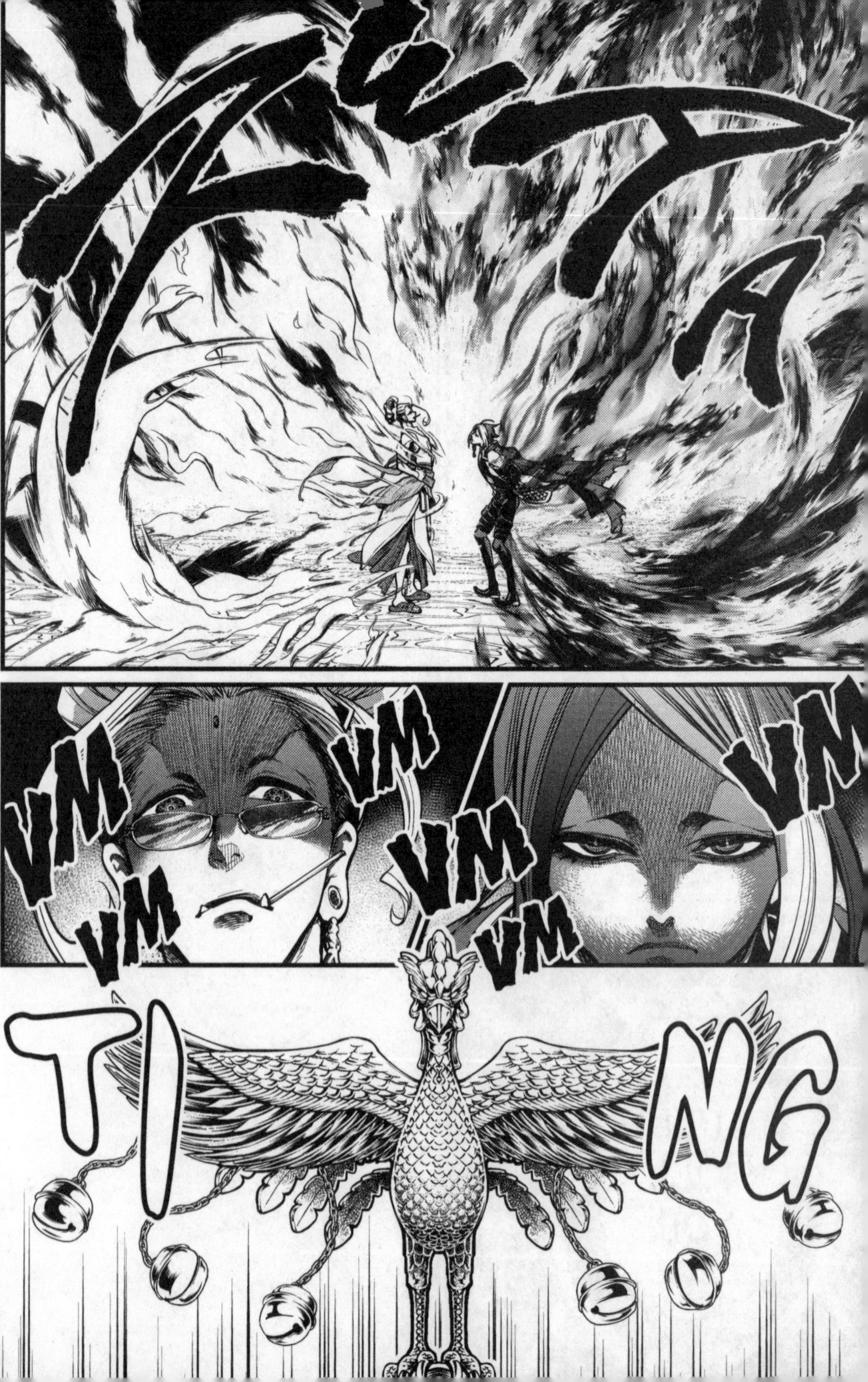
VM
VM
VM
VM
VM
VM
TING

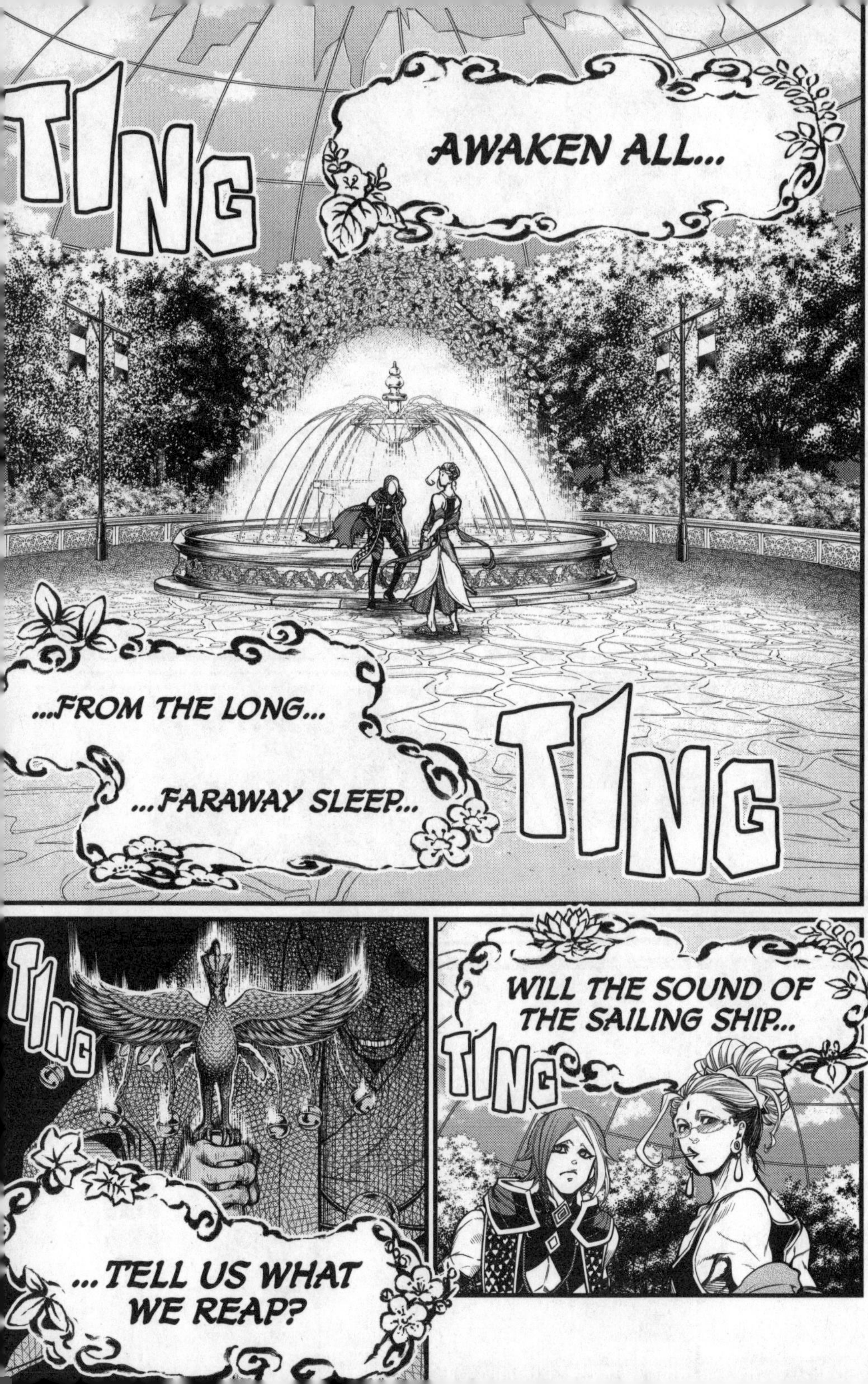
AWAKEN ALL...
TING
TING
...FROM THE LONG...
...FARAWAY SLEEP...
WILL THE SOUND OF THE SAILING SHIP...
TING
TING
...TELL US WHAT WE REAP?

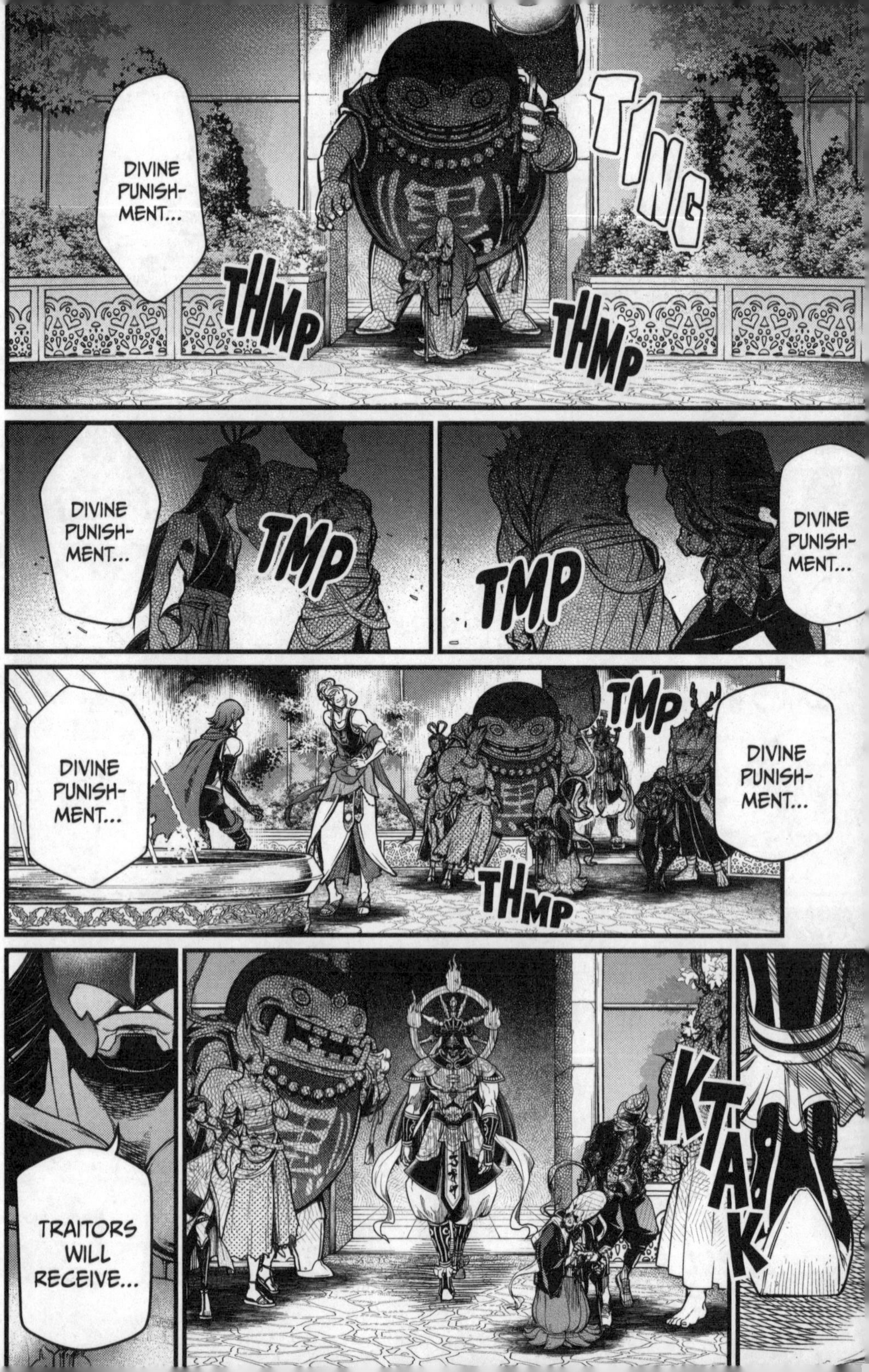
TING
DIVINE PUNISH-MENT...
THMP
THMP
DIVINE PUNISH-MENT...
TMP
TMP
DIVINE PUNISH-MENT...
TMP
DIVINE PUNISH-MENT...
DIVINE PUNISH-MENT...
THMP
KTAK
TRAITORS WILL RECEIVE...

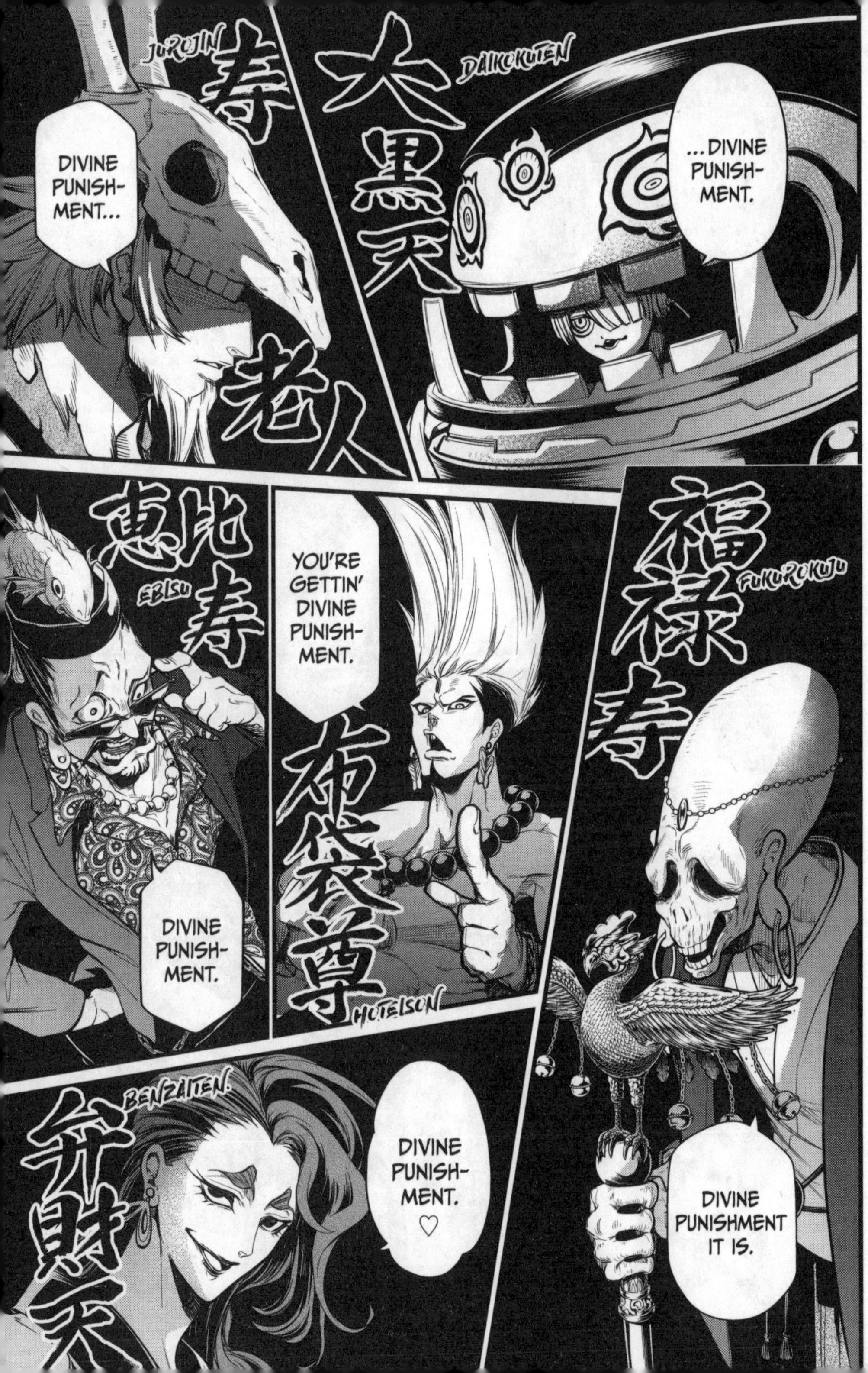
大黒天
DAIKOKUTEN
...DIVINE PUNISHMENT.
寿老人
JUROJIN
DIVINE PUNISHMENT...
福禄寿
FUKUROKUJU
DIVINE PUNISHMENT IT IS.
YOU'RE GETTIN' DIVINE PUNISHMENT.
布袋尊
HOTEISON
恵比寿
EBISU
DIVINE PUNISHMENT.
弁財天
BENZAITEN.
DIVINE PUNISHMENT. ♡

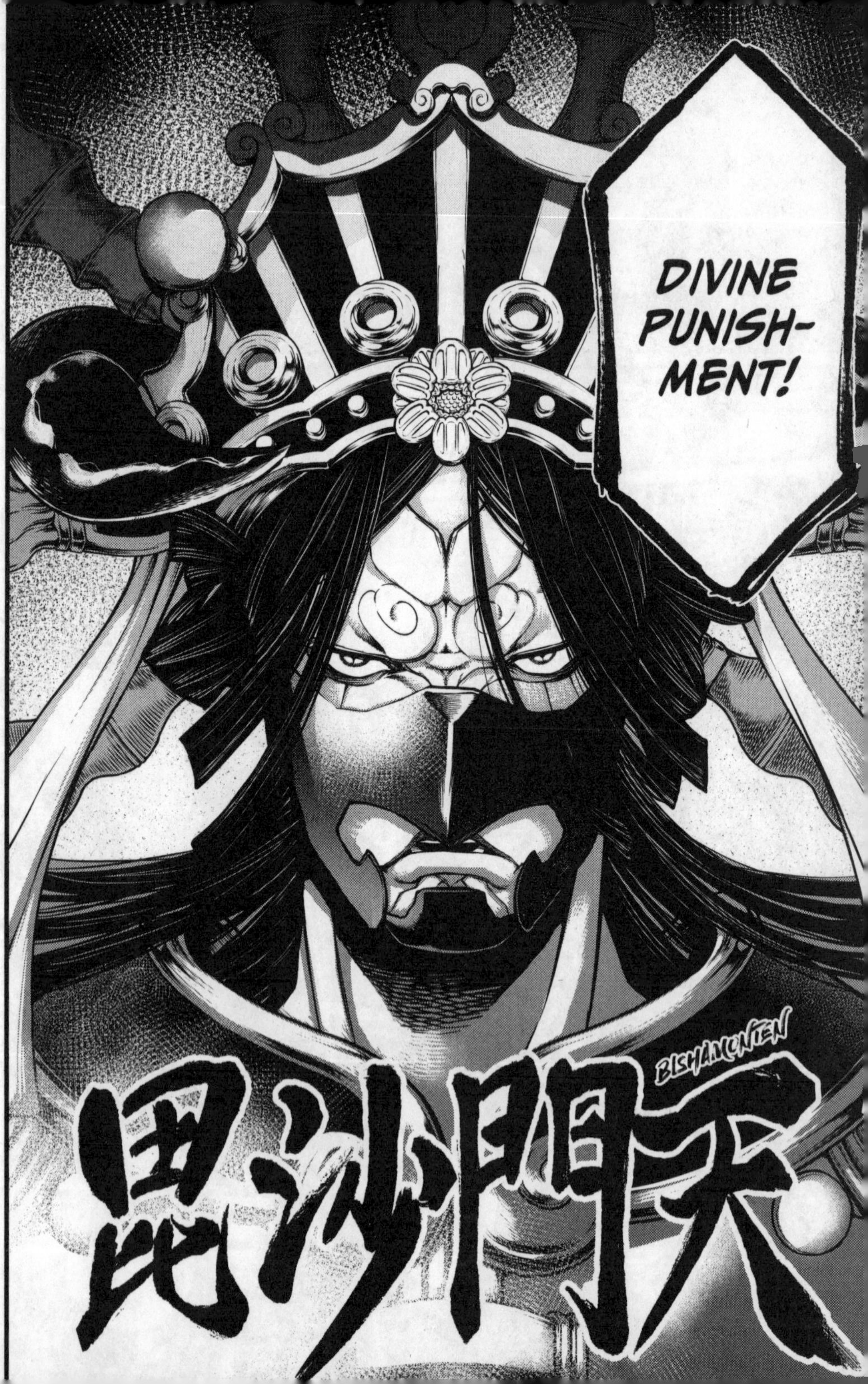
DIVINE PUNISH-MENT!
BISHAMONTEN
毘沙門天

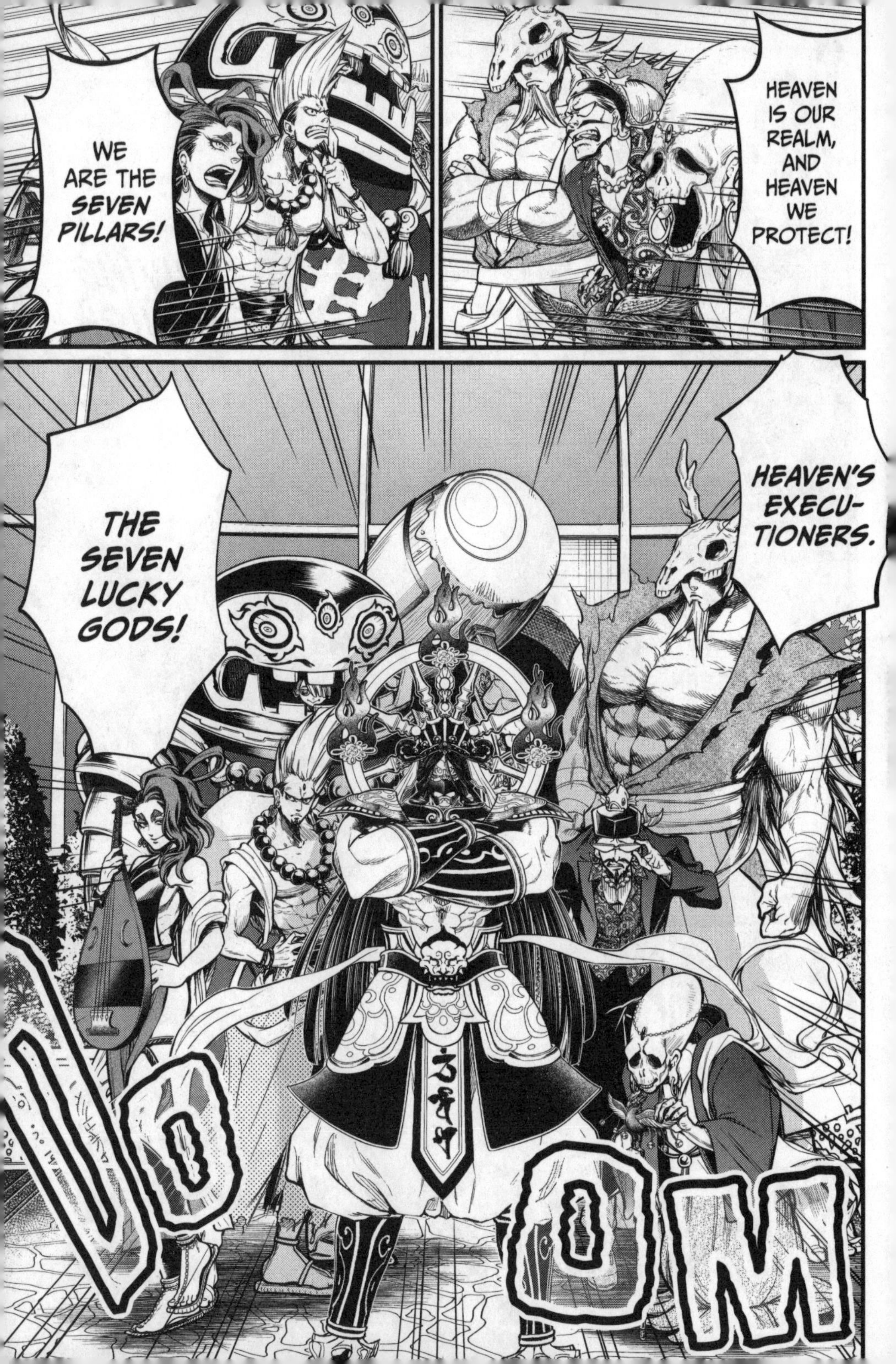
HEAVEN IS OUR REALM, AND HEAVEN WE PROTECT!
WE ARE THE SEVEN PILLARS!
HEAVEN'S EXECUTIONERS.
THE SEVEN LUCKY GODS!
VOOM

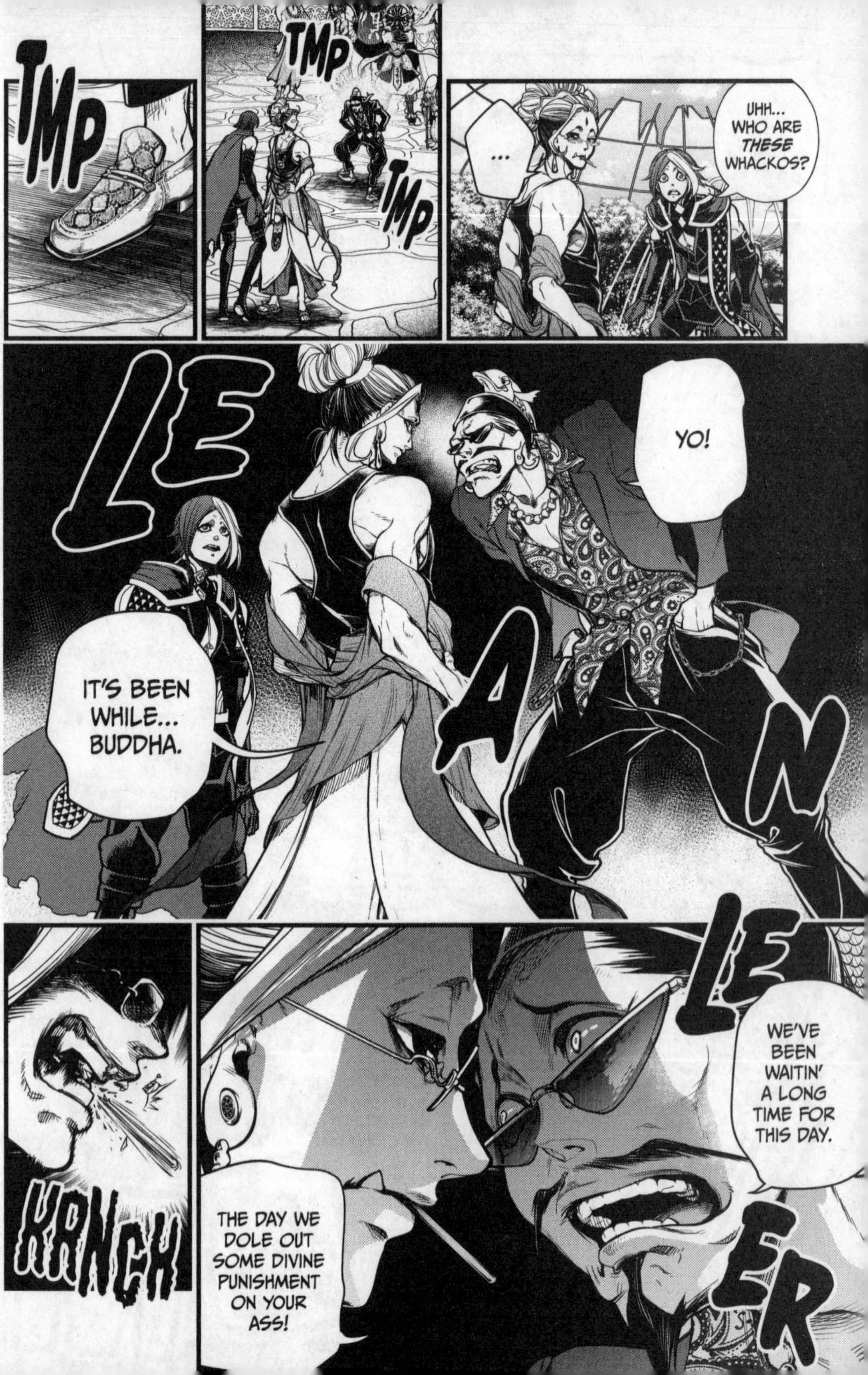
UHH... WHO ARE THESE WHACKOS?
...
TMP
TMP
TMP
YO!
LEAN
IT'S BEEN WHILE... BUDDHA.
LEER
WE'VE BEEN WAITIN' A LONG TIME FOR THIS DAY.
THE DAY WE DOLE OUT SOME DIVINE PUNISHMENT ON YOUR ASS!
KRNCH

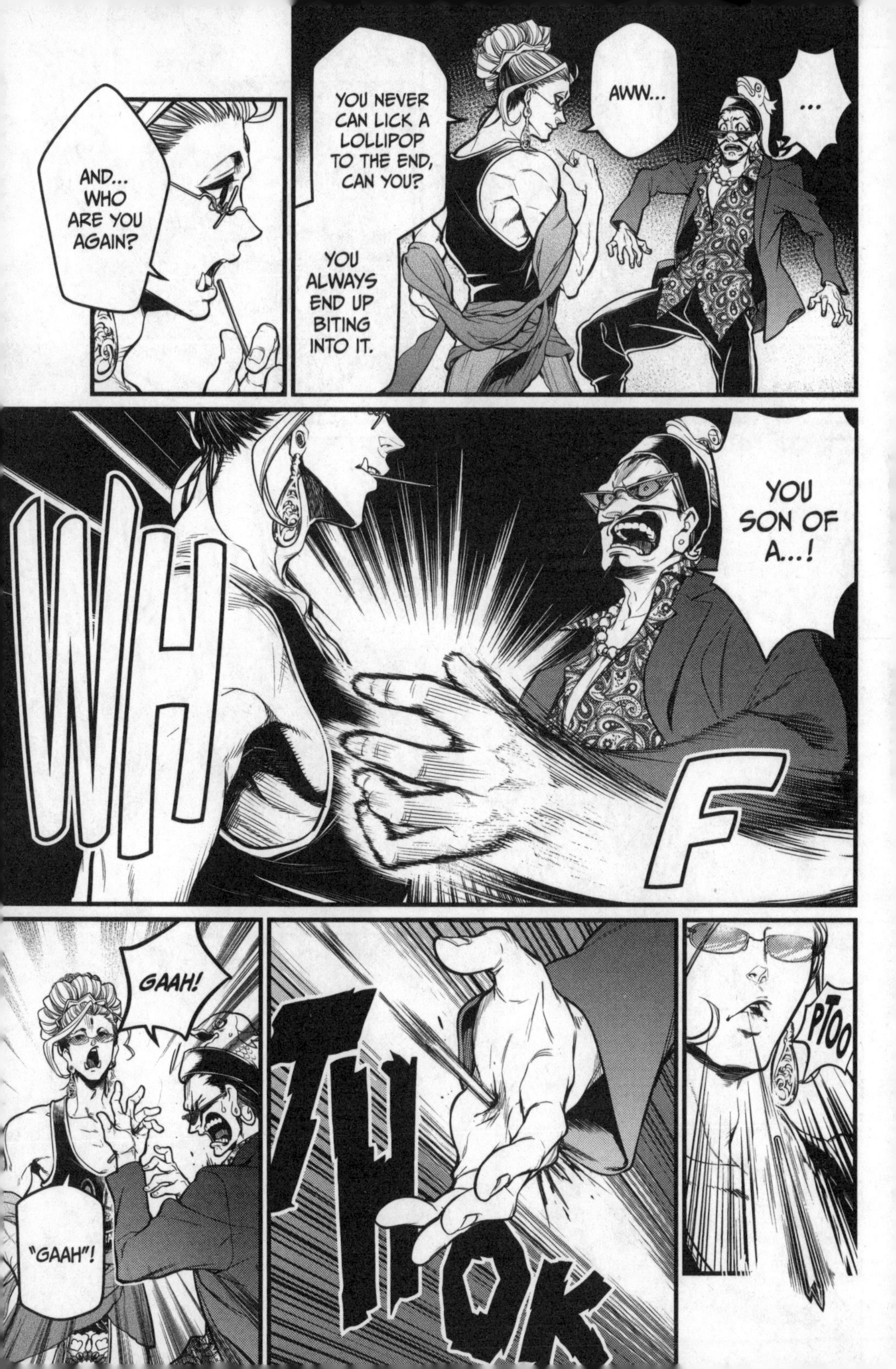
...
AWW...
YOU NEVER CAN LICK A LOLLIPOP TO THE END, CAN YOU?
YOU ALWAYS END UP BITING INTO IT.
AND... WHO ARE YOU AGAIN?
YOU SON OF A...!
WHF
PTOO
THOK
GAAH!
"GAAH"!

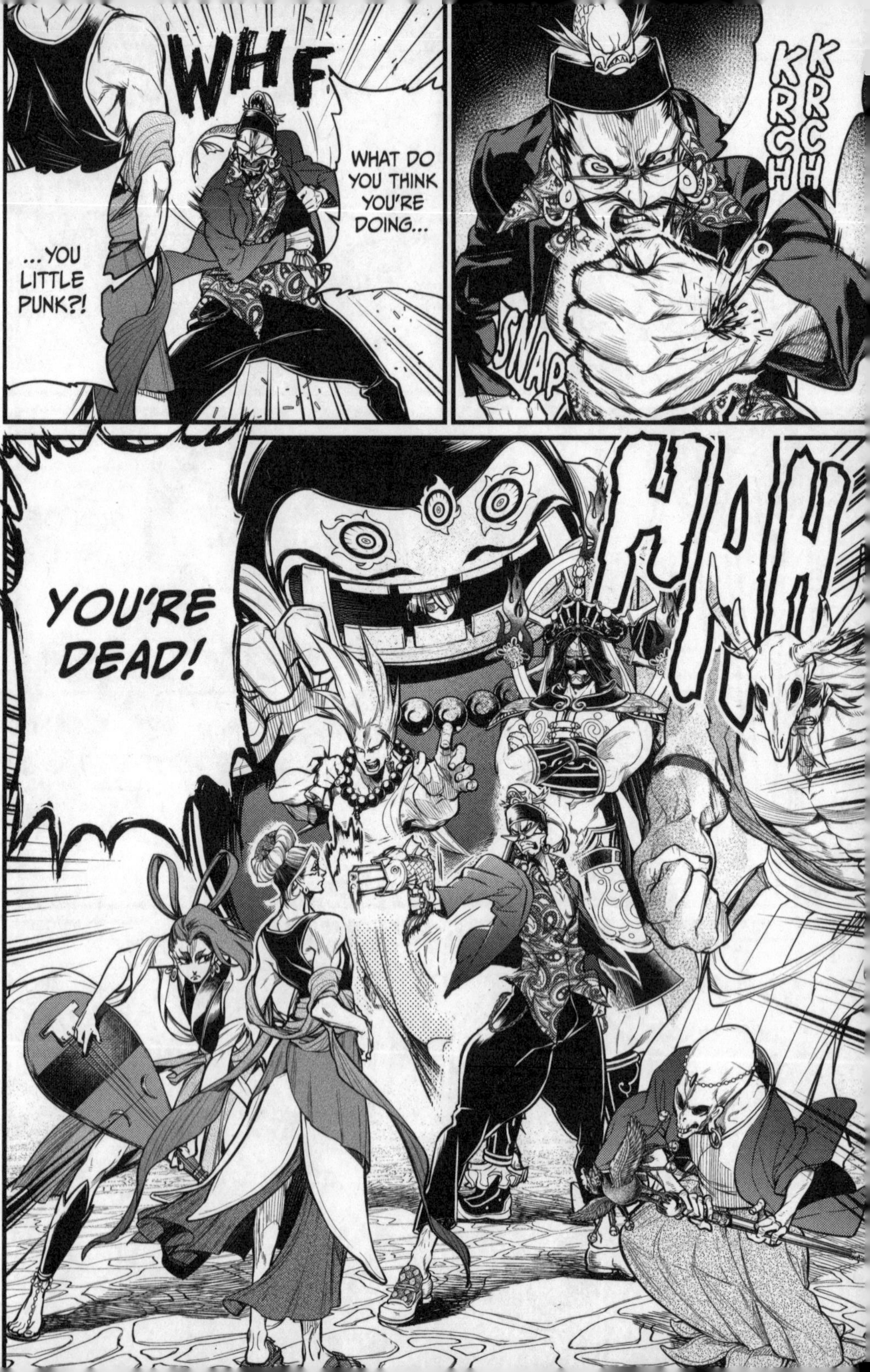
KRCH KRCH
SNAP
WHF
WHAT DO YOU THINK YOU'RE DOING...
...YOU LITTLE PUNK?!
HAH
YOU'RE DEAD!

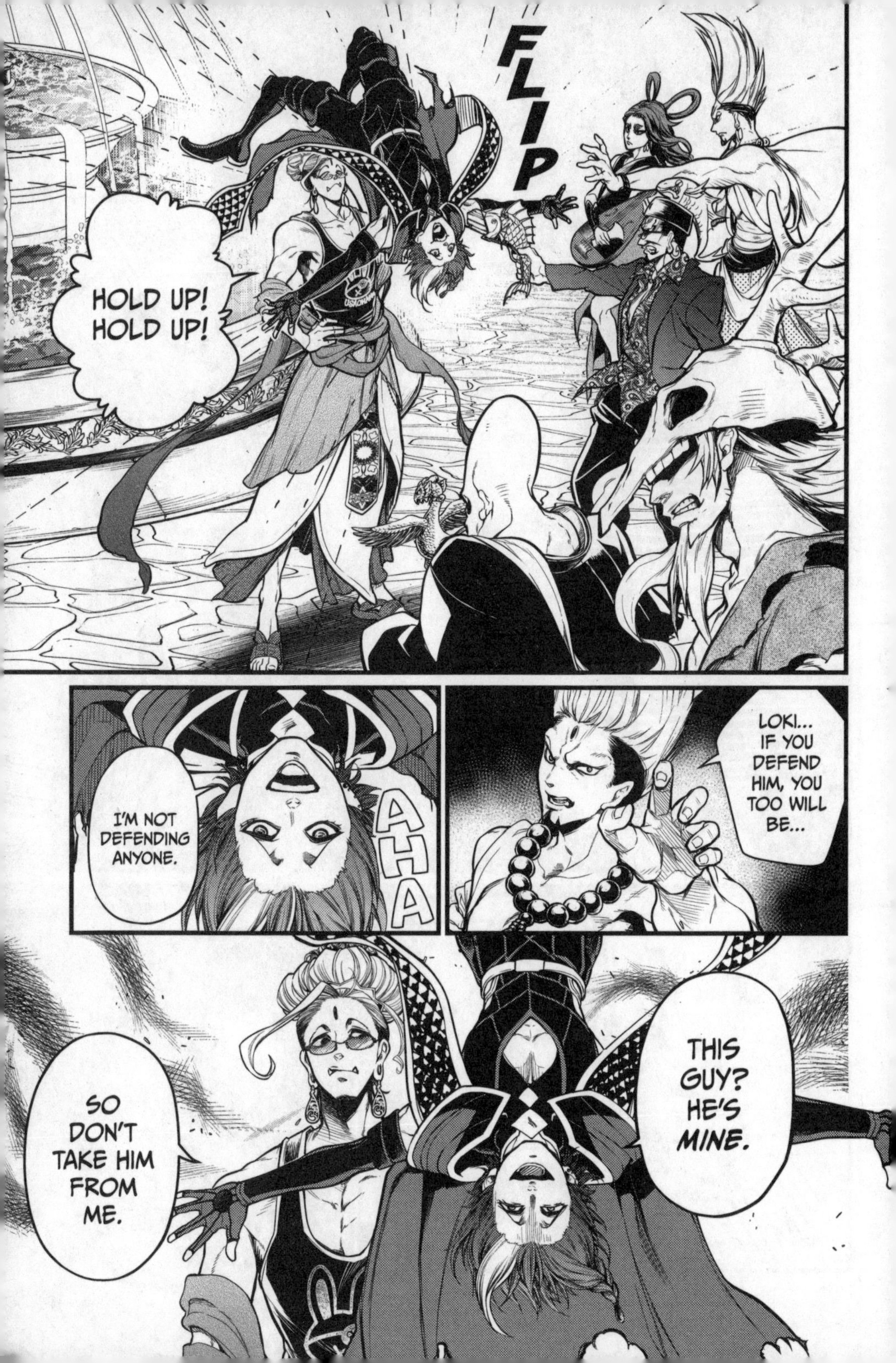
FLIP
HOLD UP! HOLD UP!
LOKI... IF YOU DEFEND HIM, YOU TOO WILL BE...
AHA
I'M NOT DEFENDING ANYONE.
THIS GUY? HE'S *MINE*.
SO DON'T TAKE HIM FROM ME.

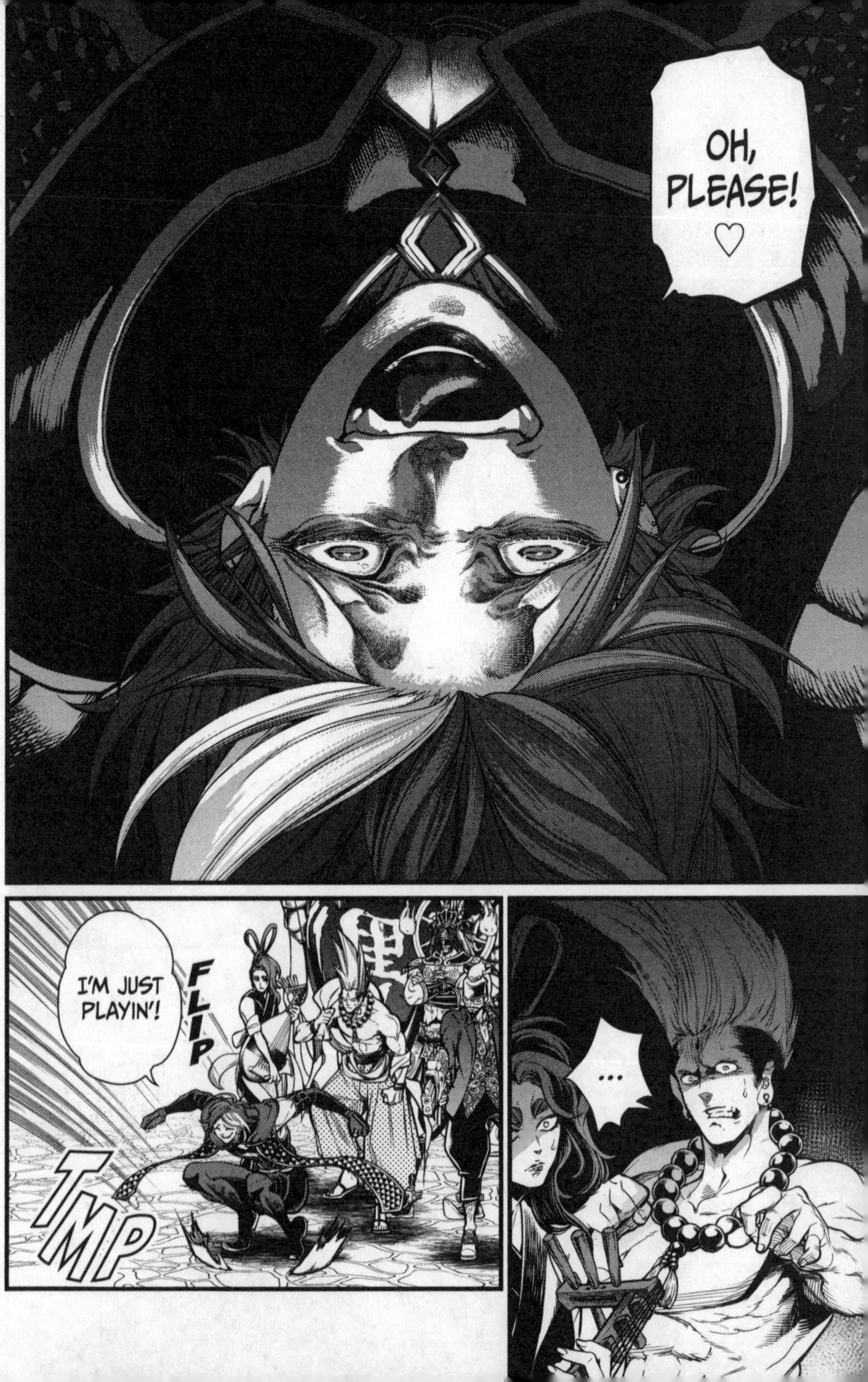
OH, PLEASE! ♡
...
I'M JUST PLAYIN'!
FLIP
TMP

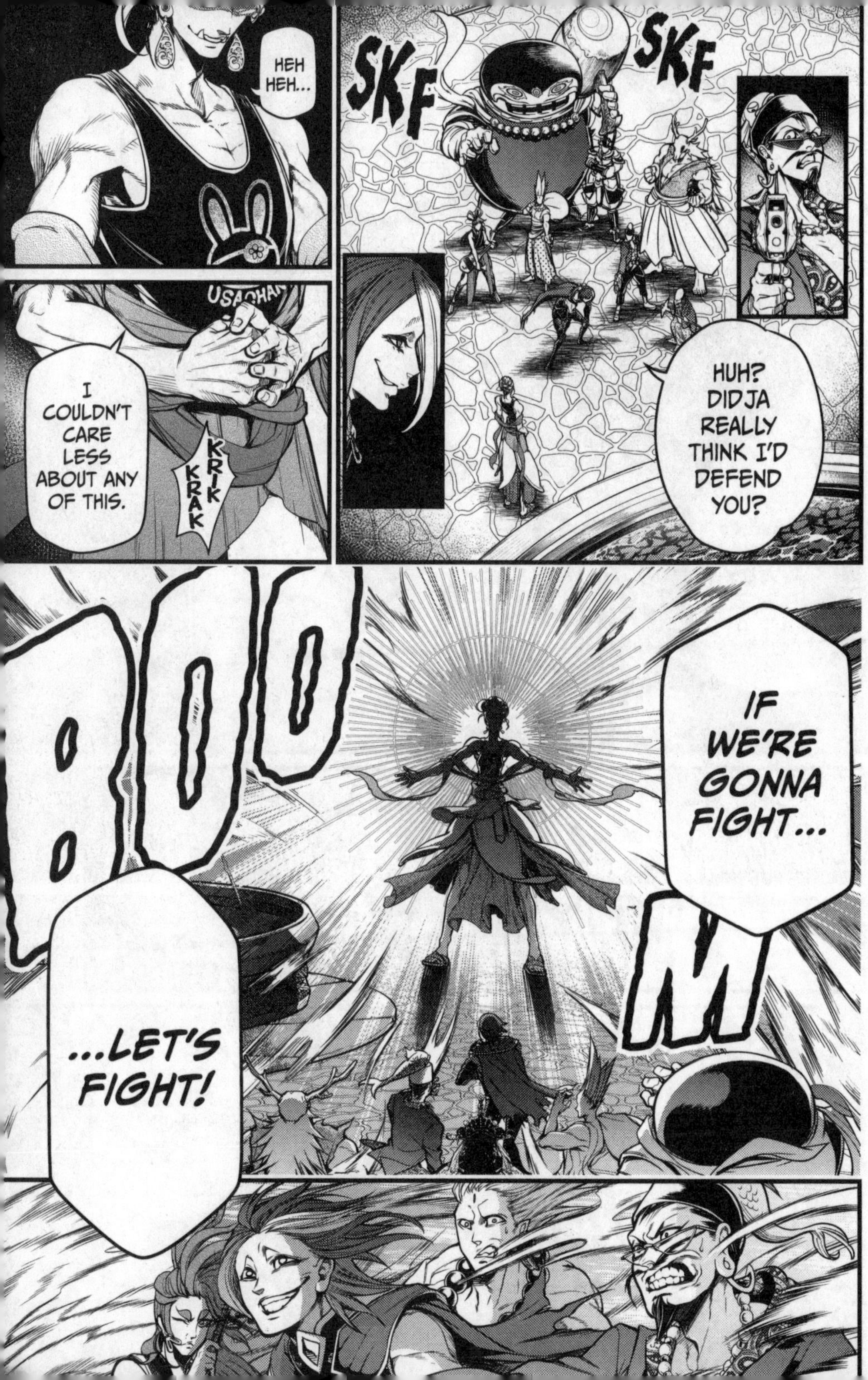
SKF
SKF
HUH? DIDJA REALLY THINK I'D DEFEND YOU?
HEH HEH...
I COULDN'T CARE LESS ABOUT ANY OF THIS.
KRIK KRAK
IF WE'RE GONNA FIGHT...
BOOOM
...LET'S FIGHT!

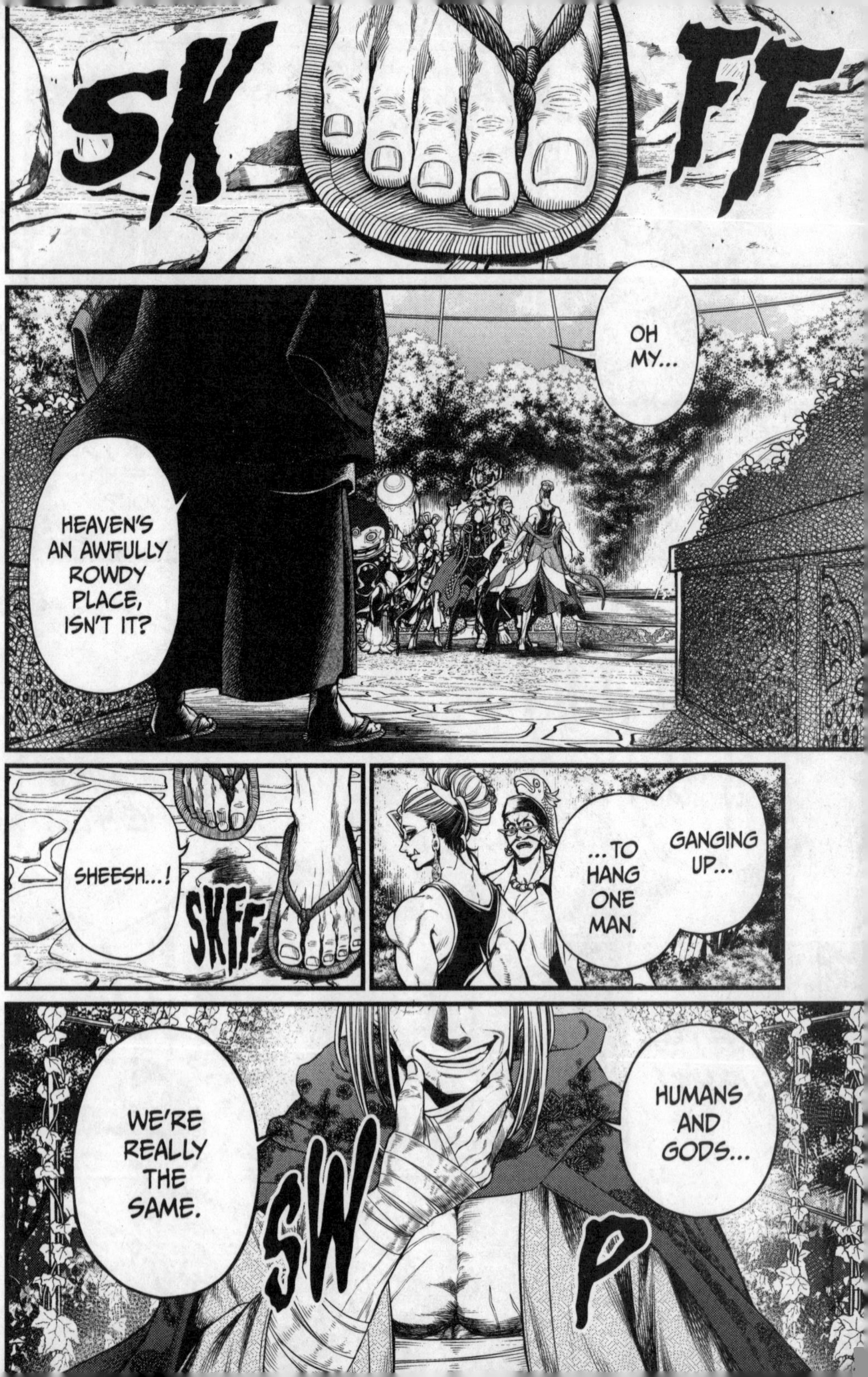
SKFF
OH MY...
HEAVEN'S AN AWFULLY ROWDY PLACE, ISN'T IT?
GANGING UP...
...TO HANG ONE MAN.
SHEESH...!
SKFF
HUMANS AND GODS...
WE'RE REALLY THE SAME.
SWP

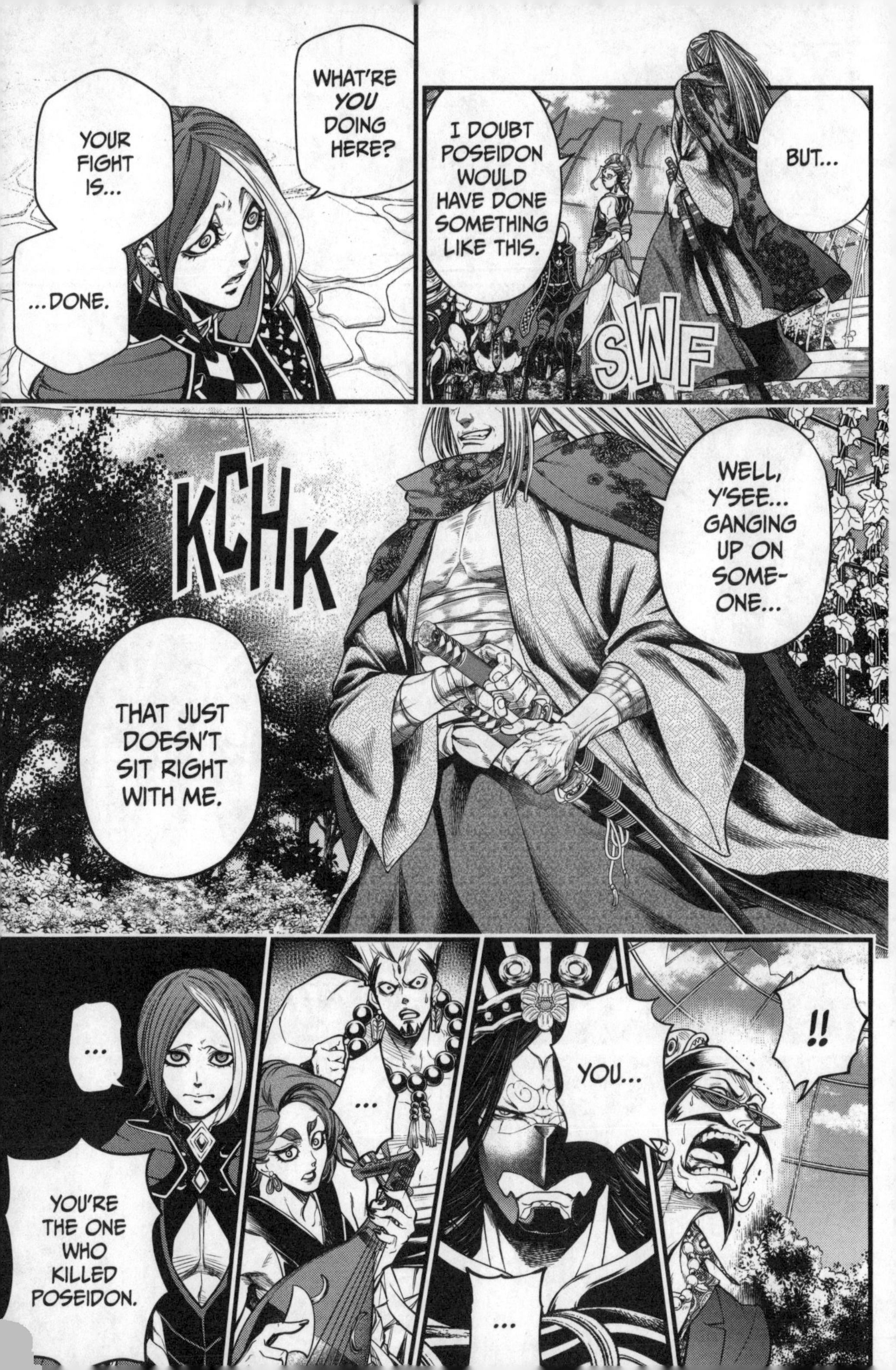
BUT...
I DOUBT POSEIDON WOULD HAVE DONE SOMETHING LIKE THIS.
SWF
WHAT'RE YOU DOING HERE?
YOUR FIGHT IS...
...DONE.
WELL, Y'SEE... GANGING UP ON SOME-ONE...
KCHK
THAT JUST DOESN'T SIT RIGHT WITH ME.
!!
YOU...
...
...
...
YOU'RE THE ONE WHO KILLED POSEIDON.

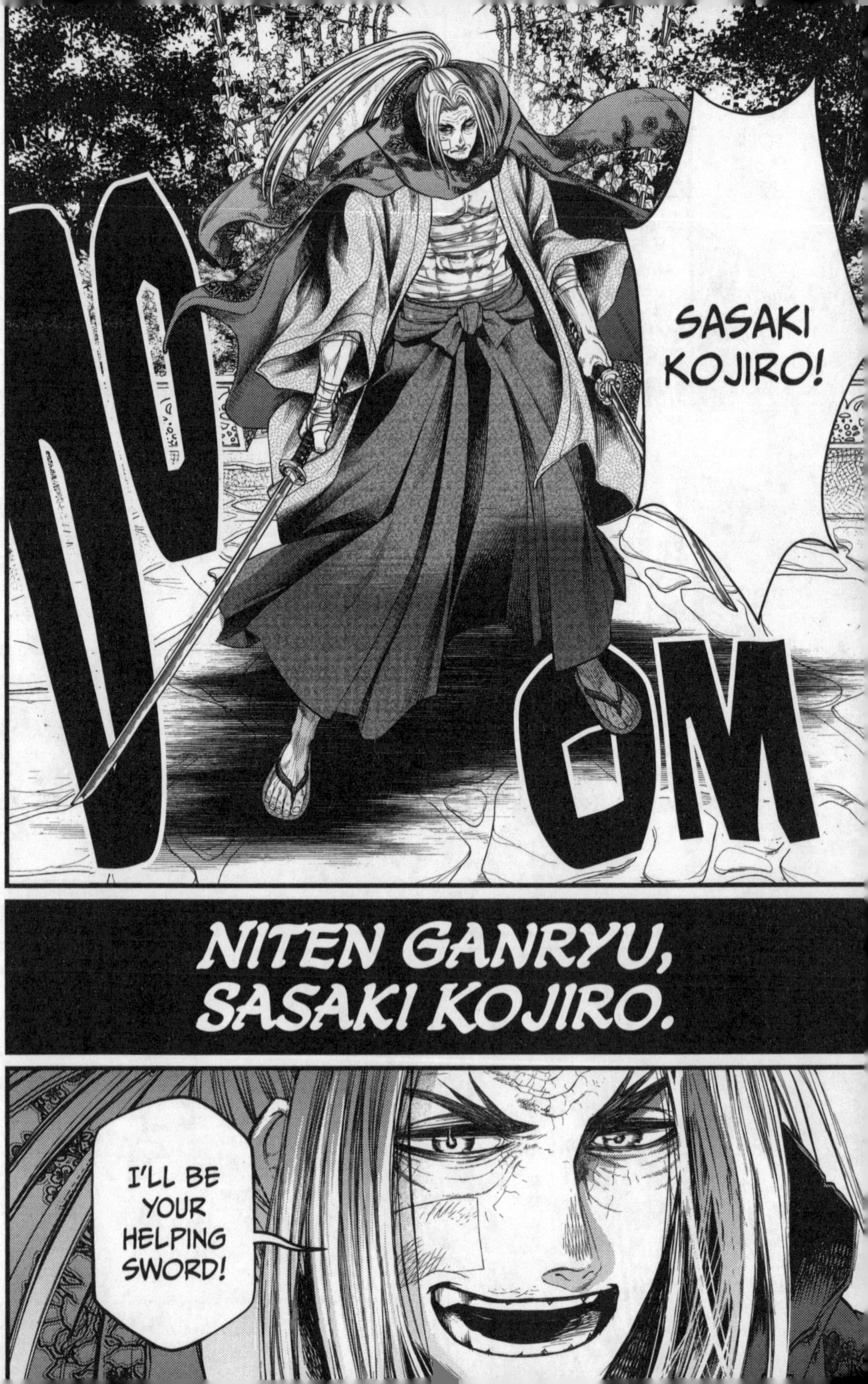
SASAKI KOJIRO!
NITEN GANRYU, SASAKI KOJIRO.
I'LL BE YOUR HELPING SWORD!

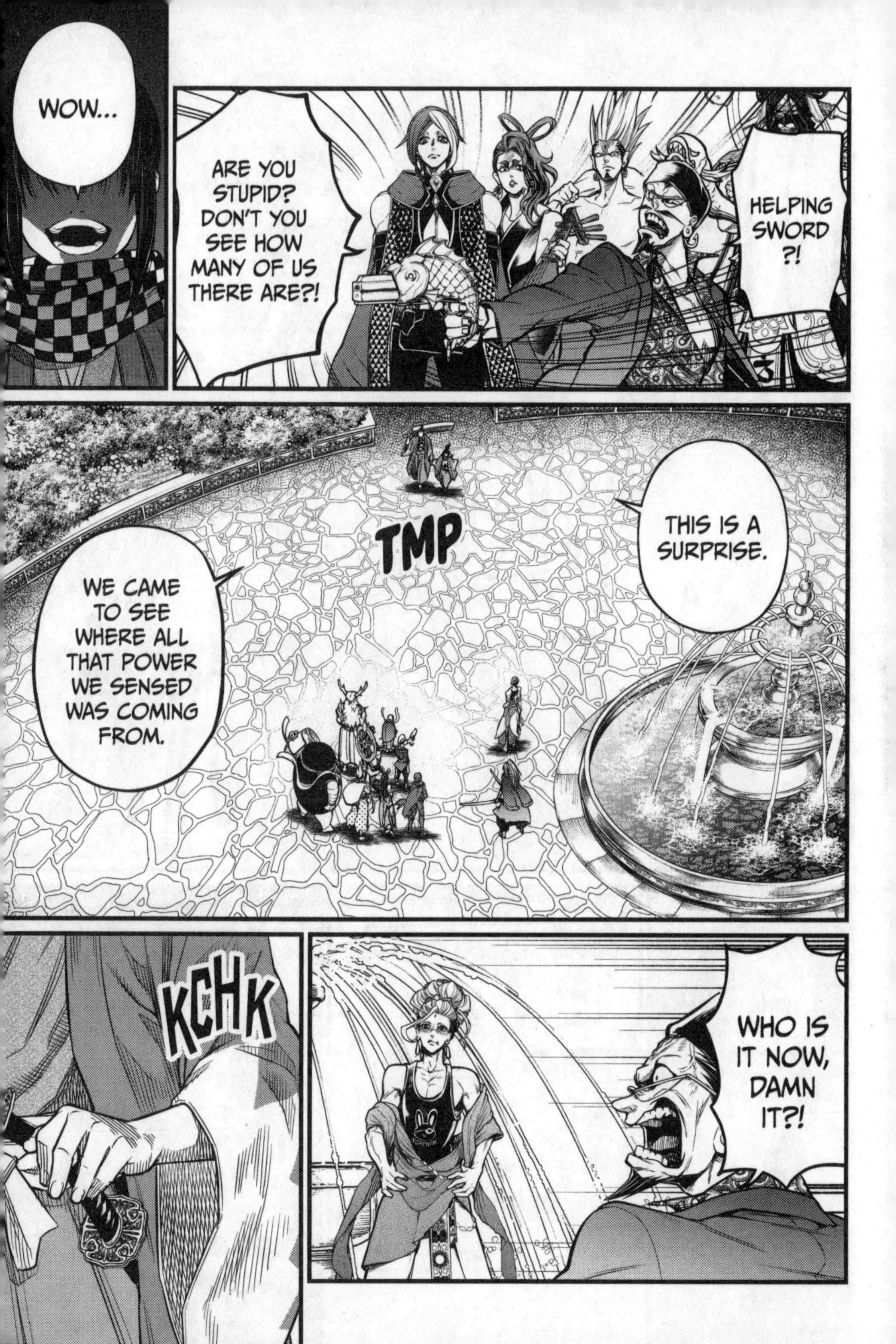
HELPING SWORD ?!
ARE YOU STUPID? DON'T YOU SEE HOW MANY OF US THERE ARE?!
WOW...
THIS IS A SURPRISE.
TMP
WE CAME TO SEE WHERE ALL THAT POWER WE SENSED WAS COMING FROM.
WHO IS IT NOW, DAMN IT?!
KCHK

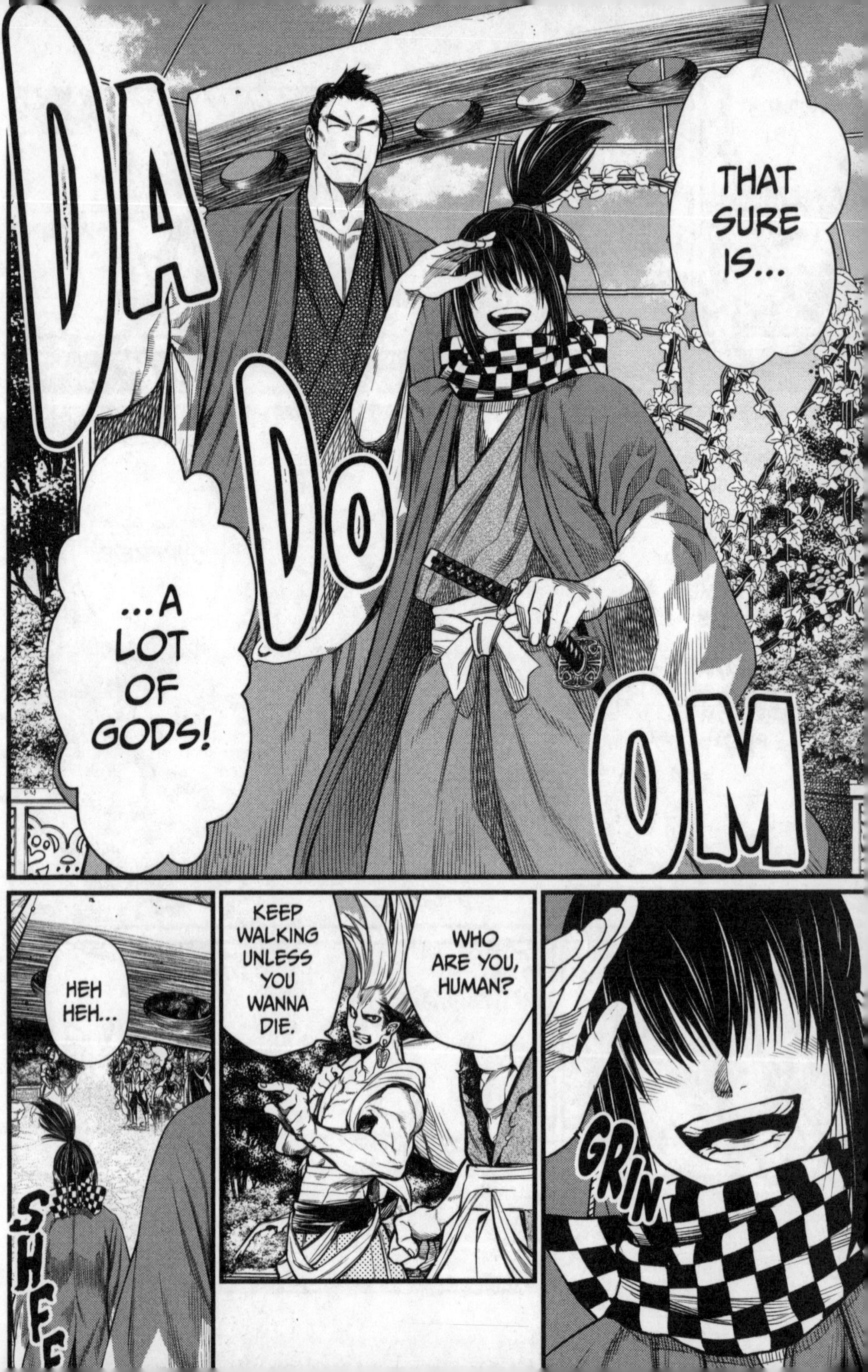
THAT SURE IS...
DA
DO
OM
...A LOT OF GODS!
GRIN
WHO ARE YOU, HUMAN?
KEEP WALKING UNLESS YOU WANNA DIE.
HEH HEH...
SHFF

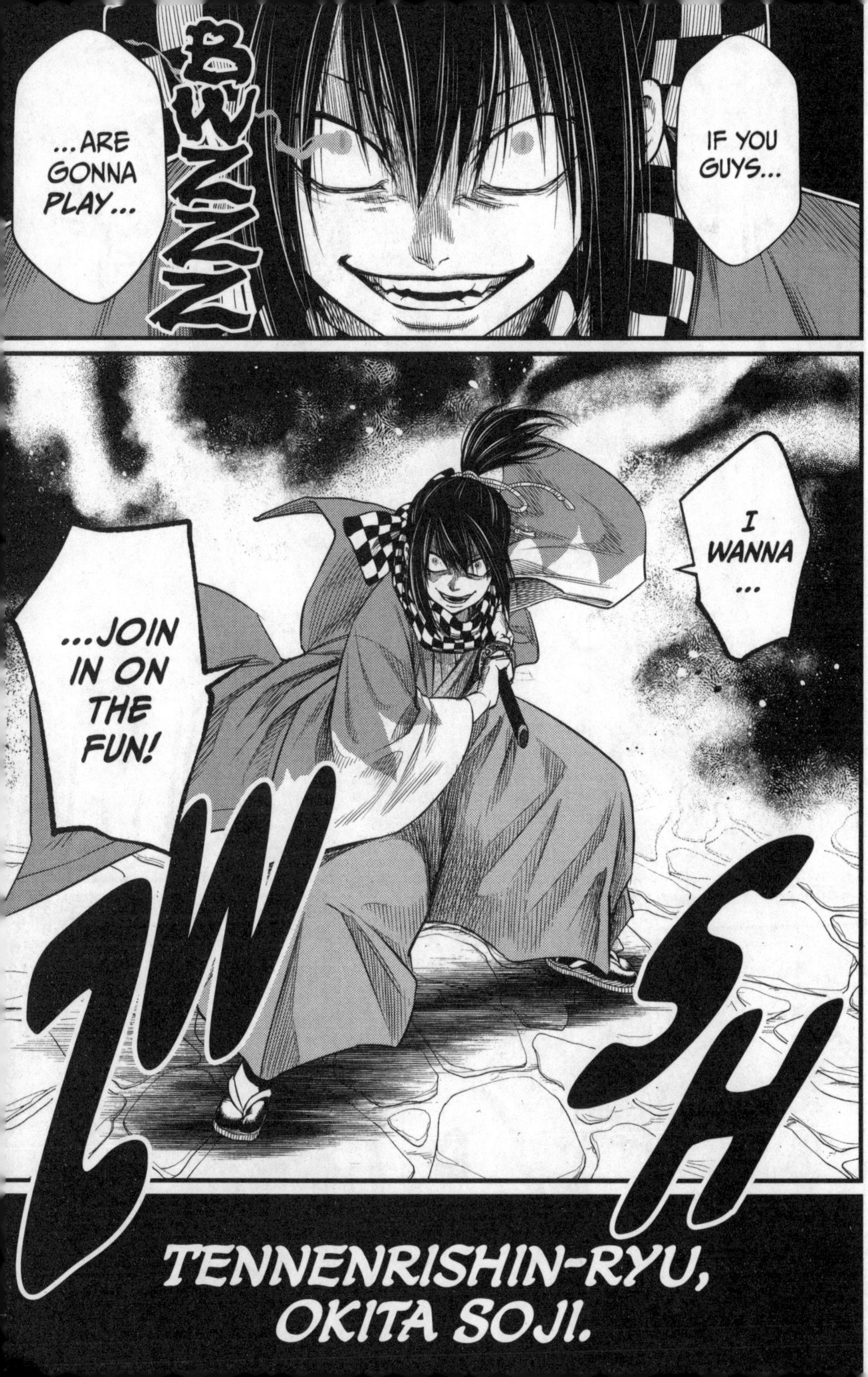
IF YOU GUYS...
BWZZZ
...ARE GONNA PLAY...
I WANNA ...
...JOIN IN ON THE FUN!
SWSH
TENNENRISHIN-RYU, OKITA SOJI.

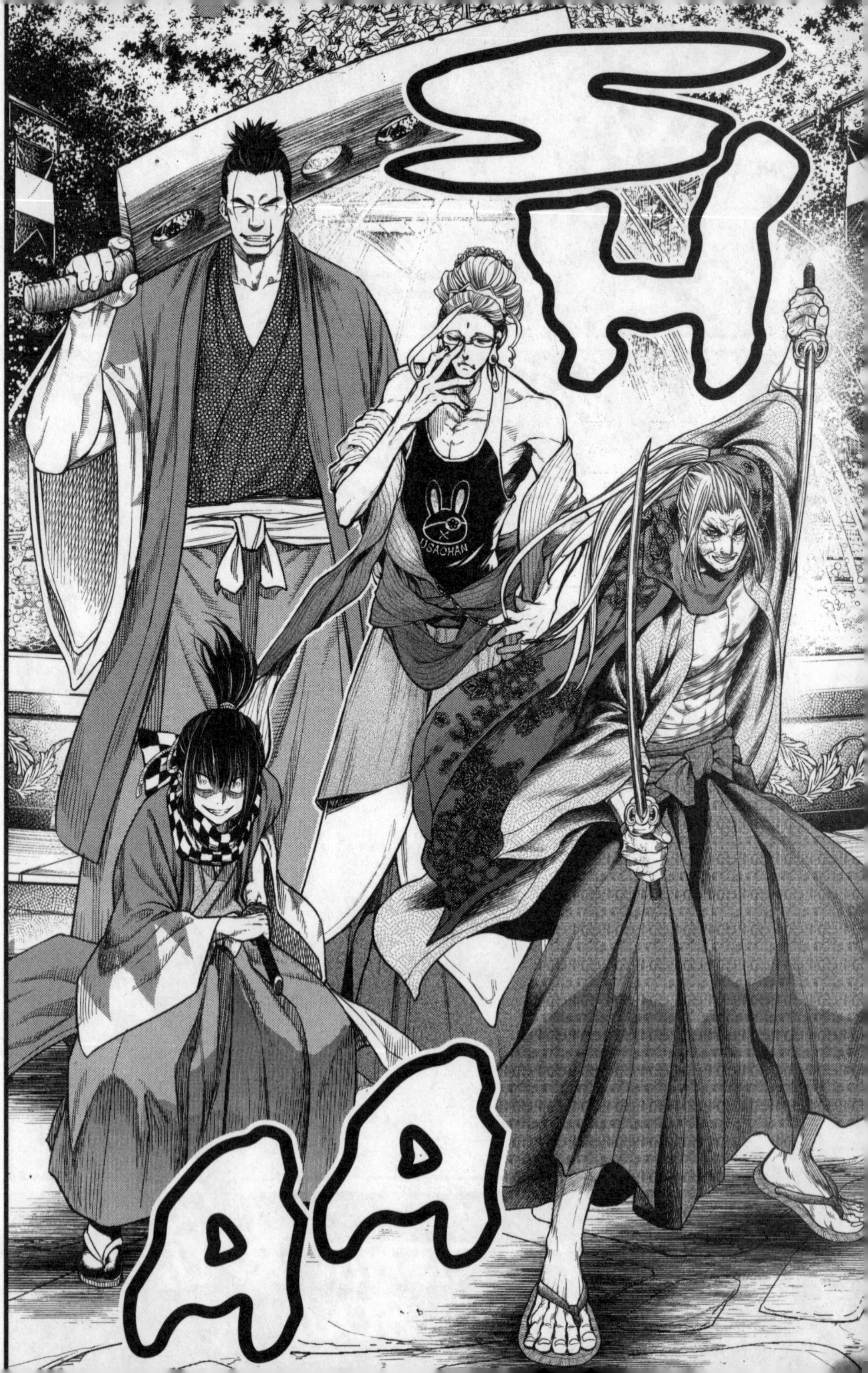
USACHAN
AA

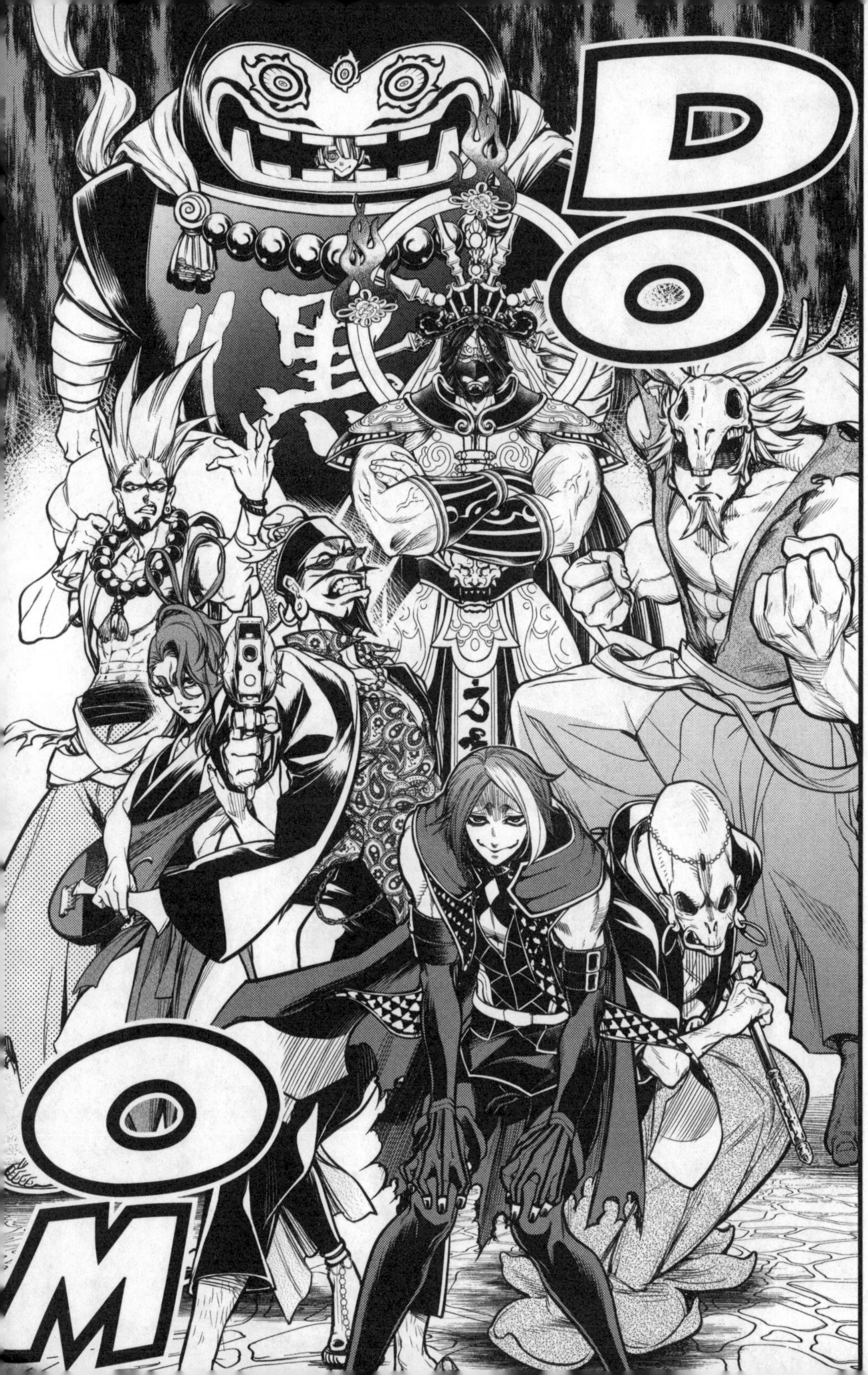
DOOM

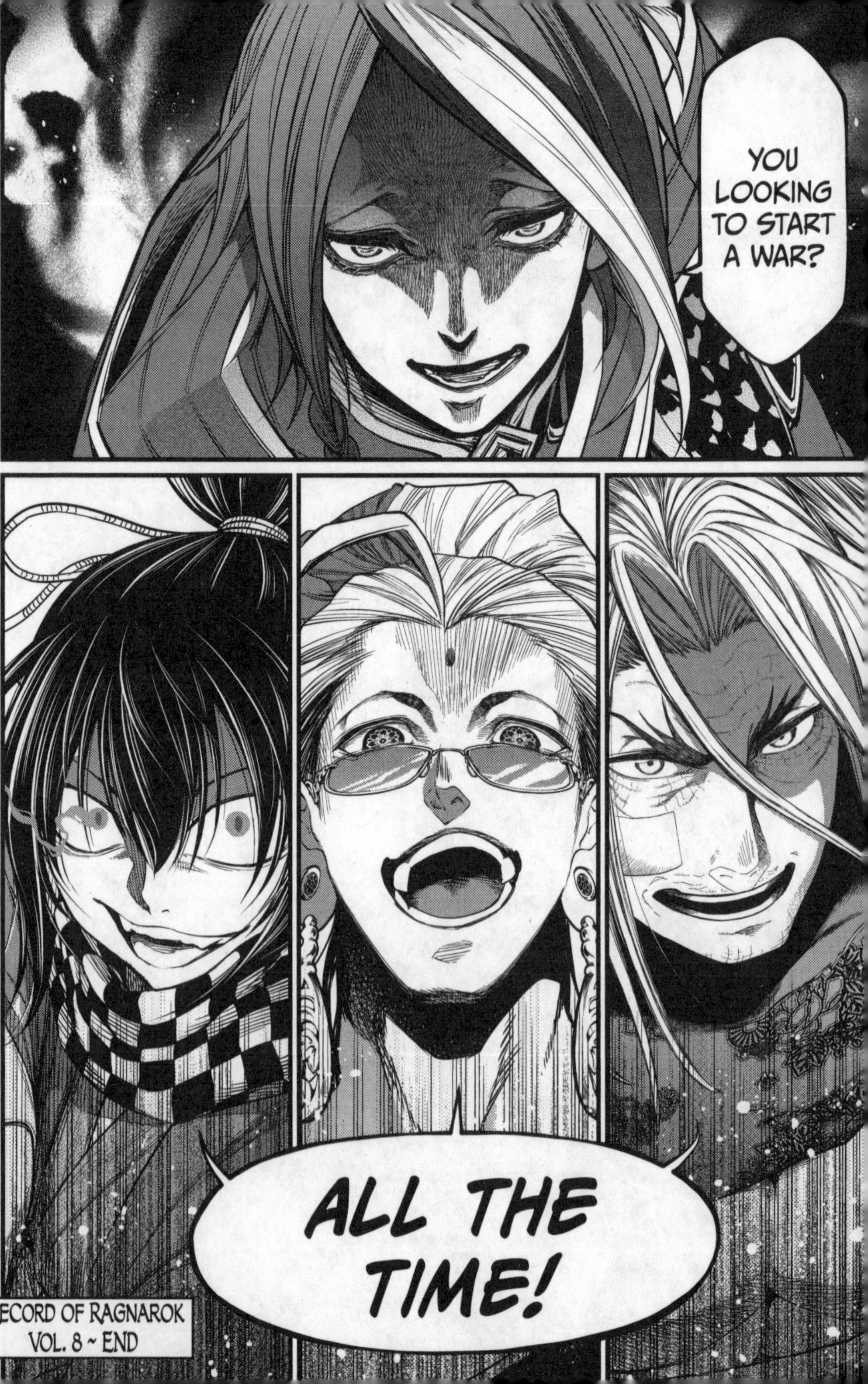
YOU LOOKING TO START A WAR?
ALL THE TIME!
RECORD OF RAGNAROK VOL. 8 ~ END

RECORD OF RAGNAROK

VOLUME 8
VIZ Signature Edition

Art by **Azychika**

Story by **Shinya Umemura**

Script by **Takumi Fukui**

Translation / Joe Yamazaki
Touch-Up Art & Lettering / Mark McMurray
English Adaptation / Stan!
Design / Julian (JR) Robinson
Editor / Mike Montesa

Shumatsu no Walkure
©2017 by AZYCHIKA AND SHINYA UMEMURA AND TAKUMI FUKUI/COAMIX
Approved No. ZCW-123W
First Published in Japan in Monthly Comic ZENON by COAMIX, Inc.
English translation rights arranged with COAMIX Inc., Tokyo
through Tuttle-Mori Agency, Inc., Tokyo

Printed in Canada

Published by VIZ Media, LLC
P.O. Box 77010
San Francisco, CA 94107

10 9 8 7 6 5 4 3 2 1
First printing, October 2023

viz.com

PARENTAL ADVISORY
RECORD OF RAGNAROK is rated T+ for
Older Teen and is recommended for ages
16 and up. Contains graphic violence.

vizsignature.com

YOU'RE READING IT WRONG!

RECORD OF RAGNAROK

reads right to left starting in the upper-right corner. Japanese is read from right to left, meaning that action, sound effects, and word-balloon order are completely reversed from English order.

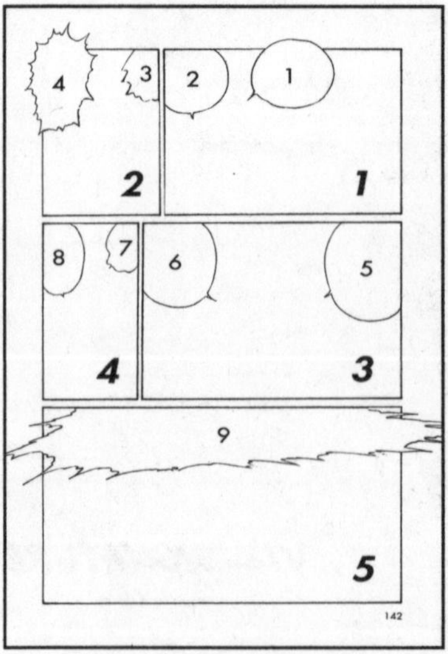

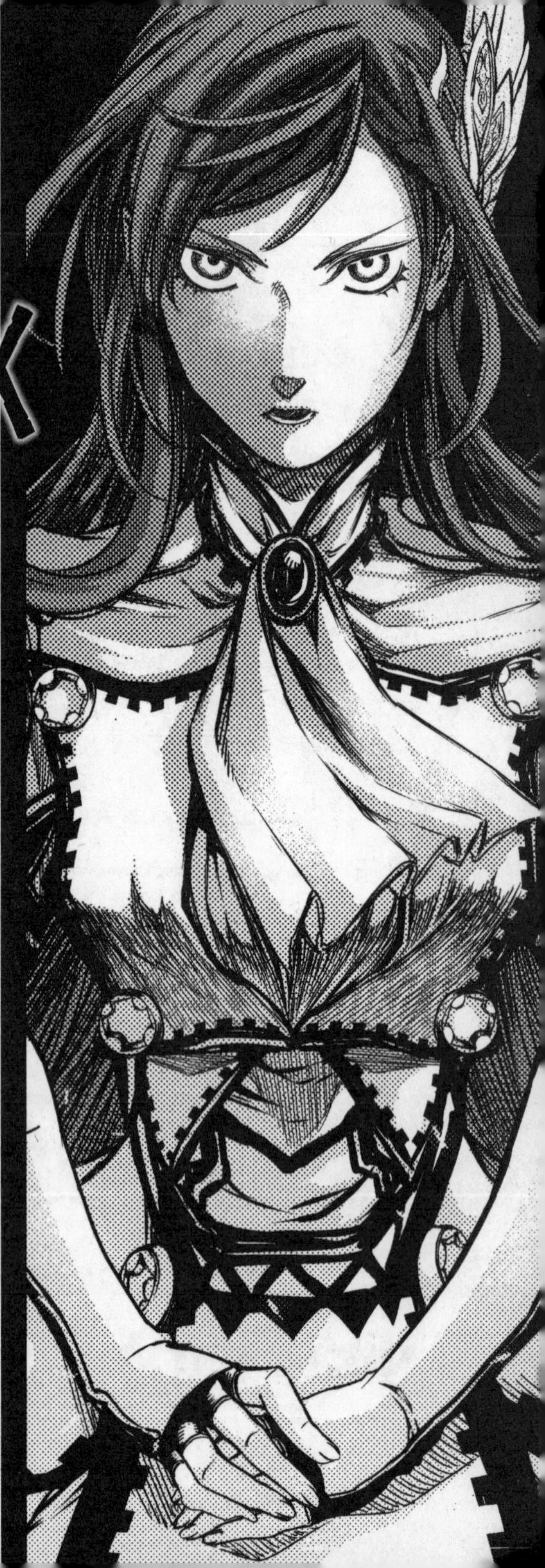